LEGAL RESEARCH:
A PRACTITIONER'S HANDBOOK

SECOND EDITION

LEGAL RESEARCH:
A PRACTITIONER'S HANDBOOK

SECOND EDITION

Peter Clinch

with contributions by
Jon Beaumont

Wildy, Simmonds & Hill Publishing

© Peter Clinch and Jon Beaumont, 2013

ISBN 9780854901234

British Library Cataloguing in Publication Data

A catalogue record for this book is available from the British Library

First edition 2010

This edition published in 2013 by

Wildy, Simmonds & Hill Publishing
58 Carey Street
London WC2A 2JF
England
www.wildy.com

Typeset by Cornubia Press Ltd, Bristol
Printed and bound by CPI Group (UK) Ltd, Croydon, CR0 4YY

MIX
Paper from
responsible sources
FSC FSC® C013604
www.fsc.org

Contents

Appendices   **289**

Figures

Introduction

> Knowledge is of two kinds. We know a subject ourselves, or we know where we can find information about it.
>
> James Boswell, Life of Samuel Johnson (1791) 18 April 1775

As its title indicates, this Handbook is for practitioners (solicitors, barristers and professional support lawyers), particularly those who do not have the benefit of access to a law librarian or information officer.

It brings together information, much of it scattered amongst many different sources, on how to carry out effective legal research. It includes tips and advice based on many years of experience finding and using legal sources both in print and online.

The Handbook is designed as a 'how to' guide as well as describing what is available. In particular it evaluates the effectiveness of many of the sources both print and online.

I believe it is the first Handbook of legal research information specifically designed for practitioners working with UK law. The first edition was greeted with such enthusiasm by overseas practitioners as to prompt this early revision of the book.

The Handbook's structure follows the three steps in the legal research process: preparation, execution and presentation.

Part A covers problem identification and analysis, followed by advice on how to select the best sources and formats (paper or electronic) for research.

Part B has chapters on twelve different types of information frequently sought by practitioners, listing sources with analytical comments and, for a selection of the most complex, 'how to use' instructions developed to a standard template.

Part C details sources on how to make the presentation of the results of legal research more effective.

These three parts are supplemented by Part D, which describes in non-technical language how a practitioner might get the best value for money when buying information from commercial law publishers. Extensive appendices provide:

- indexes to abbreviations for Acts, journals and law reports;
- a glossary of technical terms used in legal research (believed to be the first time such a list has been compiled for use in the UK);

- a summary of the practice directions, statements and decisions of the UK courts relating to legal research (also another first in the UK);

- a table of guidance on how to devise more effective searches on the four most popular commercial databases; and

- a popular names index for legislation and cases relating to the UK and the EU.

Parts A and C cover principles on thinking about legal problems and presenting the results of legal research applicable to work in any jurisdiction. Part D includes principles, tips and techniques with universal application.

Part B has a jurisdictional coverage which includes sources for the UK (including details of the sources for legal research in all three devolved administrations), the EU, with the addition of information on key sources in European human rights and international law. It would be impossible to cover all jurisdictions – so the jurisdictional coverage is restricted, yet pragmatic. Devolution has added new dimensions to finding and researching legal information – the structure of most of the chapters in Part B attempts to ease the practitioner's path through the jungle.

The appendices adhere to the jurisdictional coverage defined for Part B, with the exception of the glossary of legal research terms. Since some UK law firms will occasionally refer to US law sources or contact US lawyers, the glossary includes references to US terminology, especially where it diverges from UK practice, so that trans-Atlantic misunderstandings might be avoided. For example, the legal term 'brief', has different meanings on either side of the Atlantic – check the glossary to see how the US and UK differ!

In the first edition, published only in 2010, I wrote: 'Over the last few years the content and range of law research sources has developed with great speed. Nevertheless, it is hoped that the core of principles here presented, based on many years of personal experience and knowledge built up by the authors, will remain dependable for some time to come'. Whilst updating this second edition, I was impressed by the fact that, whilst the principles remained sound, so much detail had changed – not just website addresses but the content and flexibility of use of many electronic sources. Also, the use by lawyers of new communication channels: the so-called Web 2.0 or social media, have become firmly established. Hardly a page in Parts B, C and D has remained unchanged.

This Handbook is neither intended nor designed to be read through from cover to cover but dipped into when a particular research difficulty arises. It tries to provide answers in three ways: lists and descriptions of a wide range of print and online sources; how to select the source appropriate to the information need; how to use key publications and databases for particular types of information. In this way I hope the path through the extensive and sometimes bewildering world of legal information will be made clearer.

I hope that by frequently referring to this Handbook lawyers might understand better the purpose and unique characteristics of particular sources in the wide range now available in different formats, and so improve the quality and value of the legal advice they provide.

Please write to me, care of the publisher, if you have any tips or techniques which you have found useful and which, with due acknowledgement, you believe ought to be included in a future edition of the Handbook.

As the acknowledgements section shows, this Handbook has benefitted from the support, information, advice and corrections provided by many people. Any errors or omissions which remain should be laid at my door.

All information, including website addresses, provided in the book is believed to be correct and up to date to 1 January 2013.

Peter Clinch
January 2013

Acknowledgements

If it had not been for Andrew Riddoch, Commissioning Editor for the publisher, this book would never have been begun. A chance meeting at the BIALL Dublin Conference in 2008 was the start of a very fruitful collaboration – I have valued his judgment, acting as a sounding board for my ideas, some of which dissolved on the way, others you see here displayed. I am also grateful for his enthusiasm for a second edition. My thanks are due to the editorial team at Wildy, Simmonds & Hill who achieved wonders in converting my complicated manuscript, especially the figures, into such a presentable and accessible form. My sincere thanks also to Jo Joyce for expertly and lucidly indexing such a vast amount of material.

James Mullan (Knowledge Management Systems Manager of Field, Fisher Waterhouse LLP) provided the essential 'practitioner spin' for the first edition. In this new edition I have been especially grateful to Jon Beaumont (Head of Knowledge Management at Harvey, Ingram, Shakespeares) for agreeing to make contributions to the Handbook from the perspective of a librarian and information officer working in a large, provincial law firm. He updated Chapters 14, 15 and 18, and looked over the rest of the book to ensure the focus remains on practitioner material. Thank you for your professionalism and keen interest.

I am also grateful to Gareth Ryan, Law, Maps and Official Publications Librarian, Andersonian Library, University of Strathclyde and John Knowles, Faculty Librarian (Arts, Humanities and Social Sciences), The Library of Queen's University Belfast, for agreeing once again to look over the sections relating to Scotland and Northern Ireland respectively, and improving the accuracy and reliability of the information provided.

Masoud Gerami, Managing Director of Justis, kindly supplied a list of the popular names of EU materials, to which, through my researches I have added UK cases. Full acknowledgement of those who responded to my request in early 2009, which was repeated in 2012, for examples is given at the beginning of Appendix 5. The combined list is used within Justis.

For the first edition, staff at both the Institute of Advanced Legal Studies Library, London (David Gee) and the Bodleian Law Library, Oxford (Helen Garner), were generous with their time and help. For the second edition, Ruth Bird at the Bodleian Law Library provided valuable assistance with updating.

The second edition has benefitted considerably from the up-to-date knowledge and experience of my former colleagues at Cardiff University Law Library, Matt Davies and Lynn Goodhew, both Subject Librarians for Law.

Over the years I have learnt so much both from close, working colleagues and the UK law librarian community in general – I am grateful for the little nuggets of information and tips and techniques which have found their way into this Handbook. It was a wonderfully, open and supportive community within which to work – I retired in July 2010.

Some of the content of the Handbook derives from my teaching materials for the Legal Research module of the Bar Vocational Course, run at Cardiff University since 1997. Over the years it has benefitted from student comments on the content and presentation of information on how to undertake practitioner research.

Grateful acknowledgement is made of the work of the following authors who have contributed to my thoughts on various topics and to a number of publishers who have granted permission to reproduce material as figures in this Handbook.

Chapter 1

McKie, S, *Legal Research: how to find and understand the law* (Cavendish Publishing Ltd, 1993).

Miskin, C (compiler), *A Legal Thesaurus* (Legal Information Resources Ltd, 1997) – the permission of Sweet & Maxwell to reproduce as Figure 1.6 part of page 68 of the thesaurus.

Stott, D, *Legal Research* (Cavendish Publishing Ltd, 2nd edn, 1999) – the permission of Taylor & Francis to reproduce as Figure 1.4 the mind-map analysis of a road accident from diagram 1 on page 19 of Stott's book.

Tunkel, V, *Legal Research: law-finding and problem solving* (Blackstone Press, 1992).

Chapter 2

Some material has been adapted from Chapter 3 of the first and second editions of the *BIALL Handbook of Legal Information Management* (edited by Loyita Worley) written by Peter Clinch.

Chapters 4 and 5

The content of the 'How to use' instructions for the *Halsbury's* publications and Figures 4.1 and 5.1 to 5.3 are based on those drawn up by my colleague Matt Davies, Subject Librarian for Law, Cardiff University Law Library, and updated by him. Matt is a fount of knowledge on both the major practitioner works and the byways of law databases and I am grateful for all his assistance.

Chapter 9

The basic text of Figures 9.1, 9.2 and 9.3 is reproduced with permission from Sweet & Maxwell.

Appendix 4

The table is based on one originally drawn up by my colleague, Matt Davies, which he and Jon Beaumont have updated for this edition.

In various places when writing the Handbook I sought information in and found clarification from Holborn, G, *Butterworths Legal Research Guide* (Butterworths LexisNexis, 2nd edn, 2001) and Duncan, N (editor), *Case Preparation 2009/2010* (Oxford University Press, 2009).

Finally, I am indebted to my wife, Verity, who yet again has had to endure my obsession over several months when updating the text. I dedicate this new edition to her.

PART A

BEFORE TOUCHING A KEYBOARD OR OPENING A BOOK …

Contents

CHAPTER 1

WHERE TO START THE RESEARCH

1.1 PREPARING TO UNDERTAKE RESEARCH

1.1.1 Basic rules to beat basic difficulties

Legal research may seem daunting, because of:

- the complexity of some legal problems lawyers have to solve;

- the vast amount of legal literature available in law libraries and on the internet;

- the inevitable dead-ends a researcher may hit;

- not knowing when to stop, so you may be unable to decide confidently your research is finished.

Avoid these negatives most of the time by:

- cultivating a patient approach to research – avoid the temptation to make a quick 'stab' at finding a particular piece of information. Be willing to follow basic research methods set out in this and the following chapters diligently;

- clarifying the research problem, so you fully understand the facts and issues (see section 1.2, below);

- analysing the problem effectively to determine the general direction of your research and the detail of the legal issues and particular sources you need to consult (see section 1.2, below, and Chapter 2);

- accepting that, because many legal issues are confused and confusing, you will experience dead-ends, misunderstandings and mental deadlock. The novice will throw up their hands in hopelessness. The experienced researcher will go back to their careful analysis of the problem and try to discover a new avenue for investigation;

- keeping a record of the process and products of your research (see section 1.1.2, below). A record of your research allows you to:

  – check back over your research to ensure it is thorough and all the avenues you identified initially have been researched comprehensively;

  – create a formal record of research to go into a client's file and which can be referred back to at a later stage in the proceedings;

  – for younger lawyers in particular, create a personal record of your learning and achievement as evidence of career development;

- knowing the questions to ask yourself so that you may confidently consider the research complete. Excepting where simple pieces of legal information are sought, legal research frequently does not provide a definitive answer to a legal problem. That is why a dispute ends up in court for the parties to present their cases and the judge or jury to decide who should win. There may not be an absolute and definitive answer to some legal problems. So, it is important to know the questions to ask yourself before you can positively answer the final, big question: 'Is my research finished?' (see section 1.1.3, below).

1.1.2   Taking notes

Careful note-taking will help to prevent you:

- failing to follow all the avenues of research set out in your analysis of the problem;

- researching the same texts or parts of a database an unnecessary number of times;

- failing to update information;

- failing to cross-check the same information found in different sources for consistency and accuracy.

Clearly indicate in the notes of your research or 'research trail' the steps you have completed so you are aware of those left to do – remember, your research may not be carried out uninterrupted and you must be confident by the end of it that you have covered all the relevant sources comprehensively and efficiently.

When using printed sources, create a research trail noting:

- the author, title, publisher, edition number (very important), date of publication;

- the parts of the book consulted – contents, index, tables – with page numbers;

- the keywords used in the index and the cross references given;

- paragraph numbers and footnotes referred to and the information they contain;

- full titles of any references to legislation, case law and other materials referred to;

- any supplement or Noter-up or newsletter associated with the publication;

- a note of the date up to which the law found in the publication is stated. This is usually found either on the title page or the pages which immediately follow or in the introduction to the book. Supplements usually carry this information on the cover.

An example of a simple research trail for *Halsbury's Statutes* is given in Figure 1.1:

Question:
Who is responsible for replacing 30 mile per hour speed limit signs damaged in a road accident in which your client was involved?

Answer:
The local traffic authority, which is either, the Secretary of State or, in Greater London, the London borough or the Common Council of the City of London or, the council of the county or metropolitan district, depending on which is designated the highway authority responsible for the road in question.

Keywords:
Speed limits
Signs
Road signs
Traffic signs

Research trail:
Halsbury's Statutes of England

Table of Statutes and Consolidated Index 2003–2004:
No entries for signs or road sign
    Traffic sign
        speed restrictions **38**, 503

Volume 38 at page 503
Road Traffic Regulation Act 1984 s85(2) as amended by the New Roads & Street Works Act 1991 s168(1), Sch 8, para 62

    answer: local traffic authority

For a definition of "local traffic authority" notes refer to s121A post.

Cumulative supplement: Changes to Regulations noted. Not relevant.

Noter-up: No changes.

Figure 1.1: Research trail for a simple research query using *Halsbury's Statutes*

When using an electronic source, create a research trail noting:

- the name of the database you searched – note any limitations in the scope of the coverage of the database in relation to the searches carried out, eg the text of legislation on *Lawtel UK* is as originally enacted, without the text of later amendments inserted or repeals indicated;

- the name of the specific library or source you searched (eg legislation on *Lexis®Library*, Archbold on *Westlaw UK*, the Articles Index on *Lawtel UK*);

- the search terms you used for each search – section 1.3, below, presents some methodical ways of deriving keywords;

- the date on which you carried out the research on the particular database – with a complex legal problem you may need to repeat the searches at a future date to bring your research up to date.

Most electronic sources now allow users to save searches, bookmark materials consulted and create alerts to warn them of new developments.

An example of a simple research trail for an electronic database is given in Figure 1.2:

Question:
Find cases establishing the principle that where a robbery is committed with an imitation firearm, it does not amount to a "violent offence". Are the cases still good law?

Answer:
R v Palin (Gareth Wayne) 1995 16 Cr App R (S) 888; *R v Baker (Wendy Ann)* 2001 1 Cr App R (S) 55. *Palin* was considered in *Baker*. Both cases still good law.

Keywords:
Violent offence
Imitation firearm
Robbery

Research Trail:
Westlaw UK: Select Cases library

Search by terms: "violent offence" and "imitation firearm"

4 hits, 2 deal with severity of sentence, 2 with principle of offence (*Palin* and *Baker*)

Check Westlaw's History of Case and Citations to Case for both *Palin* and *Baker*.

No negative judicial comment.

Searched Westlaw UK 10/11/2009

Figure 1.2: Research trail for a simple query using *Westlaw UK*

A more complex piece of research using both print and electronic sources should be recorded as in Figure 1.3:

Research into substantive law surrounding a client's case involving their theft of local authority funds as an employee, and likely sentence to be passed.

Keywords:
Theft Act 1968 s1 and s7
Breach of trust by an employee
Breach of trust by an employee employed by a public body
Theft and dishonesty
Sentencing guidelines
Guilty plea and sentencing discount

Strategy:
Key sources:
Westlaw UK for legislation and judicial interpretation
Blackstone's Criminal Practice 2008
Archbold 2008 – including Cumulative Supplements and Archbold News
Thomas – Current Sentencing Practice, including Newsletter
Crown Court Index 2008

Other sources:
Journals Index on Westlaw
Articles in Criminal Law Review

Research Trail:
Blackstone's Criminal Practice 2008
    Index: Theft
        Breach of trust
            Guideline cases
ETC, etc.

Figure 1.3: Research trail for a more complex query involving the use of both print and electronic sources

Note that an additional and vital step has been listed in this research trail. It is important to devise a research strategy, listing the print and electronic sources you believe to be relevant to satisfying the research problem. Setting down a research strategy will:

- provide a guide to the general direction the research task should take;

- help you to avoid wasting time and effort by using inappropriate sources and following irrelevant avenues;

- allow you at any time to measure how far along the research process you have reached, and how much further you need to go to complete it.

1.1.3   Knowing when to stop

Ask yourself these questions to determine whether your research is finished:

- Have you used the most reputable sources available, selecting full-text versions rather than summaries of the law?

- Have you logically answered the question you wanted to answer when you began? Ask a colleague to look over your answer and research trail.

- Is the statement of law in the legislation and cases relevant to the facts of the situation? Carefully compare the facts of your research problem with the statement of law and consider whether the differences could alter your answer.

- Have you checked that the legislation and cases you cite are current?

- Have you checked all the major research sources that might improve your understanding of the area of law? Always use as many sources in an area of law as possible, rather than relying on one, hoping that it will be the fullest and most up-to-date source. The ideal is to 'triangulate' your research, checking one source with two other sources to verify the accuracy of your findings.

- Can you explain your reasoning in writing? As you write up the results of your research and compile an answer, holes may appear in your logic and will indicate further research is required.

When you can answer YES to all the questions, you have done as much as is possible.

1.2   ANALYSING THE PROBLEM

Legal problems dealt with in law firms and barristers chambers comprise a mass of facts which require translation into legal issues.

The first step is to collect and order the facts from the various papers and statements. The second step is to apply a logical analysis to the facts to isolate the legal issues which are to be researched.

A number of techniques are available to assist with both steps.

1.2.1   Fact collection

A systematic method of collecting data is to create a list of the facts under the headings:

Who?
What?
When?
Where?
Why?
How?

It is possible that having collected the existing facts under these headings omissions and uncertainties may be apparent, and further and better particulars will need to be sought. When the fact collection exercise has been completed, progress to analysing the facts.

1.2.2   Fact analysis

Several techniques are available including West's technique (PPOBR), 'mind-mapping' and 'brainstorming'.

West's technique – This requires that the factual material be allocated to the appropriate heading, as follows:

- *Parties* – What is the status of the parties in terms of their relationship to each other or as individuals? For example: landlord and tenant, husband and wife, employer and employee, etc. One party may have a special status or characteristic: minor, trespasser, bankrupt, policeman, etc.

- *Places* – Is the place where the event took place significant? For example: public or private, domestic or commercial, in a place of employment or on premises to which one is invited.

- *Objects* – Do any of the objects in the factual situation have significance? For example, in a road traffic accident, the make and year of the car and motor-bike involved in the collision may not be important, but the fact that one of the parties wears glasses may indicate a visual impairment which might be significant.

- *Basis and defence* – What is the legal basis on which the action will be founded and the potential defences? For example, an action founded on the breach of duty of care, with the main defence based on contributory negligence.

- *Relief* – What does the law allow? What are the client's wishes and preferences? For example, in the case of faulty goods, is it a refund, or the goods exchanged for new, or a different model, or the goods repaired, and compensation for inconvenience.

'Mind-mapping' – This is a very structured, diagrammatic technique in which the main theme or proposition is placed at the centre of the page and branches from it identify facts (or omissions) and inferences. An example relating to the analysis of a road accident is given in Figure 1.4.

The facts behind this 'mind-map' are given as follows:

A sixth form schoolboy, Robert Tee, riding a moped he bought second-hand and driven under a provisional licence, was involved in an accident with a car driven by a middle-aged person, Eileen M. The schoolboy, your client, has no recollection of the accident. He was seriously injured and spent six weeks in hospital. He has suffered permanent injury to his right leg. He has had to give up his Saturday job, will be unable to take a booked holiday abroad and may need to defer taking his 'A' levels. He had hoped to go to university but is now not confident of obtaining the required grades because of the severity of the headaches he now suffers. His sporting activities have been curtailed also. There are witness statements from an elderly passenger in the car (Noreen) and a local resident, Maureen Bell. The police, who attended the scene of the accident, intend to prosecute the car driver.

The mind-map identifies the host of factual and legal issues arising from this scenario with which many personal injury action lawyers deal frequently.

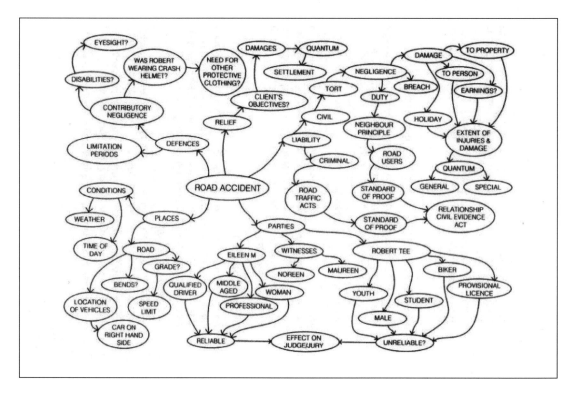

Figure 1.4: Mind-map of legal analysis of a road accident (Stott, 1999)

'Brainstorming' – This is an unstructured approach to factual analysis. It is more successful if undertaken by a group but can be employed by an individual working alone. After absorbing all the facts of the problem, write down single words and short phrases relating to the issues affecting your client. Then reverse the process and look at the problem from the other side's point of view. When the flow of words and phrases has dried up fully evaluate the lists and organise them into a logical sequence.

Two further questioning techniques will help to clarify a legal problem:

- *Funnelling questions* help focus-in from the general to the particular:

    'In which particular aspects of the law of carriage of goods by sea am I interested?'

    'Why do I need this information?'

    'Am I concerned with the law effective in the United Kingdom or internationally?'

- *Probing questions* seek further details:

    'When I say Europe, do I mean cases heard in the courts of the individual countries or cases heard in the European Court of Justice or the European Court of Human Rights?'

    'What forms of discrimination do I have in mind: racial, gender, age, religious?'

Having successfully analysed the legal problem the next stage is to derive research questions such as:

'What is the most recent case law on "nervous shock" especially in relation to medical evidence and proximity of personal relationship in time and space? What is the current position regarding defences and limitation periods?'

As they stand, these types of question cannot be researched effectively without selecting relevant keywords (legally significant terms). Before deriving keywords it is essential to carry out a further categorisation to clarify these questions:

'Am I concerned with international, European, national, or local law?'

'Am I concerned with a criminal or a civil matter?'

'What is the principal area of law?'

'Am I concerned with substantive or procedural issues?'

Answering these questions will not only help to identify further keywords for your search of sources but also indicate the most relevant source publications and databases (see Chapter 2).

The next section describes a technique which will help you develop more keywords for use in searches of indexes to publications and in databases.

1.3   DERIVING KEYWORDS

A systematic method of deriving keywords is essential because:

- the legal concept or issue you are investigating may be indexed in any number of different ways, given the richness of the English language in general, and legal language in particular;

- a general source might use a general index term, such as 'family law', while a more specialised source might select 'domestic relations' or 'divorce', when referring to the same topic;

- although many indexes to publications are well constructed with 'see' references to preferred terms or 'see also' references to associated terms, you need to be confident you have covered all the possibilities by cycling your full list of terms against the entire index;

- it is important to identify relevant legal jargon, since some law indexes may use these terms in preference to others;

- whilst some electronic sources now offer 'Did you mean?' functions or similar recommendations via predictive text when searching, these sophisticated features can mislead the unprepared and unfocussed researcher;

- it can be difficult for some lawyers familiar with very specific areas of law to formulate general keywords to search more widely if searches using specialised keywords fail;

- some law databases do not have a conventional index for you to search, but directly search the full text of each document for the words you type in. Judges in case law, authors in journal articles and books and, to a lesser extent, Parliament in legislation, may use alternative words or phrases to refer to the same topic. You need to be confident that you have searched the database using all the words relevant to your research and retrieved everything of relevance.

To derive all the possible words which might be used in an index or database to refer to a concept in which you are interested, adopt a word association technique such as 'cartwheeling'. An example, using the word employees, is given in Figure 1.5:

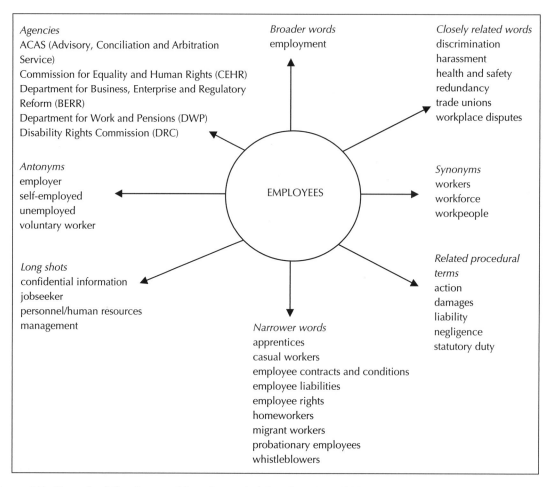

Figure 1.5: Cartwheel for the word 'employees'. After Statsky (1982)

Place the concept in which you are interested at the centre of the page, then cluster in groups around it words which have a broader meaning, closely related terms, synonyms (words with similar meaning), related terms, narrower words and so on.

To help you compile these groups of words use:

- a student textbook on the general topic area;

- an ordinary *Oxford English Dictionary*;

- a law dictionary – there are many on the market but here are a few: *Mozley and Whiteley's Law Dictionary* (Oxford University Press, 12th revised edn, 2001); *Osborn's Concise Law Dictionary* (Sweet & Maxwell, 12th edn, 2013); *Jowitt's Dictionary of English Law* (Sweet & Maxwell, 3rd revised edn, 2010) and supplements; *Stroud's Judicial Dictionary of Words and Phrases* (Sweet & Maxwell, 8th edn, 2012) and supplements; *Glossary of Scottish and European Union Legal Terms and Latin Phrases* (LexisNexis UK, 2nd edn, 2003); *Glossary of Legal Terms* (W Green, 5th edn, 2009);

- the index volumes to a general law encyclopedia such as *Halsbury's Laws of England* or the *Laws of Scotland* (the fullest lists of law terms to be found in a library) – see Chapter 4;

- a legal thesaurus, such as that edited by Christine Miskin, last published in 1997 but now out of print – see Figure 1.6 for an extract:

HOUSING BENEFIT (G)
    BT: INCOME RELATED BENEFITS
    RT: HOUSING BENEFITS

HOUSING BENEFITS (G)
    NT: RENT ALLOWANCES
    NT: RENT REBATES
    BT: HOUSING
    RT: HOUSING LAW
    RT: LOCAL AUTHORITIES POWERS AND DUTIES

HOUSING CONTROL (G)
    NT: CLEARANCE AREAS
    NT: DEFECTIVE PREMISES
    NT: DEMOLITION
    NT: HOUSING ACTION AREAS
    NT: IMPROVEMENT AREAS
    NT: MULTIPLE OCCUPATION
    NT: OVERCROWDING
    NT: REHOUSING
    NT: REPAIRS NOTICE
    BT: HOUSING
    RT: ENVIRONMENTAL HEALTH
    RT: LOCAL AUTHORITIES POWERS AND DUTIES

HOUSING LAW (G)
    BT: HOUSING
    RT: HOUSING BENEFITS
    RT: LANDLORD AND TENANT

Figure 1.6: Extract from *A Legal Thesaurus* (1997)

The thesaurus is an alphabetical listing of legal terms against each of which are noted words of broader meaning (labelled BT in the example from the thesaurus), narrower terms (labelled NT) and related terms (labelled RT). It is electronic versions of a thesaurus like this which are embedded within many commercial law databases, such as *Westlaw UK* and *Lexis®Library*, and which drive the search engines responding to the enquiries typed in by lawyers. More about this at section 2.2, below.

Having compiled your cartwheel, run the list of terms against the index entries in books, encyclopedias and databases to be more confident you will retrieve the maximum amount of relevant information.

Now you should be ready to select the particular sources most relevant to the topic of research in hand.

Summary

- Clarify the research problem carefully.

- Collect facts using a logical and comprehensive method.

- Analyse the facts using a logical method – select from the range of methods available the one which you feel best suits your way of working.

- Use a systematic method to derive keywords from your analysis, in preparation for searching print and electronic sources.

- Devise a research strategy listing the particular print and electronic sources you consider relevant to the solution of the problem, especially with complex research problems.

- Create a research trail of your use of print and electronic sources, for all but the simplest research tasks.

- Know how to recognise the time when it is appropriate to stop your research.

CHAPTER 2

WHICH SOURCES TO USE

2.1   CLASSIFYING THE TYPES OF INFORMATION NEEDED

Towards the end of section 1.2.2, above, four basic questions were posed, which every researcher should ask themselves when undertaking all but the simplest research task:

'Am I concerned with international, European, national, or local law?'

'Am I concerned with a criminal or a civil matter?'

'What is the principal area of law?'

'Am I concerned with substantive or procedural issues?'

Now you should be ready to classify the research into one or more of the following categories:

- *Substantive law* – the actual law embodied in treaties, conventions or domestic legislation and the decisions of the international, European and national courts, as opposed to procedural law – see Chapters 4, 5 and 6;

- *Procedural law* – law dealing with the procedure of the courts (litigation) or with the preparation of legal documents for use in transactions outside the courts (non-litigious procedure) such as wills, mortgages, leases and so on – see Chapter 7;

- *Words and phrases* – where the meaning of a legal term is required, defined either by treaty, convention or statute or through interpretation by the judges in case law – see Chapter 8;

- *Updating known law*

    - for legislation: checking if there are proposals which will affect known law; tracing the progress of draft legislation through the legislature; checking whether a known treaty, convention or piece of primary or secondary legislation is still good law and whether there have been any protocols, amendments, or repeals which affect the validity of the legislation; checking if the legislation has been interpreted by the courts.

– for case law: similarly, tracing the progress of a case through the courts; establishing whether the judgment is still good law or has been adversely commented on in court or overruled by a later decision – see Chapter 9;

• *Commentary on the law* – opinions and explanations of the law, whether on a particular piece of legislation or case or a subject in general – see Chapter 10;

• *Pre-legislative proposals* – consultation papers, working papers, official reports – see Chapter 11;

• *Other official information produced by international organisations and national governments, such as circulars, memoranda and policy papers issued by official organisations to assist public bodies in applying the law* – see Chapter 12;

• *Business information* – company accounts, annual reports, directories and business news – see Chapter 14;

• *Information about people and personalities connected with the law, law firms or chambers, government ministers and key civil servants* – see Chapter 15.

2.2 CHOOSING THE BEST SOURCE: PRINT OR ELECTRONIC?

Legal and business information is available in two different formats: printed and electronic. Electronic sources are accessed almost entirely over the internet, only a small proportion of materials is still available on CD-ROM, and the format is being actively phased out by publishers.

In addition to the well known legal databases, the advent of social media has opened a further research medium, with a number of providers of legal information embracing technology to provide relevant material. Sites hosting or providing tools such as forums, blogs, picture or video sharing, discussions boards, micro-blogging, wikis, RSS feeds and social networking are now plentiful. These developments are popularly known as Web 2.0. Whilst ever more useful, users must be aware (as with all content) of the source of the information provided. However, a user who embraces and learns to use such resources well shall certainly find benefit from them. For more on how law firms are using the new technology, see Lustigman, A, 'Web 2.0: how is it being used? What can it do for law firms?' (2010) 10 *Legal Information Management* 235–238.

When deciding which format to use, carefully consider the following characteristics.

2.2.1 Printed sources

• *Cost to the client* – there are no charges to search a paper publication held in your own library or available in a larger library to which your firm has access.

• *Availability* – a considerable number of important books on practice and precedent aimed at the law practitioner are available only in print format.

- *Access to information* – print publications have indexes compiled by experts which not only highlight all the references to a topic but frequently indicate by the use of bold type where the fullest treatment of the matter is to be found.

- *Currency* – print publications usually include a clear statement of how up to date is the information provided – see section 1.1.2, above; *but*, the speed with which the publisher updates the information through supplements, newsletters or a Noter-up can be slow and the statement of law therefore dated.

2.2.2   Electronic sources

- *Cost to the client* – all electronic databases make charges for access, whether as an annual subscription (sometimes based on overall use or the number of partners in the firm) or as 'pay-as-you-go'. Using an electronic database to research all of a problem will probably incur a greater charge to the client than if the bulk of the research was undertaken through print sources, and electronic sources employed only to cross-check and update the information already found. Like for like, law firm librarians usually assume that there will be more cost incurred using an electronic source.

- *Availability* – each database usually makes available a wide range of information sources, more than might be found in even a very large print-based library. Some databases, such as *Lawtel UK*, perform functions which print materials cannot match effectively; they are purposely designed to provide an updating service across a wide range of the categories presented at section 2.1, above, such as pre-legislative materials, legislation, case law and commentary.

- *Access to information* – some databases do not include a conventional index for the user to browse. Some databases may search the full text of documents (legislation and case law). So, in response to the word/s or phrase/s typed in, these databases retrieve a large number of results, sometimes ordered by date rather than relevance. It may not be possible to sort the results to quickly focus on the most relevant material. If you have searched using general or frequently used words or phrases, the list of results will be considerable and it will take valuable time for you to read and sort those relevant to the solution of your research problem from those which are not.

- *Currency* – some databases do not clearly state how up to date is the information they contain, nor clearly list the titles of the publications over which a search has been conducted. Electronic versions of encyclopedias and practitioner texts are often no more up to date than their print equivalents.

Research tip

Rather than relying solely on print or solely on electronic sources, consider whether the research might be best conducted using a mixture of both: begin with a good practitioner work on the topic in print form to identify the key legislation and case law, then update the legislation and cases mentioned and obtain more background material (journal commentary) using electronic databases.

2.3   WHICH SOURCES SHOULD I SEARCH FIRST?

Unless you are already very familiar with the area of law in which the legal problem is set, it is often more productive to begin your research with the secondary sources: a general law encyclopedia such as *Halsbury's Laws of England* or the *Laws of Scotland* (also referred to as the *Stair Memorial Encyclopedia*), textbooks (both student and practitioner) and journals. Why?

- *Halsbury's Laws* and the *Stair Encyclopedia* are both valuable starting points because their coverage of the law of each jurisdiction is comprehensive. Looking up one point of law may uncover a reference to another point you had not thought of.

- *The indexes to general law encyclopedias* are rich in legal terminology and if you had not used them when deriving keywords for your research (see section 1.3, above), using them now should prompt further keywords and avenues to explore.

- *Textbooks* provide a narrative explanation of the law, frequently with a critical evaluation. Practitioners' books provide a detailed treatment of a subject, focusing on as up-to-date a statement of the law as possible, with commentary on both practice and procedure. Student textbooks are less concerned with detail but more with describing general principles of law and identifying and commenting on areas of doubt or conflict in legislation and case law. Areas for future law reform will be noted. Use the catalogue to your law library to trace relevant textbooks, searching by broad topic (eg contract) rather than detailed subject (eg rescission). Most library catalogues index books by title and general subject, not the contents of particular chapters. If your organisation does not have a library catalogue use the web catalogue of one the libraries listed at section 15.6, below or even the printed or electronic catalogue of a major law bookshop such as Hammicks <http://www.hammickslegal.com/live> or Wildy <http://www.wildy.com>.

- *Journals* provide commentary and analysis, case notes, notes on practice and procedure and comments on the latest legal developments. To find relevant journal articles search a journals index – the most comprehensive for UK law is the Journals Index on *Westlaw UK*. The Articles Index on *Lawtel UK* covers around only approximately 10% of the titles included in the Journals Index on *Westlaw UK*. The contents of Journals Index Plus on *Lexis®Library* may vary according to the subscription your organisation has taken out with the database provider. Whilst Journals Index Plus indexes a large number of titles, many are overseas publications.

Research tip

It is often best to start research using secondary sources, that is, practitioner encyclopedias, textbooks and journals, to identify the key primary sources – the titles of treaties, conventions or domestic legislation and/or names of cases, details of the latest developments and possible reforms. Then move to the full text of the primary sources themselves.

Figure 2.1 brings together material discussed in Chapters 1 and 2 to display a suggested sequence for undertaking problem-solving legal research.

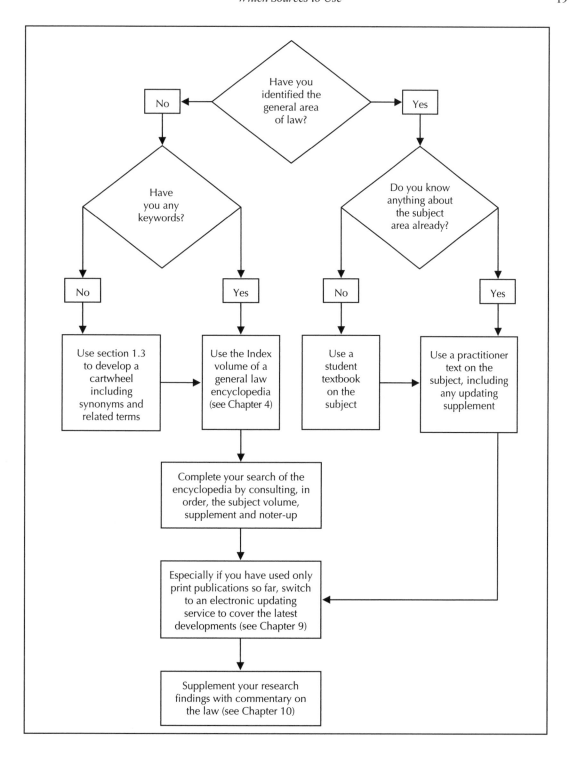

Figure 2.1: Sequence for problem-solving legal research

CHAPTER 3

HOW TO CHOOSE THE SOURCES

3.1 ASKING FUNDAMENTAL QUESTIONS ABOUT A SOURCE

Regardless of whether you use an electronic or a paper source to research the law always ask yourself three questions when using a publication or database:

'Is the statement of law I have found authoritative?'

'Is it an accurate statement of the law?'

'Is the statement of law as up to date as possible?'

3.1.1   Authority

Legislation

- Does the version of the legislation carry an indication that it is official, such as a copyright statement by the official government or parliamentary printer? Especially if you are using the internet, never automatically assume that the text you are looking at is the authoritative will of the legislature.

- If there is no evidence that the version is official, can you trust the source?

Case law

- Has the case report been prepared by a law reporter (a barrister)?

  Check the end of the report to make sure a barrister's name is attached. Historically, the courts will only accept the report of a decision compiled by a barrister. Although the law reports in newspapers are not signed or even initialled, they are believed to be compiled by barristers. Those in *The Times* are known to be compiled by staff of the Incorporated Council of Law Reporting (ICLR).

- If the text is given only as a 'case note' or as an edited or summarised version (such as a law report in a newspaper like *The Times*) can you trace a fuller and more authoritative version?

  Use the sources described in Chapter 6 and/or the citators described in Chapter 9 to check for other, fuller versions of the case.

Commentary

- Is there a named author or organisation?

- Is the author or organisation an expert in the field?

- Are the author's or the organisation's contact details given?

3.1.2   Accuracy

Legislation and case law

- Are you looking at a summary or the full text?

  Wherever possible, use the full text.

- Have you verified the statement of the law uncovered in one source, with a similar statement in a second and, if possible, a third source?

  The ideal is to triangulate your research findings, checking each statement of the law in one source against at least one other. Mistakes, errors and misinterpretations can occur in publications and databases. Adopting the triangulation method should uncover them. Using this technique is particularly important if you found material from the internet (see section 3.2, below).

Commentary

- Are the sources of the information presented identified, referenced and cited?

- Does the information seem biased?

3.1.3 Currency

Legislation

- Does the publication or database carry a statement of how up to date is the text of the legislation or should you assume it is only 'as enacted' originally?

- Have you checked the sources described in Chapter 9 to trace amendments, repeals and revocations?

Case law

- Is a publication date or a phrase such as 'the statement of the law is correct to …' given?

- How recent is it?

- Is there any indication when the information was last updated?

3.2 BE 'STREETWISE' ABOUT USING THE INTERNET

The internet is a rich source of legal information. But remember that law found on the internet is:

- Not all accessible to everyone.

- Not comprehensive.

- Not all free.

Further, even if they look legitimate, some sources may not be trustworthy.

If you are happy to accept these propositions at face value, take a look at the summary in Figure 3.1, memorise them now and apply them when using the sources listed in Part B, below.

If you want to know the detail behind the three propositions, then read on.

Figure 3.1: Quick Guide to the contents of the major UK law databases

Material	Provider	Characteristics	Dates	Fee/Free
Acts/SIs	BAILII	Generally Acts and SIs, unconsolidated.	Acts: selection in force 1215–1987. All Acts: 1988– SIs: selection in force 1947–2001. All SIs: 2002–	Free
	Legislation.gov.uk	Acts: consolidated or 'revised' up to end 2002; about 50% Acts 2003– 'revised' to date – 'point in time from 1991–'. SIs: not consolidated.	In force	Free
	Lexis®Library	Acts: consolidated, 'point in time' by using Historical Versions E-mail Service within database to send request to editors; no repealed legislation; links to *Halsbury's Statutes* commentary; full history of amendments; links to cases discussing the section; direct link to related journal articles only if in full text on this database. SIs: consolidated.	In force	Fee
	Westlaw UK	Acts: all in force in 1991 and all published subsequently. Consolidated, 'point in time' from 1/2/1991 onwards – use Advanced Search; no repealed legislation before this date; full history of amendments; links to cases discussing the section; direct link to related journal articles only if in full text on this database. SIs: selection 1948–1991 plus all published subsequently. Consolidated, 'point in time' search from 1948 onwards using Advanced Search.	In force	Fee
	Lawtel	Acts: unconsolidated, text of Acts reproduced similarly to TSO version; statutory status table records repeals and amendments; rapid reporting of summaries; no direct link to journal articles discussing the section; progress of bills with links to full text. SIs: unconsolidated, text of SI reproduced in TSO version.	Acts and SIs: 1987–	Fee
	Justis	Acts and SIs: as enacted. Acts: diagrammatic links to amendments and repeals. PDF versions available.	Acts: 1267– SIs: 1948–	Fee

Material	Provider	Characteristics	Dates	Fee/Free
	PLC	Part consolidated – text of acts linked to *Westlaw UK* (where text is available if users have a subscription to *Westlaw UK*) or *Legislation.gov.uk* (free).	Dependent on particular legislation to which PLC materials refer.	Fee
Cases	Westlaw UK	Both reported cases (starting with *The Law Reports*, 1865–) and transcripts (WL reference); link to a case citator compiled by *Westlaw UK* staff to discover: 'Is the decision still good law?'; Graphical History of case displaying direct history of decision; link to journal articles discussing each decision. Includes access to *The English Reports* (1220–1873). PDF versions of Sweet & Maxwell law reports available as part of an additional subscription.	Reported 1220– Bulk from 1970s onwards.	Fee
			Transcripts 1980– plus selected cases 1948–1979.	Fee
	Lexis®Library	Both reported cases (starting with *The Law Reports*, 1865–) and transcripts; link to citator compiled by *Lexis®Library* staff to discover: 'Is the decision still good law?'; no direct link to extensive journal articles database discussing each decision. Includes access to *The English Reports* (1220–1873).	Reported 1220– Bulk from 1936–	Fee
			Transcripts 1980–	Fee
	BAILII	Transcripts and full text of 2,380 historic landmark decisions. PDF versions not available.	Mainly 1996–	Free
	Lawtel	Digest of each case (LTL reference) with link to transcript for majority.	1980– plus selected cases pre-1980.	Fee
	Justis	Restricted selection of reported decisions: ER, LR, WLR, ICR, some criminal cases; transcripts of CA (Civil) from 1951–, CA (Crim) 1963–, other courts from 1990s. PDF versions of both reported cases and transcripts available.	Oldest 1485– Mainly 1960–	Fee
			Transcripts 1951–	Fee
	PLC	Comments with links directly to *BAILII* and also official transcripts of EAT.	Dependent on particular cases to which PLC materials refer.	Fee
Journals	Lexis®Library	Full text of over 90 UK and nearly 200 overseas titles; index of articles from over 500 UK and overseas titles.	Dates not specified but index 1995–	Fee
	Westlaw UK	Full text of over 100 titles and, for additional subscription, access to PDF versions of 32 Sweet & Maxwell titles 2003–; index of articles from 1986– covering over 1,000 titles – most comprehensive journal index available.	Full text 1990s– Index 1986–	Fee

Material	Provider	Characteristics	Dates	Fee/Free
	Lawtel	Digest of articles from about 100 titles – link to full text at extra cost.	Full text late 1990s– Index 1980s–	Fee
Books / Commentary	Westlaw UK	Full text of over 100 Sweet & Maxwell practitioner publications. Some available only on payment of additional annual subscription.		Fee
	Lexis®Library	Full text of range of LexisNexis titles available under 'Commentary' library, only on payment of additional annual subscription.		Fee
	Lawtel	Full text of *Kemp & Kemp on Quantum of Damages* (excluding anatomy and medical information section) available on payment of additional annual subscription.		Fee
	PLC	Practice notes, checklists, PLC magazine and standard documents along with links to a selection of book titles from Bloomsbury Professional (included within a separate subscription).		Fee
	Lexis®PSL	Practice notes, checklists, flowcharts and links through to LexisLibrary (content available with separate subscription).		Fee

Key:

BAILII	British and Irish Legal Information Institute <http://www.bailii.org>
EAT	Employment Appeal Tribunal <http://www.justice.gov.uk/tribunals/employment-appeals/judgments>
Justis	<http://www.justis.com>
Lawtel	<http://www.lawtel.com/login/default.aspx>
Legislation.gov.uk	'The official home of revised, enacted UK legislation 1267– present' <http://www.legislation.gov.uk>
Lexis®Library	<https://www.lexisnexis.co.uk/our-solutions/legal/research-knowledge-solutions/find-unrivalled-information/lexislibrary.aspx>
Lexis®PSL	<http://www.lexisnexis.co.uk/our-solutions/academic/online-services/lexispsl.aspx>
PLC	Practical Law Company <http://uk.practicallaw.com>
TSO	TSO (The Stationery Office) <http://www.tsoshop.co.uk/bookstore.asp?FO=1160005>
Westlaw UK	<http://www.westlaw.co.uk>

3.2.1 Not all accessible to everyone

There are two parts to the web – the free sites available to everyone and a vast area called the 'hidden web'. The 'hidden web' includes sites which:

- are password protected – that includes all the quality law databases such as *Justis*, *Lawtel UK*, *Lexis®Library* and *Westlaw UK*;

- include other design features which prevent search engines such as Google searching them – for example, although a freely accessible database for individuals, *BAILII* purposely prevents all search engines entering its site and indexing material it displays – a reply on the *BAILII* website to a FAQ (Frequently Asked Question) explains why this is considered necessary.

Google

Using a search engine such as Google will retrieve information from free websites only, but only those which choose to allow it in to index material. Nevertheless, Google may display a little information about material on a 'hidden' site which it is prevented from entering. This occurs when Google picks up references to a case or legislation held on a 'hidden web' location from a link on an open, free site. Google indexes the only information it has been able to gain, which is usually only the title of the material.

A Google search can never enter the 'hidden web' of quality law databases to find information. So, if you do use Google you must evaluate the information you find by asking the questions at sections 3.1.1–3.1.3, above (authority, accuracy and currency).

Remember, when you put a request to Google it merely searches its index of archived web pages. It can take days if not weeks for Google to locate, index and incorporate within this index the addresses of recently created web pages, especially in specialist subjects such as law.

Further, Google indexes official, commercial and personal websites, and jumbles them up in the results list according to their popularity. Lawyers in particular need to check whether a site appearing in the results list is a personal page with no official sanction – look for a personal name in the website address, usually preceded by a tilde sign ~ or devised by an organisation, the name of which may appear in the website address. The domain name extension can also provide information on site ownership, and therefore authority:

    .ac (UK academic institutions – the US equivalent is .edu);
    .com (commercial);
    .gov (governmental organisation);
    .info (information which any person or organisation can register);
    .int (international organisations, offices or programmes endorsed by an international treaty);
    .org (mainly non-profit organisations).

In addition, a Google search may find material drawn from jurisdictions across the world. This may be of some value in answering a limited number of research problems, but you must 'sort the wheat from the chaff' and evaluate whether this cornucopia is of any value to the particular research problem in hand.

So, the statement of law retrieved through a Google search is usually:

- Not the most authoritative.

- Not the most accurate.

- Not the most up to date.

But, to be fair, the free web includes valuable law material (eg the *BAILII* website and the other sites forming the Legal Information Institutes worldwide). However, always carefully evaluate information gleaned from the free web in general and, if possible, cross-check it with quality controlled sources.

Lexis now offers a free online service in the form of LexisWeb <http://lexisweb.co.uk>, which provides access to some legal information. Links to *Lexis®Library* supplement the basic information available.

Commercial databases

Quality legal information is found in the commercial databases. But, the content of each is determined by the licences and agreements which the particular database provider has made with the original publishers of the information it contains. *Lawtel UK* and *Westlaw UK* are run by the long-established law publishers, Sweet & Maxwell (now owned by Thomson Reuters); similarly *Lexis®Library* owned by the LexisNexis Group, includes material originally published by Sweet & Maxwell's competitor: Butterworths. To a great extent, the full text information contained within each database is restricted to that published by each of the parent companies. So, a user of *Lexis®Library* is unlikely to find there the full text of a law report, journal or practitioner book published by Sweet & Maxwell, and vice versa. Also, some independent publishers (for example, the Incorporated Council for Law Reporting (ICLR), publisher of a range of titles including the *Law Reports* and *Weekly Law Reports*) have chosen to licence either one or more of the big database providers to display their publications. Other smaller, law publishing firms, have not granted licences to display on the big databases the full text of some of their publications, but set up their own electronic databases in competition (for example, i-law, publishers of the various 'Lloyds' series of law reports).

Similarly, valuable content can be found on other commercial databases which provide access to material published only by the organisation itself (examples include Jordan Publishing, Estates Gazette (EGi) and *Solicitors Journal*). Users need to examine such sites to see which best meets their research requirements.

A relatively new provider is the *Practical Law Company* (*PLC*). Access to *PLC*, especially in law firms, is now as commonplace as that to *Westlaw UK* and *Lexis®Library*. Rather than aiming to provide comprehensive case law and legislation coverage, *PLC* produces more in the way of standard precedent documents and drafting notes for a wide range of practice areas and a range of jurisdictions.

Developments within all commercial databases continue, although providers are usually good at keeping interested individuals up to date. LexisNexis has recently redeveloped and re-launched its *Lexis®PSL* product. *PLC*, *Westlaw UK*, *Lawtel UK* and *Justis* continue to expand content and develop their platforms, whilst all other providers are constantly looking at ways to provide relevant legal information to users in the most suitable way.

Especially within law firms, users potentially also have access to internal information within intranet or specific Knowledge Management systems. Often this supplements external information with internal know-how. The value of such systems differs greatly between organisations and it is once again be for the user to examine this resource diligently.

That is a major reason why it is important to think carefully about what each database contains. If you have access to only one database, recognise the limitations. If you have access to two or more, select the correct one for the research task in hand. See the descriptions under Part B, below, to make this decision easier.

3.2.2   Not comprehensive

Never assume that the internet contains all the law. Different websites and databases perform different functions and provide different pieces of law information. It should be clear from the description above that there is really no 'one stop shop' in which to find the law. Recognise this and develop your knowledge of where to find which piece of legal information on the internet, and you will be able to use it with more confidence.

Jurisdictions covered

Not all commercial databases include the legislation and cases applying to all the constituent parts of the United Kingdom (England, Wales, Scotland and Northern Ireland). In Part B, below, the inclusions and omissions are noted as far as it is possible to glean from each of the databases in question.

Dates available

No website or database covers all the law up to date from the year dot.

Some include the text of primary and secondary legislation in force now (*Lexis®Library* and *Westlaw UK*), while another includes the text of all legislation from 1267 onwards (*Justis Statutes*). Others include the text as enacted but from a date in the 1980s only (*Lawtel UK*). Some permit the user to undertake a 'point in time' search, where it is possible to retrieve the text of legislation on any specified date in the relatively recent past, such 1 April 1995 (*Westlaw UK, Legislation.gov.uk*).

Different databases owned by different publishers include different law report publications in full text. Each database therefore has different levels of coverage of the total output of reported decisions. *Lexis®Library* probably has the most comprehensive collection of older cases because it has the licence to display the *Law Reports* and the *All England Law Reports*. *Westlaw UK* has a licence to display *The English Reports* carrying the full text of cases from 1220 to 1865, and *The Law Reports* from 1865–, but is perhaps less comprehensive in its coverage of the 20th century in general than *Lexis®Library*. *Justis*, on the other hand, carries *The English Reports* but, as compared with *Lexis®Library* and *Westlaw UK* has very few more recent series of law reports.

Some databases include unreported cases, that is, cases which have not been published in a bona fide series of law reports (for as fuller explanation of 'unreported case' see Chapter 6 and also the entry in the glossary in Appendix 2), but the courts and dates included vary.

Full text or summary

Some databases contain either summaries only or the full text of cases and journal articles, depending on either the licenses the database provider has agreed with the original publisher or the purpose of the database (either for sophisticated searching or merely to keep users up to date with the latest developments). Knowing what is available where will speed your research – see Part B, below.

3.2.3   Not all free

The internet contains free sites of great value such as *BAILII*. The *British and Irish Legal Information Institute (BAILII)* was set up in 2001 as a registered charity, providing open, free access to quality legal information. It has 90 separate databases containing legislation, case law and secondary materials, such as Law Commission documents, held in over 290,000 searchable documents. *BAILII* has a reputation for being one of swiftest to display the text of recent, unreported cases. It also has an extensive collection, starting in 1996, of transcripts of cases (that is, the version of a case as issued by the firm of shorthand writers which made the record for the court – for a fuller explanation of 'transcript' see Chapter 6 and the entry in the glossary in Appendix 2). However, it lacks:

- the historical depth of case law (apart from a selection of 2,380 landmark decisions from before the 1990s);

- 'value-added' services available in the commercial, subscription databases, such as linkage from a particular case directly into:

  – a case citator to check whether the case is still good law;

  – the text of relevant, cited legislation;

  – relevant commentary in journals and practitioner books;

- the text of legislation in force now;

- sophisticated indexing of materials, using 'catchwords' (see the glossary in Appendix 2 for an explanation of this term), rather than simply searching for the word to appear in the full text, regardless of the significance of its use in the particular judgment (see section 1.3, above, for the limitations of some database search software).

Summary

- Understand and check each source (both paper and electronic) for its authority accuracy and currency.

- Be streetwise about using the internet – Google has severe limitations as a research tool for lawyers; each of the commercial databases has particular qualities and characteristics which it is essential to understand, to carry out the most comprehensive and effective research. A research task is not only about conducting a search, but also knowing which further resources to use, such as creating updates based upon results, finding related information and examining the search history.

- Recognise that there is a limit to the quality of the information which can be obtained from even the most valuable of free internet sites, and good legal research will often depend on a blend of free and fee-paid information.

PART B

SELECTING THE RIGHT SOURCE AND USING IT EFFECTIVELY

Contents

CHAPTER 4

GENERAL LAW ENCYCLOPEDIAS

4.1   INTRODUCTION

General law encyclopedias are best used when you:

- have no clear idea of the area/s of law involved in the research problem – you are cold starting (see Appendix 2 for a definition);

- are unfamiliar with the area/s of law which you have identified and need to obtain some general, contextual information;

- are not sure whether legislation or case law or both are involved in the solution – encyclopedias link the two sources together in the commentary.

General law encyclopedias usually focus more on substantive than procedural law. So, if your problem is procedural you may find the sources described in Chapter 7 a better starting point.

If you are sure of the area/s of law at the heart of the problem you need to research, rather than using a general law encyclopedia you may find it better to start by consulting a practitioner text – it will provide more detail than a general law encyclopedia.

4.2　　UNITED KINGDOM

4.2.1　*Westlaw UK – Insight*

At the end of 2012 *Westlaw UK* launched *Insight*, an online encyclopedia due to cover UK law. At the time of writing, however, its initial focus is on the law of England. The *Insight* tab is at the left hand end of the menu bar at the top of every *Westlaw UK* page. Access to commentary is via either a search facility or an alphabetical list of topics. Each entry is to a standard format with common headings under which succinct guidance and references to statute and case law are provided, with links into the rest of the *Westlaw UK* database for the full text. The Analysis section towards the end of every entry is a unique feature, providing commentary on key areas of complexity or uncertainty and details of future developments. The encyclopedia is being compiled by a combination of Westlaw's own editorial staff, practitioners and academic lawyers. A Watch Topics feature lists the entries the user has recently consulted and alerts the user to entries which have been updated. At this early stage, with only a limited number of entries, the service is highly intuitive, well presented and easy to use.

4.3　　ENGLAND AND WALES

4.3.1　*Halsbury's Laws of England*

> *Halsbury's Laws of England* (LexisNexis, 4th and 5th edns)

Also available as an additional subscription to the Commentary library of *Lexis®Library*.

Purpose

Commentary written by editorial staff on the whole law of England and Wales. No original legal materials reprinted but copious references to statutes, statutory instruments and cases. Invaluable guide to unfamiliar areas of law, especially those not available in more detailed practitioner texts.

Structure

The 4th edition (brown covers) is being updated over a period of many years to a 5th edition (black covers). The structure of the publication and how to use it is a little more complicated than previously. Libraries ought to be shelving the 5th edition volumes in a separate sequence following after the volumes of the 4th edition:

- Fifty-two Main Volumes in the 4th edition containing commentary arranged by subject title, gradually, being replaced by over 100 Main Volumes in the 5th edition;

- Annual Abridgments recording changes to the law in any one year not yet included in the Main Volumes, with brief summaries of statutes and cases – a consolidation of the information included in the year's Monthly Reviews, see below;

- Two volume Cumulative Supplement, replaced annually around March/April, in bound volumes, recording changes affecting both the Main Volumes and Annual Abridgements;

- Noter-up booklet, issued each month, containing citations to new legislation and cases since the preparation and publication of the Cumulative Supplement;

- Monthly Review booklet containing summaries of legislation and cases referred to in the Noter-up and Cumulative Supplement;

- Consolidated Index in three bound volumes, replaced annually around September/October, providing a subject index to the Main Volumes;

- Consolidated Table of Statutes, single bound volume;

- Consolidated Table of Statutory Instruments and other materials, in a single bound volume;

- Consolidated Table of Cases, two bound volumes.

How to use the print publication

Five step search:

Consolidated Index $\Rightarrow$ Current Service Noter-Up, Arrangement of Titles $\Rightarrow$ Main Volume $\Rightarrow$ Cumulative Supplement $\Rightarrow$ Noter-up

The second step is into a booklet which is replaced each month. At the front consult the 'Table of Correspondence' and 'Arrangement of Titles'. It displays a list of 4th and 5th edition titles and their subject headings. Titles not in bold print have been replaced or partially replaced in later volumes.

Use the flowchart in Figure 4.1.

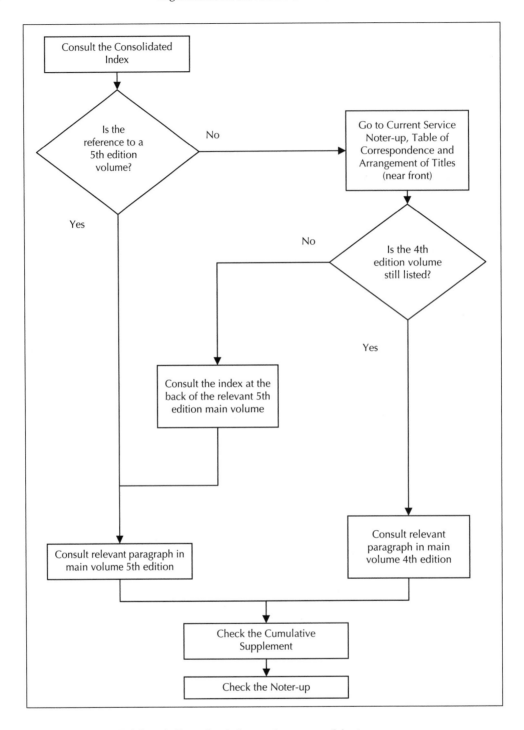

Figure 4.1: Searching *Halsbury's Laws* for information on a subject

Examples of the layout of entries in the Consolidated Index:

ANIMALS
  highway
        obstructing,   21 (4th), 350

meaning Main Volume 21 of the 4th edition at paragraph 350

ANIMALS
  ownership
        offspring of,   35 (4th), 1238n[1]

meaning Main Volume 35 of the 4th edition at paragraph 1238, footnote 1

ANIMALS
  poisoning   2 (5th), 829

meaning Main Volume 2 of the 5th edition at paragraph 829

Research tips relating to the Consolidated Index:

- the Consolidated Index is published annually but 5th edition volumes replacing those of the 4th edition are appearing all the time. There is a chance that after the Consolidated Index was published the topic you are looking for may have transferred from the 4th to the 5th edition, and so to an entirely different volume and paragraph number from that given in the Consolidated Index. So, check the listing near the front of the Noter-up booklet entitled 'Table of Correspondence and Arrangement of Titles' to see details of the latest replacements and rearrangement of volumes and titles, to trace the 5th edition Main Volume and title you need;

- as the 5th edition develops, it is probable that the publishers will adopt the same updating practice with Main Volumes as with the 4th edition. Once the law in a Main Volume became very dated and subscribers had to consult the Cumulative Supplement, Noter-up and Annual Abridgments for many new materials, the publishers published an updated, Reissue Main Volume. It totally replaced the former Main Volume, incorporating references to material previously only described elsewhere in *Halsbury's Laws*. So, if the paragraph references to a Main Volume given in the Consolidated Index do not lead to the text you expected to find, refer to the subject index at the back of the Reissue Main Volume to discover where the information you need is now printed.

Research tips relating to the Main Volumes:

- find your way around a volume by checking the subject title on the headers – the information printed across the top of each page;

- when each 4th edition Main Volume that has been partially replaced by a 5th edition volume a red label is fixed on the front cover stating where the subject titles have been moved to in the 5th edition Main Volume(s). Check if the 4th edition you are using has a red label on the front cover. If it does, check if the subject title you are researching has been moved to a new 5th edition volume. If it has, check the subject index at the back of the new 5th edition volume to discover where the updated information is now printed. Then follow the three research tips on using the Cumulative Supplement and Noter-up given below.

Research tips relating to the Cumulative Supplement and Noter-up:

- the Cumulative Supplement and Noter-up list legal developments to the text of the two editions as separate sections under each Main Volume number. So, if you are checking updates for a 5th edition volume, always look for a list following after the entries for the 4th edition volume number;

- if the Cumulative Supplement still carries entries relating to any 4th edition Main Volume since replaced by a 5th edition volume, ignore the updating information given for the 4th edition Main Volume. The changes should have been incorporated in the new 5th edition Main Volume. But still check the Noter-up for any developments since the 5th edition Main Volume was published;

- if there is no entry in the Cumulative Supplement and Noter-up for the Main Volume and paragraph number in which you are interested, you must assume that there have been no changes to the area of law between the publication of the relevant Main Volume and the publication of the Cumulative Supplement and Noter-up.

How to use the online version

Halsbury's Laws is available online via *Lexis®Library* only as an additional subscription to the Commentary library:

At any main search screen on *Lexis®Library*, click Commentary in the menu bar across the top of the screen
Open the 'Sources' dialog box and select *Halsbury's Laws of England*

Choose one route from the three different search routes available:

- *Route 1* – Consulting the online equivalent of the Consolidated Index and follow entries displayed there – probably the best route for novice users.

- *Route 2* – A subject term search across the full text of all the Main Volumes – only use this if you are familiar with the terminology used in *Halsbury's Laws* and the techniques used to link search terms together effectively. Otherwise your search may by less than effective with either too many, irrelevant results returned or no results at all.

- *Route 3* – Browsing amongst the list of Main Volume titles to find the most relevant – a technique probably best left to the more experienced user who understands the allocation of subjects to volumes.

Route 1 explained

Using the online Consolidated Index:

- Opening and browsing the Index as you might in paper form:

  At the Commentary search screen, click 'Browse' at the left side.
  Open the 'View' dialog box at the top of the screen and select Index.

An A–Z list appears in the centre of the screen. Where + appears against any entry, sub-headings can be opened up to narrow the search. When the search has reached the level of an individual paragraph clicking on the paragraph reference will bring the full text of the Main Volume into the right-hand screen. Where there is updating material which appears in the paper version of the Cumulative Supplement or Noter-Up, the word UPDATE appears below the paragraph number in the list in the left-hand screen. Click the link to reveal the text in the right-hand screen

Route 2 explained

Using a subject term search.

Lexis®Library provides links to help at the left side of the main subject search screen. Also see Appendix 4 for advice on constructing searches more effectively.

Here are some general matters to consider when compiling a search across the full text of all the Main Volumes:

- the technical terms which *Halsbury's* uses – for example, a search on the term 'roads' will not retrieve as good material as 'highways';

- how far distant from each other the keywords might appear in the text of *Halsbury's Laws*.

This knowledge only comes as a result of familiarity with the subject area and the way terminology is used in the publication.

Route 3 explained

Browsing amongst the list of Main Volumes:

At the Commentary search screen, click 'Browse' at the left side.
Open the 'View' dialog box at the top of the screen and select Table of Contents.

Subject headings appear in the centre of the screen. Where + appears against any entry, sub-headings can be opened up to narrow the search. When the search has reached the level of an individual paragraph clicking on the paragraph reference will split the screen, bringing the full text of the Main Volume into the right-hand screen and moving the subject headings to the left. Where there is updating material which appears in the paper version of the Cumulative Supplement or Noter-Up, the word UPDATE appears below the paragraph number in the list in the left-hand screen. Click the link to reveal the text in the right-hand screen

As an alternative to browsing, a 'quick search' can be performed across the Main Volumes by using the box near the top of the search screen. See Appendix 4 for advice on constructing searches more effectively.

Making access to Halsbury's Laws easier

Users can select *Halsbury's Laws* (along with other subscribed sources) for insertion into the 'My Bookshelf' area of *Lexis®Library*. This will permit searching or browsing of a specific source from the homepage.

4.4   SCOTLAND

4.4.1   The Laws of Scotland: Stair Memorial Encyclopedia

The Laws of Scotland: Stair Memorial Encyclopedia (LexisNexis)

Also available by subscription through *Lexis®Library*.

Purpose

To provide commentary with copious footnote references to original sources of the law of Scotland.

Structure

There are similarities with *Halsbury's Laws* (see section 4.3, above), in structure, content and use, except that the *Stair Encyclopedia* is not undergoing a major overhaul:

- Twenty-five Main Volumes containing an alphabetical subject arrangement of commentary of the law of Scotland;

- Reissue Booklets housed in thirteen binders, containing revisions to the Main Volumes. Each Reissue Booklet usually covers only one topic though the editorial re-categorisation of topics may cause one or more of the topics in the Main Volumes to be included;

- A Cumulative Supplement published annually updating both the Main Volumes and the Reissue Booklets;

- Updating Service, published twice a year in looseleaf format, updating the Main Volumes, Reissue Booklets and the Cumulative Supplement;

- Consolidated Index, published annually as a softback volume, indexing the Main Volumes and Reissue Booklets;

- Consolidated Table of Statutes, published annually as a softback volume, indexing the Main Volumes and Reissue Booklets and containing separate tables of Statutes; Orders, Rules and Regulations; EC legislation; Treaties and Conventions;

- Consolidated Table of Cases, published annually as a softback volume, indexing the Main Volumes and Reissue Booklets.

How to use the print publication

There are three possible searches: by subject, for a statute or for a case.

- Subject search:

    Consolidated Index then

    either ⇒ Main Volume ⇒ Cumulative Supplement ⇒ Updating Service

    Delict
                carelessness 15 256

    meaning Main Volume 15, paragraph 256

or ⇒ Reissue Booklet ⇒ Cumulative Supplement ⇒ Updating Service for reissues (at the back of the volume)

> Delict
>> carriage by sea, title to sue shipowner Carr 206

meaning Reissue Booklet: Carriage, paragraph 206

- Statute or case search:

  Consolidated Table of Statutes or Consolidated Table of Cases then

  > either ⇒ Main Volume
  > or ⇒ Reissue Booklet

  Index entries contain references either to the Main Volumes or Reissue Booklets in the same style as for the subject search. A key to the abbreviations used for the titles of the Reissue Booklets is printed at the front of each of the Consolidated Indexes.

How to use the online version

Laws of Scotland is available online via *Lexis®Library* only as an additional subscription to the Commentary library:

> At any main search screen on *Lexis®Library*, click Commentary in the menu bar across the top of the screen
> Open the 'Sources' dialog box and select *Stair Memorial Encyclopedia* from the list of sources

Choose one route from the three different search routes available:

- Searching across the entire publication:

  A search across the entire publication will retrieve documents matching the search words appearing anywhere. In the results list follow the document title link to view the full text. The disadvantage of this approach is the possibility of retrieving many irrelevant results.

- Browsing amongst the list of Main Volumes:

  Use the +/- symbols to expand or collapse headings, sub-headings and numbered paragraphs within a title.

  Browsing limits results to the particular title/s selected but provides greater focus than searching.

- Browsing or searching the online index.

Reading the online text

Each numbered paragraph comprises original text and updated text. The updating text appears as separate 'TEXT' and 'NOTE' entries below the original text and footnotes. Updates are not incorporated into the main text so the entire paragraph must be read.

4.5   NORTHERN IRELAND

There is no encyclopedia equivalent to *Halsbury's Laws* (for England and Wales) or the *Stair Memorial Encyclopedia* (for Scotland). SLS Legal Publications published the *Digest of Northern Ireland Law as* a fairly irregular pamphlet series by various authors until 2007. The last published were:

- Dickson, B, *A Short Guide to Contract Law in Northern Ireland* (as above, 2006).

- Dickson, B, *Legal Services in Northern Ireland: a short guide* (as above, 2006).

- Grattan, S, *Social Security Law in Northern Ireland: a short guide*; new edition by Eileen Evason (as above, 2006).

- Grattan, S, *Wills and Intestacy: a short guide* (as above, 2007).

As an introduction to the Northern Ireland legal system, the following is recommended:

- Dickson, B, *Law in Northern Ireland: an introduction* (SLS Legal Publications (NI), 2011).

4.6   EUROPEAN UNION

4.6.1   Law of the European Union

Vaughan, D, and Robertson, A, *Law of the European Union* (Oxford University Press, 2007–)

Purpose

To provide commentary on EU law; no original materials are reprinted but the footnote references are copious. Commentary written by a large number of expert contributors.

Structure

Six looseleaf volumes updated quarterly. The set is divided into thirty sections, mainly by practice area.

How to use the print publication

There is no comprehensive index to the whole set.

Contents pages to the entire set found at the front of each volume ⇒ section index at the back of the relevant section ⇒ main text of that section.

4.7   INTERNATIONAL

4.7.1   Encyclopaedia of Public International Law

Max Planck Encyclopaedia of Public International Law (Oxford University Press, 2012)

Good for background information but of limited use for recent developments and in-depth research.

Some 1,600 articles, each often several pages in length, describing the basic principles and rules governing aspects of international law with summaries of the more important decisions of courts and tribunals. Each article is fully referenced and written by one of over 800 experts contributing to the publication. The online version (subscriber-only) is regularly updated with revised articles: <http://www.mpepil.com>

4.7.2   International Encyclopedia of Comparative Law

> *International Encyclopedia of Comparative Law* (Sijthoff & Noordhoff)

A highly authoritative publication but suffers from rather slow updating. Good at providing foundations and context rather than detail and current references.

Purpose

A broad, systematic, descriptive compendium of international comparative law providing commentary with copious references to original legal materials.

Structure

In seventeen volumes:

- Volume I – national reports on nearly 150 countries, each report providing a concise outline of each country's legal system, including its constitutional system and sources of law, with particular emphasis on private and commercial law. Each national report is to a common, broad structure to facilitate comparison.

- Volume II – legal systems of the world, their comparison and a description of the steps towards unification.

- Volumes III to XVII – each on a different topic, eg volume IV on persons and family with chapters on divorce (Chapter 5), parents and guardians (Chapter 7) and intra-family torts (Chapter 9).

Each chapter is written by subject specialists drawn from a panel of about 400 who have contributed to the encyclopedia. On completion chapters are published rapidly as individual paperbacks. When all the chapters in a volume are complete all are updated and revised and published as a hardback volume with a full index.

How to use the print publication

Since there is no index to the entire set, select the appropriate volume and chapter from the list at the back of the guide volume published in 1974. Then use the index at the back of the relevant bound volume or the contents list at the front of the paperback chapter to find the material required.

4.7.3   Encyclopaedic Dictionary of International Law

Grant, JP and Barker, JC (eds), *Parry and Grant Encyclopaedic Dictionary of International Law* (Oxford University Press USA, 3rd edn, 2009)

Combined encyclopedia and dictionary containing both definitions of terms and concepts with a lengthy commentary on the context in which each term is employed and a list of primary and secondary publications. Covers mainstream international law – the law of peace, law of war, humanitarian and human rights law and the law of international organisations. Includes biographies of a selection of leading figures in international law. Available as an online e-reference on the Oxford University Press Digital Reference Shelf.

4.8   HOW TO CITE AN ENCYCLOPEDIA

OSCOLA (see section 17.4.3, below) recommends that these publications should be cited much as one would a book, but excluding the author or editor and publisher and including the edition and year of issue or reissue. However, where an author is credited with a particular segment, different standards apply. Encyclopedias can be compiled by editorial teams as well as individuals, and are available online and in print, so OSCOLA helpfully provides examples for each eventuality.

CHAPTER 5

LEGISLATION

5.1   INTRODUCTION

To ensure you get the best from this chapter, check that you know the type of information you are trying to find.

Are you looking for:

(1) a particular piece of legislation the title or citation you know?; or

(2) legislation in a practice area, or on a topic or subject, the particular titles or citations you do not yet know?

If (1), decide whether you wish to find:

- an unconsolidated version of the legislation, that is, without subsequent amendments or repeals or revocations noted;

- the consolidated version;

- a summary; or

- revoked legislation.

Publications and databases in most sections of this chapter, apart from those on international law, are discussed under those four headings. In addition, databases which permit searching for historical versions of the text as at a user-specified date are highlighted.

Details of how to cite each type of legislation are given at the end of each section.

If (2), a practice area, topic or subject search, do not use the commercial full text online databases, for they usually search every word in the legislation library and the results will contain every mention of the search word or phrase, both significant and insignificant. Better to refine your search using the controlled listing of subject words (that is, indexes where only significant mentions of the keyword are listed) in the subject indexes to publications such as:

- *Encyclopedia of European Union Law: Constitutional texts* (see section 5.6.2 below);

- *Encyclopedia of European Community Law: Community secondary legislation* (see section 5.6.2, below);

- *Halsbury's Statutes of England* (covering England and Wales) (see section 5.2.1, below);

- *Halsbury's Statutory Instruments* (covering England and Wales) (see section 5.2.3, below);

- *Parliament House Book* (Scotland) (see section 5.4.1, below).

If a commercial database is used for a subject search, many now have features such as predictive text or the ability to limit the search over title only, which may help focus the search results.

Alternatively, use the keyword or subject indexes in the sources mentioned in Chapter 10 and/or a practitioner work to identify particular pieces of legislation.

Some services use an abbreviation for the title of a particular piece of legislation. A list of abbreviations most frequently used for UK legislation is found in Appendix 1.1.

To check whether legislation is in force, has been amended, repealed or revoked or the courts have interpreted the meaning of a provision, see Chapter 9.

To check for draft legislation, see section 9.2, below and Chapter 11.

5.2   UNITED KINGDOM

5.2.1   Public General Acts passed at Westminster

To check if an Act is still in force, has been amended or repealed, or if its meaning has been interpreted by the courts, see section 9.2.2, below.

Unconsolidated Acts

Loose copies of Acts published as soon as possible after Royal Assent by TSO (The Stationery Office): <http://www.tso.co.uk>

Alerts to new Acts passed: <http://www.legislation.gov.uk/new>

The original full text of Acts made at Westminster since 1 January 1987, with a selection from earlier years, and access to original print pdf versions: <http://www.legislation.gov.uk/ukpga>

Both *Lawtel UK* (subscriber-only service) and the free service *British and Irish Legal Information Institute* (*BAILII*) reproduce material from the TSO source: <http://www.bailii.org>

Public General Acts and General Synod Measures (TSO – The Stationery Office)
Annual bound volume set, not updated.

Law Reports Statutes (Incorporated Council of Law Reporting)
Annual bound volume set reprinting the text of the Act as at Royal Assent.

Current Law Statutes (Sweet & Maxwell)
The full text of individual Acts is issued in individual booklets soon after Royal Assent, together with, from the 1980s onwards, increasingly extensive annotations and commentary on the meaning and effect of the Act in general and individual sections in particular. The booklets are filed in a Service Binders 1, 2 and 3. At the year end, the individual booklets are replaced by a bound volume. Unfortunately, the text of the Act and the commentary are not updated.

Knight's Local Government Reports
From 1903 to 1990 *Knight's* carried the full, unconsolidated text of Acts published each year, of relevance to local government in England and Wales.

Consolidated Acts in force now

Print sources

Many looseleaf subject specialist encyclopedias reprint the consolidated text of Acts relevant to their topic area. But the only general 'encyclopedia' of Acts is *Halsbury's Statutes of England.*

| *Halsbury's Statutes of England* (LexisNexis, 4th edn, 1985) |

Bound volumes and looseleaf, continuously updated (Butterworths). Partly incorporated within the Legislation library of *Lexis®Library* (subscriber-only service).

Purpose

Provides up-to-date versions of all Public General Acts (except Consolidated Fund Acts and Appropriation Acts) in force in England and Wales and, in addition, provides copious commentary and notes. Public General Acts which affect only Scotland are generally omitted.

Structure

- Fifty Main Volumes containing an alphabetical subject-by-subject arrangement of the Public General Acts in force at the time of the publication of each volume – the date is given on the spine of each volume along with the titles of the subjects included. When the law in any Main Volume has changed considerably a 'reissue' volume is compiled and published to replace the original Main Volume;

- Current Statutes Service of six looseleaf volumes containing the text of recent Acts not yet included in the Main Volumes, arranged in parallel order with them – on the spine of each volume is a list of the volumes to which the updating information refers. Note that recently, the updating information about large and complex pieces of legislation, such as the Finance Act 2011, is printed as covering a group of volumes (42–49(S)) not a single volume;

- Cumulative Supplement, a single bound volume issued each year in April or May, containing details of changes which have affected both the Main Volumes and the Current Statutes Service since they were published;

- Noter-up, a single looseleaf volume containing updating information issued quarterly, bridging the gap between the compilation of the Cumulative Supplement and the present day, filed behind the Noter-up guide card or tab;

- Consolidated Index, issued annually, usually in the autumn, containing three indexes: a list in alphabetical order of the names of all statutes included in *Halsbury's Statutes*, a second index arranging the statutes in chronological order and finally a subject index (called the Consolidated Index) to the whole work;

- Consolidated Table of Statutory Instruments, a single volume issued annually, usually in the autumn;

- Consolidated Table of Cases, a single volume issued annually, usually in the summer;

- *Is it in force?*, a single softbound volume, issued twice a year (winter and summer), recording the exact commencement date of every section of every Public General Act since 1 January 1960, with details of the authority (such as a Statutory Instrument) by which it was brought into force;

- Destination Tables, a single volume issued irregularly, providing information on the origin of law now included in sections of consolidation or similar Acts passed since 1957;

- Statutes Citator, a single volume issued twice a year (winter and summer) detailing the current status (in force, amended, repealed) of every section of the 7,600 Acts which have appeared in *Halsbury's Statutes* since publication began in 1929.

How to use the print publication

Halsbury's Statutes contains a vast amount of information and can be searched in at least four different ways: to find the text of an Act, to check if a section is in force, to check the status of a section and to check the derivation of a section within a consolidation Act or similar legislation. In this chapter the instructions below focus on finding the text of an Act only. The use of *Halsbury's Statutes* for the three other purposes is covered in Chapter 9.

There are three different searches in *Halsbury's Statutes* which may be carried out to find the text of an Act:

(1)   Searching for an Act by subject:

Table of Statutes and General Index (use the Consolidated Index (subject index) towards the back of the volume) ⇒ Main Volume ⇒ *Halsbury's Statutes Checklist*. At the front of *Current Statutes Service* Binder A, to check the reissue year of the volume which is current and you should be using ⇒ Cumulative Supplement ⇒ Noter-up

Use the flowchart in Figure 5.1.

See below on how to use each of the parts of the publication effectively.

(2)   Searching for an Act by its title:

Table of Statutes and General Index (use the Table of Statutes, the alphabetical title index at the front of the volume) ⇒ Main Volume ⇒ *Halsbury's Statutes Checklist*. At the front of *Current Statutes Service* Binder A, to check the reissue year of the volume which is current and you should be using ⇒ Cumulative Supplement ⇒ Noter-up

Use the flowchart in Figure 5.2.

See below on how to use each of the parts of the publication effectively.

(3)   Searching for the text of an Act recently given the Royal Assent:

Current Statutes Service Binder A (check the list of recent statutes at the front) ⇒ appropriate Current Statutes Service binder ⇒ Cumulative Supplement ⇒ Noter-up

Use the flowchart in Figure 5.2.

See below on how to use each of the parts of the publication effectively.

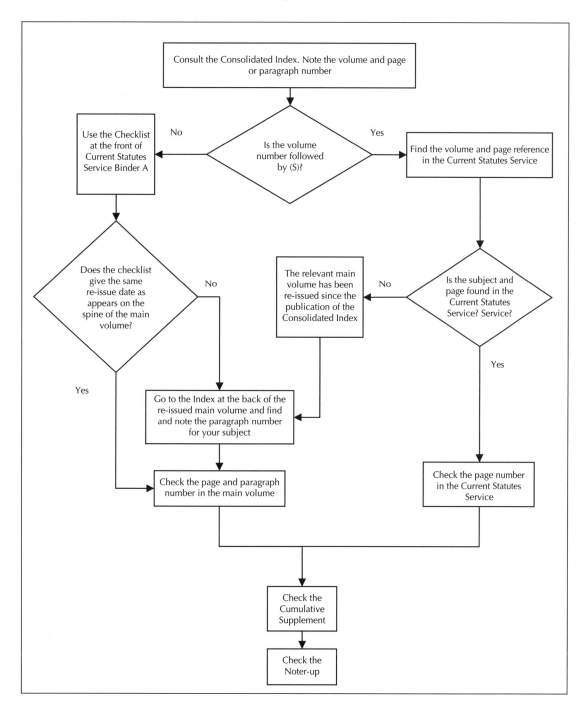

Figure 5.1: Searching *Halsbury's Statutes* for information on a subject

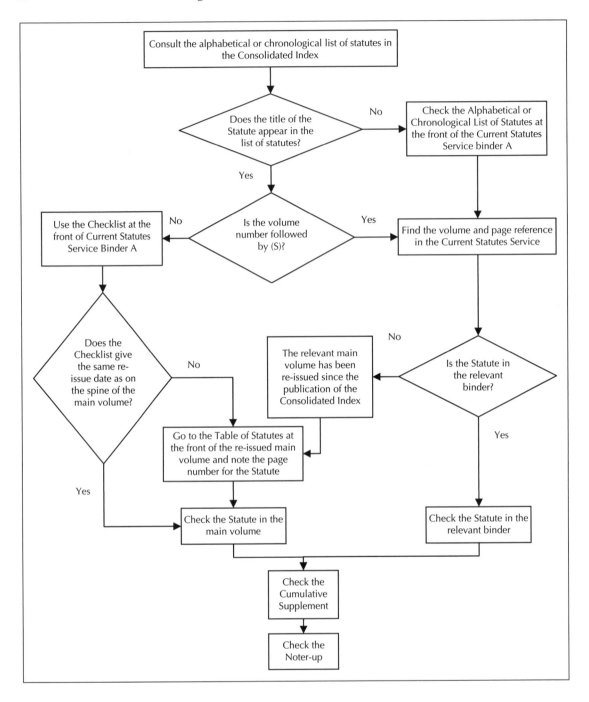

Figure 5.2: Searching *Halsbury's Statutes* for a Statute by title

How to use the Index to *Halsbury's Statutes* effectively
Examples of different types of entry in the Consolidated (subject) Index:

family proceedings
    child involved in, privacy for,   6 [428]

meaning Main Volume 6 at paragraph 428

family proceedings
    officers, risk assessments,   6(S),18

meaning Current Service Volume containing updates to Main Volume 6 at page 18

laundry
    self operated,   26, 710–11

meaning Main Volume 26 at pages 710–711

Examples of different types of entry in the Alphabetical (title) Index:

Football Spectators Act 1989   13, 362

meaning Main Volume 13 at page 362

Forced Marriage (Civil Protection) Act 2007   27(S), Matrimonial 1

meaning Current Service Volume containing updates to Main Volume 27, subject title Matrimonial at page 1

Foreign Enlistment Act 1870   12(1), 160

meaning Main Volume 12, part 1 at page 160

Human Tissue Act 2004   28 (2008R), 1038

meaning Main Volume 28, reissued in 2008, at page 1038

If there is no entry in the Alphabetical or Chronological Index for the Act you require it may be very recent, so check the Alphabetical or Chronological List of Statutes at the front of the Current Statues Service Binder A.

Research tip
The basic unit of reference throughout *Halsbury's Statutes* has been changed from page number to paragraph number given in brackets for all but a few volumes. The Consolidated Index features a few entries to the old scheme until all Main Volumes have been reissued to the new scheme. Ensure you note carefully whether the Index is leading you to a page or a paragraph. Note that references to the Current Statutes Service Binders are always to page numbers.

How to use the Main Volumes of *Halsbury's Statutes* effectively

- To find the subject you require look at the subject titles printed at the top of each left-hand page; to find the Act you require look at the titles printed at the top of the right-hand page.

- Paragraph numbers are printed at the right-hand side of the body of the text on each page.

- Take care as some subjects are printed across at least one Main Volume.

- If the subject, page or paragraph numbers do not match with the information found in the Index, the Main Volume may have been published after the Index volume was issued. So, check the index at the back on the Main Volume for the new location of the subject or Act you require. Write down this new location to use when the Cumulative Supplement and Noter-up are searched for more recent changes to the law.

- Amended text appears in square brackets [ ].

- Repealed text appears as three dots … .

- Editorial commentary is in a smaller typeface.

How to use the Current Statutes Service of *Halsbury's Statutes* effectively

- Each binder is arranged in parallel order with the Main Volumes listed on its spine.

- Red guide cards or tabs separate information on each Main Volume or, in few cases, a group of Main Volumes.

- Grey guide cards or tabs separate information on individual subject titles into which the Main Volumes are divided.

- Subject titles are printed at the top of each left-hand page.

- The title of each statute is printed at the top of the right-hand page.

- If there is no material behind the relevant guide card, an updated Main Volume has been issued since the index volume was compiled, and all the updating information is now included within its covers. Go to the relevant Main Volume, then the Cumulative Supplement followed by the Noter-up, looking under the new page and paragraph numbers found in the updated Main Volume.

- The layout of the text of each statute is the same as found in the Main Volumes.

How to use the Cumulative Supplement of *Halsbury's Statutes* effectively

- The Cumulative Supplement is arranged in parallel with the Main Volumes.

- To find the correct entry for the Main Volume look for the volume number and subject printed at the top of the page (the header), then look down the left-hand margin for the page number.

- Any updates applying to information found in the Current Statutes Service are printed in a separate section after the updates for the Main Volume. The header includes the volume number but with an (S) after the volume number: 28(S).

- If there is no entry for the volume and page numbers you may assume there have been no changes up to the time the Cumulative Supplement was published.

- If the Main Volume was published after the Cumulative Supplement there will be no entries to it in the Cumulative Supplement, but there will be entries to the out of date Main Volume which should be ignored.

How to use the Noter-up of *Halsbury's Statutes* effectively

- Look for the Noter-up tab in the Noter-up Service looseleaf binder.

- The Noter-up is arranged in parallel with the Main Volumes and Cumulative Supplement.

- Always check the Noter-up regardless of how recently the Main Volume or Cumulative Supplement were published. New material could have been published.

Online sources

Legislation.gov.uk (free):
<http://www.legislation.gov.uk>
Full text of Acts in force on 1 February 1991 and all published subsequently. Open the 'Type' drop-down box and select appropriate material from list. Some materials are not fully up to date – watch for warning notices at the top of the contents page of such Acts. Under Advanced Search can undertake a 'point in time' search for text of an Act on any particular date from 1 February 1991 onwards.

Practical Law Company (subscriber-only service)
PLC has been working with The National Archive for some time to provide access to legislation for its subscribers, via links to the *Legislation.gov.uk* website, which was launched in 2010. Not all legislation is currently available and only some is consolidated, although where the latter is relevant this is clearly stated. Access to the legislation itself is free of charge.

Lexis®Library (subscriber-only service)
Legislation library – full text of all Public General Acts currently in force, incorporating some features of *Halsbury's Statutes*. The main features from *Halsbury's Statutes* are listed in the box at the top right-hand side of any screen bearing the text of a particular section of an Act. There are links to *Halsbury's Is it in Force?* and the *Halsbury's Statute Citator*. At present the link to commentary does not carry the same text that appears in *Halsbury's Statutes* but displays commentary created by the editorial staff of *Lexis®Library*. The Statute Snapshot facility provides a pop-up of the relevant annotations from *Halsbury's Statutes* both for individual provisions and the Act as a whole. The Snapshot sets out commencement and amendment information. Historical versions of Acts are not available directly from the *Lexis®Library* database but can be requested from *Lexis®Library* staff – at the main Legislation Library search screen click the link at the left: 'Historical Versions' for details.

Westlaw UK (subscriber-only service)
Includes all Public and General Acts still in force on 1 February 1991 and all published subsequently. Basic Search contains the most up-to-date version of legislation. Earlier versions of legislation can be accessed via the Advanced Search with the Historic Law or Point in Time options selected. They can also be accessed via the Legislation Analysis or by using the version navigation buttons in full text legislation

documents. Annotations are provided for all Acts back to 1992 and for a selection before that date. Search for Acts in the normal way and in the results list an A will indicate annotations are available.

Justis UK Statutes (subscriber-only service)
See 'Repealed Acts', below.

Repealed Acts

Justis UK Statutes (subscriber-only service)
Original text, from 1235 onwards, but with information about amending and repealing legislation – the user has to piece together the consolidated version of the text of an Act. But this is a unique database, containing repealed and live legislation back to 1235.

How to cite Public General Acts

OSCOLA (see section 17.4.3, below) recommends citing modern Acts by title and year only and including the chapter number for older statutes without short titles. However, the inclusion of the chapter number makes it easier to locate the text of the Act in print volumes from all periods, since they frequently reproduce Acts in chapter number order.

Public General Acts of Westminster, since 1 January 1963:

> Title | year | chapter number

Example:

> Explosives (Age of Purchase, etc) Act 1976 c.26

Public General Acts of Westminster, before 1 January 1963:

> Title | year (regnal year | chapter number)

Example:

> Abandonment of Animals Act 1960 (8 & 9 Eliz. 2, c.40)

Official print versions of pre-1963 Acts were bound in volumes according to the regnal year (see Appendix 2 for an explanation of this term). Omitting the regnal year from the citation makes finding the text in these older volumes more difficult.

Some services use an abbreviation for the title of a particular piece of legislation. A list of the most frequently used for UK legislation is found in Appendix 1.1.

5.2.2   Local, Personal and Private Acts passed at Westminster

To check if a Local, Personal and Private Act is still in force, has been amended or revoked, or if its meaning has been interpreted by the courts, see Chapter 9.

Official sources

Loose copies of Local, Personal and Private Acts (TSO – The Stationery Office) published soon after Royal Assent:
<http://www.tso.co.uk>

Local, Personal and Private Acts (TSO – The Stationery Office):
<http://www.tso.co.uk>
Annual bound volume set.

Local Acts of the UK Parliament:
<http://www.legislation.gov.uk/ukla>
Full text of Local Acts only from 1991 onwards, as originally enacted, with a selection back to 1857. Access to the original print pdf versions available. See the entry below for *Justis UK Statues* for a more comprehensive collection of material.

Legislation.gov.uk (free):
<http://www.legislation.gov.uk>
Full text of Local Acts in force on 1 February 1991 and all published subsequently. Open the 'Type' drop-down box and select appropriate material from list. Note that only a few Local Acts will be displayed in their revised form, most have not been updated. Watch for warning notices at the top of the contents page of such Acts. It is not possible to use Advanced Search to undertake a 'point in time' search for the text of a Local Act on any particular date from 1 February 1991 onwards.

Pre-1991 local, personal or private legislation may be held by the local studies library of the Central Public Library in the area to which the local Act applies, or by the County Records Office or the archives section of the public corporation or landed family or estate in question.

The website of the National Archives at Kew provides a list of major collections of local legislation in the United Kingdom, see:
<http://yourarchives.nationalarchives.gov.uk/index.php?title=Major_Collections_of_Local_Legislation_in_the_United_Kingdom>
But note that the list has not been updated since 30 September 2012 and is available as read-only. At a future date the content will be transferred to the UK Government Web Archive:
<http://webarchive.nationalarchives.gov.uk/*/http:/yourarchives.nationalarchives.gov.uk>

In addition, the following libraries are noted for their good collections of local Acts:

Guildhall Library, London:
<http://www.cityoflondon.gov.uk/things-to-do/visiting-the-city/archives-and-city-history/guildhall-library/Pages/default.aspx>

Law Society Library, London:
<http://uk1.lexisnexis.com/LawSocietyLibrary/HomePage.aspx>

Cardiff University Law Library
<http://www.cardiff.ac.uk/insrv/libraries/law/index.html>
An incomplete print collection of local, personal and private Acts from the early years of the 19th century onwards.

Otherwise, a master set is held in print form by the Parliamentary Archives. Images of printed local and personal Acts from 1799 to 1990 (with some gaps) are available to use on CD at the Parliamentary Archives, see:
<http://www.parliament.uk/business/publications/parliamentary-archives/archives-electronic/primary-and-secondary-legislation>

Unofficial sources

Current Law Statutes (Sweet & Maxwell)
Includes text of all Local and Personal Acts from 1992 onwards. Booklets containing the text of Acts not yet incorporated in an annual bound volume are filed at the back of Binder 3.

Lexis®Library (subscriber-only service)
Excludes Local, Personal and Private Acts.

Westlaw UK (subscriber-only service)
Includes Local Acts published since 1991 but excludes Personal and Private Acts.

Justis UK Statutes (subscriber-only service)
A collection of all local Acts from 1797 onwards, as originally enacted, with a constantly growing collection of personal and private Acts being added. The private Act collection is complete from 1834 onwards and work progresses on adding earlier material.

How to cite Local and Personal Acts

> Title | year | chapter number (lower case roman numeral)

Example:

> Transport for London Act 2008 c.i

5.2.3   Statutory Instruments of General Application passed at Westminster

To check if a Statutory Instrument is still in force, has been amended or revoked, or if its meaning has been interpreted by the courts, see Chapter 9.

Unconsolidated Statutory Instruments

Loose copies of Statutory Instruments published by TSO (The Stationery Office):
<http://www.tso.co.uk>

Alerts to new Statutory Instruments:
<http://www.legislation.gov.uk/new>

The original full text of Statutory Instruments made at Westminster since 1 January 1987. Prior to 1987, only those Statutory Instruments that were still at least partly in force in April 2011. Access to original print pdf versions:
<http://www.legislation.gov.uk/uksi>

Both *Lawtel UK* (subscriber-only service) and the free service *British and Irish Legal Information Institute* (*BAILII*) reproduce material from the TSO source:
<http://www.bailii.org>

Legislation.gov.uk (free):
<http://www.legislation.gov.uk>
Full text of Statutory Instruments in force on 1 February 1991 and all published subsequently. Prior to 1987, only those Statutory Instruments that were still at least partly in force in April 2011. Unlike Acts, the text of most Statutory Instruments on the *Legislation.gov.uk* database are in unrevised form, as originally enacted. Open the 'Type' drop-down box and select appropriate material from list. It is not possible to use Advanced Search to undertake a 'point in time' search for text of a Statutory Instrument on any particular date from 1 February 1991 onwards.

Statutory Instruments (TSO – The Stationery Office)
Annual bound volume set. It includes all Statutory Instruments in force at the end of the year – it excludes instruments of temporary application and which are 'spent'.

Knight's Local Government Reports
From 1903 to 1990 *Knight's* carried the full, unconsolidated text of Statutory Instruments published each year, of relevance to local government in England and Wales.

Consolidated Statutory Instruments in force now

Many subject specialist encyclopedias reprint the text of Statutory Instruments relevant to their topic area.

Lexis®Library (subscriber-only service)
Legislation library – full text of all Statutory Instruments of General Application except for those relating purely to areas outside London currently in force.

Westlaw UK (subscriber-only service)
Includes a selection of UK Statutory Instruments of General Application published between 1948 and 1991. All subsequent Statutory Instruments made at Westminster are included. *Westlaw UK* Basic Search contains the most up-to-date version of legislation. Earlier versions of legislation can be accessed via the Advanced Search with the Historic Law or Point in Time options selected. They can also be accessed via the Legislation Analysis or by using the version navigation buttons in full text legislation documents.

Justis UK Statutory Instruments (subscriber-only service)
See 'Revoked Statutory Instruments', below.

Revoked Statutory Instruments

Justis UK Statutory Instruments (subscriber-only service)
Original text, from 1671 onwards, but with information about amending and repealing legislation – the user has to piece together the consolidated version of the text of a Statutory Instrument. But this is a unique database, containing revoked and live SR&O and Statutory Instruments back to 1671. Available on the internet and as a DVD.

Revoked Statutory Rules and Orders, pre-1894

London Gazette (free)
<http://www.london-gazette.co.uk>
The text of pre-1894 Statutory Rules and Orders was printed in full in the *London Gazette*. At the home page, there is a box labelled 'Historians'. Click 'Search the Archive'. Search for the required SR&O by date and/or words. When searching by date it is possible to select a range as well as the specific date of the issue of the gazette in which the SR&O appeared.

Summaries of Statutory Instruments

Halsbury's Statutory Instruments (LexisNexis, 2nd edn, 1986–)

Bound volumes and looseleaf, continuously updated.

Purpose
Summarises, and in a few cases reprints the full text of, Statutory Instruments in force in England and Wales (except for local Statutory Instruments) made at Westminster and summaries of Statutory Instruments made by the National Assembly for Wales. It does not include Statutory Instruments extending only to Scotland.

Structure

- Consolidated Index, published annually (usually in June/July) and includes a subject index (called the Consolidated Index) and a title index: Alphabetical List of Instruments, which appear in *Halsbury's Statutory Instruments*.

- Twenty-two Main Volumes containing subject titles arranged alphabetically. When the law in a Main Volume becomes badly out of date, the volume is reissued incorporating the changes. This occurs frequently. The year of reissue is printed at the foot of the spine and at the bottom of the title page. The date up to which the statement of law is correct is also printed at the bottom of the title page. The subject titles covered in each volume are noted on the spine.

- Looseleaf Service Binder, updated monthly, includes many sections:

   – a Chronological List of Instruments included in the Main Volumes and the Monthly Update;

   – a subject index called the Monthly Index which supplements the Consolidated Index;

– a Monthly Update which brings the information found in the Main Volumes up to date and is arranged in the same subject title sequence used in the Main Volumes. It achieves this through four separate sections included in each subject title sequence:

— a Chronological List of new instruments that have come into force since the publication of a Main Volume;

— a List of Changes recording developments to instruments since the publication of each Main Volume;

— summaries of some Statutory Instruments that have come into force since the publication of the relevant Main Volume.

— Commencement of legislation, detailing commencement dates for a selection of Acts;

– an Alphabetical list of instruments for the current year;

– a Table of statutes listing enabling powers under which instruments of the current year were made;

– further sections in the looseleaf binder include:

— a Chronological List of Scottish Statutory Instruments issued since 1999;

— a Table of European Legislation for [the current year] which details EU Directives and Decisions implemented in England and Wales by instruments, and continues the table in Part 1 of the EC Legislation Implementator (see below).

• Statutory Instrument Citator, issued each October, detailing the status of each Statutory Instrument in the service.

• EC Legislation Implementator, issued each March, detailing the implementation in England and Wales of EC Directives. Instruments relating purely to Scotland and Northern Ireland are excluded.

How to use the print publication

Three different types of search may be carried out: for Statutory Instruments on a particular subject; finding a Statutory Instrument from a citation; finding a Statutory Instrument by its title:

(1) Subject search

To trace all Statutory Instruments on a subject, see Figure 5.3.

Three step search:

Consolidated Index ⇒ Main Volume ⇒ Service Binder (Monthly Update)

Example of entries in the Consolidated Index:

disability discrimination
public transport   4, [1564]

meaning Main Volume 4 at paragraph 1564 – paragraph numbers are found at the right-hand side of the page in Main Volumes

Note: If the paragraph numbers obtained from the Consolidated Index do not match with the paragraphs found in the Main Volume, the Main Volume has been reissued since the Index was compiled. So, look up the subject again in the index at the back of the new Main Volume:

> disability discrimination
> qualification bodies   4 (S), (2007/1764)

meaning Service Binder – search the Chronological List of Instruments in the Service Binder to find the Main Volume title ⇒ Monthly Update, look at the headers across the tops of the pages to find the appropriate title header

To trace a very recent Statutory Instrument on the subject:

> Service Binder (Monthly Index) ⇒ Service Binder (Monthly Update)

In the Monthly Update check both the List of Changes and Revocations and the Noter-up.

(2)   Citation search
Three step search:

> Service Binder (Chronological List of Instruments) ⇒ Main Volume (Chronological List of Instruments, at front of volume) ⇒ Service Binder (Monthly Update)

Example of entry in Service Binder (Chronological List of Instruments):

> 2002/2817   Carriers' Liability Regulations 2002........Nationality

meaning this Statutory Instrument will be found in the Main Volume dealing with Nationality; since neither the volume nor paragraph number are given for entries in the Chronological List of Instruments, it is necessary to follow the second and third steps set out above

If the Statutory Instrument cannot be traced then either it is no longer in operation or it is outside the scope of the publication.

(3)   Title search:

> Consolidated Index (Alphabetical List of Instruments) ⇒ Main Volume (Chronological List of Instruments, at front of volume) ⇒ Service Binder (Monthly Update)

Example of entry in Consolidated Index (Alphabetical List of Instruments):

> 1965   Lands Tribunal (Amendment) Rules 1997.....Comp Acquisition

meaning the Lands Tribunal (Amendment Rules 1997 (SI 1997/1965) will be found in the Main Volume dealing with Compulsory Acquisition; since neither the volume nor paragraph number are given for entries in the Alphabetical List of Instruments, it is necessary to follow the second and third steps set out above

If the Statutory Instrument cannot be traced then either it is no longer in operation or it is outside the scope of the publication.

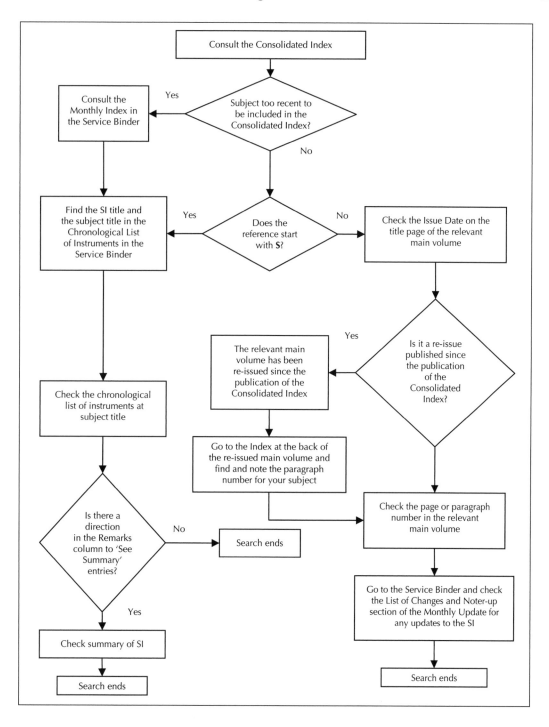

Figure 5.3: Searching *Halsbury's Statutory Instruments* by subject

Search tips

When using the Main Volume always make a note of the page number as well as the subject title heading (given in the header at the top of the page) to find update information required from the Service Binder more efficiently.

Amended text appears in square brackets [...].

Text which has been repealed appears as '...'.

How to cite Statutory Instruments of General Application

A full reference includes the following elements:

> Title | year | SI year/sequence number

Example:

> The Working Time (Amendment) Regulations 2009 SI 2009/1567

An abbreviated citation is frequently used:

> SI year/sequence number

Example:

> SI 2009/1567

5.2.4   Local Statutory Instruments passed at Westminster

Note: Statutory Instruments which apply to localities in Wales only are covered at section 5.3.3, below.

Official sources

Local Statutory Instruments are numbered in the sequence of general Statutory Instruments and are listed in the annual, bound volume set of Statutory Instruments (see section 5.2.3, above). A few are reprinted there. The majority are not printed or sold and do not appear in either those bound volumes or the *Legislation.gov.uk* website.

There are at least five routes to obtain copies:

(1)   unpublished local Statutory Instruments issued in the current year and the last two years and in force for a limited period only are obtainable on request from HMSO;

(2)   earlier local Statutory Instruments (from 1922 onwards) are obtainable from the National Archives, Kew, Richmond, Surrey TW9 4DU, phone +44 (0) 20 8876 3444, <http://www.nationalarchives.gov.uk>. The National Archives department code and series reference for these Statutory Instruments is TS 37. Quote this reference in any correspondence to aid your search;

(3) contact the central government department which drew up the Statutory Instrument – the *Civil Service Yearbook* (see Chapter 15) details public enquiry points – the departmental library may be a good place to start;

(4) contact the Bodleian Law Library – a Legal Deposit Library – which holds copies of local Statutory Instruments, and also operates a document delivery service <http://www.bodleian.ox.ac.uk/law/services/ill/docdel>;

(5) the British Library also has a collection of local Statutory Instruments (from 1922 onwards). The title of the collection is 'Statutory instruments [of a local nature]'. They are held on microfiche at the shelfmark: General Reference Collection SPR.Mic.E.349. Statutory Instruments can be ordered by searching the main catalogue: 'Explore the British Library' using the collection title and, once the catalogue record is on the screen, click 'I want this' and choose the delivery option desired.

Unofficial sources

There are none. *Westlaw UK*, *Lexis®Library* and *Justis Statutory Instruments* subscriber-only services exclude local statutory instruments.

How to cite local Statutory Instruments

See 'How to cite Statutory Instruments of General Application', above.

5.3 WALES

Additional help in gaining an understanding of Welsh law and legal materials will be found in the concise and useful bibliographic guide: 'Researching Welsh Law: What is unique in Wales?', compiled by Lillian Stevenson and Dr Catrin Huws, which provides an introduction to the legal system of Wales and the sources of legislation relating to the Principality. It is on the GlobaLex website: <http://www.nyulawglobal.org/Globalex/Wales.htm>

5.3.1 Acts made at Westminster applying to Wales and Acts and Measures of the National Assembly for Wales

To check if an Act made at Westminster applying to Wales is still in force, has been amended or repealed, or if its meaning has been interpreted by the courts, see section 9.2.2, below. To check if a an Act or Measure of the National Assembly for Wales is still in force, has been amended or if its meaning has been interpreted by the courts, see 'Is it is force?; Has this legislation been amended, repealed or interpreted by the courts?', at section 9.4.1, below.

Unconsolidated versions

Acts made at Westminster applying to Wales

Public General Acts and General Synod Measures (TSO – The Stationery Office)
Annual bound volume set.

Law Reports Statutes (Incorporated Council of Law Reporting)
Annual bound volume set merely reprinting the text of the Act as at Royal Assent.

Acts made at Westminster applying to Wales and Acts and Measures of the National Assembly for Wales Loose copies of Acts are published by TSO (The Stationery Office) and issued soon after Royal Assent:
<http://www.tso.co.uk>

Updates on new legislation passed:
<http://www.legislation.gov.uk/new>

Original legislation (no details of revisions or amendments), with access to original print pdf versions:
<http://www.legislation.gov.uk/browse/wales>

Both *Lawtel UK* (subscriber-only service) and the free service *British and Irish Legal Information Institute* (*BAILII*) reproduce material from the TSO source:
<http://www.bailii.org>

Consolidated versions

Acts made at Westminster applying to Wales and Acts and Measures of the National Assembly for Wales

Legislation.gov.uk (free):
<http://www.legislation.gov.uk>
Full text of Acts in force on 1 February 1991 and all published subsequently, and Acts and Measures of the National Assembly for Wales (in English, Welsh or mixed language). Open the 'Type' drop-down box and select appropriate material from list. Some materials not fully up to date – watch for warning notices at the top of the contents page of such Acts. Under Advanced Search can undertake a 'point in time' search for text of an Act on any particular date from 1 February 1991 onwards.

Lexis®Library (subscriber-only service)
Includes only English language versions of Acts and Measures made by the National Assembly for Wales:

> Click Sources, Browse Sources, in Country field select United Kingdom, open All Regions drop-down menu and select England & Wales, select Legislation from list of categories of material, click 'OK – continue' to reach search screen.

Westlaw UK (subscriber-only service)
Includes only English language versions of Acts and Measures made by the National Assembly for Wales.

Justis UK Statutes (subscriber-only service)
Does not appear to include Measures of the National Assembly for Wales.

Repealed Acts made at Westminster applying to Wales

Justis UK Statutes (subscriber-only service)
Original text, from 1235 onwards, but with information about amending and repealing legislation – the user has to piece together the consolidated version of the text of an Act. This is a unique database, containing repealed and live legislation back to 1235.

How to cite Acts and Measures of the National Assembly for Wales

Note: the information given here is taken from original versions of Acts and Measures. The *Legislation.gov.uk* website uses only the 'anaw' code for both the English and Welsh versions of an Act of the National Assembly of Wales and, similarly, the 'nawm' code for a Measure.

Acts

English language version:

> Title | year | anaw | running number

Welsh language version:

> Title | year | dccc | running number

Examples:

> Local Government Byelaws (Wales) Act 2012 anaw 2
> Deddf Is-ddeddfau Llywodraeth Leol (Cymru) 2012 dccc 2

Measures

English language version:

> Title | year | nawm | running number

Welsh language version:

> Title | year | mccc | running number

Examples:

> NHS Redress (Wales) Measure 2008 nawm 1
> Mesur Gwneud Iawn am Gamweddau'r GIG (Cymru) 2008 mccc 1

5.3.2   Local, Personal and Private Acts passed at Westminster relating to Wales

See section 5.2.2, above.

In addition, there is a searchable, free database of Welsh Local Acts 1900–1999, in MS Access format which, according to the website is useable with Internet Explorer only as your browser. It appears to work with Firefox also. It is possible to search by subject or date or both. Details of repeals are provided but the full-text of each Act is not available on the website. The database is on the website of Cardiff University Special Collections and Archives (SCOLAR):
<http://cardiff.ac.uk/insrv/libraries/scolar/special/welsh/index.html>

SCOLAR, together with the University's Law Library, has an extensive collection of Welsh Local Acts.

5.3.3   Statutory Instruments applying to Wales

To check if a Statutory Instrument is still in force, has been amended or revoked, or if its meaning has been interpreted by the courts, see 'Is it is force?; Has this legislation been amended, revoked or interpreted by the courts?', at section 9.4.2, below.

Statutory Instruments made at Westminster

Unconsolidated versions

Loose copies of Statutory Instruments are published by TSO (The Stationery Office) soon after Royal Assent:
<http://www.tso.co.uk>

Updates on new legislation passed:
<http://www.legislation.gov.uk/new>

Statutory Instruments (TSO – The Stationery Office):
<http://www.tso.co.uk>
Annual bound volume set.

Original legislation (no details of revisions or amendments) and access to original print pdf versions:
<http://www.legislation.gov.uk/browse/wales>

Both *Lawtel UK* (subscriber-only service) and the free service *British and Irish Legal Information Institute* (*BAILII*) reproduce material from the TSO source:
<http://www.bailii.org/uk/legis/num_reg>

Legislation.gov.uk (free):
<http://www.legislation.gov.uk>
Full text of Statutory Instruments in force on 1 February 1991 and all published subsequently, and all Statutory Instruments made at Westminster and Cardiff. Prior to 1987, only those Statutory Instruments that were still at least partly in force in April 2011. Unlike Acts, the text of most Statutory Instruments on the *Legislation.gov.uk* database are in unrevised form but as originally enacted:

> Open the 'Type' drop-down box and select appropriate material from list. It is not possible to use Advanced Search to undertake a 'point in time' search for the text of a Welsh Statutory Instrument on any particular date from 1 February 1991 onwards.

Consolidated versions

Lexis®Library (subscriber-only service)
Appears to include only Statutory Instruments made at Westminster applying to Wales but not Statutory Instruments made by the National Assembly for Wales:

> Click Sources, Browse Sources, in Country field select United Kingdom, open All Regions drop-down menu and select England & Wales, select Legislation from list of categories of material, click 'OK – continue' to reach search screen.

Westlaw UK (subscriber-only service)
Includes a selection of UK Statutory Instruments of general application published between 1948 and 1991. All subsequent Statutory Instruments applying to Wales made at Westminster are included as are all English language Statutory Instruments made by the National Assembly for Wales. Use the Legislation library in the usual way – see 'Consolidated Statutory Instruments in force now', at section 5.2.3, above.

Justis UK Statutory Instruments (subscriber-only service)
Original text of Instruments relating to Wales made at Westminster from 1671 onwards, but with information about amending and repealing legislation – the user has to piece together the consolidated version of the text of a Statutory Instrument. This is a unique database, containing revoked and live legislation back to 1671.

Statutory Instruments enacted by the National Assembly for Wales

Unconsolidated versions

Welsh Statutory Instruments, 1999– (TSO – The Stationery Office):
<http://www.tso.co.uk>
Loose issues published soon after being passed.

Legislation.gov.uk (free):
<http://www.legislation.gov.uk>
Full text of Welsh Statutory Instruments made from 1999 onwards. Unlike Acts, the text of most Statutory Instruments on the *Legislation.gov.uk* database are in unrevised form but as originally enacted:

> Open the 'Type' drop-down box and select appropriate material from list. It is not possible to use Advanced Search to undertake a 'point in time' search for the text of a Welsh Statutory Instrument on any particular date from 1999 onwards.

National Assembly for Wales (free)
Text of local Statutory Instruments in English and Welsh.

- English language version:
  <http://new.wales.gov.uk/legislation/subordinate/localstat/?lang=en>

- Welsh language version:
  <http://new.wales.gov.uk/legislation/subordinate/localstat/?skip=1&lang=cy>

British and Irish Legal Information Institute (*BAILII*) (free):
<http://www.bailii.org/wales/legis/num_reg>
Includes Statutory Instruments made by the National Assembly for Wales.

Consolidated versions

Westlaw UK (subscriber-only service)
Includes all English language versions of Statutory Instruments made by the National Assembly for Wales. Excludes all Statutory Instruments in the Welsh language.

How to cite Statutory Instruments applying to Wales

Statutory Instruments made at Westminster

> Title | year | SI | year/running number | (W or Cy running number in sequence of Welsh Statutory Instruments)

Example of English language version:

> The Non-Domestic Rating (Demand Notices) (Wales) (Amendment) Regulations 2008 SI 2008/7 (W.3)

Example of Welsh language version:

> Rheoliadau Ardrethu Annomestig (Hysbysiadau Galw am Dalu) (Cymru) (Diwygio) 2008 SI 2008/7 (Cy.3)

Statutory Instruments made by the National Assembly for Wales

> Title | year | SI | year/running number | (W or Cy running number in sequence of Welsh Statutory Instruments)

Example of English language version:

> The Childcare Act 2006 (Local Authority Assessment) (Wales) Regulations 2008 SI 2008/169 (W.22)

Example of Welsh language version:

> Rheoliadau Deddf Gofal Plant 2006 (Asesiadau Awdurdodau Lleol) (Cymru) 2008 SI 2008/169 (Cy.22)

5.4   SCOTLAND

5.4.1   Acts applying to Scotland

To check if an Act passed at Westminster applying to Scotland is in force, has been amended or repealed, or if its meaning has been interpreted by the courts, see section 9.2.2, below. To check if an Act of the Scottish Parliament is in force, has been amended or if its meaning has been interpreted by the courts, see section 9.5.2, below.

Unconsolidated versions of Acts either made at Westminster applying to the United Kingdom or to Scotland alone or Acts of the Scottish Parliament or by the pre-1707 Parliaments of Scotland

Acts made at Westminster applying to the United Kingdom or to Scotland alone or Acts of the Scottish Parliament

Loose copies of Acts published as soon as possible after Royal Assent by TSO (The Stationery Office):
<http://www.tso.co.uk>

Alerts to new Acts passed:
<www.legislation.gov.uk/new>

The original full text of Acts made at Westminster since 1 January 1987, with a selection from earlier years, and access to the original pdf versions:
<http://www.legislation.gov.uk/ukpga>

Both *Lawtel UK* (subscriber-only service) and the free service *British and Irish Legal Information Institute* (*BAILII*) reproduce material from the TSO source:
<http://www.bailii.org>

Public General Acts and General Synod Measures (TSO – The Stationery Office)
Annual bound volume set, not updated.

Scottish Current Law Statutes Annotated (1949–1990) then merged with *Current Law Statutes Annotated* – original text (with annotations) only (both publications of W Green, Edinburgh).

Current Law Statutes (Sweet & Maxwell)
The full text of individual Acts is issued in individual booklets soon after Royal Assent, together with, from the 1980s onwards, increasingly extensive annotations and commentary on the meaning and effect of the Act in general and individual sections in particular. The booklets are filed in a Service Binder. At the year end, the individual booklets are replaced by a bound volume. Unfortunately the text of the Act and the commentary are not updated.

Acts of the Scottish Parliament only

Loose issues of individual Acts of the Scottish Parliament are published by TSO (The Stationery Office), Edinburgh, soon after Royal Assent.

Acts of the Scottish Parliament (TSO – The Stationery Office, Edinburgh)
Annual bound compilations reprinting the loose issues.

The original full text of Acts of the Scottish Parliament:
<http://www.legislation.gov.uk/asp>

Both *Lawtel UK* (subscriber-only service) and the free service *British and Irish Legal Information Institute* (*BAILII*) reproduce material from the TSO source:
<http://www.bailii.org>

Statutes Revised (Stationery Office)
This reprint contains UK/English statutes from 1235 to 1948 which were still in force in 1948 and incorporating amendments to that date.

Scots Statutes Revised, 1700–1900 (W Green)
This commercial reprint, in ten volumes, reproduces the text of those post-1707 public general statutes applicable to Scotland which were still in force in 1900 incorporating amendments to that date.

Scots Statutes 1901–1948 (W Green)
This commercial reprint reproduces the text of public general statutes applicable to Scotland between 1901 and 1948.

Acts of the Parliaments of Scotland (Record Edition)
This 19th century publication, published 'by Royal Command' in eleven volumes, reproduces Acts of the Parliaments of Scotland from 1124–1707 ('old Scots Acts').

The Acts of the Parliaments of Scotland 1424–1707 (HMSO, 2nd edn, 1966)
This work reproduces the text of those 'old Scots Acts' still in force when it was published in 1966.

Records of the Parliaments of Scotland to 1707:
<http://www.rps.ac.uk>
Fully searchable, free database of the proceedings of the Scottish Parliaments (including Acts in their original unrevised form) from 1235 to 1707. However, the version of the Acts on the site makes no claim to be authoritative. Devised by the Scottish Parliament Project of the University of St Andrews.

Consolidated versions

Acts made at Westminster applying to Scotland and Acts of the Scottish Parliament

Parliament House Book (W Green & Son, 1982–)

Purpose
To reproduce statutes and statutory instruments, other regulations, tables and notes for guidance, relating to Scots private law and court procedure, made at Westminster and by the Scottish Parliament. Some, though not all, legislation includes annotations.

Structure
Six looseleaf volumes, volumes 1, 2 and 3 containing material relating to the Scottish courts themselves, their procedure, solicitors and legal aid. Volumes 4–6 contain materials arranged according to practice area – rather confusingly the practice areas are not listed alphabetically. Within each division, statutes appear first, then statutory instruments and other regulations and finally tables and notes for guidance.

How to use the print publication

'Indices' ⇒ main text

Note: The indexes are filed at the front of each volume under the 'Indices' guide card, and comprise: an alphabetical list of the titles of statutes and statutory instruments, a chronological list, a list of report series cited (note: not a list of cases cited; that appears in section C), and a table of regnal years.

Example from the alphabetical list:

Cheques Act 1957   H105

meaning division H, paragraph 105

Note: Paragraph numbers are printed at the top, outside corner of the page and are referred to in the checklist as 'pages'.

Some subject specialist encyclopedias specific to Scots law reprint the text of Acts relevant to their topic area.

Legislation.gov.uk (free):
<http://www.legislation.gov.uk/browse/scotland>
Full text of Acts in force on 1 February 1991 and all published subsequently, and all Acts of the Scottish Parliament and all Acts of the Old Scottish Parliament, 1424–1707, including repealed Acts. Some materials not fully up to date – watch for warning notices at the top of the contents page of such Acts. Under Advanced Search can undertake a 'point in time' search for text of an Act on any particular date from 1 February 1991 onwards.

Lexis®Library (subscriber-only service)
Includes the full text of Public and General Acts made by the Scottish Parliament currently in force. Provisions of pre-devolution UK legislation which relate to Scotland only are not included:

> Click Sources, Browse Sources, in Country field select United Kingdom, open All Regions drop-down menu and select Scotland, select Legislation from list of categories of material, click 'OK – continue' to reach search screen. Alternatively, search at the main Legislation screen across 'All subscribed legislation sources'.

Westlaw UK (subscriber-only service)
Includes all Public and General Acts in force of 1 February 1991 and all published subsequently. Basic search includes the most up to date version of the legislation. Also includes Acts made by the Scottish Parliament since its inception. An initial archive of annotations back to 2007 is available on *Westlaw UK* and will be extended back further. Search for Acts in the normal way and in the results list an A will indicate annotations are available.

Justis UK Statutes (subscriber-only service)
See 'Revoked Acts …', below.

Revoked Acts made at Westminster applying to Scotland and Acts of the Scottish Parliament

Justis UK Statutes (subscriber-only service)
Original text, from 1707 onwards, of Acts made at Westminster relating to Scotland, and Acts of the Scottish Parliament from 1999 onwards, but with information about amending and repealing legislation – the user has to piece together the consolidated version of the text of an Act. A unique database.

How to cite Acts of the Scottish Parliament

Title | year | asp | Act number

Example:

Public Finance and Accountability (Scotland) Act 2000, 2000 asp 1

How to cite pre-1707 Scots Acts ('old Scots Acts')

The form of citation given below will apply in most circumstances that a practitioner may come across. However, in the event of the Act being cited from an authoritative text other than the Record Edition, (such as Murray of Glendook's *Laws and Acts of Parliament*, sometimes known as the *duodecimo* (12mo) edition), then the abbreviation (12mo edition) should be placed after the initial chapter number and the reference to the APS and all that follows after, removed:

Short title | year | chapter number | reference to 'Record Edition' of Acts of Parliaments of Scotland

Example:

Breach of Arrestment Act 1581 c 23, APS III, 223, c23

Note: Chapter numbering begins at the start of each session. If there was more than one session in a year this is identified by the date of the session.

5.4.2   Scottish Statutory Instruments

To check if a Scottish Statutory Instrument is still in force, has been amended or revoked, or if its meaning has been interpreted by the courts, see 'Is it is force?; Has this legislation been amended, revoked or interpreted by the courts?', at section 9.5.3, below.

Unconsolidated Statutory Instruments

Statutory Instruments passed at Westminster

Loose copies of Statutory Instruments published by TSO (The Stationery Office):
<http://www.tso.co.uk>

Alerts to new Statutory Instruments:
<http://www.legislation.gov.uk/new>

The original full text of Statutory Instruments made at Westminster since 1 January 1987. Prior to 1987, only those Statutory Instruments that were still at least partly in force in April 2011. Access to original print pdf versions:
<http://www.legislation.gov.uk/uksi>

Both *Lawtel UK* (subscriber-only service) and the free service *British and Irish Legal Information Institute* (*BAILII*) reproduce material from the TSO source:
<http://www.bailii.org/uk/legis/num_reg>

Legislation.gov.uk (free):
<http://www.legislation.gov.uk/uksi>
Full text of Statutory Instruments in force on 1 February 1991 and all published subsequently. Prior to 1987, only those Statutory Instruments that were still at least partly in force in April 2011. Unlike Acts, the text of most Statutory Instruments on the *Legislation.gov.uk* database are in unrevised form, as originally enacted. Open the 'Type' drop-down box and select appropriate material from list. It is not

possible to use Advanced Search to undertake a 'point in time' search for text of a Statutory Instrument on any particular date from 1 February 1991 onwards.

Statutory Instruments passed at Holyrood

Scottish Statutory Instruments (TSO – The Stationery Office, Edinburgh)
Legislation.gov.uk (free):
<http://www.legislation.gov.uk/ssi>

Both *Lawtel UK* (subscriber-only only) and the free service *British and Irish Legal Information Institute* (*BAILII*) reproduce material from this source:
<http://www.bailii.org/scot/legis/num_reg>

Legislation.gov.uk (free)
<http://www.legislation.gov.uk/sdsi>
List of draft Scottish Statutory Instruments awaiting approval.

Legislation.gov.uk (free):
<http://www.legislation.gov.uk/ssi>
Full text of Statutory Instruments in force on 1 February 1991 and all published subsequently, and all Scottish Statutory Instruments made at Holyrood. Unlike Acts, the text of most Statutory Instruments on SLD are in unrevised form, as originally enacted. It is not possible to use Advanced Search to undertake a 'point in time' search for the text of a Statutory Instrument or SSI on any particular date from 1 February 1991 onwards.

Consolidated Statutory Instruments

Parliament House Book (W Green & Son, 1982–)
See section 5.4.1, above.

Some subject specialist encyclopedias specific to Scots law reprint the text of Statutory Instruments relevant to their topic area.

Lexis®Library (subscriber-only service)
Includes the full text of Scottish Statutory Instruments made by the Scottish Parliament currently in force. Click Sources, Browse Sources, in Country field select United Kingdom, open All Regions drop-down menu and select Scotland, select Legislation from list of categories of material, click 'OK – continue' to reach search screen. Alternatively, search at the main Legislation screen across 'All subscribed legislation sources'.

Westlaw UK (subscriber-only service)
Includes all Scottish Statutory Instruments (SSI) made by the Scottish Parliament since inception. Basic search includes the most up to date version of the legislation.

Justis UK Statutes (subscriber-only service)
See 'Revoked Statutory Instruments', below.

Revoked Statutory Instruments

Justis UK Statutory Instruments (subscriber-only service)
Original text of both Instruments applying to Scotland made at Westminster from 1707 onwards and all Scottish Statutory Instruments made at Holyrood, but with information about amending and repealing legislation – the user has to piece together the consolidated version of the text of a Statutory Instrument or Scottish Statutory Instrument. This is a unique database.

How to cite Statutory Instruments relating to Scotland

Statutory Instruments made at Westminster

Title | year | SI year/running number | (S running number in sequence of Statutory Instruments relating to Scotland)

Example:

The Absent Voting (Transitional Provisions) (Scotland) Regulations 2008 SI 2008/48 (S.1)

Scottish Statutory Instruments made at Holyrood

Title | SSI | year/running number

Example:

The Scottish Register of Tartans Fees Order 2009 SSI 2009/6

5.5 NORTHERN IRELAND

5.5.1 Acts passed at Westminster or Belfast applying to Northern Ireland – excluding those made by the Northern Ireland Assembly

To check if an Act is still in force, has been amended or repealed, or if its meaning has been interpreted by the courts, see section 9.6.1, below.

Unconsolidated versions of Acts passed at Westminster applying to Northern Ireland

In most publications Northern Ireland Acts are not separated out from other Westminster statutes. See the following sources fully described in 'Unconsolidated Acts', at section 5.2.1, above.

Loose copies of Acts published by TSO (The Stationery Office):
<http://www.tso.co.uk>

Alerts to new Acts passed:
<http://www.legislation.gov.uk/new>

Lawtel UK (subscriber-only service) and the free service *British and Irish Legal Information Institute* (*BAILII*)

Public General Acts and General Synod Measures (TSO – The Stationery Office)

Current Law Statutes (Sweet & Maxwell)

Consolidated versions of Acts passed at Westminster applying to Northern Ireland

Halsbury's Statutes of England (LexisNexis, 4th edn, 1985–)
Volume 31 reprints Acts made at Westminster applying exclusively to Northern Ireland. Bound volume and looseleaf, continuously updated. See section 5.2.1, above, for instructions on how to use. Partly incorporated within the Legislation library of *Lexis®Library* (subscriber-only service).

Westlaw UK (subscriber-only service)
Includes Acts passed at Westminster relating to Northern Ireland.

5.5.2   Northern Ireland Statutes (including Northern Ireland Orders in Council)

Northern Ireland Statutes 1921– (TSO – The Stationery Office, Belfast) – spine title to 1967: *Public General Acts: Northern Ireland* – annual bound volumes but after 2000/2001 looseleaf binders only. Unconsolidated, original versions only.

Statutes Revised, Northern Ireland (TSO – The Stationery Office, Belfast, 2nd edn, 1982 and annual cumulative supplement)
The main cumulation of statute law applying to Northern Ireland. Legislation in force in Northern Ireland on 31 May 1981. It includes Acts of the Irish and British Parliaments up to 1800, and the UK Parliament to 1921 and Orders in Council to 1981. Original bound volumes supplemented from 1982 onwards by looseleaf binders. A supplement binder lists all revisions to Northern Ireland statutes since 1981.

Legislation.gov.uk (free)
<http://www.legislation.gov.uk>
Full text of Acts of the old Irish Parliament where still in force; Acts of the Northern Ireland Parliament (revised versions where in force); Orders in Council (revised versions where in force, some as enacted); Acts of the Northern Ireland Assembly (revised and as enacted).

British and Irish Legal Information Institute (*BAILII*) (free):
<http://www.bailii.org>
Includes Orders in Council 1972–2009 (partially revised); Acts of the Northern Ireland Assembly from 2000 onwards (unconsolidated).

Westlaw UK (subscriber only service)
Northern Ireland Orders in Council as in force, 1991 onwards; Acts of the Northern Ireland Assembly, as in force.

Acts of the Northern Ireland Assembly (unconsolidated) are also included in:

Justis UK Statutes (subscriber-only service)
Original text of Acts of the NI Assembly from 2000 onwards, but with information about amending and repealing legislation – the user must piece together the consolidated version of the text of an Act.

How to cite Acts passed at Westminster applying to Northern Ireland

> Title | year | chapter | number

Example:

> Pension Schemes (Northern Ireland) Act 1993 ch.48

How to cite Acts of the Parliament of Northern Ireland and Acts of the Northern Ireland Assembly

OSCOLA (see section 17.4.3, below) recommends citing modern Acts by title and year only and including the chapter number for older statutes without short titles. However, the inclusion of the chapter number does make it easier to locate the text of the Act in print volumes from all periods, since they frequently reproduce Acts in chapter number order.

Acts of the Parliament of Northern Ireland

> Title | (NI) | year | chapter number

Example:

> Poultry Improvement Act (NI) 1968 ch.12

Acts of the Northern Ireland Assembly

> Title | (Northern Ireland) | year

Example:

> Child Maintenance Act (Northern Ireland) 2008

How to cite Orders in Council Relating to Northern Ireland

OSCOLA (see section 17.4.3, below) makes no recommendation on citing Orders in Council. The Northern Ireland courts have made Practice Direction 6/2011 which appears to require only the title, Statutory Instrument year/running number, and omitting the number sequence relating to Northern Ireland. However, this appears to be out of step with practice in Scotland and Wales:

> Title | SI year/running number | (number in sequence of Orders in Council for Northern Ireland)

Example:

> Water (Northern Ireland) Order 1999 SI 1999/662 (NI 6)

5.5.3 Statutory Instruments passed at Westminster applying to Northern Ireland only

To check if a Statutory Instrument is still in force, has been amended or revoked, or if its meaning has been interpreted by the courts, see section 9.6.2, below.

Unconsolidated version

Statutory Instruments (TSO – The Stationery Office):
<http://www.tso.co.uk>
Annual bound volume set. It includes all Statutory Instruments in force at the end of the year – it excludes instruments of temporary application and which are 'spent'.

Legislation.gov.uk (free):
<http://www.legislation.gov.uk>
Full text from 1987 onwards. Northern Ireland Statutory Instruments not separated from other Statutory Instruments made at Westminster.

Consolidated version

Lexis®Library (subscriber-only service)
Specifically excludes NI Statutory Instruments.

Westlaw UK (subscriber-only service)
Includes selected Statutory Instruments 1949–1990 but all Statutory Instruments 1991 onwards.

How to cite Statutory Instruments passed at Westminster applying to Northern Ireland only

> Title | SI | year/running number

Examples:

> The Guardian's Allowance Up-rating (Northern Ireland) Order 2009 SI 2009/797
> Northern Ireland Assembly (Elections) (Amendment) Order 2009 SI 2009/256

See also above for Orders in Council relating to Northern Ireland. These are UK Statutory Instruments, but are not included in UK Statutory Instrument sources.

5.5.4 Northern Ireland Statutory Rules

To check if a Statutory Rule is still in force, has been amended or revoked, or if its meaning has been interpreted by the courts, see section 9.6.2, below.

Statutory Rules are made by the Northern Ireland Executive or the Northern Ireland Office.

Unconsolidated version

Northern Ireland Statutory Rules 1973–; *Statutory Rules and Orders* 1922–1972 (TSO – The Stationery Office, Belfast)
Annual bound volumes.

Legislation.gov.uk (free):
<http://www.legislation.gov.uk>
Full text from 1996 onwards. Some earlier Statutory Rules included (1986–1995).

British and Irish Legal Information Institute (*BAILII*) (free):
<http://www.bailii.org/nie/legis/num_reg>
Includes Statutory Rules from 2001 onwards.

Consolidated version

Westlaw UK (subscriber only service)
Includes Statutory Rules in force from 1991 onwards.

How to cite a Northern Ireland Statutory Rule

OSCOLA (see section 17.4.3, below) makes no recommendation on citing NI Statutory Rules. The Northern Ireland courts have made Practice Direction 6/2011, which appears to require the following, though some eminent Northern Ireland lawyers drop the No from the citation:

> Title | year | SR | No | running number

Example:

> The River Bann Navigation Order (Northern Ireland) 2010, SR No 126

5.6   EUROPEAN UNION

5.6.1   Unconsolidated EU legislation

Official Journal of the European Union (free):
<http://eur-lex.europa.eu/en/index.htm>
Official text of secondary legislation in unconsolidated form (Regulations, Directives and Decisions), in full text from the first issue in December 1952 onwards. The *Journal* was not printed in English until after the accession of the United Kingdom:

> Click link left-side of screen to Official Journal for a search by the issue number or date. Subject searching is available via another link at the left-side of the screen: Simple Search. More advanced searching using the European Union's own EUROVOC thesaurus and terminology (which can be confusing) is available using yet another link at the left-side of the screen: Advanced Search.

Summaries of EU legislation (free):

<http://europa.eu/legislation_summaries/index_en.htm>

Provides the main aspects of EU legislation 'in a concise, easy-to-read and unbiased way'. Approximately 3,000 summaries of European legislation are divided into 32 subject areas corresponding to the activities of the European Union.

Justis CELEX (subscriber-only service)

Comprehensive database of data taken directly from the official EU publisher: Office for the Official Publications of the European Communities, coverage starting in 1951. Full text of treaties establishing the EC, including articles, protocols, annexes and declarations, treaties of accession and other EC treaties; external agreements between the European Union and both member and non-member states; secondary legislation, and supplementary legislation. Materials reproduced in original form (unconsolidated) with amendments not inserted. Materials from 1998 onwards reproduced as pdfs.

Justis OJ Daily (subscriber-only service)

Daily update of the tables of contents of the Official Journal both L and C series, with web links to the pdf version of the full text. Archive back to 1998.

To check for national implementation of secondary legislation, see section 9.7.2, below.

5.6.2   Consolidated EU legislation

Treaties and agreements

Treaties: text in consolidated form, EUR-Lex website (free):
<http://eur-lex.europa.eu/en/treaties/index.htm>

Agreements: text in consolidated form, EUR-Lex website (free):
<http://eur-lex.europa.eu/en/accords/accords.htm>

Encyclopedia of European Union Law: Constitutional texts (Sweet & Maxwell)

Purpose

To reproduce, with commentary, almost all the constitutional legislation of the European Community and European Union.

Structure

Seven looseleaf volumes:

- Volume 1: constitutional law (origin of the European Union's legal system, its structures and institutions)

- Volumes 2–8: reproducing the substantive constitutional law of the European Union. Each chapter begins with a general commentary. Then the relevant legislation is reproduced with commentary, in a smaller typeface, attached to individual articles, protocols or declarations.

How to use the print publication
Either:

> General table of contents to all eight volumes printed at the front of volume 1, and select the relevant volume and chapter

Or:

> General table of contents at the front of each individual volume covering only the contents of that volume, and select the relevant chapter

Or:

> Detailed subject index to all eight volumes printed at the front of volume 1. Confusingly this is in two parts: a main index and a supplementary index of additional entries omitted from the main index. In a looseleaf publication it ought to be possible to consolidate the two indexes into one.

> Main Index $\Rightarrow$ Supplementary Index $\Rightarrow$ paragraph

Example:

> Credit institutions
>   Supervision of, 97.0247

> meaning paragraph 97.0247

Unfortunately the paragraph numbers are not printed on the spines of the looseleaf binders, so it is necessary to open up the binders to find the relevant location.

Secondary legislation

Text in consolidated form, EUR-Lex website (free):
<http://eur-lex.europa.eu/RECH_consolidated.do>
The results of a search provide links to not only the latest but all previous consolidations.

Text of original with access to consolidations, EUR-Lex website (free):
<http://eur-lex.europa.eu/RECH_naturel.do>
This is an alternative route to consolidations: search for the piece of legislation then, on the results page, click 'Bibliographic notice' to display links to other consolidations. The bibliographic notice also displays links to all amending legislation.

> *Encyclopedia of European Community Law: Community secondary legislation* (Sweet & Maxwell)

Purpose
To reprint the secondary legislation of the European Community with annotations. It provides consolidated versions of legislation with amendments and revocations noted.

Structure
Twelve looseleaf binders arranging the reprints in broad subject areas.

How to use the print publication
Two searches are possible: by subject or by Regulation, Directive, Decision or Recommendation reference number.

Subject search
Two important matters to note:

- First, there are two subject indexes located at the back of the last binder. A Main Index and a Supplementary Index of additional subjects – since it is a loose leaf publication it is surprising that the publisher is unable to merge the two indexes into a single, user-friendly sequence.

- Second, the Roman numerals printed on the spines of the looseleaf binders merely label the binders and have no significance in relation to navigating the contents. The contents are arranged in Parts bearing Arabic numerals, as in the example below. So, ignore the Roman numerals and look at the guide cards inside the volume to find the location of the material required.

Main Index $\Rightarrow$ Supplementary Index $\Rightarrow$ paragraph

Example:

Company law
    Directors, C3-011

meaning Part C3, paragraph 011

Reference number search
There are two lists to choose from:

- Near the back of the final binder is a guide card: Checklist. Behind it are two sequences: Regulations in reference number order (running number/year) and a second list with Directives, Decisions and Recommendations merged into a single sequence by reference number (year/running number).

- Near the front of the first binder is a red guide card: Tables, which is a condensed version of the above Checklist, omitting the titles of the individual instruments.

Comprehensive online sources

In alphabetical order:

Eurolaw (subscriber-only service)

Justis CELEX (subscriber-only service)
See section 5.6.1, above.

Lawtel EU (subscriber-only service)
Although this database includes the full text of the EU treaties with article by article links between the versions, its main strength and purpose is to provide an updating service on the progress of proposals for legislation and alerts to the latest case law decisions of the European Court of Justice and Court of First Instance. These aspects are dealt with more fully at section 9.7.4, below.

Lexis®Library (subscriber-only service)
European Union library:

> At the main search screen click tab 'Sources', ensure secondary tab 'Browse sources' is coloured red, open dialog box 'Filter by country' and select 'European Union', then select sources required, either 'Treaties and Agreements' or 'Legislation'.

Westlaw UK (subscriber-only service)
European Union library:

> At the bottom of the initial EU library search screen, select either Treaties or [Secondary] Legislation.

5.6.3   How to cite EU legislation

Treaties

OSCOLA (see section 17.4.3, below) recommends that treaties should be cited by providing:

> Legislation title | [year] | OJ series | issue/first page

Example:

> Treaty on European Union (Maastricht Treaty) [1992] OJ C191/1

For the first reference in a document use the shortened or popular title followed by the formal title. For further references in the same document, use the shortened or popular title only.

Example:

> Maastricht Treaty

Secondary legislation

OSCOLA (see section 17.4.3, below) recommends that EC legislation (Regulations, Directives and Decisions) and other instruments (Recommendations, Opinions, etc) should be cited by providing:

> Legislation type | number | title | [year] | OJ L issue/first page

Example for a regulation:

> Council Regulation (EC) 1984/2003 of 8 April 2003 introducing a system for the statistical monitoring of trade in bluefin tuna, swordfish and big eye tuna within the Community [2003] OJ L295/1

The OJ citation is given in the order: [year] OJ series letter issue number/page. The capital letter 'L' indicates the series stands for Legislation (the C series contains EU information and notices, and the S series contains invitations to tender).

5.7   INTERNATIONAL – BILATERAL TREATIES

5.7.1   Where to start

Tens of thousands of treaties have been signed between just two international entities. Usually bilateral treaties are concluded between two states, but can be concluded between a state and an international entity representing many states, such as the European Union. They establish legal rights and obligations between the two signatories.

Because there are so many they can be difficult to trace, unless one of the signatories systematically publishes the treaties to which it is party in either print or web format. Only Australia and the Netherlands have placed their complete treaty series on the web.

A useful guide to researching bilateral treaties is available free at:
<http://www.llrx.com/features/non_ustreaty.htm>
Click the link to the specific text on bilateral treaties.

Bilateral treaties to which the United Kingdom is party

The official text of each bilateral treaty that the United Kingdom has signed but which Parliament at Westminster has yet to ratify, is laid before Parliament and published in the Country Series of Command Papers, published by TSO (The Stationery Office). When Parliament has ratified the treaty and it comes into force, the text is published a second time in the United Kingdom Treaty Series (UKTS) of Command Papers.

A list of Treaty Command Papers from January 1999 onwards, with links to the full text, is given on the Foreign and Commonwealth Office website:
<http://www.fco.gov.uk/en/publications-and-documents/treaty-command-papers-ems>
Note that the FCO website is due to move to a new website in 2013:
<http://www.gov.uk/fco>
In addition, there is a searchable database carrying details of treaties, including bilaterals, but not offering access to the full text of the treaty, on a different part of the FCO website:
<http://www.fco.gov.uk/en/treaties/search>

A specialised list of bilateral treaties on investment promotion and protection agreements, enforcement of judgments and prisoner transfer agreements is given at:
<http://www.fco.gov.uk/en/publications-and-documents/treaties/treaty-texts>

To trace the Command Paper number and other publication details of a bilateral treaty which the United Kingdom has signed or ratified, use the catalogues of TSO (The Stationery Office): the Daily List, monthly and annual issues. They are available in print and web form:
<http://www.tsoshop.co.uk/parliament/bookstore.asp>

Bilateral investment treaties

For bilateral investment treaties (BITs) the best print source is:

International Centre for the Settlement of Investment Disputes (ICSID) (compiler), *Investment Promotion and Protection Treaties* (Oxford University Press USA, looseleaf, 1983–)
Nine-volume, looseleaf set reprinting the text of over 1,000 BITs for over 130 countries, concluded from 1959 onwards. Cumulative alphabetical and chronological indexes.

There are several specialist databases available.

ICSID Database of Bilateral Investment Treaties (free):
<https://icsid.worldbank.org/ICSID/FrontServlet>
Lists BITs made under its auspices providing the date of signature and the date of entry into force. The list can be searched by country, date of treaty and the parties. The full text is not available on this site.

ITA (free):
<http://italaw.com>
Run by Professor Andrew Newcombe of the University of Victoria Law Faculty, investment treaty arbitration (ita) provides a wealth of links, including many to country websites carrying further information on investment and free trade treaties. The full text of treaties is not available on this site but as a portal to others it is very useful.

UNCTAD (United Nations Conference on Trade and Development) (free):
<http://www.unctadxi.org/templates/DocSearch.aspx?id=779>
Lists bilateral treaties made under its auspices, providing the date of signature and the date of entry into force. The list can be searched by the name of a single country or by the names of both parties. A link on the results screen leads to the full text of the treaty held on the site.

Investment Claims (subscriber-only service):
<http://www.investmentclaims.com>
Includes amongst a wide range of international investment materials, the full text of an undisclosed number of bilateral investment treaties concluded by twenty 'key jurisdictions' including the following states: Canada, China, Czech Republic, France, Germany, Pakistan, Russia, Switzerland and the United States. The service includes official English translations, if available, otherwise the material is in the languages of the states in question.

Bilateral tax treaties

Diamond, D and Diamond, W, *International tax treaties of all nations* (Oceana, looseleaf, 1973–)
Series A: treaties published by the United Nations (fifteen looseleaf volumes) and series B: treaties not published by the United Nations (forty looseleaf volumes); both series also available online, as a subscriber-only service, from Oxford University Press.

UNCTAD (United Nations Conference on Trade and Development) (free):
<http://unctad.org/en/Pages/DIAE/International%20Investment%20Agreements%20%28IIA%29/Country-specific-Lists-of-DTTs.aspx>
Lists details of double taxation treaties concluded by 185 countries (including the United Kingdom) as at 1 June 2012. Searchable only by the name of the country. Provides details of the partners, the type of taxation treaty and the date of entry into force. The full text is not available on this site.

5.7.2   How to cite a bilateral treaty

There are no formal, internationally recognised rules. OSCOLA in its latest (2006) recommendations on citing international law (see section 17.4.3, below) suggests that the full form of citation should be given, as set out in the example below. Only use an abbreviated or popular title in subsequent references within the same document. If only the abbreviated or popular title is provided readers can be hindered making effective use of indexes and catalogues to trace the publication. The following citation principles are based on good practice:

> *Full, formal title* | place of signature | date of signature | date the treaty entered into force | UK Treaty Series and Command Paper references

Example:

> *Agreement between the Government of the United Kingdom and Northern Ireland and the Government of Australia providing for the reciprocal recognition and enforcement of judgments in civil an commercial matters* Canberra 23 August 1990 with exchange of notes London 1 September 1994 (entered into force 1 September 1994) UKTS 45 (1995) Cm 2896

5.8   INTERNATIONAL – MULTILATERAL TREATIES (INCLUDING COUNCIL OF EUROPE)

5.8.1   Where to start

Multilateral treaties are treaties concluded between more than two legal entities, states or international bodies representing a number of states.

Treaties are amended by means of protocols. The reputable web version of a treaty (ie the version found on the website of the particular body which prepared the treaty) usually incorporates the changes made by a protocol or directs users from the original version to the protocol. The *FLARE Index to Treaties*, see the following section, includes such links.

If you do not know which organisation prepared the treaty or convention

Use one of these three finding tools.

FLARE Index to Treaties (FIT) (free):
<http://193.62.18.232/dbtw-wpd/textbase/treatysearch.htm>
Searchable index to over 2,000 of the most significant multilateral treaties concluded from 1353 to 2011. Can be searched using a single word or combination of words from the title or subject, or the exact date or just the year of the treaty, or the place where it was concluded. Each entry in FIT includes details of where the full text is printed in paper publications with links to free versions on the internet.

Electronic Information System for International Law (EISIL) (free):
<http://www.eisil.org>
Database developed by the American Society of International Law, listing authoritative websites for primary and secondary international law materials, arranged under broad subject headings. Although it covers more than just treaties, searching the database is not as easy or as flexible as with FIT, above, since websites and their descriptions are arranged in subject hierarchies and not searchable on so many entry points as FIT. Dates on web pages suggest that maintenance of the database ceased in 2010. Nevertheless, EISIL is a useful starting point to research a wide range of internet resources on international law.

The Multilaterals Project, Fletcher Law School, Tufts University, Massachusetts (free):
<http://fletcher.archive.tusm-oit.org/multilaterals>
Project to make available on the web the text of multilateral treaties and conventions in the areas of environmental law, human rights, commerce, trade, law of war and arms control, mostly concluded from 1945 to 2002. May be searched by keyword and browsed by topic listings.

If you do know which organisation prepared the treaty or convention

Either use the indexes listed in the previous section, or go to the website of the organisation, using Google to help you locate it, if necessary. Here is a selection of the key multilateral treaty-preparing organisations and their web locations.

Council of Europe Treaties (free):
<http://conventions.coe.int>

Hague Conventions on Private International Law (free):
<http://www.hcch.net/index_en.php?act=conventions.listing>

International Institute for the Unification of Private Law (UNIDROIT) (free):
<http://www.unidroit.org>

International Labour Organization (ILO) (free):
<http://www.ilo.org/global/standards/lang--en/index.htm>

United Nations Treaty Collection Database (free):
<http://treaties.un.org/pages/UNTSOnline.aspx?id=1>

United Nations Commission for International Trade Law (UNCITRAL) (free):
<http://www.uncitral.org>

Searching collections of treaties

These are all subscriber-only services.

Lexis®Library
At main search screen:

> Click tab 'Sources', ensure secondary tab 'Browse sources' is coloured red, open dialog box 'Filter by country' and select 'International', then 'Treaties and International Agreements', and select sources required.

Westlaw International
Accessible from *Westlaw UK*:

> Click the 'Services' tab towards top right of screen, and clicking 'Westlaw International' tab several times to reach the International Directory, then 'International/Worldwide Materials', 'Multi-National Materials', 'Legislation', for a listing of the range of treaty collections available.

HeinOnline: Treaties & Agreements Library
Contains the text of *United States Treaties in Force*, *International Legal Materials* and *British Yearbook of International Law*.

5.8.2   How to cite multilateral treaties

There are no formal, internationally recognised rules, but OSCOLA in its latest (2006) recommendations on citing international law (see section 17.4.3, below) suggests that the full form of citation should be given, as set out in the example below. Only use an abbreviated or popular title in subsequent and repeated references within the same document. If only the abbreviated or popular title is cited it can hinder readers wanting to trace a copy of the treaty since most indexes and catalogues use only the formal title of the publication. The following principles are based on good practice:

> *Full, formal title* | place of signature | date of signature | treaty series references

Example:

> *International Covenant on Civil and Political Rights* (adopted 16 December 1966, entered into force 23 March 1976) 999 UNTS 171 (ICCPR)

5.9   UK TREATIES AND AGREEMENTS

5.9.1   Where to start

Depending on whether you believe it is a bilateral or multilateral treaty, follow the steps at section 5.7.1 or section 5.8.1, above.

Unfortunately there is no online database of treaties to which the United Kingdom is party. A list of Treaty Command Papers from January 1999 onwards, with links to the full text, is given on the Foreign and Commonwealth Office website:
<http://www.fco.gov.uk/en/publications-and-documents/treaty-command-papers-ems>
Note that the FCO website is due to move to a new website in 2013:
<http://www.gov.uk/fco>

5.9.2   How to cite treaties to which the United Kingdom is party

See section 5.7.2, above (bilateral treaties) or section 5.8.2, above (multilateral treaties).

CHAPTER 6

CASE LAW

6.1   INTRODUCTION

To ensure you get the best from this chapter check that you know the type of information you are trying to find.

Are you looking for:

(1)   the text of a particular case the title or citation you know or,
(2)   any cases in a practice area, or on a topic or subject.

If (1), a wide range of free and fee-paying services is available.

If (2), a more restricted range of sources is available, but this is where the large commercial databases come into their own, offering sophisticated searching across a very wide range of reported and unreported cases (see Appendix 2 for a definition).

To make the best use of expensive subscriber-only databases, do not use the keyword or subject search function in one of the comprehensive, commercial databases without having taken time to research in other sources for the most focused and appropriate search terms to use. First undertake a subject search in the commentary sources mentioned in Chapter 10 and/or practitioner books, to discover the key cases on the topic. Then, read the judgments and look at the catchwords (definition in Appendix 2) at the beginning of the key, reported decisions to generate a list of more focused keywords which when used in the commercial database will offer the best chance of identifying further, relevant cases.

The sources for each jurisdiction listed below are divided into the free sources, followed by the subscriber-only. The contents of each website or database are described, focusing in particular on whether reported or unreported cases are available, over what time period and whether subject searches may be undertaken.

Finally, clarify whether you need the full text of the case or just a summary – you may assume that all the sources featured in this chapter provide the full text of cases unless it is specifically noted that only summaries are available.

Abbreviations for publications can be converted into their full title by using any of the following:

- Cardiff Index to Legal Abbreviations (free):
  <http://www.legalabbrevs.cardiff.ac.uk>
  Includes over 17,000 abbreviations to over 10,000 law publications worldwide. Can search from abbreviation to title and vice-versa. Also lists the preferred citation where it has been stipulated by the publisher.

- Raistrick, D, *Index to legal citations and abbreviations* (Sweet & Maxwell, 3rd edn, 2008).

- *Osborn's concise law dictionary* (Sweet & Maxwell, 12th edn, 2013).

- The list given in Appendix 1.2.

Details of how to cite cases are given at the end of each section on a particular jurisdiction – details of the system of 'neutral citation' (see Appendix 2 for a definition) in the jurisdiction are given.

To check the progress of a case through the courts and whether a particular case is still good law, see Chapter 9.

To check whether a particular court in the United Kingdom has made administrative and/or practice directions about the citation of case law before it, see Appendix 3.

6.2 ENGLAND AND WALES

6.2.1 Free sources

Warning

Free sources usually provide either the transcript (see Appendix 2 for a definition) of the decision or a summary. Some, such as *BAILII*, include transcripts of many unreported decisions. The courts have placed restrictions on the use of unreported decisions in litigation – see Appendix 3.

A proportion of cases appearing in the free services will also appear as reported decisions in print publications and online services. The courts have made Practice Directions regarding the hierarchy of law reports to be cited in litigation. See Appendix 3 for details of these requirements.

Full-text sources

Here are the key websites. *BAILII* is an excellent portal for cases from a wide selection of courts and tribunals. It now comprises 90 databases with over 290,000 searchable documents. Use the *Legal Resources in the UK and Ireland, etc.* website <http://www.venables.co.uk/caselaw.htm> to trace links to even more websites for particular courts and tribunals which may carry transcripts. A final route to obtain a transcript is to contact some nearby law firms (especially in the City of London) and see if they have a copy on file they are prepared to loan. The lis-law email discussion list (see section 13.4.6, below) is one of the best ways of contacting information staff across many law organisations. The list has over 1,000 members world-wide, most based in the United Kingdom; the majority of members are law firm librarians.

British and Irish Legal Information Institute (BAILII) (free):
<http://www.bailii.org/databases.html#uk>
<http://www.bailii.org/databases.html#ew>
The first link above is to UK courts and tribunals, the second to those specifically within the jurisdiction of England and Wales.

Cross-court subject searching is available at:
<http://www.bailii.org/form/search_cases.html>
Transcripts of cases from a wide selection of courts and tribunals from 1996 onwards. But note that there are circumstances when a transcript of a case will not appear on *BAILII*, and should not appear anywhere, for that matter:
<http://www.bailii.org/bailii/faq.html#ewhc>
In addition to the recent case law, about 1,500 landmark judgments from earlier years, selected by academic lawyers have been added to *BAILII*.

Scottish Council of Law Reporting: list of British courts and tribunals (free):
<http://www.scottishlawreports.org.uk/resources/links/courts.html>
Extensive and valuable list of links to British and international courts and tribunals with a note of whether decisions of the court or tribunal are available at the court website.

Transcripts of Judicial Proceedings in England & Wales: A Guide to Sources, compiled by Sally McLaren (Inner Temple Library, March 2011)
A revised and expanded version of the invaluable 2006 edition, listing by court, organisations holding copies of transcripts of unreported cases. A major new feature is the greatly expanded coverage of tribunals. The transcript content of the major commercial databases is not included. Available to buy only as an online version:
<http://www.innertemplelibrary.org.uk/Transcripts/TranscriptsGuide.htm>

Here are some links to other sources of decisions.

Supreme Court (free):
<http://www.supremecourt.gov.uk/decided-cases/index.html>
Provides access to full text of decisions and associated press summaries from 1 October 2009 onwards.

House of Lords: Judgments Archive (free):
<http://www.publications.parliament.uk/pa/ld/ldjudgmt.htm>
Provides access to full text transcripts of judgments from the Appellate Committee from 14 November 1996 to 30 July 2009.

Judicial Committee of the Privy Council (free):
<http://www.jcpc.gov.uk/decided-cases/index.html>
Provides access to full-text of judgments and associated press summaries from 1 October 2009 onwards.

Judicial Committee of the Privy Council Archive (free):
<http://privycouncil.independent.gov.uk/judicial-committee/judgments>
Provides access to full text transcripts of judgments up to 31 July 2009.

Asylum and Immigration Chambers (free):
<http://www.judiciary.gov.uk/media/tribunal-decisions/immigration-asylum-chamber.htm>
No details of the extent of the archive of the tribunals. Contrast with *BAILII* which includes reported and starred decisions from 1973 onwards – only a handful before the mid-1990s.

Employment Tribunals (free):
<http://www.justice.gov.uk/tribunals/employment/part-time-workers/judicial-decisions>
Carries a selection of Employment Tribunal and higher court decisions on part-time workers only.

Employment Appeal Tribunal (free):
<http://www.justice.gov.uk/tribunals/employment-appeals/judgments>
Includes judgments from full hearings from 1999 onwards and selected other hearings.

Lands Chamber (free):
<http://www.justice.gov.uk/tribunals/lands/decisions>
Searchable database of decisions from 2000 onwards and list of cases appealed to the Court of Appeal.

Leasehold Valuation Tribunal (free):
<http://www.residential-property.judiciary.gov.uk/search/decision_search.jsp>
The Residential Property Tribunal Service (RPTS) provides the full text of all Rent Assessment Committees and Leasehold Valuation Tribunal decisions from 1 January 2006. Decisions before this date made by the Leasehold Valuation Tribunals are available on the Leasehold Advisory Service website:
<http://www.lease-advice.org/lvtdecisions>

Solicitors Disciplinary Tribunal (free):
<http://www.solicitorstribunal.org.uk/search/JudgementSearch.aspx>
Searchable database of judgments, and based on the earlier simple list of hearings which was available on this site. Results carry a link to the full text of the tribunal's judgments, where available. Older judgments are available by post or email from the Tribunal's Office, see:
<http://www.solicitorstribunal.org.uk/about-us/frequently-asked-questions>

The Judgment Publication Policy is complex; some judgments will be available on the website for only three years, see:
<http://www.solicitorstribunal.org.uk/Content/ documents/Judgment%20publication%20policy.pdf>

Coroner's Inquest Reports
Coroner's Inquest files are closed to the public for 75 years. To view records falling within that time period apply to the Coroner's Office in the area concerned. Only 'properly interested persons' may inspect records. *Jervis on Coroners* (13th edn, 2013) notes that there is no definition of the phrase for the purposes of the provisions on access to documents, but states that the phrase 'should mean what it means elsewhere in the Coroners Rules, that is, a person entitled to be represented at the inquest.' Files outside the time period are usually transferred to the local authority to be added to the local records or archives collection. Failing either avenue, local newspapers are the best source of information. Older newspaper reports (19th century and early 20th century) appear to be almost a transcript of the proceedings. Some local authority local history/records/archive collections also maintain indexes to local newspapers. Alternatively, see section 10.3.2, below for information on how to trace copies.

BAILII's JISC-supported leading cases (free):
<http://www.bailii.org/openlaw>
A selection of 2,380 leading cases identified by academic lawyers, the full text organised under a range of broad subject headings.

Casetrack (subscriber-only)
See 'Full-text sources', at section 6.2.2, below.

Legal Resources in the UK and Ireland maintained by Delia Venables: free case law on the web (free):
<http://www.venables.co.uk/caselaw.htm>
Portal to a number of court and other websites.

For pre-1865 cases use:
English Reports (period covered 1220–1873) available free on
Commonwealth Legal Information Institute (CommonLII):
<http://www.commonlii.org/int/cases/EngR>

Summaries

Law Reports:
<http://www.lawreports.co.uk>
Free summaries of recent cases appearing in *The Law Reports*, *Weekly Law Reports* and *Industrial Cases Reports*.

Daily Law Notes, on the same website, contains brief summaries of forthcoming cases to be reported. The summaries are added the night after the decision was given.

The law reports which appear in *The Times* newspaper are summaries published soon after the decision was handed down and are prepared by staff of the Incorporated Council of Law Reporting, the publishers of *The Law Reports*, etc. Note that journalists on many newspapers write reports of court cases but only those reports written by a barrister may be cited during argument in court in subsequent cases, to establish precedent.

6.2.2 Subscriber-only services

Full-text sources

Casetrack (subscriber-only):
<http://www.casetrack.com/index.html>
Database of transcripts of Court of Appeal (Criminal and Civil Divisions) from April 1996 onwards; Administrative Court from April 1996 onwards; all divisions of the High Court from July 1998 onwards; selected judgments of the European Court of Justice and the European Court of Human Rights. Subscriber-only service to firms but free to academic institutions, charities and welfare organisations.

Justis (subscriber-only service)
Includes a limited range of full-text reports comprising the *Law Reports, Weekly Law Reports, The Times Law Reports* (1990–), *English Reports* (1220–1873), *State Trials* (1163–1858), *Daily Cases* (1999–) based on the case report summaries from the *Daily Law Notes* website (see 'Summaries', at section 6.2.1, above), and a number of specialist law reports, separately priced. A collection of transcripts has been developed and includes all decisions of the House of Lords/Supreme Court (1996–), Judicial Committee of the Privy Council (1999–), Court of Appeal (Civil Division) (1951–), Court of Appeal (Criminal Division) (1963–, except 1990–1992) and High Court 1996–. Full subject searching facility. Cases available as pdfs.

Lawtel (subscriber-only service)
Carries transcripts of cases from 1984 onwards. As well as official transcripts its own team of reporters provide unofficial transcripts of extempore judgments. A transcript search service: Transcripts Express is available.

Lexis®Library (subscriber-only service)
Full text of cases published by Butterworths and a few other publishers with whom Butterworths has a licence agreement. Extensive collection of reported cases including the *English Reports* back to the 13th century, the *All England Law Reports Reprint* and *Reprints Extension* volumes (1558–1935), the *Law Reports* from 1865 including the *All England Law Reports* but not the *Weekly Law Reports* or law reports published under the Lloyds imprint. Certainly the most comprehensive set of transcripts available, extending as far back as 1980 for decisions of the Court of Appeal (Civil Division), and now including the Supreme Court, House of Lords, Privy Council, Court of Appeal (both divisions) and all divisions of the High Court. A recently developed service providing approved judgments, which are made available immediately and have been approved by the judge, though they may be subject to minor editorial corrections subsequently. They are a pre-transcript stage in the preparation of judgments and, according to *Lexis®Library* editorial staff, should not be used if a transcript is available:

> To access them, click Cases on the *Lexis®Library* home page then, from the drop-down Sources menu, select Judgments. If Judgments does not appear in the drop-down box, click the 'More sources' line, then click Cases, click in the box next to Judgments, then click OK-Continue.

To search all case materials, both reported cases and transcripts, click the Cases library (tab at top of screen) and select whether you want a case name or search term (subject) or citation search.

Westlaw UK (subscriber-only service)
Full text of cases published by Sweet & Maxwell and a few other publishers with whom Sweet & Maxwell has licence agreements. Extensive collection of reported cases, including the *English Reports* back to 13th century. Does not include the *All England Law Reports* or the law reports published under the Lloyds imprint but does have the *Weekly Law Reports*. Collection of transcripts back to 1980, with a selection back to 1948, which can be searched or browsed independently by using the Cases library, then click Law Reports and Official Transcripts, then Official Transcripts. Subscribers to *Westlaw UK* who also subscribe to *Lawtel* (see above) are now able to access Lawtel Next Day Transcripts and Official Transcript pdfs on *Westlaw UK*. For searches across the whole cases library, click Cases (tab at top of screen) and select whether you want a subject search (use the free-text search box) or a case name search or a citation search. Hover the mouse over the 'i' symbol adjacent to any search box to see an example of what to type. Be aware that when using Advanced Search, a search for keywords searches only the Case Analysis summaries and not the full-text of decisions.

There is a considerable range of specialist databases covering the case law of particular practice areas. They include *Kemp & Kemp: Quantum of Damages* (available online via *Lawtel UK* for an added subscription), EGi (covering property law) and Family Law Online (Jordan Publishing). One way to trace what is available is to look up some of the publisher and subscription agent websites noted in Chapter 18, or join the lis-law email discussion lists mentioned in section 13.4.6, below.

Historic reprints

All England Law Reports Reprints Extension (period covered 1558–1935)
Print volumes usually shelved before the *All England Law Reports* proper start. Cases from 1861 to 1935 are incorporated within the cases library of *Lexis®Library*.

English Reports (period covered 1220–1873)
Also available online via *Westlaw UK, Lexis®Library, Justis, HeinOnline* (free module embedded within a subscriber-only service) – but available free on *Commonwealth Legal Information Institute* (CommonLII):
<http://www.commonlii.org/int/cases/EngR>

Revised Reports (period covered 1785–1865)
Selection of cases many duplicating what is available in the *English Reports*. Not available online.

Summaries

The services listed below index only summaries of cases. They also provide web links to the full text of a significant number. It is worth remembering that *Lexis®Library* and *Westlaw UK* (mentioned above under full-text sources) default to providing summaries of cases which they are not able to display in full.

Lawtel UK (subscriber-only service)
Summaries of over 70,000 cases from 1 January 1980 onwards – extremely wide coverage of the courts. Summaries loaded the day after the judgment is given. Links to transcripts of significant number. Case name and subject searching available, but remember that the search software is scanning summaries, not the full-text of decisions. If an in-depth practice or subject search is contemplated, this database may not prove as effective when compared with the full-text services.

David Swarbrick's *Lawindexpro*:
<http://swarb.co.uk/the-cases>
This site created and run by David Swarbrick, a solicitor in Halifax, Yorkshire, has indexed over 230,000 cases dating from January 1992 onwards, with well over 57,000 as case summaries. Links to full-text decisions of over 195,000, searchable by subject, date and court.

Current Law Monthly Digest (Sweet & Maxwell)
Each issue carries short summaries of recent cases, mainly reported decisions except for personal injury actions, arranged under broad practice areas. Subject and case name indexes are provided. During the summer of the year following publication, the summaries are re-published in the sister publication: *Current Law Yearbook*, edited in the light of subsequent events. For two reasons CLMD and CLYB might not be the first place to go to carry out comprehensive and in-depth research of a topic:

- there are no consolidated indexes to all the issues of CLMD and CLY since first publication in 1947;

- the subject indexes do not differentiate between summaries of cases and summaries of the wide range of other law material included, eg Acts and statutory instruments.

CLMD is best used for keeping up to date with developments by reading the summaries of materials in each current issue under the practice area/s within which you are normally working.

An online version of *Current Law Monthly Digest* is not available.

The Digest (LexisNexis, 3rd edn)

Purpose
Three main purposes:

- to summarise over 500,000 cases drawn from over 1,000 series of law reports covering the case law of not just England and Wales but also Scotland, Ireland and a number of Commonwealth countries;

- to act as a citator – see 'Is this case still good law?', at section 9.3.1, below.

- to act as a finding tool for the correct citation of cases not included in *Current Law Case Citator* – see 'Is this case still good law?', at section 9.3.1, below.

Structure

- Over 90 Main Volumes, arranging summaries under a similar subject arrangement as found in *Halsbury's Laws* (see section 4.2, above);

- Cumulative Supplement, issued annually, containing summaries of recent cases not included the Main Volumes;

- Quarterly Survey, summarising the latest cases – this is not a cumulative publication, so all the Surveys published since the Cumulative Supplement will need to be retained – three sections: list of new cases; updates to cases already summarised in the Main Volumes or Cumulative Supplement; summaries of new cases;

- Consolidated Table of Cases, an alphabetical list of cases summaries in the Main Volumes and Cumulative Supplement;

- Index, subject index to the Main Volumes and Cumulative Supplement.

How to use the print publication

Three searches are possible:

- a subject search for cases on a wide area of law;

- a highly specific subject search;

- a search for a summary of a case the name of which is known.

Broad subject search

Cumulative Supplement ⇒ Main Volume ⇒ Cumulative Supplement ⇒ Quarterly Survey

At the front of the Cumulative Supplement is a list of the titles of the Main Volumes. Select the Main Volume required and follow the search through ending with the Quarterly Survey.

Specific subject search

Index ⇒ Main Volume ⇒ Cumulative Supplement ⇒ Quarterly Survey

Two steps in the Index: first use the subject index; example of the layout of entries in the Index:

Formation of contract
telephone communication   12(1) Contr 938

meaning volume 12, part 1, Contracts at paragraph 938

Second, check the contents pages at the front of the Index to see from which issue of the Main Volume it has been prepared.

Then, check the spine of the Main Volume to ensure it is the same as used to compile the Index. If not, use the Reference Adaptor at the back of the new Main Volume to find where the case is now summarised. Take care, for the Reference Adaptor is sometimes in two parts, one for English cases, the second for other jurisdictions.

Search by case name

Consolidated Table of Cases ⇒ Main Volume ⇒ Cumulative Supplement ⇒ Quarterly Survey

Example of the layout of entries in the Consolidated Table of Cases:

Cooper v Bill (1865) 32(2) Lien; 39(2) Sale of Goods

meaning *Cooper v Bill* (1865) is summarised in two places in the Main Volumes: volume 32, part 2 on Lien and volume 39 part 2 on Sale of Goods. Paragraph numbers are not given in this Index

So, in the relevant Main Volume consult the case name index to find where the case summary is located.

An online version of *The Digest* is available on *Lexis®Library* for an additional subscription.

Neligan, D, *Social Security Case Law: Digest of Commissioners Decisions* (HMSO, 1979–)

Popularly know as Neligan's Digest and sometimes as 'the red books'.

Since 2006 the publication has not been available in print form but as a free download from the Department for Work and Pensions website:
<http://www.dwp.gov.uk/publications/specialist-guides/neligans-digest>

The following instructions are retained in the second edition of this Handbook to assist researchers use the online version, which is a facsimile of the print version. It is possible for users with print versions to make copies of the revised pages provided in the online supplements, and maintain the print copy up to date.

Purpose
To digest reported decisions of the Social Security Commissioners.

Structure
Two looseleaf volumes with brief digests of decisions arranged in chapters according to the particular benefit.

How to use the print publication

General index (back of volume 2) ⇒ text of digest

Example:

Child support
earnings
income tax R(CS) 1/05, 21.5.3 i

meaning: reported decision on child support, 2005 number 1, at chapter 21, part 5, section 3, paragraph i

The correct way to cite Commissioners Decisions is complex and an authoritative note is provided in Appendix 1, at the back of volume 2.

On the web page given at the top of this entry it is possible to register on a emailing list for notification when this and associated social security publications have been updated.

Equal Opportunities Review and *Employment Law Brief* (subscriber only services):
<http://www.eordirect.com>
Equal Opportunities Review through its free *EOR Online* website (above) offers access to summaries of EAT cases which have appeared in the journal, but a subscription in required to access any full text material. Its sister publication, *Employment Law Brief* occasionally includes the full text of EAT decisions, but more often carries only summaries.

Litigation documents

A variety of documents is filed with the court during litigation. Court documents in civil litigation have only been available to non-parties since 2 October 2006 under the Civil Procedure Rules. Anything deposited before then is not available. The rights of non-parties to view the documents are set out in the Civil Procedure Rules, Part 5, supplemented by the Practice Direction 5A:
<http://www.justice.gov.uk/courts/procedure-rules/civil/rules/part05>
See paragraphs 5.4C and 5.4D of Part 5 of the foregoing Rules.

High Court litigation records are transferred to the National Archives at Kew, London (formerly the Public Record Office). The records of lower courts are normally transferred to the County Record Office in the area concerned. Links from the research guide given below will assist in tracing if and where litigation materials are available to view:
<http://www.nationalarchives.gov.uk/records/research-guides/crime-and-law.htm>

Two recent articles which appeared in *Legal Information Management* describe the patterns of access to the judicial records of the House of Lords from the 16th century to 2009, and access to litigation documents from the Court of Appeal through to Coroners' Courts and Administrative tribunals:

> Shenton, C, 'The historic records of the judicial function of the House of Lords' (2011) 11 *Legal Information Management* 35–41

> Clinch, P, 'Answering queries about access to law court documents' (2011) 11 *Legal Information Management* 42–44.

There appear to be no equivalent rules on access to criminal litigation documents.

6.2.3   How to cite cases from England and Wales

Reported cases

> *Names of parties* | date | volume number – if more than one | abbreviation for publication | first page number of the report | (abbreviation for the court).

Note the year should appear in:

- square brackets where it is essential to finding the report of the case in the series of law reports. It will be the year the case was published (reported), not the year it was decided;

- round brackets where it is not essential to finding the report of the case, usually because the publication has a running volume number from its inception. In this case, the year *is* the year the case was decided, not the year it was published.

Examples:

> *Pepper v Hart* [1993] AC 593 (HL)
> *Pepper v Hart* (1992) 65 TC 241 (HL)

To translate abbreviations for publications into their full title use any of the following:

- Cardiff Index to Legal Abbreviations (free):
<http://www.legalabbrevs.cardiff.ac.uk>
Includes over 17,000 abbreviations to over 10,000 law publications worldwide. Can search from abbreviation to title and vice-versa. Also lists the preferred citation where it has been stipulated by the publisher.

- Raistrick, D, *Index to legal citations and abbreviations* (Sweet & Maxwell, 3rd edn, 2008).

- *Osborn's concise law dictionary* (Sweet & Maxwell, 12th edn, 2013).

- The list given in Appendix 1.2.

Neutral citation

Since 2001 the courts in England and Wales have developed a system of neutral citation. This enables the unique identification of a case on the internet even though it may not have been published in print. The neutral citation is allocated to each case by the court. A neutral citation comprises:

> *Names of parties* | [year] | abbreviation for the court | running number

Example:

> *R v Secretary of State for Employment* [2001] UKHL 23

The Cardiff Index to Legal Abbreviations (see above) will expand the abbreviations used for all courts. Some neutral citation abbreviations and their meaning are given in Practice Direction (Judgments: Form and Citation) [2001] 1 WLR 194, supplemented by Practice Direction (Judgments: Citations) [2002] 1 WLR 346. The Consolidated Criminal Practice Direction 28 March 2006, 2006 WL 1887076 (unreported, but transcript available online via *Westlaw UK*), incorporates the intentions of the earlier Directions at Part I paragraph 12.1 and following (see Appendix 3).

By Practice Direction (Judgments: Form and Citation) [2001] 1 WLR 194 (see Appendix 3), the neutral citation must always follow immediately after the names of parties, and any print versions of the case may be cited following the neutral citation.

Example:

> *R v Secretary of State for Employment* [2001] UKHL 23; [2001] 2 WLR 1389

Unreported cases without a neutral citation

OSCOLA (see section 17.4.3, below) recommends the following:

> Names of parties | (abbreviation for court | date)

Example:

> *Berk v Hair* (DC 12 September 1956)

Pre-1865 cases from a reprint publication

OSCOLA (see section 17.4.3, below) recommends the following:

> *Names of parties* | (date) | original report reference, | reprint report reference

Example:

> *Boulton v Jones* (1857) 2 H&N 564, 157 ER 252

Pinpoint citation

A pinpoint citation refers the reader to the exact point in the case report where the authority or proposition is located. See OSCOLA (see section 17.4.3, below) for detailed recommendations:
<http://www.law.ox.ac.uk/publications/oscola.php>

Decisions of the Social Security, etc Commissioners

These decisions differ from all other series of law reports in the form of citation used. The names of parties are not given in the report at all. Useful guides and information on Commissioners Decisions, how they are cited and how reported, are given at:
<http://www.osscsc.gov.uk/Decisions/decisions.htm>

In addition, the website includes a searchable list of reported decisions from 2001 onwards with links to the full-text of decisions since 2008. In addition, Appendix 1 of Neligan's Digest provides similar, authoritative information (see 'Summaries', at section 6.2.2, above).

6.3   SCOTLAND

6.3.1   Free sources

Warning

Unlike the courts in England and Wales, the use of unreported cases seems to be less contentious in Scotland. The position was stated in *Leighton v Harland & Wolff Ltd* 1953 SLT (Notes) 34 that the authority of a case 'depends not upon whether it is to be found in a series of reports but upon the fact that it is a judicial decision'. The Scottish courts appear not to have issued any more modern direction via a Practice Note, on the citation of unreported cases.

However, a proportion of cases appearing in the free services will also appear as reported decisions in print publications and online services. The Scottish courts have made Practice Notes regarding the hierarchy of law reports to be cited in litigation. See Appendix 3 for details of these requirements.

Full-text sources

Scottish Courts Website (free):
<http://www.scotcourts.gov.uk/search-judgments>
Sophisticated and well presented free search facility of transcripts from September 1998 onwards. Can search by keyword or on a number of elements within each opinion, such as the type of opinion, date, name of judge or judges, pursuer/appellant, defender/respondent and type of action.

Scottish Council of Law Reporting (free):
<http://www.scottishlawreports.org.uk/resources/open-access.html>
Fully searchable database of a selection of the opinions (Judgments) of the Scottish courts delivered in over 650 cases, from 1873 onwards. The archive is searched using JustCite software and can be searched in a number of ways: by subject terms, the name of the case or its citation.

Supreme Court of the United Kingdom (free):
<http://www.supremecourt.gov.uk/index.html>
Provides full text transcripts of decisions under 'Decided Cases'. Jurisdiction includes Scottish civil appeals and devolution issue cases from the Scottish courts (from 1 October 2009 onwards).

House of Lords: Judgments Archive (free):
<http://www.publications.parliament.uk/pa/ld/ldjudgmt.htm>
Provides access to full text transcripts of judgments from the Appellate Committee from 14 November 1996 to 30 July 2009. Jurisdiction includes Scottish civil appeals.

Judicial Committee of the Privy Council Archive (free):
<http://privycouncil.independent.gov.uk/judicial-committee/judgments>
Provides access to full text transcripts of judgments (under 'Judgments'). From 1999 to July 2009 its jurisdiction included cases on devolution issues appealed from the Scottish courts.

Judiciary of Scotland
<http://www.scotland-judiciary.org.uk/1/0/Home>
Provides information about judges and their work in the different courts. The site includes sentencing statements, summaries of court opinions and summaries of some fatal accident enquiries.

Scottish Council of Law Reporting: list of British courts and tribunals (free):
<http://www.scottishlawreports.org.uk/resources/links/courts.html>
Extensive and valuable list of links to British and international courts and tribunals with a note of whether decisions of the court or tribunal are available at the court website.

British and Irish Legal Information Institute (BAILII) (free):
<http://www.bailii.org/databases.html#uk>
<http://www.bailii.org/databases.html#scot>
Cross-court subject searching is available at:
<http://www.bailii.org/form/search_cases.html>
Takes a feed from the *Scottish Courts Website* (see above). Transcripts of cases from three Scottish courts with a selection back to 1879. The first link above is to UK courts and tribunals, the second to those specifically within the jurisdiction of Scotland.

CaseCheck (free, with optional registration):
<http://www.casecheck.co.uk>
Provides access to case summaries written by legal practitioners which can be browsed or searched. Coverage includes Scottish Courts case reports, Employment Appeal Tribunal Decisions, Employment Tribunal decisions and House of Lords/UK Supreme Court decisions. Where available, links are provided to the full-text transcripts on official court and tribunal sites.

Legal Resources in the UK and Ireland maintained by Delia Venables: free case law on the web (free):
<http://www.venables.co.uk/caselaw.htm>
Portal to a number of court and other websites.

6.3.2   Subscriber-only services

Full-text sources

Justis Electronic Sessions Cases (subscriber-only service)
Includes *Session Cases* from 1873 to the present. Full subject searching facility. Cases available as pdfs. In addition, available as a separate package, *Session Cases Archive* includes cases from 1821 to 1872.

Lexis®Library (subscriber-only service)
Full text of cases published by Butterworths and a few other publishers with whom Butterworths has a licence agreement. Includes *Scottish Civil Law Reports*, *Scottish Court Opinions* (not available in print form), *Scottish Criminal Case Reports*, *Scottish Transcripts* from selected courts and *Session Cases* from 1930–:

> At the *Lexis®Library* home page, click Sources, Browse Sources, in Country field select United Kingdom, open All Regions drop-down menu and select Scotland, select Cases from list of categories of material, click 'OK – continue' to reach search screen.

Westlaw UK (subscriber-only service)
Full text of cases published by Sweet & Maxwell and a few other publishers with whom Sweet & Maxwell has licence agreements. Includes *Session Cases* (1873–), *Scots Law Times* (1893–), plus a small number of specialist series. However, Case Analysis information attached to each case includes references to materials published in the rest of the United Kingdom which cite or report Scottish cases:

> At *Westlaw UK* home page, click tab 'Services' on menu bar and select Scots Law. Use the Cases library (tab at top of screen) and select whether you want a subject search (use the free-text search box) or a case name search or a citation search. Hover the mouse over the 'i' symbol adjacent to any search box to see an example of what to type.

Historic reprints

Scots Revised Reports (1540–1873)
Reprints a selection of cases of 'practical utility' from the following:

- Morison, WM, *Decisions of the Court of Session Digested under Proper Heads in the Form of a Dictionary* (1540–1808);
- Various series of House of Lords cases;
- Faculty Collection (1807–1825);
- Early volumes of Session Cases; and
- *Scottish Jurist* (1829–1865).

There is no online version of *Scots Revised Reports*.

Summaries

Current Law Monthly Digest and *The Digest*
See 'Summaries', at section 6.2.2, above. Summaries of cases decided in Scotland are printed in a section of *Current Law Monthly Digest* after the sections of summaries for: (a) England and Wales; and (b) Northern Ireland.

Green's Weekly Digest (1986–)
Digests all Scottish judicial decisions received by the publisher, W Green & Son. It is published in forty parts throughout the year. Cumulative indexes for the year's issues are produced three times during year. A consolidated index covering the period 1986–1995 is available. The indexes provide a table of cases and a subject index. While many cases may be reported later elsewhere, the digest may remain the only 'report' available.

Citation to *Green's Weekly Digest* is in the form:

> Party Names | Year | G.W.D. | issue number-paragraph number

Example:

> *Al-Megrahi v H.M.A.* 2009 G.W.D. 29-467

6.3.3   How to cite Scottish cases

Reported cases

Names of parties | date | volume number – if applicable | abbreviation for publication | first page number of the report

The conventional use of brackets when citing Scottish law reports is as follows:

- round brackets are used to denote the year when this is not required to locate the case (ie when there is a distinct volume number);

- no brackets are used when the year is required to locate the case (ie when the year also refers to the volume of reports).

Examples:

> *Stewart v Chalmers* (1904) 12 SLT 468
> *Stewart v Malik* 2009 SLT 205

Both *Session Cases* and *Scots Law Times* are published in separately paginated sequences of reports from different courts. It is important to be certain which sequence is being referred to. This can be made clear by the use of abbreviations:

- SC   for Court of Session cases in *Session Cases*
- SC (HL)   for House of Lords cases in *Session Cases*
- SC (PC)   for Privy Council cases in *Session Cases*
- SC (UKSC)   for Supreme Court cases in Session Cases
- JC   for Justiciary cases in *Session Cases*
- SLT   Scots Law Times 'reports' section (cases from superior courts)
- SLT (Land Ct)   for Land Court cases in *Scots Law Times*
- SLT (Land Tr)   for Lands Tribunal cases in *Scots Law Times*
- SLT (Lyon)   for Court of the Lord Lyon cases in *Scots Law Times*
- SLT (News)   for News section in *Scots Law Times*
- SLT (Sh Ct)   for Sheriff Court cases in *Scots Law Times*

To translate abbreviations for publications into their full title use any of the following:

- Cardiff Index to Legal Abbreviations (free):
  <http://www.legalabbrevs.cardiff.ac.uk>
  Includes over 17,000 abbreviations to over 10,000 law publications worldwide. Can search from abbreviation to title and vice-versa. Also lists the preferred citation where it has been stipulated by the publisher.

- Raistrick, D, *Index to legal citations and abbreviations* (Sweet & Maxwell, 3rd edn, 2008).

- *Osborn's concise law dictionary* (Sweet & Maxwell, 12th edn, 2013).

- The list given in Appendix 1.2.

Neutral citation

In 2004 both the Court of Session and the High Court of Justiciary developed a system of neutral citation. This enables the unique identification of a case on the internet even though it may not have been published in print. The neutral citation is allocated to each case by the court. A neutral citation comprises:

Names of parties [year] abbreviation for the court running number

Example:

Stewart v Malik [2009] CSIH 5

The Cardiff Index to Legal Abbreviations (see above) will expand the abbreviations used for all courts. The neutral citation abbreviations for the Court of Session and their meaning are given in Practice Note (No 5 of 2004) and those for the High Court of Justiciary in Practice Note (No 2 of 2004) (see Appendix 3).

By the same Practice Notes the neutral citation must always follow immediately after the names of parties, and any print versions of the case may be cited following the neutral citation.

Example:

Syed v Ahmed [2005] CSIH 72; 2006 S.C. 165

Unreported cases without a neutral citation

OSCOLA (see section 17.4.3, below) makes no recommendation relating to Scotland. The practice set out for England and Wales may be used – see section 6.2.3, above:
<http://www.law.ox.ac.uk/publications/oscola.php>

Scottish cases from a reprint publication

OSCOLA (see section 17.4.3, below) makes no recommendation relating to Scotland. The practice set out for England and Wales may be used – see section 6.2.3, above:
<http://www.law.ox.ac.uk/publications/oscola.php>

Pinpoint citation

A pinpoint citation refers the reader to the exact point in the case report where the authority or proposition is located. See OSCOLA (see section 17.4.3, below) for detailed recommendations:
<http://www.law.ox.ac.uk/publications/oscola.php>

Decisions of the Social Security, etc Commissioners

See section 6.2.3, above.

6.4   NORTHERN IRELAND

6.4.1   Free sources

Warning

The courts in Northern Ireland have made a Practice Direction regarding the hierarchy of law reports to be cited in litigation. For details of these requirements, see Annex E1 of the extract from the Direction reproduced in Appendix 3, below.

Full-text sources

Note: Although the Northern Ireland jurisdiction came into existence in 1921, the Incorporated Council for Law Reporting for Northern Ireland only started publishing the *Northern Ireland Law Reports* in 1925. Reports of cases in the Northern Ireland courts between 1921 and 1924 can be found in the *Irish Reports* and the *Irish Times Reports*.

Time lags in the publication of the official law reports led in 1970 to the *Northern Ireland Law Judgments Bulletin* (which has undergone several minor changes of title since).

Northern Ireland Court Service Website (free):
<http://www.courtsni.gov.uk/en-GB/Judicial%20Decisions/PublishedByYear/Pages/Home.aspx>
List of judgments from 1999 onwards with links to the full text. No subject search facility.

British and Irish Legal Information Institute (*BAILII*) (free):
<http://www.bailii.org/databases.html#uk>
<http://www.bailii.org/databases.html#nie>
Cross-court subject searching is available at:
<http://www.bailii.org/form/search_cases.html>
Takes a feed from the *Northern Ireland Courts Website* (see above). Transcripts of cases from seven courts and three tribunals mainly back to 1998 but some courts/tribunals back a little earlier. The first link above is to UK courts and tribunals, the second to those specifically within the jurisdiction of Northern Ireland.

Legal Resources in the UK and Ireland maintained by Delia Venables: free case law on the web (free):
<http://www.venables.co.uk/caselaw.htm>
Portal to a number of court and other websites.

6.4.2   Subscriber-only services

Full-text sources

Lexis®Library (subscriber-only service)
Includes *Northern Ireland Law Reports* 1945 onwards and selected *Northern Ireland Unreported Judgments 1989* onwards:

> Use the *Lexis®Library* 'Cases' search and narrow results by source name.

Westlaw UK (subscriber-only service)
Does not include Northern Ireland cases.

Historic reprints

There are none.

Summaries

Current Law Monthly Digest and *The Digest*
See section 6.2.2, above. Summaries of cases decided in Northern Ireland are printed in a section of *Current Law Monthly Digest* after the main body of summaries for England and Wales.

Bulletin of Northern Ireland Law (SLS Publications (NI))
Monthly publication which provided lengthier summaries of Northern Ireland cases than provided by *Current Law Monthly Digest* or *The Digest*. Ceased publication December 2012.

6.4.3   Index to cases

Index to the Northern Ireland cases 1921–1997 (Butterworths, in association with Incorporated Council of Law Reporting for Northern Ireland, 1998)
Includes an alphabetical list of cases names, subject index and tables of statutes, cases and rules judicially considered.

6.4.4   How to cite cases from Northern Ireland

Reported cases

> *Names of parties* | [date] | neutral citation; | [date] | abbreviation for publication | first page number of the report

Example:

> *Re Misbehavin' Ltd's Application for Judicial Review* [2005] NICA 35; [2006] NI 181

Neutral citation

The Northern Ireland courts have adopted a system of neutral citation. This enables the unique identification of a case on the internet even though it may not have been published in print. The neutral citation is allocated to each case by the court. A neutral citation comprises:

Names of parties | [year] | abbreviation for the court | running number

Example:

Salt v Helly [2009] NIQB 69

The Cardiff Index to Legal Abbreviations (see above) will expand the abbreviations used for all courts. In addition, an appendix to the fourth edition of OSCOLA (see section 17.4.3, below) lists abbreviations for Northern Ireland courts at paragraph 4.1.4.

Unreported cases without a neutral citation

OSCOLA (see section 17.4.3, below) makes no recommendation relating to Northern Ireland. The practice set out for England and Wales may be used – see section 6.2.3, above:
<http://www.law.ox.ac.uk/publications/oscola.php>

6.5   EUROPEAN UNION

There have been delays in the publication of the decisions of the European Court of Justice for many years. The main reason is that in direct actions, cases may be submitted to and argued before the court in any one of the 23 official languages currently recognised (the language of the case). Preliminary judgments are given in the language of the national court which made the application. The judges of the ECJ deliberate in a common language, which is usually French, see:
<http://curia.europa.eu/jcms/jcms/Jo2_7024/#jurisprudences>
The official text of the judgment is not released until an agreed translation has been made of all elements of the case report, into all the official languages.

6.5.1   Free sources

Court of Justice of the European Communities (European Court of Justice)

<http://eur-lex.europa.eu/JURISIndex.do?ihmlang=en>
The text of the 15,000 or so judgments, opinions and orders of the European Court of Justice from 1954 onwards is available free, but there is no subject search facility – use the search boxes at the bottom of the list to search by year, case name or official case number or type of document.

The text of judgments, opinions and orders delivered by the Court since 1954 and published in *European Court Reports* (see section 6.5.2, below) are also available free on the Court's own website. For further details of what this database contains see the note at:
<http://curia.europa.eu/jcms/jcms/Jo2_14954>
The advantage of this site is that a subject search facility is available at:
<http://curia.europa.eu/juris/recherche.jsf?language=en>

All judgments of the Court, but only the judgments, are available free on the *British and Irish Legal Information Institute* (*BAILII*) website, with a subject search facility:
<http://www.bailii.org/eu/cases/EUECJ>

Decisions of the European Commission

Decisions relating to competition law, anti-trust law and mergers are published in the Official Journal, as also are the decisions of the Merger Task-Force and Competition Directorate. The full text of Official Journal from 1952 onwards, is available free at:
<http://eur-lex.europa.eu/en/index.htm>

Follow the links for the Official Journal at the left side of the page.

In addition, the EC Directorate-General Competition has a case search page for a database of decisions but there is no information on the contents of the database:
<http://ec.europa.eu/competition/index_en.html>

6.5.2   Subscriber-only services

Print sources

Official Reports of Cases before the Court – better known as *European Court Reports* (ECR) 1954–
The official print version of the judgments of the European Court of Justice. They are published with some delay owing to the requirement to translate the judgment and associated materials into all the official languages of the European Community before any version is released.

Other print versions of judgments are published unofficially in:

- *All England Law Reports*: European Cases (Butterworths)

- *Common Market Law Reports* (Common Market Law Reports Ltd)

- *European Community Cases* (Sweet & Maxwell)

- *European Union Law Reporter* (Sweet & Maxwell)

For sources on the interpretation and application of EU law by national courts see section 9.7.3, below.

Online sources

Justis CELEX (subscriber-only service)
Uses data provided by the Office for Official Publications of the European Communities. A segment includes the full text of all judgments, orders, opinions and other acts issued by the European Court of Justice and Court of First Instance, as well as the opinions of the Advocates-General. Full subject search facility.

Lexis®Library (subscriber-only service)
Click Sources, Browse Sources, in Country field select European Union, select Cases from list of categories of material, select one or more categories and click 'OK – continue' to reach search screen.

Westlaw UK (subscriber-only service)
Click EU on main toolbar and select Cases from the Browse list towards the bottom left of screen.

6.5.3   How to cite judgments of the European Court of Justice

The mode of citation recommended by the editors of the *European Court Reports* is:

> Case registration number | *Names of parties* | [year] | ECR | part number (only from 1990 onwards) | page number

Examples:

> Case C-3/87 *The Queen v Ministry of Agriculture, Fisheries and Food, ex parte Agegate Ltd* [1989] ECR 4459
> Case T-119/89 *Teissonnié re v Commission* [1990] ECR II-7

If an official ECR reference is not available OSCOLA (see section 17.4.3, below) recommends using *Common Market Law Reports* next in the hierarchy of reports, or failing that, the *Law Reports*, the *Weekly Law Reports* or the *All England Law Reports*, see:
<http://www.law.ox.ac.uk/publications/oscola.php>

OSCOLA also details how to cite Commission Decisions published in the Official Journal.

6.6   EUROPEAN COURT OF HUMAN RIGHTS

6.6.1   Free sources

European Court of Human Rights HUDOC database (free):
<http://www.echr.coe.int/ECHR/EN/Header/Case-Law/Decisions+and+judgments/HUDOC+database>
Has subject search facility. The HUDOC database is easy to access and its use is recommended. There are disadvantages in the indexing and currency of all the official paper sources.

Many of the larger university law libraries have all or a selection of the three publications listed below. See section 13.4.2, below on how to gain access.

European Court of Human Rights. Series A: Reports of Judgments and Decisions (1996–) (formerly, *Judgments and Decisions* (1959–1995)) (Carl Heymanns Verlag KG)
Earlier set popularly cited as ECHR or Series A. Continuation from 1996 onwards cited as ECHR. Usually shelved in issue number order. No consolidated index to the set. Some annual indexes published years after issues originally appeared. These indexes are useful, having for a single year separate lists of cases arranged by: the name of the applicant, the name of the state, the convention article under which the action has been brought, a list of states and the national provisions at issue, a subject index.

European Court of Human Rights. Series B: Pleadings, oral arguments and documents (1959–1988) (Carl Heymanns Verlag KG)
Popularly cited as Series B.

European Commission of Human Rights; Decisions (later *Decisions and Reports*) (1955–1998) (Carl Heymanns Verlag KG)
Usually shelved in case number order. The Council of Europe published these occasional volumes of summaries of cases arranged under the convention article under which the action was brought, and indexes by case number, applicant's name, the name of the respondent state, the convention article under which the action was brought and a subject index.

6.6.2   Subscriber-only services

For sources on the application and interpretation of European Court of Human Rights decisions in national courts, see section 9.8.4, below.

Print sources in full text

European Human Rights Reports (European Law Centre)
The widely available alternative to the official published reports of the European Court of Human Rights. Note that from and including 2001, Volume 31, these reports have adopted case numbering as the method of citation rather than page numbering. For example, (2001) 31 EHRR 1 refers to the first case reported, (2001) 31 EHRR 2 refers to the second; do not treat the final number/s as page numbers. The reports are available online via *Westlaw UK*, in the EU library.

Butterworths Human Rights Cases (LexisNexis)
Publishes a selection of the most significant human rights cases from international tribunals, including the European Court of Human Rights, and national courts in the United Kingdom. Available online via *Lexis®Library.*

Although the following publication does not include European Court of Human Rights materials, and is placed here for convenience, it provides reprints of materials within the wider international context of human rights:

International Human Rights Reports (Human Rights Law Centre, Department of Law, University of Nottingham)
Reprints human rights treaties promoted by the United Nations and other documents, including decisions and opinions, adopted within the United Nations and by other international organisations. Published four times a year. Also available as a subscriber-only online service, see:
<http://www.nottingham.ac.uk/hrlc/publications/internationalhumanrightsreports.aspx>

Print sources of summaries

The *Yearbook* and *Human Rights Case Digest* are the only digests still actively published and both are of value for their coverage. The latter contains longer summaries and is more current. Gomien's *Judgments of the European Court of Human Rights: Reference Charts* is unique, summarising case law made under the Convention in chart form. Sikuta and Hubelova's book is more up to date and contains useful case-finding aids.

Yearbook of the European Convention on Human Rights (Martinus Nijhoff, 1955–)
Official publication containing in part 2, brief summaries of judgments and, in part 4 (when included, as not appearing in every issue), summaries of national court decisions concerning the Convention.

Human Rights Case Digest: the European Convention system prepared by the British Institute of Human Rights (Martinus Nijhoff, 1990–)
Available online through several subscriber-only e-journal hosts including Hein-Online and Academic Search Complete.

Published bi-monthly carrying summaries of up to five or six pages in length of judgments of the European Court of Human Rights, decisions on admissibility of the European Commission of Human Rights and summaries of Reports of the Commission on case references to the Court. It also summarises all significant activities of the Council of Europe. Each issue includes editorial comment on the contents.

The following digests have ceased publication but are still of use for historical research.

Digest of Strasbourg case-law relating to the European Convention on Human Rights prepared by the Council of Europe Directorate of Human Rights and the Europa Instituut at the University of Utrecht (Carl Heymanns Verlag KG, 1970–1997)
Six looseleaf volumes arranging summaries of cases under the articles of the Convention under which the action was brought. Although issued by the Council of Europe it is not regarded as an official source of published law. Appears to have ceased publication in 1997.

Berger, V, *Case law of the European Court of Human Rights* (Round Hall, 1989–1995)
Three volumes containing case summaries, each summary extending to two or three pages and placed in chronological order, with an index by article of the Convention. Covers the period 1960–1993 only.

Kempees, P, *A systematic guide to the case-law of the European Court of Human Rights* (Martinus-Nijhoff, 1996–2000)
Four volume set with of excerpts from the judgments of the Court, arranged according to the articles of the Convention. Covers the period 1960–1998.

Gomien, D (compiler), *Judgments of the European Court of Human Rights: Reference Charts* (Council of Europe Press, 1995)
Four charts, which are correct to the end of 1994, list cases alphabetically by case name; by case number; alphabetically by country (and numerically within each country listing); by article number (and numerically by judgment number within each article. Unfortunately a 'one-off' publication and not updated.

Sikuta, J and Hubelova, E (editors), *European Court of Human Rights: Case-law of the Grand Chamber 1998–2006* (Asser Press, 2007)
A selection of decisions and judgments containing the facts of each case and a summary of the considerations and conclusions. Annexes list judgments and decisions in chronological and alphabetical order, by articles of the Convention and Protocols and by subject matter.

Online sources

Full-text sources

Justis Human Rights (subscriber-only service)
Includes the full text of all cases from the inception of the European Court of Human Rights. Also includes the full text of the European Convention for the Protection of Human Rights and Fundamental Freedoms with protocols. Full subject search facility.

Lexis®Library (subscriber-only service)
Includes official and unofficial reports of the European Court of Human Rights and *Butterworths Human Rights Cases*:

> Click Sources, Browse Sources, in Country field select International, select Cases from list of categories of material, select one or more categories and click 'OK – continue' to reach search screen.

Westlaw UK (subscriber-only service)
Contains *European Human Rights Reports* and *Human Rights Law Reports – UK Cases* but does not include the official reports of the European Court of Human Rights.

Summaries

One Crown Office Row (free):
<http://www.1cor.com/resources-introduction>
Amongst a variety of resources on this very popular website is Human Rights and Public Law Update, a database of over 1,000 summaries with commentary on cases decided by the European Court of Human Rights and domestic courts, since 1998. Click the Cases link to a list of broad subject headings under which the summaries and commentary are arranged. The database has been compiled by Rosalind English, Chambers Academic Consultant, who also prepares material for the *Lawtel Human Rights* service. To view most of the content it is necessary to register and log in but access is free.

Lawtel Human Rights (subscriber-only service)
Searchable database of summaries of all European Court of Human Rights cases plus selected Admissibility Decisions of the European Court of Human Rights since 1997. Summaries appear online within 48 hours of the judgment being made available with over 2,000 European Court of Human Rights Case Reports linked to full text transcripts. Commentary is provided by barristers from 1 Crown Office Row chambers (see above).

6.6.3   How to cite judgments of the European Court of Human Rights

The Court has prepared a detailed two-page note on how to cite its judgments and decisions which is printed at the front of each issue and is also available at:
<http://www.echr.coe.int/NR/rdonlyres/0D5B9647-A83F-43CD-88E1-44B7312A29D6/0/COURT_ n2316817_v2_Note_explaining_the_mode_of_citation.pdf>

Alternatively, Google HUDOC which should take you to the 'home page' for the database – click Reports Collection at left side of screen and a link to the Note on Citation is at the bottom of the page.

6.7   INTERNATIONAL LAW

6.7.1   Permanent Court of International Justice and International Court of Justice: free sources

Permanent Court of International Justice

Reports of Judgements and Advisory Opinions 1922–1946, available online via *World Legal Information Institute* (WorldLII) free website:
<http://www.worldlii.org/catalog/55613.html>

Another source of Permanent Court of International Justice cases is the collection of full text reports with editorial summaries:

Hudson, MO, *World Court Reports* (Carnegie Endowment for International Peace, 1934–1943, reprinted Oceana, 1969) but not available on the web.

International Court of Justice

Reports of Judgements, Advisory Opinions and Orders, 1947– (Sijthoff); International Court of Justice: *Pleadings, Oral Arguments and Documents*, 1947– (Sijthoff). Both available through the International Court of Justice website (free) but with only a basic subject search function:
<http://www.icj-cij.org/docket/index.php?p1=3>

World Court Digest (Max Plank Institut) 1985– is a digest (brief summaries) of decisions of the International Court of Justice. Available in print and online (but no detailed subject searching available on website):
<http://www.mpil.de/ww/de/pub/forschung/forschung_im_detail/publikationen/institut/wcd.cfm? fuseaction_wcd=aktdat&aktdat=100000000000.cfm>

6.7.2   International Court of Justice: subscriber-only services

A range of materials including filings, advisory opinions and judgments is available online via *Lexis®Library*:

> Select tab: Sources; Click: Browse sources; In the country dialog box select International, select Cases from list of categories of material, then select one or more publications and click OK-continue button top right.

Reports of Judgments, Advisory Opinions and Orders, from 1947 onwards, are available online via *Westlaw International*, which may be reached from *Westlaw UK* (subscriber-only service) as follows:

> Click tab 'Services' towards top right of screen
> Click tab 'Westlaw International' and continue clicking this tab on subsequent screens until the International Directory is reached.
> In 'Search these databases' box (left-hand side of screen) type INT-ICJ and click Go
> In the search screen which appears, either:

- type in the search box the names of parties in a particular case or subject keywords,
- or click the tab 'Terms and connectors' and construct a search using the principles set out in Appendix 4.

More comprehensive coverage

International Law Reports (formerly *Annual Digest of Public International Law Cases*), 1919– (Butterworths/Grotius Publications Ltd), covers decisions of the ICJ, Court of Justice of the European Communities and the Administrative Tribunal of the International Labour Organization and municipal (ie national) courts – available in full text from *Justis International Law Reports*.

Oxford Reports on International Law (subscriber-only)
An ambitious project, still developing, to bring together full text reports of cases from a wide range of international courts, tribunals, domestic courts and ad hoc tribunals. The cases are allocated to one of five modules according to subject matter. Each case will be accompanied by commentary and analysis.

6.7.3 Arbitral awards

Permanent Court of Arbitration, *Reports of International Arbitral Awards* (United Nations, 1948–) – continues *Reports of the Permanent Court of Arbitration* (1902–1931)
These official reports searchable both by parties and full-text subject search of judgments (free):
<http://untreaty.un.org/cod/riaa/index.html>

Permanent Court of Arbitration website (free):
<http://www.pca-cpa.org/showpage.asp?pag_id=1029>
Clickable list of decisions leading to the full text but the site's subject search function retrieves material from across the entire PCA website, not just the cases.

Westlaw International (subscriber-only service)
Has selected coverage of PCA Awards from 1980 onwards within its International Directory (see section 6.7.2, above) under the abbreviation PCA-AWARDS.

6.7.4 Specialised courts

International Criminal Court (free):
<http://www2.icc-cpi.int/Menus/ICC>
Click link: Situations and cases.

For other international courts, see links on *World Legal Information Institute* (WorldLII) (free):
<http://www.worldlii.org/catalog/2561.html>

6.7.5 National adjudicatory decisions

Parry, C and Hopkins, J (eds), *British International Law Cases* (Oceana, 1964–1969)
Parry, C and Hopkins, J (eds), *Commonwealth International Law Cases* (Oceana, 1974–1985)
These print publications cover very brief time periods and are of little practical use.

6.7.6　Comprehensive sources

Lexis®Library (subscriber-only service)
Apart from full text of ICJ judgments (1947–), it also includes WTO cases (1995–) and GATT Panel Decisions (1948–1994):

> Click Sources, Browse Sources, in Country field select International, select Cases from list of categories of material, click 'OK – continue' to reach search screen.

Westlaw UK (subscriber-only service)
In the *Westlaw International* Library (see section 6.7.2, above), apart from the full text of ICJ judgments (1947–), *Westlaw International* provides access to WTO cases (1995–) and GATT Panel Decisions (1948–1994):

> At the International Directory screen, click International/Worldwide Materials, Multi-National Materials, Court and Tribunal Cases – click source to be searched.

WorldLII (free):
<http://www.worldlii.org/catalog/2561.html>

6.7.7　How to cite international law cases

There is a variety of official materials published by each international court as a case passes through the various judicial stages. There are also unofficial versions of the case published. It is best to consult the free OSCOLA publication (Oxford Standard for the Citation of Legal Authorities – see section 17.4.3, below) for guidance. The section on Citing International Law has not been updated or included in the 4th edition of OSCOLA, so follow the link on the home page to the 2006 edition:
<http://www.law.ox.ac.uk/publications/oscola.php>

CHAPTER 7

PROCEDURAL LAW

7.1 CRIMINAL PROCEDURE

7.1.1 United Kingdom

The Supreme Court – procedures:
<http://www.supremecourt.gov.uk/procedures/index.html>
Links to forms, rules and practice direction for the Supreme Court.

Judicial Committee of the Privy Council – procedures:
<http://www.jcpc.gov.uk/procedures/index.html>
Links to the rules and practice directions of the Judicial Committee of the Privy Council.

7.1.2   England and Wales

Ministry of Justice – Criminal Procedure Rules official website:
<http://www.justice.gov.uk/courts/procedure-rules/criminal/rulesmenu>

Criminal Procedure Rules (TSO – The Stationery Office)
The official publication containing the CPR, supplied to criminal courts across England and Wales for use by judges, magistrates and clerks.

Judicial College (Magistrate and Legal Advisor Training):
<http://www.estudo.co.uk/jsb/course/view.php?id=9&topic=all>
This body replaced the Judicial Studies Board. Links to the Adult Court, Family Court, Youth Court and Equal Treatment Bench Books plus a range of other guidance materials provided to magistrates.
The Equal Treatment Bench Book can also be accessed at:
<http://www.judiciary.gov.uk/publications-and-reports/judicial-college/Pre+2011/equal-treatment-bench-book>

Sentencing Guidelines Council:
<http://sentencingcouncil.judiciary.gov.uk/sentencing-guidelines.htm>
Reproduces Sentencing Guidelines.

Anthony & Berryman, *Magistrates' Court Guide* (Butterworths, annual publication)

Archbold, *Criminal Pleading, Evidence and Practice* (Sweet & Maxwell)

Also available online via *Westlaw UK*. Commonly referred to as '*Archbold*'. Published biennially.

Purpose
The old established, authoritative work on criminal practice, reproducing legislation and procedural guidance with commentary. Some courts and practitioners have a preference for citation from *Archbold* over the more modern, *Blackstone's Criminal Practice*.

Structure of the print publication

- 3,000 page Main Volume, issued each December in a new edition;
- Cumulative Supplement issued three times a year;
- *Archbold News* – an updating newsletter published ten times a year.

How to use the print publication
Four step search:

Subject index at the back of the Main Volume ⇒ paragraph in Main Volume ⇒ paragraph in latest Cumulative Supplement ⇒ scan copies of *Archbold News* published since the date of the latest Cumulative Supplement

How to use the electronic version

Archbold is available online via *Westlaw UK* as an additional subscription to the Books library.

> At the *Westlaw UK* main search page, click Books (on the menu bar across the top of the screen) ⇒ Browse, By title ⇒ *Archbold* then click the link to either Main Volume, Supplement

Blackstone's Criminal Practice (Oxford University Press, published annually)
Also available electronically on OUP website and *Lexis®Library*.

> *Stone's Justices' Manual* (LexisNexis)

Also available as CD. Commonly referred to as '*Stone's*'. Published annually.

Purpose

Reprints Acts, rules and forms relating to the business of Magistrates' Courts. Editorial notes also provided. Although the contents are 'basic', with limited added value in terms of commentary, it is the key reference work used by the Clerk to the Justices to check points of law raised by Counsel and advise the Bench.

Structure of the print publication

Three, bound volumes published in a new edition early each year, updated by a supplement published the following autumn. Each bound volume is divided into Parts.

How to use the print publication

> Index or tables at the back of vol.3 ⇒ body of text ⇒ supplement (if published)

All references in the index, tables and contents are to Part and paragraph numbers. Example:

> EXPLOSIVES, search for, 8-14042, 8-14187

> meaning Part 8 paragraph 14042 and paragraph 14187

There is a CD-ROM version of *Stone's* but no internet version.

7.1.3   Scotland

Scottish Courts:
<http://www.scotcourts.gov.uk>
Links to High Court of Justiciary, the Sheriff Courts, Justice of the Peace Courts and, under the Rules and Practice tab, links to Rules, Practice Notes, Fees, Forms and Guidance Notes.

Scottish Sentencing Council:
<http://www.scotland.gov.uk/Topics/Justice/legal/criminalprocedure/17305/Responses>
The Council is due to be set up under the provisions of the Criminal Justice and Licensing (Scotland) Act 2010 and will be required to publish sentencing guidelines.

> *Sentencing Practice* (W Green/Sweet & Maxwell, 2000–)

Purpose

A guide to the appropriate range of sentence for a particular case being considered, listing sentences passed in individual cases under each offence. Does not deal with the principles of sentence.

Structure

One looseleaf volume, the material in divisions by categories of crime and offences. Within each division the material is presented in the following standard order:

- name of the crime or sentence;

- maximum penalties;

- guidelines provided by the High Court of Justiciary;

- recent cases, the case notes compiled from material in *Green's Weekly Digest*, the *Scots Law Times*, *Scottish Criminal Case Reports* and some unreported cases.

How to use the print publication

Index, at the back of the volume ⇒ main text

Example:

Cocaine
possession, G6.0003.3

meaning Division G, paragraph 6.0003.3

Note: paragraph numbers are displayed in the margins of the text. Ignore page numbers at the centre, foot of each page in the format G35

Gordon, GH, *Criminal Procedure according to the Law of Scotland* by Robert Wemyss Renton and Henry Hilton Brown (*Renton & Brown's Criminal Procedure*) (W Green, 6th edn, 1996–)
Two looseleaf volumes of commentary with footnotes.

Also available online via *Westlaw UK* for an additional subscription.

> *Criminal Procedure Legislation* (W Green/Sweet & Maxwell, 1996–)

Purpose

A comprehensive collection of the full text of Scottish primary and secondary legislation relating to criminal procedure, with commentary.

Structure

Three looseleaf volumes, in divisions: A, primary statutes; B, Acts of Adjournal; C, Practice Notes and D to G, tables of penalties for various offences.

How to use the print publication

Index ⇒ main text

Example:

BAIL CONDITIONS
    breach, 10-13 – 10-19

meaning chapter 10, paragraphs 10–19

Note 1: Rather confusingly, the guide cards between chapters mention Parts in roman type face yet the index provides directions to the chapter and paragraph numbers. There are several chapters within each Part.

Note 2: The commentary is presented in the style of *Current Law Statutes* (in fact the contents are a reproduction of material which also appears in that service). Each Act commences with an introductory commentary, sometimes at great length and in a small typeface, and many individual sections of the Act are followed by short commentary also in a smaller typeface.

Also available online via *Westlaw UK* for an additional subscription.

Renton & Brown's Statutory Offences (W Green/Sweet & Maxwell, 1999)

Purpose
Reproduces the full text of statutes and statutory instruments, with annotations and commentary, relating to crimes and offences.

Structure
Two looseleaf volumes with statutes and statutory instruments arranged in divisions by offence. Statutes are reproduced first in each division, followed by statutory instruments.

How to use the print publication

Index at back of volume 2 ⇒ main text

Example:

ANIMALS
    abandonment, F-182

meaning division E, paragraph 182

Note 1: Paragraph numbers are printed in the margins. Ignore the page numbers printed at the centre, foot of the page in the style E-80/19.

Note 2: The commentary is presented in the style of *Current Law Statutes* (in fact the contents are a reproduction of material which also appears in that service). Each Act commences with an introductory commentary, sometimes at great length and in a small typeface, and many individual sections of the Act are followed by short commentary also in a smaller typeface.

Also available online via *Westlaw UK* for an additional subscription.

7.1.4   Northern Ireland

Magistrates' Courts Rules (Northern Ireland) 1984 (TSO – The Stationery Office, Belfast, 1984)
Single volume looseleaf reproducing the rules without commentary or index.

Links to the web version of amendments only may be found at:
<http://www.courtsni.gov.uk/en-GB/Publications/Legislation/Pages/default.aspx>

7.1.5   Regional courts

European Court of Human Rights (free) – rules of court:
<http://www.echr.coe.int/ECHR/EN/Header/Basic+Texts/Other+texts/Rules+of+Court>

Leach, P, *Taking a case to the European Court of Human Rights* (Oxford University Press, 3rd edn, 2011)
Advice and guidance in the form of a step-by-step approach to the litigation process. Concise analysis of each article of the Convention. Commentary and guidance on the Court's rules and a set of key Court forms and other precedents.

European Court of Justice (free) – texts governing procedure:
<http://curia.europa.eu/jcms/jcms/Jo2_7031>

European Courts Procedure (Sweet & Maxwell)
Single, looseleaf volume, reproducing the rules of procedure for the European Court of Justice (including the Court of First Instance) and the EFTA Court. Rules are arranged by topic and printed in a small typeface. Following most individual rules is commentary in a larger typeface together with a list of further reading. Also reproduces forms and specimen pleadings.

Subject index at back. Example:

> **Appeals to the European Court of Justice**
>   Content of the notice, **35.050**, 35.051-059

meaning the text of the rule is at paragraph 35.050 and the commentary starts at paragraph 35.051 and extends to paragraph 35.059

7.1.6   International law

International Criminal Court (free):
<http://www.icc-cpi.int/en_menus/icc/legal%20texts%20and%20tools/Pages/legal%20tools.aspx>
Regulations and codes relating to the procedure of the court.

7.2   CIVIL PROCEDURE

7.2.1   England and Wales

Ministry of Justice – Civil Procedure Rules:
<http://www.justice.gov.uk/courts/procedure-rules/civil>

Civil Procedure Rules: the consolidated edition (TSO – The Stationery Office)
The official version of the CPR used by judges in courts in England and Wales. CD-ROM included with every subscription and update.

Judicial College (Magistrate and Legal Advisor Training):
<http://www.estudo.co.uk/jsb/course/view.php?id=9&topic=all>
This body replaced the Judicial Studies Board. Links to the Adult Court, Family Court, Youth Court and Equal Treatment Bench Books plus a range of other guidance materials provided to magistrates.
The Equal Treatment Bench Book can also be accessed at:
<http://www.judiciary.gov.uk/publications-and-reports/judicial-college/Pre+2011/equal-treatment-bench-book>

Judicial College, *Guidelines for the Assessment of General Damages in Personal Injury Cases* (Oxford University Press, 11th edn, 2012)
The standard reference work for general damages in personal injury claims. Available in electronic format on *Lexis®Library* and *Lawtel* for additional subscriptions, and *Lexis®PSL* as part of the service.

HM Courts & Tribunal Service – procedure rules:
<http://www.justice.gov.uk/courts/procedure-rules>
Includes Civil, Criminal and Family Procedure Rules.

HM Courts & Tribunal Service – tribunals guidance:
<http://www.justice.gov.uk/tribunals>
Links on this page to 'Rules and Legislation' and 'Practice Directions & Statements', Additionally, in the body of the page, links to websites for each of the many tribunals. Their websites routinely include further links to 'Rules and Legislation'.

Atkin's Court Forms (Butterworths, 2nd rev edn, 1961, inc Noter-up)

Full title: *Atkin's Encyclopedia of Court Forms in Civil Procedure*; often referred to simply as '*Atkins*'.

Purpose
Reproduces court forms and procedural documents used in civil proceedings. It also provides commentary and checklists for practice and procedure.

Structure of the print publication
Three units:

- Forty-one Main Volumes

- One looseleaf Service Binder

- Consolidated Index volume (a subject index), issued annually.

Each Main Volume is divided into a number of subject groups or **Titles**.

Within each **Title** there are two or three **Parts**, as appropriate:

- Practice: an explanation of the courts and their practice and procedure on the topic;

- Procedural tables: set out step-by-step procedures to be followed in an action – only printed in titles devoted to a particular course of proceedings;

- Forms: reprints of the relevant forms and precedents used before, at the commencement, throughout and following actions.

The looseleaf Service Binder contains a Noter-up with details of developments since each Main Volume was published. Each Main Volume is replaced at intervals (which can be as short as every two years or as long as ten years) by a new volume including all the relevant, recent material from the Service Binder.

How to use the print publication
Three step search:

Consolidated Index ⇒ Main Volume ⇒ Service Binder

Check that the Consolidated Index is the latest available.

The index entries provide the volume in bold type and a paragraph number in [ ] brackets.

Example:

MONEY
    judgment
            foreign currency, in, **27** [357]

    meaning Main Volume 27 at paragraph 357

Once you have found material in the Main Volume, note not only the paragraph number in [ ] but also the page number, to assist your search in the Service Binder for updating information.

Guide cards in the Service Binder divide the updating information relevant to each Main Volume.

How to use the electronic version
Atkin's Court Forms is available for an additional subscription on *Lexis®Library*, as part of the Commentary library:

At the *Lexis®Library* homepage, click Commentary (on the menu bar across the top of the screen) ⇒ Browse ⇒ *Atkin's Court Forms*

Three search routes are possible:

- a keyword search across the entire set of volumes;

- use 'Browse' to drill down to a specific volume; or

- view the 'Indexes' to *Atkin's Court Forms*, to either create a search or click Browse and change the View box to Index to display an alphabetical list of the index terms employed in the publication.

This tool, with virtually all of the *Lexis®Library* sources, may be added to a user's 'My Bookshelf'.

Bullen & Leake & Jacob's Precedents of Pleadings (Sweet & Maxwell, 17th edn, 2011, and supp)

Also available online via *Westlaw UK*. Often referred to simply as '*Bullen & Leake*'.

Purpose
Classic work on civil litigation procedure. Combines valuable commentary with many examples of statements of case and other transactional documents, compiled by barristers and submitted to the publication.

Structure of the print publication

- Two bound Main Volumes.

- One soft-back Cumulative Supplement.

How to use the print publication
Three step search:

Index at the back of either Main Volume ⇒ Main Volume text ⇒ Cumulative Supplement

In the index references are to paragraph numbers (those given as numbers only (eg 32-05) are to commentary; those to a mixture of numbers and letters (eg 32-H7) are to examples of documents).

How to use the electronic version
Bullen and Leake is only available online via *Westlaw UK* as an add-on subscription to the Books library:

At the *Westlaw UK* main search page, click Books (on the menu bar across the top of the screen) ⇒ Browse, By title ⇒ Bullen & Leake. Either conduct a search at this screen or select from under 'Browse' and narrow your search on a particular element of the publication.

Where material in a Main Volume has been updated by material in the print version Supplement, in the electronic version the updating material is inserted at the relevant point in the text of the Main Volume. There is no need for a link to a Supplement.

Butterworths Civil Court Precedents (LexisNexis, 1991–)

Also available online via *Lexis®Library*.

Purpose
To provide precedents in support of litigation under the Civil Procedure Rules.

Structure of the print publication
Two looseleaf volumes, the contents divided into twenty divisions, mainly according to practice area. Most divisions commence with an introductory commentary on the topic, followed by numerous precedents.

How to use the print publication

Index (at back of volume 3) ⇒ main body of text

Example of index entry:

Accidents at work
asthma, **M** 478

meaning Division M, paragraph 478

Note: The index displays the paragraph numbers without square brackets, but in the body of the text the paragraph numbers are given with square brackets [478] and noted at the top outside corner of the page. When moving from the index to the text, ignore the page numbers given at the centre bottom of pages.

Butterworths Costs Service (LexisNexis, 1996–)

Purpose
To provide comprehensive and authoritative guidance on all aspects of costs to users at all levels of experience.

Structure of the print publication
Three looseleaf volumes, the contents divided into thirteen divisions, either by practice area or by proceedings within a particular court, for example the Court of Protection. An additional section on court fees is provided at the back of volume 2. Divisions are further sub-divided into three, but not all instances. Sub-division A is commentary, B materials (statutes, statutory instruments and practice directions), and C precedents.

A bulletin, filed at the front of volume 1, is issued four times a year carrying brief summaries/headnotes of recent cases, some with a sentence or two of comment by the editor, and summaries of statutory and practice material.

How to use the print publication

Index (near front of volume 1) ⇒ main body of text

The index is in two parts, a main index covering the bulk of material and a supplementary index including material recently added. Make sure to check both.

Examples of index entries:

Court fees
    criminal proceedings
          hardship paying   M5004

meaning Division M, paragraph 5004

Court fees
    civil proceedings
          generally   Fees 1–10

meaning Fees Division at the back of volume 2, paragraphs 1–10

Note 1: The index displays the paragraph numbers without square brackets, but in the body of the text the paragraph numbers are given with square brackets [5004] and noted at the top outside corner of the page. When moving from the index to the text, ignore the page numbers given at the centre bottom of pages.

Note 2: The material in the precedents sub-divisions appears not be indexed.

   | *Civil Court Practice* (LexisNexis) |

Popularly know as *The Green Book*, owing to the colour of its cover. Also available online via *Lexis®Library* entitled *Green Book*. Published annually, including supplements.

Purpose
Reproduces primary legislation, rules of court and practice directions dealing with matters of procedure and practice in the High Court and county courts, supported by expert commentary.

Structure of the print publication

- Two Main Volumes – published annually

  - Volume 1: comprises Part I (rules and procedure) and reproduces the entire Civil Procedure Rules with associated Practice Directions, the Supreme Court Rules, County Court Rules, Protocols, Guides to court procedure, Procedural Tables and Tables of Fees.

  - Volume 2: reproduces in Part II (general jurisdiction of courts) the text of five key Acts relating to civil procedure plus material relating to specialist areas of practice and procedure, and in Part III (special powers and procedure) Acts and commentary relating to particular courts and jurisdictions.

- Single, soft-cover volume, published annually, reproducing all the forms referred to in Practice Directions which supplements Part 4 of the CPR, plus some additional forms.

- *Civil Court News* booklet, published three times a year summarising recent cases, providing commentary on topics of current interest and developments since the last edition of the Main Volumes was published.

- Single, soft-cover volume Supplement, published as and when required, reproducing the text of new legislation introduced since the last edition of the Main Volumes.

- Single, soft-cover volume Supreme Court Supplement including legislation, new rules, practice directions and commentary relating to the practice and procedure of the new Supreme Court.

How to use the print publication
Note: there is no consolidated index to the entire set.

Four step search:

Decide which of the two Main Volumes will be relevant to the problem ⇒ use the Index at the back of the volume selected ⇒ text of Main Volume ⇒ *Civil Court News*

Short cut to information:

Key reference list on green card at the front of volume 1 and volume 2 ⇒ text of Main Volume ⇒ *Civil Court News*

Index entries used in Volume 1:

Registration for enforcement
    awards
        generally,   CPR 70.5 *2146*

meaning Volume 1, Part I, CPR part 70, paragraph 5 at page 2146

Registration for enforcement
    awards
        Practice Direction,   CPR PD 70.5 2151

meaning Volume 1, Part I, CPR Practice Direction supplementing part 70, paragraph 5 at page 2151

Registration for enforcement
    ICC orders
        definitions,   RSC 115r37 *2452*

meaning Volume 1, Part I, Rules of the Supreme Court 1965, Order 115, Rule 37 at page 2452

Other abbreviations used in the Volume 1 index are:

- CCR   County Court Rules
- FEE   Fees
- PRO   Protocols
- TAB   Procedural tables

Index entries used in Volume 2 are different forms of entry for each of the two parts into which Volume 2 is divided. Example:

Civil proceedings orders
   Appeals, II SCA[44.2] *4057*

meaning Volume 2, Part II, Supreme Court Act 1981, paragraph 44.2 at page 4057

Part II of *Civil Court Practice* reprints the text of several Acts with commentary. The abbreviations used in the Volume 2 index are:

- CA   Courts Act 2003
- CCA   County Court Act 1984
- HCJ   High Court and County Courts Jurisdiction Order 1991
- SCA   Senior Courts Act 1981
- TCE   Tribunals, Courts and Enforcement Act 2007

Example:

Civil legal aid
   Assessment o costs, III FUND[1.5] *5293*

meaning Volume 2, Part III, Costs of Assessment paragraph 1.5 at page 5293

Part III of *Civil Court Practice* is split into 30 practice areas, each with its own three-letter abbreviation, for example:

- FMY   Family Provision
- HUM   Human Rights
- L&T   Landlord & Tenant & Housing
- PID   Personal Injury and Death

How to use the electronic version
Civil Court Practice (The Green Book) is available for an additional subscription on *Lexis®Library* as part of the commentary library:

> At the *Lexis®Library* homepage, click Commentary (on the menu bar across the top of the screen) ⇒ Browse ⇒ Civil Court Practice (The Green Book)

Two search routes are possible:

- a keyword search across the entries set of volumes; or

- use 'Browse' to drill down to a specific volume.

The electronic version of *Civil Court Practice 2009* (The Green Book) also includes the 'Special Issue' published in conjunction with the opening of the new UK Supreme Court in October 2009.

This tool, with virtually all of the *Lexis®Library* sources, may be added to a user's 'My Bookshelf'.

Civil Procedure (Sweet & Maxwell)

Widely known as *The White Book*, owing to the colour of its cover. Published annually, including supplements. Also available online via *Westlaw UK*.

Purpose
Reproduces primary legislation, rules of court and practice directions dealing with matters of procedure and practice in the High Court and county courts, together with case law interpreting and applying those sources, supported by expert commentary.

Structure of the print publication

- Two Main Volumes – published annually

  - Volume 1: reproduces the entire Civil Procedure Rules (with a few exceptions) in bold type, together with associated Practice Directions in normal typeface, and expert commentary in a smaller font size.

  - Volume 2: reproduces material relating to specialist areas of practice and procedure, for example, particular courts or proceedings, drawn from the Civil Procedure Rules (in bold type), primary legislation (in normal type) and commentary in a smaller font.

- Cumulative Supplement, issued twice a year updating the two Main Volumes

- Permanent ring binder of CPR Forms, updated three times a year

- *Civil Procedure News*, published ten times a year containing news of new developments

How to use the print publication
Four step search:

Index at the back of either Main Volume ⇒ Main Volume text ⇒ Cumulative Supplement ⇒ *Civil Procedure News*

Examples:

Judicial review
    application   [9A-84] – [9A-85]

meaning Volume 2, section 9A at paragraphs 84–85; all references to Main Volume 2 are in square brackets [ ]

Judicial review
    bundles   54PD.16

meaning Volume 1, part 54, Practice Direction supplementing CPR Part 54 at paragraph 6. Practice Directions are reproduced in Volume 1 following the Civil Procedure Rule and associated editorial commentary to which they refer

Judicial review
    filing
        generally   54.16.4

meaning: Volume 1, Part 54, Civil Procedure Rule 16, commentary at paragraph 4

How to use the electronic version
Civil Procedure (White Book) is available online via *Westlaw UK* as an additional subscription to the Books library:

At the *Westlaw UK* main search page, click Books (on the menu bar across the top of the screen) ⇒ White Book [year]. Either conduct a search at this screen or select from under 'Browse' and narrow your search on a particular element of the publication

In the online version Main Volume 1 is designated Sections A–F and Main Volume 2 is designated Sections 1–15.

Where material in a Main Volume has been updated by material in the print version Supplement, in the electronic version the updating material is inserted at the relevant point in the text of the Main Volume. There is no need for a link to a Supplement.

Lawtel Litigator
Free addition to the *Lawtel* subscriber-only service. Searchable database of civil procedure forms, precedents and procedural guides, together with news update service.

Practical Civil Court Precedents (Sweet & Maxwell, 1999–)

Purpose
To provide precedents, with commentary, for use in the civil courts.

Structure
Two looseleaf volumes, volume 1 on general court procedure and volume 2 containing precedents in particular practice areas. Each division commences with commentary on the Civil Procedure Rules, followed by precedents.

How to use the print publication
Either:

> Contents at the front of volume 1 ⇒ main text

Or:

> Index, at the back of volume 2 ⇒ main text

Example from index:

> Appeals
> Grounds for, G1.005
>
> meaning division G, part 1, paragraph 005

Note 1: Unfortunately the guide cards which separate the divisions do not bear the division letter so hampering quick navigation of the contents.

Note 2: Paragraph numbers are printed at the top outside corner of each page. Ignore the page numbers at the bottom outside corner, in the style P2-38.

Stone's Justices Manual (LexisNexis, published annually)
See section 7.1.2, above.

Westlaw UK Civil Procedure (online subscription service)

Practical Law Company (PLC) (online subscription service)
Provides practical 'know-how' (standard forms, precedents and checklists) alongside articles written by PSL's own and other staff, in practice areas including company, commercial, employment, environment, finance, property and tax In addition, a news updating service is provided.

7.2.2   Scotland

Scottish Courts:
<http://www.scotcourts.gov.uk>
Links to the Supreme Courts (Court of Session and High Court of Justiciary), the Sheriff Courts, Justice of the Peace Courts and, under the Rules and Practice tab, links to Rules, Practice Notes, Fees, Forms and Guidance Notes.

Court of Session Practice (Bloomsbury Professional Publishing, 2005–)

Purpose
Commentary on the practice and procedure of the Court of Session. 'Written by practitioners for practitioners'. No original legislation or cases are reproduced.

Structure
One looseleaf volume.

How to use the publication
Either:

> Contents at the front ⇒ main text

Or:

> Subject index at the back ⇒ main text

Example from the subject index:

> **Adoption**
>   adoptable children G [1201]
>
> meaning division G, paragraph [1201]

Note: Paragraph numbers are printed at the top outside corner of the page. Ignore the page numbers at the bottom, centre of the page in the style G/903.

Parliament House Book (W Green & Son, 1982–)
See section 5.4.1, above.

Sections also reproduced in annual reprints, eg:

- *Green's Annotated Rules of the Court of Session*

- *Green's Sheriff Court Rules*

- *Green's Solicitors Professional Handbook*

Lord MacPhail, *Sheriff Court Practice*, edited by T. Welsh (SULI/W Green, 3rd edn, 2006)
A 'textbook, manual and *vade mecum* for all those who work, practice and sit in the sheriff court': Preface to 3rd edition.

Andrew M Hajducki, *Civil Jury Trials* (Avizandum, 2nd edn, 2006)

Charles Hennessy, *Civil Procedure and Practice* (W Green, 4th edn, 2013)
Offers guidance on 'the many diverse forms of civil procedure, from small claims to the Court of Session Rules': blurb on back cover.

| *Employment Tribunal Practice in Scotland* (W Green, 2nd edn, 1998–) |

Single, looseleaf volume. Comprises a narrative (describing the history, rules, jurisdiction and practice of the tribunals) and appendices including legislation, forms, and practice directions.

How to use the publication
Either:

> Contents at the front ⇒ main text

Or:

> Subject index at the back ⇒ main text

Example from the subject index:

> **Abandonment of claims**
> consequences 7-56

> meaning chapter 7, paragraph 7-56

Note: Paragraph numbers are printed at outs. Ignore the page numbers at the bottom, centre of the page in the style 718.

| *Green's Litigation Styles* (W Green & Son, 1994–) |

Also available as a CD received as part of the looseleaf subscription.

Purpose
To provide forms and precedents for use in civil litigation.

Structure
Two looseleaf volumes, the material presented in divisions.

How to use the print publication

Index at the back of volume 2 ⇒ main text

Example:

Answers
averments D3

meaning division D, paragraph 3

Note: Paragraph numbers are printed at the top, outside corner of the page, but are referred to in the checklist as 'pages numbers' (sic).

Bennett, SA, *Style Writs: an illustrative guide to written pleading in general and Sheriff Court writs in particular* (Barnstoneworth Press, 4th edn, 2009)
Provides examples of well-drafted pleadings from 80 fictitious cases, presented in five groups covering petitory actions, declaratory actions, family proceedings, heritage proceedings and miscellaneous proceedings. All previous three editions have been critically well received.

7.2.3   Northern Ireland

Rules of the Supreme Court (Northern Ireland) 1980 (TSO – The Stationery Office, Belfast, 1980)
Single, looseleaf volume, reproducing the rules without commentary or an index.

An updated electronic edition of the Rules is provided at:
<http://www.courtsni.gov.uk/en-GB/Publications/court-rules/Pages/default.aspx>

Links to the web version of amendments only may be found at:
<http://www.courtsni.gov.uk/en-GB/Publications/Legislation/Pages/default.aspx>

Valentine, BJAC and Barry, JAC, *Civil Proceedings: the County Court* (SLS Legal Publications (NI), 1999)

Valentine, BJAC and Barry, JAC, *Civil Proceedings: the Supreme Court* (SLS Legal Publications (NI), 1997)

Valentine, BJAC and Barry, JAC, *Supplement to Civil Proceedings: the Supreme Court* (SLS Legal Publications (NI), 2000)

7.2.4   Regional courts

European Court of Human Rights (free) – rules of court:
<http://www.echr.coe.int/ECHR/EN/Header/Basic+Texts/Other+texts/Rules+of+Court>

European Court of Justice (free) – texts governing procedure:
<http://curia.europa.eu/jcms/jcms/Jo2_7031>

European Courts Procedure (Sweet & Maxwell)
Single, looseleaf volume, reproducing the rules of procedure for the European Court of Justice (including the Court of First Instance) and the EFTA Court. Rules are arranged by topic and printed in a small typeface. Following most individual rules is commentary in a larger typeface together with a list of further reading. Also reproduces forms and specimen pleadings.

Subject index at back:

> **Appeals to the European Court of Justice**
> Content of the notice, **35.050**, 35.051-059

meaning the text of the rule is at paragraph 35.050 and the commentary starts at paragraph 35.051 and extends to paragraph 35.059

Lasok, KPE, *European Court: Practice & Procedure* (Bloomsbury Professional, 3rd edn, forthcoming December 2013)
Probably the most detailed and authoritative guide since the publisher maintains that the Court itself turns to the book when seeking confirmation or guidance on practice and procedure.

7.2.5   International law

There are none.

7.3   NON-LITIGIOUS SITUATIONS

7.3.1   England and Wales

Encyclopedia of Forms and Precedents (Butterworths, 5th edn, 1985, inc Noter-up)

Also available online via *Lexis®Library* (subscription service).

Purpose
Reproduces forms and precedents with annotations and commentary, mainly relating to non-litigious business in the core practice areas of property, commercial and private client law, and also associated subject areas such as advertising and marketing, building and engineering, charities, contracts for services, education, the environment, health and safety and local government.

Structure of the print publication

- Forty-two Main Volumes (the contents arranged under broad practice headings; each volume includes contents pages at the front and index at the back).

- Five looseleaf Service Volumes labelled A to E containing updating material.

- One looseleaf Service Volume labelled volume F, containing copies of the occasional bulletin of new developments, budget information, fees, stamp duties and taxation tables.

- Consolidated Index arranged by subject, replaced twice a year.

- Form Finder, index replaced twice a year.

- Consolidated Tables, containing lists of Statutes, Statutory Instruments, cases, European and other material referred to in the encyclopaedia, replaced twice a year.

How to use the print publication
Two alternative routes, depending on how familiar you are with the contents of the publication:

Novice – four step search:

Either, for a search by subject use the Consolidated Index or, if the Form's name is known, use the Form Finder ⇒ Main Volume ⇒ Service Binder (A to E) ⇒ Service Binder F bulletin, only if no relevant forms or precedents found so far

Expert – four step search:

Main Volume using contents pages at front ⇒ Main Volume, text of form ⇒ Service Binder (A to E) ⇒ Service Binder F bulletin, only if no relevant forms or precedents found so far

Examples from Indexes:

LAND REGISTRATION
    Restrictions
         Entry without application,   **25(1)** [816]

meaning Main Volume 25, Part 1 at paragraph [816]

LAND REGISTRATION
    Restrictions
         Execution, evidence of,   **25(1)(S)** [2643.7]

meaning Service Volume relating to Main Volume 25(1) at paragraph [2643.7]

Commentary is printed at the front of each practice section in the main volumes.

Guide cards in the Service Binder divide the updating information relevant to each Main Volume.

An asterisk * against any entry in the contents pages of the Service Binders indicates this is entirely new material.

Form Finder

Split into seven separate indexes:

- Deeds, agreements and contractual forms.

- Whole non-contractual forms.

- Letters.

- Notices.

- Clauses.

- Official forms.

- Checklists.

The format of entries in all these separate indexes is the same:

> Clubs
>   Application for membership   **7** 2006 [5851]

> meaning Volume 7, published in 2006, at paragraph [5851]

Where (S) appears in an index after the volume number, this material is found in the relevant Service Binder.

Where (O) appears in an index after the volume number, this material is to be retained until the publication of future volumes.

How to use the electronic version

EFP is available online via *Lexis®Library* but as an additional module subscription:

> On the menu bar at the top of any search screen on *Lexis®Library*, click Forms & Precedents
> Open the 'Sources' dialog box and select *Encyclopedia of Forms and Precedents*
> *Lexis®Library* defaults to a search screen designed to search by form title or subject
> To exclude the commentary sections from a search, open the 'Search within' dialog box and select from the options
> To select a particular volume of EFP in which to browse, click the 'Browse' link at the left of the search screen
> To search the Index, FormFinder or Table of Contents stay in the 'Browse' screen and open the 'View' dialog box and select from the options

The online version also includes the EFP Key Document Finder which provides a more user-friendly list of precedents within the Company/Commercial, Employment, Property and Private Client practice areas. Documents are listed within more specific subject areas under the four headings above, whilst each also provides a full list of linkable content with the requisite paragraph number. This tool, with virtually all of the *Lexis®Library* sources, may be added to a user's 'My Bookshelf'.

EveryForm available on CD from *LexisNexis Butterworths* (subscription service).

7.3.2   Scotland

Green's Practice Styles (W Green & Son, 1995–)

CD issued as part of looseleaf subscription.

Purpose
Provides forms and precedents for use in non-litigious business.

Structure
Two looseleaf volumes.

How to use the print publication

Index at the back of volume 2 ⇒ main text

Example:

Banking
facility letters, B01-01

meaning division B, paragraph 01-01

Note: Paragraph numbers are printed at the top, outside corner of the page. There are no page numbers.

7.3.3   Northern Ireland

County Court Rules (Northern Ireland) (TSO – The Stationery Office, Belfast, 1987–)
Single, looseleaf volume reproducing the text of the rules without commentary. Index at the back.

Links to the web version of amendments only may be found at:
<http://www.courtsni.gov.uk/en-GB/Publications/Legislation/Pages/default.aspx>

CHAPTER 8

WORDS AND PHRASES

8.1   INTRODUCTION

Some legal problems revolve around discovering a precise definition for a word or phrase used in an Act or a regulation or in a legal document such as a contract, lease or agreement. The situation might arise not just within the context of litigation but also when drafting a legal document.

Print sources come into their own for this type of research, in terms of the intellectual effort which has gone into compiling the sources.

The various dictionaries of words and phrases and other sources featured below have been compiled by expert lawyers, so that the publications contain genuine instances where the word or phrase is defined by statute or through judicial interpretation.

There are drawbacks in attempting a words or phrases search on one of the commercially available, comprehensive online databases, especially within the huge case law libraries they contain. Even the following searches may not retrieve all the relevant material.

On *Lexis®Library*:

> the word to be defined w/10 construe! or defin! or mean! or interpret!

On *Westlaw UK*:

> the word to be defined /10 construe! or defin! or mean! or interpret!

The reasons are that in the text of the case, the catchwords or headnote, the definition may not have been 'flagged' by the judge or law reporter using these terms. Further, the word 'construction', sometimes used in the interpretation of a word, cannot be used, for it may retrieve building and engineering law cases.

However, *Westlaw UK* does provide a searchable list of definitions contained in Acts and Statutory Instruments. At the Legislation search screen open the dialog box labelled Statutory Definitions and select the word or phrase required.

If an added subscription is taken to *Halsbury's Laws* on *Lexis®Library* then it is possible to search the words and phrases section of the *Halsbury's Laws* index for the terms sought – see section 4.2, above, towards the end describing use of the online version. If a number of 'commentary' publications are subscribed to then within the Commentary library, open the Search form, use the default to search All Subscribed Commentary Sources. In Search terms, enter the word or phrase for which you require a definition, followed by w/15 (mean! or defin! or interpret!). For example, to find the definition of a shadow director, type shadow director w/15 (mean! OR defin! OR interpret!). Click on Search to retrieve your results.

Information on publications within each jurisdiction listed below is divided into conventional law dictionaries and judicial dictionaries. Conventional law dictionaries provide definitions of legal terms either not defined in a statute or by the courts, for example, 'tort'; or provide simple definitions with the minimum of citation to statute and case law. Judicial dictionaries, on the other hand, contain definitions drawn solely from statute and case law.

Figure 8.1 provides a suggested research sequence featuring sources discussed in this chapter and elsewhere, to discover the definition of words and phrases appearing in a statute published in the United Kingdom.

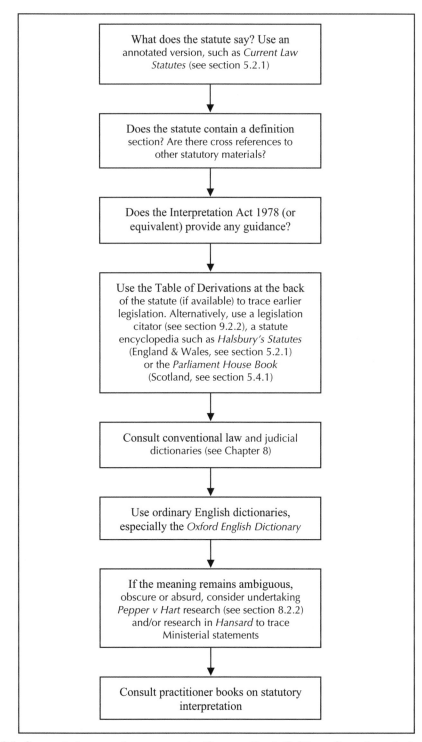

Figure 8.1: Suggested research sequence to discover the definition of words and phrases appearing in a statute published in the United Kingdom

8.2   ENGLAND AND WALES

8.2.1   Conventional law dictionaries

Jowitt's Dictionary of English Law (Sweet & Maxwell, 3rd edn, 2010)
Jowitt has established itself as the most comprehensive dictionary of legal terms. The latest edition focuses only on the inclusion of terms not defined in statute and case law. For statutory or judicial definitions, see the sister publication: *Stroud* (see section 8.2.2, below).

There are many compact, conventional law dictionaries, perhaps the most popular being *Osborn's Concise Law Dictionary* (Sweet & Maxwell, 12th edn, 2013). However, the definitions they provide are not sufficiently detailed and scholarly for use in practice and *Jowitt* is the best to use for legal research.

8.2.2   Judicial dictionaries

Stroud's Judicial Dictionary of Words and Phrases (Sweet & Maxwell, 8th edn, 2012) plus annual cumulative supplement
Published in three volumes and kept up to date by annual supplements, provides details of judicial interpretation and well as definitions contained in statutes. The jurisdictions from which entries are drawn are not stated in the work's introduction but law reports from England and Wales, Scotland, Northern Ireland, Ireland, Australia, New Zealand, Canada and the United States are cited. Some entries extend to a page and all are fully referenced to the original material.

Words & Phrases Legally Defined (LexisNexis, 4th edn, 2007) plus annual supplements
Covers definitions in Acts and judicial interpretation from England, Wales and Scotland, with extracts of cases from Australia, Canada and New Zealand. Entries are lengthier than those in *Stroud* and include verbatim extracts from speeches and judgments. *Words and Phrases* carries cross references to *Halsbury's Laws*, 4th edition (see below and section 4.2, above).

Halsbury's Laws (LexisNexis, 5th edn, 2008–) plus Cumulative Supplement and Noter-Up
The final Index volume of this encyclopedia includes near the back a separate index to Words and Phrases with references to the appropriate Main Volume. Always carry through the search from the Main Volume to the Cumulative Supplement and Noter-Up for the latest developments. The online version of *Halsbury's Laws* is available as a separately priced module on *Lexis®Library*, complete with an online Index (see section 4.3, above)

The *Law Reports* Pink and Red Indexes (Incorporated Council of Law Reporting for England and Wales)
The ten-year and annual indexes (red) and current year indexes (pink) include a words and phrases index listed under 'W' in the subject matter index. The words and phrases references are drawn not only from the ICLR's own publications: the *Law Reports* and the *Weekly Law Reports*, but also some dozen other major series of law reports, including the *All England Law Reports*, *Criminal Appeal Reports*, *Industrial Cases Reports*, *Lloyds Law Reports*, *Road Traffic Reports* and *Simons Tax Cases*. An online version of this index is incorporated within *Justcite* (subscriber-only service), see section 9.3.1, below.

Current Law Monthly Digest and *Current Law Yearbook* (Sweet & Maxwell)
Each monthly issue carries a cumulative list of references to the definition of Words and Phrases during the calendar year, drawn from cases decided in England and Wales, Scotland and Northern Ireland. The

list is located separately from the subject index and can be located by using the contents at the front of the latest issue. After the year-end, the entries are reprinted in the sister publication *Current Law Yearbook*, usually towards the back of volume 2. Whilst probably the most quickly updated source for words and phrases the list appears to be not as extensive as provided by other sources.

8.2.3   Undertaking *Pepper v Hart* research

The House of Lords' decision in *Pepper v Hart* [1993] AC 593 has permitted lawyers, subject to limitations, to 'go behind the Act' and cite in court what was said in Parliament during the passage of the Bill, as an aid to statutory interpretation. The circumstances when reference to Parliamentary materials is now permitted where stated by Lord Browne-Wilkinson:

> where (a) legislation is ambiguous or obscure, or leads to an absurdity; (b) the material relied upon consists of one or more statements by a Minister or other promoter of the Bill together if necessary with such other Parliamentary material as is necessary to understand such statements and their effect; (c) the statements relied upon are clear: [1993] AC 593 at 640.

Whilst *Pepper v Hart* was concerned with 'going behind the Act', an earlier decision *Pickstone v Freemans* [1989] 1 AC 66 held that it was permissible to look at Parliamentary debates on a Statutory Instrument. It concerned the implementation of an EC Directive by a Statutory Instrument. The procedure for researching what was said in Parliament about a Statutory Instrument is described at 'Researching a Statutory Instrument', below.

The Law Society Library in London provides a Parliamentary Debates Research Service for a fee, which will research a section of an Act as it progressed through Parliament – for contact details see section 13.1.1, below.

This type of research in Parliamentary materials can take a considerable time. Here is a suggested sequence of activities when carrying out *Pepper & Hart* research.

Brush up knowledge of Parliamentary procedure and the stages through which legislation passes in both Houses of Parliament

An authoritative guide is available on the Parliament website:
<http://www.parliament.uk/about/how/laws/passage-bill>

The stages which often provide the best chance of obtaining information on the intentions of the Bill's proposer behind the precise wording of a clause are the Commons Committee stage, where there is detailed scrutiny clause-by-clause, and the Lords Committee stage. The Commons Committee stage is taken in a room away from the floor of the House and usually involves up to twenty MPs only. The reports of these debates are printed in the Public Bill Committee debates series of *Hansard* and not the main series covering business on the floor of the House. In the Lords, the Committee stage is usually taken as a Committee of the Whole House and the debates *are* printed in House of Lords *Hansard*.

Trace when the Bill was debated

Debates will have taken place: (a) on the floor of the House of Commons; (b) in Public Bill Committee (or prior to session 2006–2007, Standing Committee); and (c) in the House of Lords. There are several different sources from which this information may be obtained:

Current Law Statutes (Sweet & Maxwell)
Since *Pepper v Hart* was decided this publication has provided near the beginning of the reprint of each Act, increasingly detailed lists of the dates, volume numbers and column numbers of the reports of debates in all three series of *Hansard*. So, to locate the list and the text of the Act in which you are interested, use the contents pages at the front of the appropriate annual volume/s. Unfortunately, prior to 1993, the list of debates provided becomes more and more sketchy the further back one searches and was not printed at all before the 1980s.

House of Commons Sessional Information Digest
This comprehensive index to the work of Parliament lists the dates, volume and column numbers of debates. It is available free online on the Parliament website back to session 1995–1996 at:
<http://www.publications.parliament.uk/pa/cm/cmsid.htm>

The final sessional issue of a sister publication: *Weekly Information Bulletin of the House of Commons Library* includes a list of the dates of all debates in both Houses on Bills of that session of Parliament. An archive back to 1995–1996 is available free on the Parliament website at:
<http://www.publications.parliament.uk/pa/cm/cmwib1995_2006.htm>

Justis Parliament (subscriber-only service)
Indexes the business of the House of Commons, the National Assembly for Wales and the Northern Ireland Assembly with coverage back to 1979. However, coverage of the National Assembly for Wales and the Northern Ireland Assembly ceased around March 2011. Quite apart from the longer archive, the advantage of this online index is that it is possible not only to obtain the dates of debates, with links to the text of *Hansard* (outside the service), but also track all the documents (including the text of the Bill, if available online outside the service) produced as it passed through Parliament. All the other services noted above provide the dates of debates only.

Lawtel UK (subscriber-only service)
The Parliamentary Bills Service tracks the progress of Bills as they pass through Parliament at Westminster, The Scottish Parliament and the Northern Ireland Assembly. It provides the dates of debates at each stage with links for Westminster Bills to *Hansard* and the *Public Bill Committee Debates* where they are available on the Parliament website. The archive starts in session 1993–1994 but comprehensive coverage commences with session 1997–1998.

If the Act you are researching dates from before the time of the services/s you have access to, contact either a large central public library, university library, or in London one of the Inns of Court libraries (they are open to barristers of any Inn) but especially Lincoln's Inn, which has the most extensive collection of parliamentary materials.

Obtain copies of the Bill as reprinted at each stage

You will need these to make sense of the clause numbers and match them with the debates found in *Hansard*, since clause numbers will change as they are deleted, added or amended during each stage of scrutiny. There is a very short archive of Public Bills back to session 2002–2003 on the Parliament website:
<http://www.parliament.uk/business/bills-and-legislation/current-bills/previous-bills>

If the Act you are researching dates from before the time of the archive on the Parliament website, contact either a large central public library, university library, or in London one of the Inns of Court libraries (they are open to barristers of any Inn) but especially Lincoln's Inn, which has the most extensive collection of parliamentary materials.

Trace copies of the relevant issues of Hansard

First, House of Commons *Hansard*: the Parliament website has transferred past issues into online format. An archive of House of Commons *Hansard* is available from two different links. Links back to session 1988–1989 are available at the bottom of this page:
<http://www.publications.parliament.uk/pa/cm/cmhansrd.htm>
The text of debates back to 1803 is available from this page – the link below is to the 20th century materials; click near the top of the page to view links to 19th century issues:
<http://hansard.millbanksystems.com/commons/C20>
Full subject searching is available and the results can be sorted by relevance and date; a great boon for researchers.

Second, *Public Bill* (formerly *Standing*) *Committee Debates*. These are available free on the Parliament website back to 1997–1998:
<http://www.publications.parliament.uk/pa/cm/stand.htm>

This is a very short archive so, if the Act you are researching is of earlier date, contact either a large central public library, university library, or in London one of the Inns of Court libraries (they are open to barristers of any Inn) but especially Lincoln's Inn, which has the most extensive collection of parliamentary materials.

Third, House of Lords *Hansard*. The full text of debates back to session 1995–1996 is available at:
<http://www.parliament.uk/business/publications/hansard/lords/by-date/#session=62738&year=2012&month=11&day=19>

The text of Archived Lords Hansard debates back to 1803 is available from this page – the link below is to the 20th century materials; click near the top of the page to view links to 19th century issues:
<http://hansard.millbanksystems.com/lords/C20>

As with the Commons version, full subject searching is available and the results can be sorted by relevance and date.

Other materials may be required

It may be useful to see documents which led up to the Bill being presented to Parliament. They will provide background information and some may have been cited during Parliamentary debates and will have to be evaluated in any case. They include:

- Relevant Law Commission, Royal Commission or official enquiry reports;

- Consultation papers (Green Papers) and Government policy documents (White Papers);

- Any Draft Bills or Select Committee Reports on Draft Bills – the pre-legislative scrutiny procedure was first introduced in 1998.

A fuller discussion of some of these documents is provided in Chapter 11.

Here are six quick ways to trace the existence of these documents:

Current Law Statutes (Sweet & Maxwell)
From the 1980s onwards this publication has provided near the beginning of the reprint of each Act under the heading 'Introduction and general note', increasingly detailed descriptions of what led up to the legislation being presented to Parliament. In addition, further commentary is given at the end of each reprinted section of the Act which may mention particular publications or cases which led to the provision being enacted.

Explanatory Notes to Bills
Since the late 1990s many Public Bills have been accompanied by a separate document of notes prepared by the Government Department sponsoring the Bill. They are available online as links from the individual pages for each Bill. Below is the general entry point for Bills back to 2002–2003. Prior to that the documents would not appear to be available online and may be difficult to trace except through major university libraries or Lincoln's Inn Library:
<http://www.parliament.uk/business/bills-and-legislation/current-bills/previous-bills>

Explanatory Notes to Acts
Since the first Public General Act of 1999 explanatory notes have been issued. They provide brief background information to the legislation and commentary on the provisions. In a table at the end they provide references to the debates published in *Hansard*. They are available free at:
<http://www.legislation.gov.uk/ukpga>
Having clicked on the particular Act in which you are interested, a tab 'Explanatory Note' may appear in the bar across the screen. Notes are prepared by the Government department which sponsored the legislation and are therefore not available for legislation sponsored by an individual MP. Explanatory Notes to Acts are included in the legislation libraries of the major subscriber access database services: *Lawtel UK*, *Lexis®Library* and *Westlaw UK*.

House of Commons Library Research Papers
Research papers or briefings are compiled for the benefit of MPs by the staff of the House of Commons Library. They are an occasional series of papers, numbered by year and sequence of publication, and usually deal with topics of current Parliamentary interest. They aim to be politically impartial and contain factual information as well as a range of opinions on each subject covered. Some research papers relate to Bills before Parliament and those issued from January 1998 onwards are available online at:
<http://www.parliament.uk/business/publications/research/research-papers>

Draft Bills of Parliament

Since 1998 a 'pre-legislative' stage of scrutiny has been introduced for Government Bills. A select Committee of the House of Commons, or House of Lords, or a Joint Committee reviews the proposed legislation. Copies of draft Bills from session 2002–2003 onwards are available through a link at: <http://www.parliament.uk/business/bills-and-legislation/draft-bills>

The Select Committee will issue a report on the Bill which will be published as a House of Commons or House of Lords Paper.

Research within the sources mentioned in Chapters 10 (journals in particular) and 11

Trace journal articles published around the time the Bill was first introduced or the Act given the Royal Assent, for references to pre-legislative materials. To write the article someone may have done your research for you. This may be quicker and more productive than using the indexes to official and unofficial publications noted in Chapter 11.

Keep an accurate and full research trail

Pepper v Hart research is probably the most complex research a lawyer is likely to undertake. Since so many different documents will be involved, it is essential to create a full record of precisely which documents need to be seen, were actually seen, what was found and where exactly the information was located (see section 1.1.2, above for techniques on developing and presenting a research trail). This will aid you by:

- providing an estimate of how far through the research you have progressed

- providing an index to the mass of material

- helping you quickly to pick up the research again at any point

- helping you to re-trace your steps accurately and quickly.

If you find the prospect of undertaking *Pepper v Hart* research daunting, the Law Society Library offers a commercial Parliamentary Debates Research Service, which can research a section of an Act or Bill. For more details, email the library staff at library@lawsociety.org.uk.

Researching a Statutory Instrument

As noted at sections 5.2.3 and 5.2.4, above, there are two types of Statutory Instrument: General and Local. Local Statutory Instruments do not have to laid before Parliament so there will be no record of them in Parliamentary materials. As to Statutory Instruments of General Application, they follow one of five different Parliamentary procedures to become law. The wording in the enabling legislation will determine which procedure the Statutory Instrument will follow.

The section of an Act specifying that any Statutory Instrument made under it must follow the affirmative resolution procedure will be worded along the lines of:

> No order shall be made under this section unless a draft of the order has been laid before and approved by a resolution of each house of Parliament.

On the Statutory Instrument itself it will state that it has been approved by a resolution of both Houses of Parliament. In this case, there may have been a debate on the Statutory Instrument which will appear in *Hansard*. So, use the sessional indexes to *Hansard* to trace the text of the debate.

The section of an Act specifying that any Statutory Instrument made under it must follow the negative resolution procedure will be worded along the lines of:

> Any regulations made under this section shall be subject to annulment in pursuance of a resolution of either House.

Usually there is no debate on Statutory Instruments following this procedure but the sessional indexes to *Hansard* ought to be checked to be absolutely sure.

The section of an Act specifying that any Statutory Instrument made under it must follow the simple laying procedure will be worded along the lines of:

> Any Order in Council under this section shall be laid before Parliament after being made.

It is unlikely that there will have been a debate on the instrument though, in theory, members now aware of its existence could question the minister on its provisions.

Many Statutory Instruments are made under enabling provisions which do not even require the instrument to be laid before Parliament. So, there will be no record of a debate.

Two final types of Order remain to be mentioned briefly. A procedure similar to the affirmative procedure but requiring scrutiny of Orders by Committees, applies, with slight variations between them, to Deregulation and Regulatory Reform Orders and Remedial Orders under the Human Rights Act. These Orders are usually submitted as a proposal for a draft order, which after debate will be revised and re-submitted as a draft. The *Sessional Information Digest* is probably the best place to track down the reports and debates arising from this specialised legislation.

The Joint Committee on Statutory Instruments is a Committee of both Houses and keeps a watching eye on Statutory Instruments as they pass through Parliament. The Committee issues more than twenty reports a year, each report covering many Statutory Instruments. Tracing this material is difficult but can be achieved successfully through the *Sessional Information Digest* though a service like *Justis Parliament* will achieve the task more quickly.

8.3   SCOTLAND

8.3.1   Conventional law dictionaries

Bell, WA, *Dictionary and Digest of the Laws of Scotland* (Bell & Bradfute, 7th edn, 1890)
The classic work.

There are many compact conventional law dictionaries, such as O'Rourke, SR, *Glossary of legal terms* (Thomson/W Green, 5th edn, 2009) and Stewart, WJ, *Collins Dictionary of Law* (Collins, 3rd edn, 2006). But the definitions may not be sufficiently detailed and scholarly for use in practice.

Trayner, J, *Latin Maxims and Phrases* (Green/Sweet & Maxwell, 4th edn, 1894 reprinted 1998)
First published in 1861 to provide an explanation of maxims and phrases used in Scottish law with illustrations of their meaning and application at the Scottish Bar. Quite lengthy explanations complete with citations to statute and case law. Now a standard work.

Styles, S, *Glossary of Scottish and European Union Legal Terms and Latin Phrases* (LexisNexis for the Law Society of Scotland, 2nd edn, 2003)

Succinct explanation of words and phrases used by Scots lawyers. Includes a large number not now in common use to aid understanding of older case decisions. At the other extreme, includes terminology on devolution and recent legislation introduced on human rights, the right to roam and community rights to buy. Well received by the critics.

8.3.2   Judicial dictionaries

Stewart, WJ, *Scottish Contemporary Judicial Dictionary of Words and Phrases* (W Green & Son, 1995)

A dictionary of words and phrases interpreted in the Scottish courts and the House of Lords. Clearly aimed at the practitioner in the Scottish courts. Does not mention every case from every court in Scotland in which a word or phrase has been judicially considered. However, it attempts to include every case in which a word has been judicially considered since 1946, with full entries only for cases in the period 1970 to the end of 1993. Supreme Court decisions receive fuller treatment where appropriate. Some entries include lengthy quotations from the judgment. All include full references to where the case discussed or quoted was reported.

Gibb, AD, and Dalrymple, AW *A Dictionary of Words and Phrases Judicially Defined and Commented on by the Scottish Supreme Courts* (Green, 1946)

See also entries at section 8.2.2, above for *Stroud, Words and Phrases* and *Current Law Monthly Digest* and *Current Law Yearbook*.

8.4   NORTHERN IRELAND

8.4.1   Conventional law dictionaries

There are none specifically relating to Northern Ireland, but see entries at section 8.2.1, above.

8.4.2   Judicial dictionaries

There are none specifically relating to Northern Ireland, but see entries at section 8.2.2, above for *Stroud, Words and Phrases, Current Law Monthly Digest* and *Current Law Yearbook*.

8.5   EUROPEAN UNION

8.5.1   Conventional law dictionaries

There are none specifically relating to EU law, but many of those featured under other jurisdictions include explanations of EU legal terminology.

8.5.2   Judicial dictionaries

Both *Stroud* and *Words and Phrases Legally Defined* (see section 8.2.2, above) include definitions of words and phrases interpreted by the European Court of Justice.

8.6 INTERNATIONAL LAW

8.6.1 Conventional law dictionaries

Grant, JP and Barker, JC (eds), *Parry and Grant Encyclopaedic Dictionary of International Law* (Oxford University Press USA, 3rd edn, 2009)
Contains definitions of terms and concepts with a lengthy commentary on the context in which each terms is employed and a list of primary and secondary publications. Covers mainstream international law – the law of peace, law of war, humanitarian and human rights law and the law of international organisations. Available as an online e-reference on the Oxford University Press Digital Reference Shelf.

8.6.2 Judicial dictionaries

There are none.

CHAPTER 9

UPDATING KNOWN LAW

9.1   INTRODUCTION

Under each jurisdiction below the sources used to update known law are placed under headings representing the six different tasks involved:

- What progress has proposed legislation made through the legislative body?

- Is the treaty or other legislation in force (including ratification and implementation as well as commencement)?

- Has it been amended, repealed or revoked?

- Has it been interpreted by the courts?

- What progress has a case made through the courts?

- Is the law embodied in a court decision still good law?

Some publications and websites address several of these research tasks together and are listed under General updating services. Not all the above headings appear under each jurisdiction for not all services are available.

A feature of the major subscriber-only services (*Justis, Lawtel UK, Lexis®Library, PLC* and *Westlaw UK*) is that they can provide tailored alerts or current awareness sent to your PC, laptop, smartphone or tablet by a choice of delivery methods (either accessible each time you log onto the database or sent to your email account each day or as an RSS feed). It is possible to focus the service on the topics or practice areas you work in regularly. This very personal and focused service may be achieved by one of several different technical means. A number of organisations prefer to use IP authentication, which is provided by most of the subscriber-only service providers at no extra cost. It allows a large number of users to access products without the need for a username or password. Setting up IP access is usually relatively straightforward (especially with the assistance of an Account Manager from the commercial provider). Whilst using IP authentication removes the hassle of password administration, there are some disadvantages regarding access for home workers, difficulties with collecting and interpreting usage statistics and also the lack of tailoring a product essential to many users. However, service providers are starting to offer various levels of IP authentication. An alternative method is to use a personal username and ID, rather than logging on with the same database identification which everyone in your firm or chambers uses. Talk to your firm or chambers librarian (if you have one) or database customer helpline to examine how your organisation might benefit from this type of focused service.

The Law Society Library in London provides a Bill tracking service (Parliamentary Debates Research Service) for a fee, which will track the progress of a clause through Parliament – for contact details see section 13.1.1, below.

Smaller law firms without access to the large commercial databases are increasingly relying on free web services to track or follow up recent developments in their practice area. Family Law Week provides free access to all the latest family law news, judgments, analysis and legislation:
<http://www.familylawweek.co.uk>

For those keen on the latest technology like blogs, wikis and RSS feeds, new communities are springing up for specific practice areas. Probably the most comprehensive coverage for England and Wales is provided by the free to use, award winning Inner Temple Library's Current Awareness Blog (renamed Current Awareness from the Inner Temple Library):
<http://www.innertemplelibrary.com>

It has been running since March 2007 with the aim of providing up-to-date information on new case law, changes in legislation and legal news from England and Wales, drawn from a huge array of sources including news feeds, other blogs, case reports, journals, websites of official bodies and barristers chambers. More than a thousand subject categories are employed.

Others covering more specific practice areas include the following.

Company Law Forum from LexisNexis (under the *New Law Journal* banner) is just one of several accessible from:
<http://www.newlawjournal.co.uk/nlj/latestblog>

Another is Thomson Reuters Accelus (formerly Complinet), which focuses on company compliance matters:
<http://accelus.thomsonreuters.com/?ref=complinet.com>

A final example is run by a respected barristers' chambers at One Crown Office Row, is the UK Human Rights blog:
<http://ukhumanrightsblog.com>

Many updating services use abbreviations to refer to law reports and journals. Abbreviations can be converted into their full title by using any of the following:

- Cardiff Index to Legal Abbreviations (free):
  <http://www.legalabbrevs.cardiff.ac.uk>
  Includes over 17,000 abbreviations to over 10,000 law publications worldwide. Can search from abbreviation to title and vice-versa. Also lists the preferred citation where it has been stipulated by the publisher.
- Raistrick, D, *Index to legal citations and abbreviations* (Sweet & Maxwell, 3rd edn, 2008).
- *Osborn's concise law dictionary* (Sweet & Maxwell, 12th edn, 2013).
- The list given in Appendix 1.2.

9.2   UNITED KINGDOM

9.2.1   Bills passing through Westminster

Tracking Draft Bills

The Government publishes a number of Bills in draft before they are introduced into Parliament as a formal Bill. They are submitted for consultation and pre-legislative scrutiny.

Draft Bills submitted this session plus an archive back to 2002–2003 can be accessed from a link at the left-hand side of:
<http://www.parliament.uk/business/bills-and-legislation/draft-bills>

Tracking Bills formally submitted

Services listed in order of increasing sophistication.

The All Follows legislative tracking service from TSO (The Stationery Office):
<http://www.tsoshop.co.uk/bookstore.asp?FO=1160005>
A subscription service, provided by the Government publisher, to all publications relating to a particular Bill of Parliament. Documents are delivered either by first class post, courier service or data post.

Weekly Information Bulletin of the House of Commons Library (WIB) (free):
<http://www.publications.parliament.uk/pa/cm/cmwib.htm>
At the time of writing the *Bulletin* is not being published and its future is under review. It was published weekly when Parliament was in session listing the progress, with details of dates of debates and stages passed and timetabled to come, for every Bill before Parliament in the current session. Unfortunately, there were no direct links to *Hansard* or other publications connected with the Bill. The web page provides links to material elsewhere on the Parliament website which the Bulletin used to bring together.

Current Law Monthly Digest (Sweet & Maxwell)
Each issue carries a 'Progress of Bills' table and a list of Acts which have received the Royal Assent.

Current Law Statutes (Sweet & Maxwell)
The looseleaf service binder carries a 'Progress of Bills' table for both Public General and Private Bills of the current session of Parliament, and a table of references to Public Bills in 'Parliamentary Debates'.

Lexis®Library (subscriber-only service)
The Bill Tracker service details the progress of Public Bills in the current session of Parliament at Westminster only. The information for each Bill is presented as a table with links to sites outside the service containing the text of the Bill as originally presented to Parliament and reports of debates in *Hansard*, including *Public Bill Committee Debates*. Setting up a Saved Search in the name of the Bill and running it across the Journals library will uncover contemporary commentary on the meaning and effect of the proposed legislation.

Lawtel UK (subscriber-only service)
The Parliamentary Bills Service tracks the progress of Bills as they pass through Parliament at Westminster. It provides links to the various versions of the Bill, amendments, and to *Hansard* and the *Public Bill Committee Debates* where they are available on the Parliament website. The archive starts in session 1993–1994 but comprehensive coverage commences with session 1997–1998.

Justis Parliament (subscriber-only service) – also known as *Parlianet*
Indexes the business of the House of Commons, with coverage back to 1979. The advantage of this online index is that it is possible not only to obtain the dates of debates, with links to the text of *Hansard* (outside the service), but also track all the documents (including the text of the Bill, if available online outside the service) produced as it passed through Parliament.

PLC (subscriber-only service)
Provides information on the progress of Bills through Parliament, taking information from the Parliamentary Bill Tracking index. This does not necessarily cover all Bills, but merely ones which the editorial staff of *PLC* believe are of most interest to practitioners.

Do-it-yourself Bill tracking free of charge

Using the various free services on the Parliament website it is possible to track Bills and obtain all the publications associated with their progress through Parliament (motions, amendments and debates).

Start with:

Weekly Information Bulletin of the House of Commons Library (WIB):
<http://www.publications.parliament.uk/pa/cm/cmwib.htm>
See above for description and note on the suspension of this service.

Then, either:

Bills before Parliament:
<http://services.parliament.uk/bills>
Lists all Bills going through Parliament, with links to all the materials published within Parliament during the progress of each Bill (motions, amendments and debates). This listing is very detailed, as is the next one.

Or:

Progress of Public Bills this session:
<http://www.parliament.uk/business/bills-and-legislation/current-bills/public-bill-list>
Link to list of current bills, with further links to details of the progress of and debates on each Bill. A link is provided to subscribe to email alerts from this page.

Or:

Go to *Hansard* directly:
<http://www.parliament.uk/business/publications>
The debates contain a wealth of information on the intended purpose and effect of the proposed legislation, as well as an indication of support for it. There are three series, one reporting what is said on the floor on the House of Commons; *Public Bill Committee Debates*, which reports what is said in the Committee Stage which is held outside the House of Commons chamber; and *Hansard* for the House of Lords. Links to all three series are available from the above website.

9.2.2 Westminster Public Acts: Is it is force?; Has this legislation been amended, repealed or interpreted by the courts?

Print sources

The two major law publishers in the United Kingdom, Sweet & Maxwell and LexisNexis, offer two contrasting services each covering most of these research questions. Sweet & Maxwell provide detailed tables and lists of information through *Current Law*; LexisNexis provide the information as part of their *Halsbury's Statutes* 'encyclopedia' service, which also includes the full and consolidated text of Acts.

Current Law Statutes and *Current Law Legislation Citator* (Sweet & Maxwell)
The Service File of *Current Law Statutes* includes two valuable tools: in Binder 1 is a list of legislation not yet in force arranged by the title of the Act. In the same binder is a *Statute Citator* for the current year. It lists Public General Acts by year and then by chapter number within each year and gives details of:

- the date and authority for commencement;
- the year and chapter number of amending or repealing legislation;
- citations to statutory instruments made under powers included within a section; and
- the names of parties and citation to cases where the wording of a section has been interpreted by the courts.

Figure 9.1 illustrates how this wealth of information is presented.

For past years, use the set of *Current Law Legislation Citator* volumes. Each covers incidents relating to an Act which occurred in the particular year or years marked on the spine and title page. They enable research to be taken back to 1947.

Research tip
Remember that each volume covers only what occurred to an Act in the year or years listed on the spine and the title page. The full set of volumes comprises the following:

- *Current Law Statute Citator 1947–1971.*
- *Current Law Legislation Citator 1972–1988.*
- *Current Law Legislation Citator 1989–1995.*
- *Current Law Legislation Citator 1996–1999.*
- *Current Law Legislation Citator 2000–2001.*
- *Current Law Legislation Citator 2002–2004.*

And annual volumes published during the following summer.

Work methodically through the set (make a list of the volumes you need to search and tick them off as you finish your search), ideally advancing through the set chronologically, so that events relating to an Act unfold in the correct order. Avoid the temptation to grab any volume in any order – your research results may become unintelligible.

Current Law Monthly Digest
Each issue carries a 'Date of Commencement' table.

Halsbury's Statutes, Cumulative Supplement and Noter-Up
See section 5.2.1, above for a full description of this publication.
Commencement and amendment information is given in notes attached to the each section of an Act.

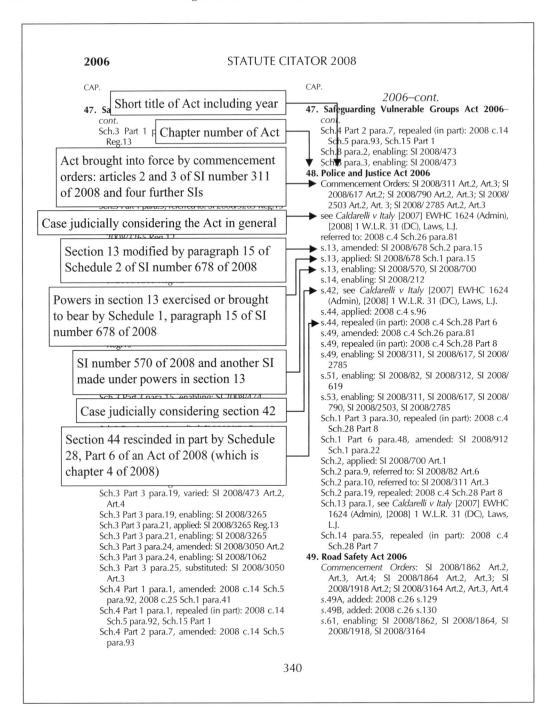

Figure 9.1: Extract from *Current Law Statute Citator 2008*

See Appendix 2 for an explanation of some of the technical terms.

Alternatively, use either:

The *Is it in force?* service: a single soft-bound volume, published annually, which records the exact commencement date of every section of every Public General Act since 1 January 1960, with details of the authority (such as a Statutory Instrument) by which it was brought into force. The volume is updated through the current year by the looseleaf *Is it in Force?* pages in the Noter-up service volume;

Or:

The *Statutes Citator*, a single volume issued twice a year (winter and summer) which details the current status (in force, amended, repealed) of every section of the 7,600 Acts which have appeared in *Halsbury's Statutes* since publication began in 1929.

Halsbury's Statutes does not provide any listing against Acts of the names and citations to cases where the courts have interpreted the meaning of the legislation.

Online sources

Free source

Legislation.gov.uk (free):
<http://www.legislation.gov.uk>
Unfortunately there are delays with the inclusion of some updating information in this database. In addition, it does not provide information on the judicial interpretation of provisions.

Subscriber-only services

The major, commercial database providers, *JustCite*, *Lawtel UK*, *Lexis®Library* and *Westlaw UK*, offer contrasting online services. They display information in different ways and each user will have a preference. Generally speaking, *Westlaw UK* provides screens less crowded with content which are easier on the eye.

JustCite (subscriber-only service)
Citation module devised by *Justis* provides searching to discover judicial interpretation of Acts. If subscriptions are taken to other relevant *Justis* products or even those of the other commercial database providers, links can be followed from the citator information to the full text held elsewhere. There are also links to case and legislative material held in the free *BAILII* service.

Lawtel UK (subscriber-only service)
Search the Statutory Law library for the Act required. Click the Act's title and a link to the Statutory Status Table will appear. This is a unique feature amongst all online services and will appeal to those who prefer to work with tables rather than text. It sets out section by section details of commencement, amendment and repeal. Caution should be used when clicking through to the text of any Acts or Statutory Instruments listed for, as noted in 5.2.1 above, this service links to the unconsolidated versions only.

Lexis®Library (subscriber-only service)
With the text of a section of an Act displayed on the screen, links to the right in the 'Find out more' box lead to *Status Snapshot*; *Find related commentary*; *Find related cases*; *Find related journals*; *Find related*

subordinate legislation; *Find related explanatory note*; *Halsbury's Statutes Citator*; and *Is it in Force?* Further, users may also view related annotations provided by *Halsbury's Statutes Notes*.

Westlaw UK (subscriber-only service)
With the text of a section of an Act displayed on the screen, links to commencement, amendments and cases citing this section are displayed on the left-hand side. Alternatively, the link Overview Document, provides similar information for the entire Act. Table of Amendments displays historic, current and future information about a provision. Details of prospective law for Acts from 2004 onwards is available now; key pre-2004 Acts will also have prospective provisions added and the remaining prospective law will be incorporated within the database over time. It is now possible to browse through three different versions of Acts on *Westlaw UK*: the historic, the current and future versions. As a result of this innovation additional status icons have been provided – more details in the database itself.

9.2.3   Westminster Local, Personal and Private Acts: Has this legislation been amended or repealed?

The four volumes of the *Chronological Table of Local Legislation (1794–1994)* (HMSO, 1996) list Local Acts in chronological order with details of amendments and repeals. The information has been supplemented and brought up to date by editorial staff working on the *Legislation.gov.uk* website, see:
<http://www.legislation.gov.uk/changes/chron-tables/local>

The Chronological Table of Private and Personal Acts 1539–1997 (HMSO, 1997) performs the same function for Private and Personal Acts, and has been updated by editorial staff working on the *Legislation.gov.uk* website, see:
<http://www.legislation.gov.uk/changes/chron-tables/private>

9.2.4   Statutory Instruments passing through Westminster

Tracking draft Statutory Instruments

Legislation.gov.uk (free):
<http://www.legislation.gov.uk/ukdsi>
The official government website provides copies of draft Statutory Instruments from 1998 onwards.
RSS or Atom feeds of draft Statutory Instruments can be set up by clicking the 'New Legislation' tab in the menu bar near the top of the page.

Lawtel UK (subscriber-only service)
Search the Statutory Instruments library for the full-text of draft Statutory Instruments.

Justis Statutory Instruments (subscriber-only service)
Provides copies of draft Statutory Instruments.

Is it is force?; Has this legislation been amended, revoked or interpreted by the courts?

Print sources

The two major law publishers in the United Kingdom, Sweet & Maxwell and LexisNexis, offer two contrasting services each covering most of these research questions. Sweet & Maxwell provide detailed tables and lists of information through *Current Law*; LexisNexis provide the information as part of their *Halsbury's Statutory Instruments* 'encyclopedia' service, which also includes the full and consolidated text of a few Statutory Instruments.

Current Law Statutes and *Current Law Legislation Citator* (Sweet & Maxwell)
The Service File of *Current Law Statutes* includes a *Statutory Instrument Citator* for the current year – printed following the citator for Acts. It lists Statutory Instruments by year and then by running number within each year and gives details of:

- the title of the Statutory Instrument;
- the year and running number of later Statutory Instruments which amend or revoke the legislation;
- references to Acts which cite the Statutory Instrument; and
- the names of parties and citation to cases where the wording of the Statutory Instrument has been interpreted by the courts.

Figure 9.2 illustrates how this wealth of information is presented.

For past years, use the set of *Current Law Legislation Citator* volumes, some of which include a Statutory Instrument Citator. A table of 'Statutory Instruments Affected' was printed at the back of the volumes for 1972–1988 and 1989–1995. But a full citator has been published only from 1993 onwards. Each volume covers incidents relating to a Statutory Instrument which occurred in the particular year or years marked on the spine and title page.

Research tip
Remember that each volume covers only what occurred to a Statutory Instrument in the year or years listed on the spine and the title page. The full set of volumes comprises the following:

- *Current Law Legislation Citator 1972–1988.*
- *Current Law Legislation Citator 1989–1995.*
- *Current Law Legislation Citator 1996–1999.*
- *Current Law Legislation Citator 2000–2001.*
- *Current Law Legislation Citator 2002–2004.*

And annual volumes published during the following summer.

Work methodically through the set (make a list of the volumes you need to search and tick them off as you finish your search), ideally advancing through the set chronologically, so that events relating to a Statutory Instrument unfold in the correct order. Avoid the temptation to grab any volume in any order – your research results may become unintelligible.

Halsbury's Statutory Instruments (LexisNexis)
This publication, which is described fully at section 5.2.3, above, does not include Statutory Instruments extending only to Scotland nor instruments made by the National Assembly for Wales, nor Northern Irish Statutory Instruments.

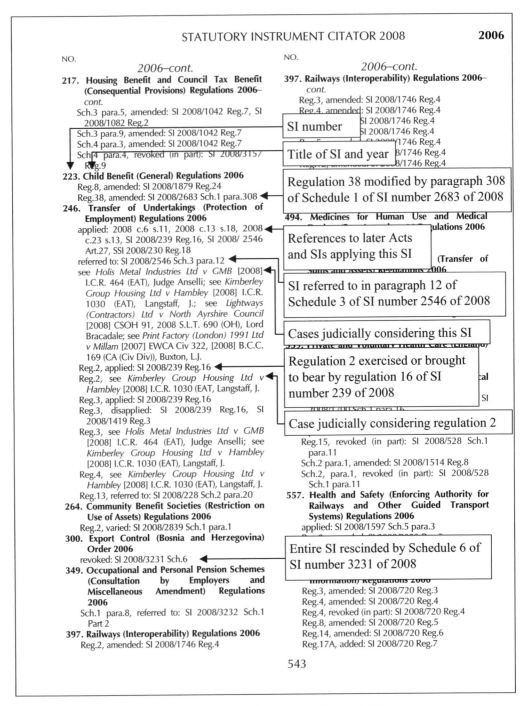

Figure 9.2: Extract from *Current Law Statutory Instrument Citator 2008*

See Appendix 2 for an explanation of some of the technical terms.

The Statutory Instrument Citator volume, issued each October or November, details the status of each Statutory Instrument included within the service. The Citator is not updated between annual issues but subscribers may contact the editorial team by phone or email for information on the latest developments – see introduction to the volume.

Online sources

The three major, commercial database providers again offer contrasting services – see the note above at 'Subscriber-only services', at section 9.2.2, above.

JustCite (subscriber-only service)

Provides the same citation service as described in 'Subscriber-only services', at section 9.2.2, above, but for Statutory Instruments.

Lawtel UK (subscriber-only service)

Search the Statutory Instruments library for the Statutory Instrument required. Click the Statutory Instrument's title for details of commencement, its effect on existing legislation and whether it has been amended or revoked. Caution should be used when clicking through to the text of any Acts or Statutory Instruments listed for, as noted at section 5.2.3 above, this service links to the unconsolidated versions only.

Lexis®Library (subscriber-only service)

With the text of an article of a Statutory Instrument displayed on the screen, links to the right in the 'Find out more' box lead to *Halsbury's Statutory Instruments* citator and related cases.

Westlaw UK (subscriber-only service)

With the text of an article of a Statutory Instrument displayed on the screen, links to commencement, amendments and cases under the article are displayed on the left-hand side of the screen. Alternatively, the link Overview Document, provides similar information for the entire Statutory Instrument.

9.3 ENGLAND AND WALES

9.3.1 Case law

Tracking the progress of cases

It is worth stating at the outset that there is no electronic filing system for cases to be heard in the courts of England and Wales.
There is no equivalent of the US PACER (Public Access to Court Electronic Records) system:
<http://www.pacer.gov>

In addition to the information given below, see the well-researched article by Nadine Fathers, 'Finding information on pending appeal cases' (2012) 12 *Legal Information Management* 56–59. The special value of this article is the information provided on tracing when an appeal has been lodged and appeal judgment given by a range of Tribunals.

There is a growing trend for third parties, often themselves involved in litigation, to seek to obtain documents not only from the court file, but also at trial, in relation to other similar or related litigation.

The Civil Procedure Rules, rule 5.4C(1), (2) and (4) governs the access of non-parties to various documents:
<http://www.justice.gov.uk/courts/procedure-rules/civil/rules/part05>
The rule needs to be read in conjunction with a burgeoning case law on the topic.

The Criminal Procedure Rules, rules 5.8 and 5.9 contain provisions relating to criminal litigation:
<http://www.justice.gov.uk/courts/procedure-rules/criminal/docs/crim-proc-rules-2012-part-5.pdf>

Tracking requests for permission to appeal to the Supreme Court:
<http://www.supremecourt.gov.uk/news/index.html>

Tracking cases which have reached the Supreme Court but await a hearing:
<http://www.supremecourt.gov.uk>
A 'Current Cases' tab links to both a search facility (by case name or case ID number) and a listing of cases awaiting a hearing. Link to full case details provides procedural progress of the case.

Tracking Court of Appeal cases going to the Supreme Court:
<http://www.supremecourt.gov.uk>
A 'Court Sittings' links on this home page provide details of sittings of both the Supreme Court and Judicial Committee of the Privy Council both for the current week and for the whole of the current law term.

Tracking decisions of the Supreme Court on applications to appeal:
<http://www.iclr.co.uk/case-search/supreme-court-applications>

To trace if a Court of Appeal decision has been appealed to the Supreme Court either email:
registry@supremecourt.gsi.gov.uk or phone: +44 (0) 20 7960 1991/1992.

Case tracker for civil appeals (free):
<http://casetracker.justice.gov.uk/listing_calendar>
Users can search for information on applications or appeals in the Court of Appeal, Civil Division for which hearing dates have been set. Three searches are possible: by case number, by title or by date.

Royal Courts of Justice and the Rolls Building: daily court hearing lists (free):
<http://www.justice.gov.uk/courts/court-lists>

Royal Courts of Justice and the Rolls Building: court hearing lists and contact details (free):
<http://www.justice.gov.uk/courts/rcj-rolls-building>
Links to a range of individual court entries which include Court Lists/Diaries and sometimes contact details.

CourtServe (subscriber-only service):
<http://www.courtserve2.net>
In partnership with the Ministry of Justice this service electronically delivers court lists to subscribers. A variety of packages is available covering different groups of courts and with different search facilities.

Casetrack (subscriber-only service):
<http://www.casetrack.com/index.html>
According to the Delia Venables website 'This is a tracking, research and full text retrieval system for all Court of Appeal, High Court and EAT cases. Casetrack is the only comprehensive source of all new judgments from these courts':
<http://www.venables.co.uk/pubmerrill.htm>

Lawtel UK (subscriber-only service)
Annotations are added to the summaries of decisions in the lower courts, where an application for leave to appeal to the Supreme Court has been made.

Lexis®Library (subscriber-only service)
The Appeal Tracker service provides appeal information (whether the parties are appealing, whether permission to appeal is being sought, whether permission has been granted or refused and the hearing dates for the appeal). The information is supplied only for cases in the All England Reporter series (same- and next-day case digest service) of particular legal importance, that is, starred cases, cases carrying * in front of the names of parties. To access the service, use the CaseSearch facility. The Appeal Tracker is shown as an additional table at the bottom of the CaseSearch screen.

Westlaw UK (subscriber-only service)
The Appeal Status Tracker service provides appeal information for the Court of Appeal (Civil Division) and the Supreme Court. An 'Appeal Outstanding' status icon will appear next to search results and at the top of Case Analysis Documents. The icon is removed once there is an outcome to the appeal. Within Case Analysis Documents the 'Appellate History and Status' section lists the direct, reported progress of the decision through to appeal, with cases displayed in chronological order. Once the appeal judgment has been received it will be published on *Westlaw UK* with citations replacing the appeal status entry. The 'Graphical History' chart of a Case Analysis Document will also be updated.

Is this case still good law?

Print sources

Current Law Case Citator and *Current Law Monthly Digest* (Sweet & Maxwell)
Each issue of the *Citator* is in three parts: Part I covers cases decided or judicially considered in the courts of England, Wales and Northern Ireland. Part II includes cases decided or judicially considered in the Scottish courts. Part III is an index to ship's names.

To obtain a *full history* of judicial consideration of English case law it is necessary to search both Part I and Part II, to include the citation of English cases before the Scottish courts.

Current Law Case Citator is an invaluable tool providing the following information:

- alternative citations to where a case has been reported;
- a judicial history of a case, listing reports of the case as it passes up the court hierarchy;
- a reference to the volume and paragraph where the case is summarised in the sister publication: *Current Law Yearbook*; and
- a reference to where in *Current Law Yearbook* there are summaries of cases in which the courts have considered the value of the original decision – the precedential value of the case.

Figure 9.3 illustrates how this wealth of information is presented.

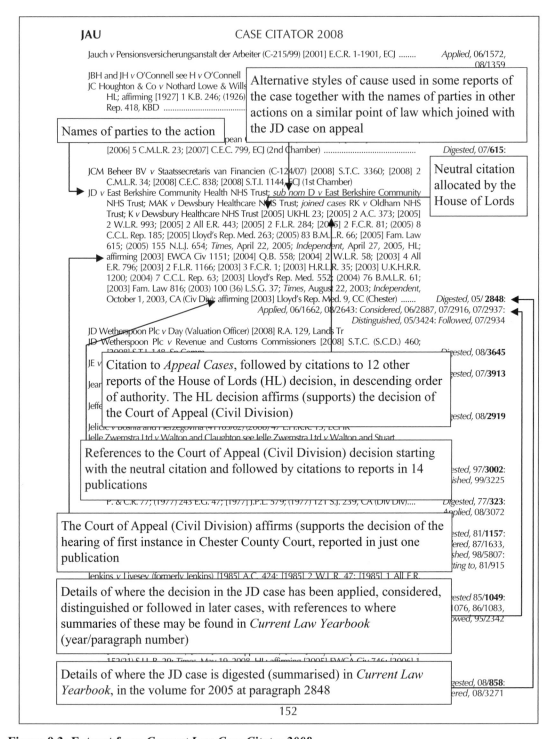

Figure 9.3: Extract from *Current Law Case Citator 2008*

See Appendix 2 for an explanation of some of the technical terms.

To research the events of the current year, use the Cumulative Table of Cases at the back of the latest issue of *Current Law Monthly Digest*. Cases names printed in upper case throughout are new decisions, those printed in upper and lower case are older cases which have been judicially considered during the year in question. The issue number and paragraph of a summary of the decision is given against each entry.

Research tip
Remember that each volume covers only what occurred to a case in the year or years listed on the spine and the title page. The full set of volumes comprises the following:

- *Current Law Case Citator 1947–1976.*
- *Current Law Case Citator 1977–1997.*
- *Current Law Case Citator 1998–2001.*
- *Current Law Case Citator 2002–2004.*

And annual volumes published during the following summer.

Work methodically through the set (make a list of the volumes you need to search and tick them off as you finish your search), ideally advancing through the set chronologically, so that events relating to a case unfold in the correct order. Avoid the temptation to grab any volume in any order – your research results may become unintelligible.

The Digest (LexisNexis, 3rd edn)
The value of using *The Digest* either as a citator or for checking the correct citation of older cases is that it ranges over case law from outside the United Kingdom as well as within, and includes cases from before 1947 (back to the 13th century in fact, for it references cases which appear in *The English Reports* and the pre-1865 nominate reports), permitting research much further back in time than *Current Law Case Citator*. For both these types of research query see section 6.2.2, above and use the third search route described: search for the summary of a case the name of which is known. At the end of each case summary are references to where the original case was reported and, under the heading Annotations, references to judicial consideration of the case decision.

Online sources

The three database providers, *JustCite*, *Westlaw UK* and *Lexis®Library*, offer case citation features on their databases. However, examples have been found when comparing the information provided in *Lexis®Library* and *Westlaw UK*, where the status of some decisions differs between the two databases. In some instances the lists of cases referring to or citing an earlier case include different decisions; in other instances the status (applied, distinguished) attached to later case law differs. The reason is likely to be the result of the providers using different teams of editors.

Research tip
If you have access to both online services, compare the status information each provides for the case in which you are interested. If they differ, read the decision online or in print and make your own mind up on how subsequent case law has affected the status of the original case.

JustCite (subscriber-only service)
Citation module devised by *Justis* provides searching to discover parallel citations, judicial interpretation of cases and journal articles discussing cases. If subscriptions are taken to other relevant *Justis* products or

even those of the other commercial database providers, links can be followed from the citator information to the full text held elsewhere. There are also links to case and legislative material held on the free *BAILII* service. A plus-point of this service is that it picks up citations across different publishers whereas there is a suspicion that some other online citation services favour citations to their own materials.

Lawtel UK (subscriber-only service)
Does not in itself provide a case citator service but if a subscription is taken to *Westlaw UK* in addition to *Lawtel UK*, users may switch between the services to use the case analysis section of *Westlaw UK*. There is a link near the end of each *Lawtel UK* case summary.

Lexis®Library (subscriber-only service)
At the main search screen for the cases library, open the sources dialog box and select CaseSearch. Type the names of parties in the 'Case name' box below. On the results screen, look down the second column for the court hearing required. Click the entry. At the next screen, in a line just above the centre, will be links to the case history, cases referring to this case and cases considered by the case.

To find all the cases which have cited your case, with the text of the case on the screen, in the 'Find out more' box click related cases. A feature of *Lexis®Library* is that where a number of results are retrieved, they can be sorted into a different sequence by opening the 'Sort' box towards the top left of the screen, and selecting the desired order.

Westlaw UK (subscriber-only service)
Having searched for a particular case, at the results screen, click the Case Analysis link for the case and a list of links at the left-hand side of the screen will include 'Cases citing this case'. The list is provided in alphabetical order by the names of parties and, unlike on *Lexis®Library*, cannot be re-arranged into date or jurisdiction or court sequences.

9.3.2   General updating services

Current Law Monthly Digest and *Current Law Yearbook* (Sweet & Maxwell)
A major part of the *Monthly Digest* consists of summaries of the latest legislative and case law developments arranged under broad subject headings. The individual issues of *Current Law* cumulate into the *Yearbook*.

9.3.3   General index to law reports

See *LawCite*, 'Citation Service', at section 9.9.2, below.

9.4   WALES

9.4.1   Assembly Bills

Draft Assembly Bills

National Assembly for Wales – Progress of Assembly Bills (free):
<http://www.assemblywales.org/bus-home/bus-legislation/bus-legislation-progress-bills.htm>
Links from this page lead to the text of individual draft Bills, summaries and information about the progress of Bills through the Assembly.

Tracking the progress of Assembly Bills

See the entry above. In addition, the website includes links into the verbatim reports of the debates in the Assembly: *The Record of Proceedings*.

Justis Parliament (subscriber-only service) – also known as *Parlianet*
Indexed the business of the National Assembly for Wales up to around March 2011. Since the official National Assembly for Wales website has been improved since 2010, the advantage of this online index (that it is possible not only to obtain the dates of debates, with links to the text held outside the service, but also track all the documents – including the text of legislation, if available online outside the service – produced as it passed through the Assembly), is not so crucial.

Is it is force?; Has this legislation been amended, repealed or interpreted by the courts?

The first Welsh Assembly Acts were passed in 2012. The text is available online in English via *Lawtel UK*, *Lexis®Library* and *Westlaw UK*. It should follow that updating information will eventually appear through their usual services.

9.4.2   Assembly Measures

As a result of a referendum held in Wales on 3 March 2011, the National Assembly for Wales was granted further powers to make legislation. Assembly Measures, along with the procedure of Legislative Competence Orders (LCO) employed by the Assembly to obtain permission from Westminster to make Measures, were replaced by Assembly Bills and Acts. Information about Measures and LCOs of the Third Assembly (2007–2011) is archived on the National Assembly for Wales website at:
<http://www.assemblywales.org/bus-home/bus-third-assembly/bus-legislation-third-assembly.htm>

Is it is force?; Has this legislation been amended, repealed or interpreted by the courts?

The oldest National Assembly Measure dates from 2008. The text is available online in English via *Lawtel UK*, *Lexis®Library* and *Westlaw UK*. It should follow that updating information will eventually appear through their usual services.

9.4.3   Welsh Statutory Instruments made at Cardiff

Draft Welsh Statutory Instruments

National Assembly for Wales (free)
Third Assembly (2007–2011):
<http://www.assemblywales.org/bus-home/bus-legislation/bus-legislation-sub.htm>
Fourth Assembly (2011–):
<http://www.assemblywales.org/bus-home/bus-legislation/bus-fourth-legislation-sub.htm>
This site splits information about draft Welsh Statutory Instruments for both periods of time according to the various procedures the legislation has to follow to become law. There are no links in the lists here to the verbatim reports of the debates in the Assembly: *The Record of Proceedings*. These need to be searched for elsewhere on the website – see links at left-hand side of screen.

The Welsh Assembly Government website (free)
Provides both English and Welsh language versions of draft Welsh Statutory Instruments:

- English language version:
  <http://new.wales.gov.uk/legislation/subordinate/draftlegislation/dfrtlocalstat/?lang=en>

- Welsh language version:
  <http://new.wales.gov.uk/legislation/subordinate/draftlegislation/dfrtlocalstat/?skip=1&lang=cy>

Tracking the progress of Welsh Statutory Instruments

There appears to be no tracking service available on either the National Assembly for Wales or the Welsh Assembly Government websites.

Is it is force?; Has this legislation been amended, revoked or interpreted by the courts?

Westlaw UK (subscriber-only service)
Since *Westlaw UK* includes all English language versions of Statutory Instruments made by the National Assembly for Wales, it should follow that they are included in its updating services.

9.4.4   Case law

Welsh cases are included within the services mentioned at section 9.3, above.

9.4.5   General updating services

Current Law Monthly Digest and *Current Law Yearbook* (Sweet & Maxwell)
A major part of the *Monthly Digest* consists of summaries of the latest legislative and case law developments arranged under broad subject headings. The individual issues of *Current Law* cumulate into the *Yearbook*.

9.4.6   General index to law reports

See *LawCite*, 'Citation Service', at section 9.9.2, below.

9.5   SCOTLAND

9.5.1   Bills passing through the Scottish Parliament

Tracking the progress of Bills

The Scottish Parliament website (free):
<http://www.scottish.parliament.uk/parliamentarybusiness/Bills/576.aspx>
A list of current Bills in alphabetical order. Links from this table lead to further information about each Bill including links to the papers presented at each stage and reports of the debate.

Current Law Monthly Digest (Sweet & Maxwell)
Each issue carries a Scottish Progress of Bills table.

Justis Parliament (subscriber-only service) – also known as *Parlianet*
Does *not* index the business of the Scottish Parliament.

Lawtel UK (subscriber-only service)
The Parliamentary Bills Service tracks the progress of Bills as they pass through the Scottish Parliament. It provides links to the various versions of the Bill, amendments, the dates of debates at each stage with links (not consistently included) to reports of debates on the Scottish Parliament website.

9.5.2   Acts of the Scottish Parliament: Is it is force?; Has this legislation been amended, repealed or interpreted by the courts?

Print sources

Current Law Statutes and *Current Law Legislation Citator* (Sweet & Maxwell)
See section 9.2.2, above but note that information about Acts of the Scottish Parliament and pre-1701 Scots Acts, is given in a section at the front of the publication before those relating to Westminster.
Information relating to Scottish legislation in the period 1947–1988 was included in two separate volumes: *Scottish Current Law Statute Citator (1948–1971)* continued by *Scottish Current Law Legislation Citator (1972–1988)*. The service then merged into the set of *Current Law Legislation Citators*.

Halsbury's Statues of England: Is it in Force? (LexisNexis)
This service is no longer included with the subscription to *The Stair Memorial Encyclopedia*.

Online sources

Legislation.gov.uk (free):
<http://www.legislation.gov.uk/asp>
Unfortunately there are delays with the inclusion of some updating information in this database. In addition, it does not provide information on the judicial interpretation of provisions.

JustCite (subscriber-only service)
See section 9.2.2, above.

Lawtel UK (subscription-only service)
See section 9.2.2, above.

Lexis®Library (subscription-only service)
See section 5.4.1, above for how to navigate to the appropriate part of the database, and then follow the instructions at section 9.2.2, above on how to find the updating information on the screen.

Westlaw UK (subscription-only service)
See section 5.4.1, above for how to navigate to the appropriate part of the database, and then follow the instructions at section 9.2.2, above on how to find the updating information on the screen.

9.5.3   Scottish Statutory Instruments

Draft Scottish Statutory Instruments

Legislation.gov.uk (free):
<http://www.legislation.gov.uk/sdsi>
The official government website provides copies of draft Scottish Statutory Instruments from 2001 onwards.
RSS Alert feeds of draft Scottish Statutory Instruments can be set up on an adjacent page:
<http://www.legislation.gov.uk/new>

Lawtel UK (subscriber-only service)
Search the Statutory Instruments library for the full-text of draft Scottish Statutory Instruments.

Justis Statutory Instruments (subscriber-only service)
Provides copies of draft Scottish Statutory Instruments.

Is it is force?; Has this legislation been amended, revoked or interpreted by the courts?

Print sources

Current Law Statutes and *Current Law Legislation Citator* (Sweet & Maxwell)
See section 9.2.2, above but note that information about Statutory Instruments issued by the Scottish Parliament is given in a section at the front of the *Statutory Instrument Citator*, before Westminster Statutory Instruments.

Information relating to Scottish legislation in the period 1947–1988 was included in two, separate volumes: *Scottish Current Law Statute Citator (1948–1971)* continued by *Scottish Current Law Legislation Citator (1972–1988)*. The service then merged into the set of *Current Law Legislation Citators*.

Online sources

JustCite (subscriber-only service)
See section 9.2.2, above.

Lawtel UK (subscription-only service)
Unfortunately this service appears not to include information about revocations and repeals of Scottish Statutory Instruments.

Lexis®Library (subscription-only service)
See section 5.4.2, above for how to navigate to the appropriate part of the database, and then follow the instructions at section 9.2.3, above on how to find the updating information on the screen. Note that information about amendments and revocations is contained in the Notes field of individual provision records (and the amendments are incorporated). There is no link to *Halsbury's Statutory Instrument Citator*. If an entire Scottish Statutory Instrument has been revoked a single document appears noting this, in place of the text.

Westlaw UK (subscription-only service)
See section 5.4.2, above for how to navigate to the appropriate part of the database, and then follow the instructions at section 9.2.3, above on how to find the updating information on the screen.

9.5.4   Case law

Tracking the progress of cases

Scottish Courts (free):
<http://www.scotcourts.gov.uk>
Searchable databases are available listing the business of the Court of Session, High Court of Justiciary and Appeals, Sheriff Courts and Justice of the Peace Court. However, some provide information only for a few business days ahead.

Is this case still good law?

Print sources

Current Law Case Citator and *Current Law Monthly Digest* (Sweet & Maxwell)
Part II of the *Citator* contains details of cases decided or judicially considered in the Scottish Courts. References to English cases judicially considered in Scotland are included in this part. Scottish cases published in English law reports and included in both the Scottish and English sections of the *Citator*. See section 9.3.1, above for details of how to use these publications but note that to obtain the full history of an English decision it will be necessary to consult both Parts I and II.

A Scottish edition of *Current Law Case Citator* existed until 1991. *Scottish Current Law Case Citator 1948–1976* covers cases reported in Scotland or judicially considered in the Scottish courts during that period, with the greater part of the volume covering English material from 1947. *Scottish Current Law Case Citator 1988* extended the coverage from 1977 to 1988 and *Current Law Case Citator 1989–1995* covered both jurisdictions. The consolidated and corrected *Current Law Case Citator 1977–1997* covers both jurisdictions.

Online sources

JustCite (subscriber-only service)
See section 9.3.1, above.

Lawtel UK (subscriber-only service)
Does not in itself provide a case citator service but if a subscription is taken to *Westlaw UK* in addition to *Lawtel UK*, users may switch between the services to use the case analysis section of *Westlaw UK*. There is a link near the end of each *Lawtel UK* case summary.

Lexis®Library (subscription-only service)
See section 6.2.2, above for how to navigate to the appropriate part of the database, and then follow the instructions at section 9.3.1, above on how to find the updating information on the screen.

Westlaw UK (subscription-only service)
See section 6.2.2, above for how to navigate to the appropriate part of the database, and then follow the instructions at section 9.3.1, above on how to find the updating information on the screen.

9.5.5   General updating services

Current Law Monthly Digest and *Current Law Yearbook* (Sweet & Maxwell)
A major part of the *Monthly Digest* consists of summaries of the latest legislative and case law developments arranged under broad subject headings. The individual issues of *Current Law* cumulate into the *Yearbook*.

9.5.6   General index to law reports

See *LawCite*, 'Citation Service', at section 9.9.2, below.

9.6   NORTHERN IRELAND

9.6.1   Bills passing through the Northern Ireland Assembly

Tracking Bills

Northern Ireland Assembly (free):
<http://www.niassembly.gov.uk/Assembly-Business/Legislation>
Follow the Current Bills link to confirm the current status of a Bill and link to debates from the 'Official Report', also known as *Hansard*.

Justis Parliament (subscriber-only service) – also known as *Parlianet*
Indexed the business of the Northern Ireland Assembly up to around March 2011. The advantage of this online index is that it is possible not only to obtain the dates of debates, with links to the text of debates outside the service, but also track all the documents (including the text of the Bill, if available online outside the service) produced as it passed through the Assembly.

Lawtel UK (subscriber-only service)
The Parliamentary Bills Service tracks the progress of Bills as they pass through the Northern Ireland Assembly. It provides links to the various versions of the Bill, amendments, the dates of debates at each stage with links to the reports of debates where they are available outside the service.

Public Information Online (subscriber-only service)
Tracks progress of Bills and provides links to the various versions of the Bill.

Is it is force?; Has this legislation been amended, repealed or interpreted by the courts?

Current Law Statutes and *Current Law Legislation Citator* (Sweet & Maxwell)
See section 9.2.2, above but note that information about Acts of the Northern Ireland Assembly is given in a section at the front of the publication between those for the Scottish Parliament and the Westminster Parliament.

Legislation.gov.uk (free):
<http://www.legislation.gov.uk>
Unfortunately there are delays with the inclusion of some updating information in this database. In addition, it does not provide information on the judicial interpretation of provisions.

Westlaw UK (subscriber only service)
Provides full text of Acts of the Northern Ireland Assembly and Northern Ireland Orders in Council as in force.

JustCite and *Lexis®Library* provide citation services for the legislation of the Northern Ireland Assembly.

9.6.2   Statutory Rules

Draft Statutory Rules

Legislation.gov.uk (free):
<http://www.legislation.gov.uk>
Full text of drafts from 2000 onwards.

Tracking Statutory Rules through the Northern Ireland Assembly

Northern Ireland Assembly (free):
<http://www.niassembly.gov.uk/Assembly-Business/Legislation/Statutory-Rules>
Provides committee referral and consideration dates along with confirmation of resolution status.

Is it is force?; Has this legislation been amended, revoked or interpreted by the courts?

Current Law Statutes and *Current Law Legislation Citator* (Sweet & Maxwell)
These publications do not appear to include information about Statutory Rules.

Westlaw UK (subscriber only service)
Provides full text of Northern Ireland Statutory Rules 1991 onwards as in force.

JustCite and *Lexis®Library* provide citation services for the legislation of the Northern Ireland Assembly.

9.6.3   Case law

Tracking the progress of cases

Northern Ireland Court Service (free):
<http://www.courtsni.gov.uk>
ICOS Case Tracking Online Service allows solicitor firms, government departments and other organisations to securely access case details for civil, criminal and family cases in which they are involved (a login needs to be assigned).

Is this case still good law?

Current Law Case Citator, and *Current Law Monthly Digest* (Sweet & Maxwell)
Part I of the *Citator* contains details of cases decided or judicially considered in the courts of Northern Ireland. See section 9.3.1, above for details of how to use these publications.

Lexis®Library (subscriber-only service)
Includes *Northern Ireland Law Reports* and selected *Northern Ireland Unreported Judgments 1989 onwards*. First follow the instructions at section 6.4.2, above to reach the appropriate library on *Lexis®Library*, and then those at section 9.3.1, above to carry out a citation search.

9.6.4   General updating services

Bulletin of Northern Ireland Law (SLS Legal Publications (NI), Belfast, 1981–)
Published approximately every five weeks, it provides a digest of legislative and case-ale developments in the province, with entries arranged under broad subject headings. The range of material included is very broad, from the highest courts in Northern Ireland to tribunals and relevant legal developments in EC law and the law of England and Wales. Individual summaries are lengthier and more detailed than those in *Current Law Monthly Digest* but, unlike the Sweet & Maxwell publication, the *Bulletin* does not cumulate into a yearbook.

Current Law Monthly Digest and *Current Law Yearbook* (Sweet & Maxwell)
A major part of the *Monthly Digest* consists of summaries of the latest legislative and case law developments arranged under broad subject headings. The individual issues of *Current Law* cumulate into the *Yearbook*.

9.6.5   General index to law reports

See *LawCite*, 'Citation Service', at section 9.9.2, below.

9.7   EUROPEAN UNION

9.7.1   Treaties, conventions and agreements

Is it in force?

Council of the European Union: agreements database (free):
<http://www.consilium.europa.eu/policies/agreements?lang=en>
Results lists include 'See details' link to status information and links to relevant EU documents.

Lawtel EU, *Lexis®Library* and *Westlaw UK* (all subscriber-only services) provide updating information for EU treaties and agreements as a matter of course.

9.7.2   EU secondary legislation

Progress of legislation

Commission Working Documents (COM Docs)
The final draft version of each proposal for new legislation is published as a Commission Working Document, more frequently referred to as a COM Doc. Versions prior to the final one are usually not available outside the Commission. COM Docs are available free on the EU website within the Preparatory Acts section, with an archive back to January 1999:
<http://eur-lex.europa.eu/COMIndex.do?ihmlang=en>

Unfortunately access to COM Docs is by year or official reference number only – there is no keyword or subject search facility.

University of Pittsburgh Archive of European Integration (free):
<http://aei.pitt.edu/white_papers.html>
A selection from 1985 to 2001 is available in full-text. The archive may be searched by subject, title, author or year. In addition, access to COM Docs can be reached through a list on the above web page.

Within the United Kingdom, the British Library (BL) European Documentation Centre has an extensive collection of EU materials, but access to the documents themselves is not available on the internet, only in person at its site at Euston Road, London, see:
<http://www.bl.uk/reshelp/findhelprestype/offpubs/eudoc/eurodoc.html>

The BL is one of about forty European Documentation Centres (EDC) in the United Kingdom established by the European Union, which receive copies of documents to support study, teaching and research. A clickable map of the United Kingdom locating the EDCs is available at:
<http://europa.eu/europedirect/meet_us/interactive_map/unitedkingdom/index_en.htm>
and a directory list at:
<http://europa.eu/europedirect/meet_us/directory/index_en.htm>

COM Docs are included within several subscriber-only services, offering full search facilities, including keyword, title, official reference number and year:

- *Westlaw UK*, the EU library, from 1974 onwards;
- *Justis OJ Daily* from 1998 onwards;
- *Justis Official Journal 'C' Series*, from 1990 onwards.

Although *Lexis®Library* has an EU materials section it does not include COM Docs in the selection of documents extracted from the *Official Journal 'C' Series*.

European Commission Register of Commission Documents (free):
<http://ec.europa.eu/transparency/regdoc/aide.cfm?page=aidedocuments&CL=en>
A link from the register should lead to a pdf file giving details of EU policy, under the Amsterdam Treaty of May 2001, on the provision on both published and unpublished information, together with details of how to apply. However, at the time of writing it did not work. The guide is available at:
<http://ec.europa.eu/transparency/access_documents/docs/guide_citoyen/citizen_guide_en.pdf>

Council of the European Union: legislative tracking database (free):
<http://www.consilium.europa.eu/policies/ordinary-legislative-procedure?lang=en>
Searchable database on the progress of EU secondary legislation under the co-decision procedure. This web page has links to the European Parliament's Legislative Observatory (OEIL) and the European Commission's Pre-Lex guides to the progress of legislation through the institutions of the European Union, with links to the relevant materials:
<http://www.europarl.europa.eu/oeil/home/home.do>
<http://ec.europa.eu/prelex/apcnet.cfm?CL=en>

European Current Law and *European Current Law Yearbook* (Sweet & Maxwell)
Each monthly issue and the cumulation volume *European Current Law Yearbook* include lists of new Regulations issued, arranged in numerical order and by subject, draft and approved Directives, in numerical and subject order. Use the contents pages at the front of the issue/volume to find the location.

Current Law Monthly Digest and *Current Law Yearbook* (Sweet & Maxwell)
Each monthly issue carries summaries of selected draft and final European legislation under the relevant subject heading and in the European Law table. The European Law Table does not carry over into *Current Law Yearbook*.

Lawtel EU – see section 9.7.4, below.

Checking national implementation of Directives

Official EU database (free)
This free database depends on EU member states notifying the European Commission with details of their implementing measures (in the United Kingdom this will consist of either an Act of Parliament or a Statutory Instrument). In the past this procedure has not been followed diligently by all states, so the information provided may be neither accurate nor up to date:
<http://eur-lex.europa.eu/en/index.htm>

Under 'Simple Search' at left-hand side of screen
Click 'More options'
Choose 'Search by Natural Number'
Click on the radio button 'National execution measures'
Enter the year and directive number

TAIEX Law Approximation Database (free):
<http://lad.taiex.be>
Searchable database providing information on the progress being made by candidate countries (that is, the enlarged European Union) towards the harmonisation of their laws with those of the rest of the Union.

European Current Law and *European Current Law Yearbook* (Sweet & Maxwell)
Each monthly issue and the cumulation volume *European Current Law Yearbook* includes a list: National Law Implementing EU Obligations. Use the contents pages at the front of the issue/volume to find the location. In the body of the publications are summaries of relevant legislation, both of the European Union and national jurisdictions.

Halsbury's Statutory Instruments (LexisNexis)
As part of the subscription to the entire *Halsbury's Statutory Instruments* publication LexisNexis publish each March a soft-back *EC Legislation Implementator*, detailing the implementation in England and Wales of EC Directives. Instruments relating solely to Scotland and Northern Ireland are excluded.

The same information provided by the free EU database is available through the subscriber-only services *Lexis®Library* and *Westlaw UK* since they take feeds from the EU's official database. *Justis CELEX* also takes the same feed but claims to offer an enhanced service in that *Justis* staff check the accuracy of the data provided, correct mistakes, and also research whether the legislation has been implemented in the United Kingdom by means of a Statutory Instrument and add that information to ensure its service is as up to date as possible.

Lexis®Library
Select the Sources tab on the Menu bar near the top of the screen. With the Browse Sources tab selected, open the Country dialog box and select European Union. Select EU Legislation, then on the next screen tick the box against EU legislation for the OK Continue button to change to red and click that button also. Information on the national implementation of EU Directives is included in a separate module: EU Tracker, reached from the General tab at the right side of the main menu bar.

Westlaw UK
Select EU library from the menu bar at the top of the screen, select Legislation under the Browse list at the left side of the screen. With the text of the particular Directive on the screen, click the link at the left hand side of the screen to 'National Measures' and select the jurisdiction required (eg United Kingdom). A little care is required in interpreting the data provided on *Westlaw UK* since Gibraltar is included within Great Britain for the purposes of the European Union and Gibraltar Ordinances are listed under the entry for Great Britain.

Justis CELEX use the Implementing Statutory Instruments field; note the comments on the high standard of accuracy and currency, above.

Lawtel EU – see section 9.7.4, below.

Citation of EU legislation in UK cases

JustCite (subscriber-only service)
Citation module devised by *Justis* allows searching to discover details of UK cases which cite from particular EU legislative materials. The coverage of EU materials is extensive and if a subscription is taken to other *Justis* modules on EU law, live links may be used between the citator and the full text.

9.7.3   Case law

Progress of cases

The progress of cases through the European Court of Justice can be slow. Apart from using the websites listed below to track progress, the Registry provides information (phone + 44 (352) 4303-1 or email ECJ.Registry@curia.europa.eu) and the Press Office has been found to be helpful (phone + 44 (352) 4303 3355/3366, the number of the named UK media representative given at <http://curia.europa.eu/jcms/jcms/Jo2_25870/collaborateurs-du-service>).

European Court of Justice, diary of future hearings (free):
<http://curia.europa.eu/jcms/jcms/Jo2_17661>
A searchable diary of hearings due to take place in the three courts which comprise the European Court of Justice during the following five weeks.

European Court of Justice, numerical access to cases (free):
<http://curia.europa.eu/jcms/jcms/Jo2_7045>
Listings of all cases from 1953 onwards in case number order, including pending cases. Links provided from each case to the full text of applications, orders and other documents, where available.

Proceedings of the Court of Justice and the Court of First Instance of the European Communities (Court of Justice of the European Communities) – information on the progress of current litigation (free)
Published weekly for many years, it ceased appearing in print a few years ago and recently has disappeared from the Court's website. It provided summaries of opinions and judgments of cases before the Court. Perhaps it will re-appear. A useful source.

European Court of Justice, press releases on judgments (free):
<http://curia.europa.eu/jcms/jcms/Jo2_16799>
Archive going back to 1996 searchable by case name or date of press release. Press releases issued on the day a judgment is given.

European Court of Justice, list of cases (free):
<http://eur-lex.europa.eu/JURISIndex.do?ihmlang=en>
Case names with html links to full-text displayed a month at a time. Also access to database of cases from 1954 onwards, searchable by year, case number and type of document.

Official Journal of the European Union, Series C:
<http://eur-lex.europa.eu/JOIndex.do?ihmlang=en>
Notices of new cases lodged and dropped appear in OJ series C, which is searchable only by issue number or year on this site.

Current Law Monthly Digest and *Current Law Yearbook* (Sweet & Maxwell)
Each monthly issue summarises recent cases decided by the European Court of Justice and the Court of First Instance, classified under the European Union subject heading. A list of the cases digested is provided in the European Law Table, which does not appear to be carried over into *Current Law Yearbook*.

European Current Law and *European Current Law Yearbook* (Sweet & Maxwell)
Each monthly issue and the cumulation volume *European Current Law Yearbook* includes lists of Competition Cases before the European Court of Justice and the Court of First Instance, and Commission merger decisions, as well as summaries of cases of the European Court of Justice and national courts relevant to the work of the Union. In addition there are summaries of relevant cases decided in national courts outside the Union, notably in Russia and Ukraine. Use the contents pages at the front of the issue/volume to find the location.

Lexis®Library and *Westlaw UK* (both subscriber-only services) provide updating information for European Court of Justice cases as a matter of course. In *Lexis®Library* search for the particular decision you wish to check and use the Case Search function to display information about subsequent decisions. In *Westlaw UK* search for the particular case and the results screen will indicate by coloured symbols whether the decision is still good law. Click the link 'Case Analysis' and then at the left side of the screen: 'Cases citing this case' for more detail of how the courts have referred to the case in subsequent decisions.

Lawtel EU – see section 9.7.4, below.

Checking the application of EU law in national courts

European Law Reports (Hart Publishing)
Reprints the decisions of national courts and tribunals in the United Kingdom and Ireland on Community law.

Caselex (subscriber-only service) – also available through *Justis*:
<http://caselex.com>
Carries decisions of national courts in the twenty-five member states of the European Union linked to EU law, which is of cross-border significance in the commercial law practice area only. Archive back to 1 January 2000. Judgments are in full-text but in the national language, with only headnotes and summaries in English.

JustCite (subscriber-only service)
Citation module devised by *Justis* includes references to cases included in *European Law Reports* (see above) and two specialist patent law report publications only. The rest of the module comprises citations to the judicial consideration of EU legislation and domestic UK law.

9.7.4   General updating services

General Report on the Activities of the European Union (free):
<http://europa.eu/generalreport/index_en.htm>
The *Bulletin of the European Union*, the official alert service produced by the European Commission, ceased in August 2009. It has been replaced by a news and media website:
<http://europa.eu/newsroom/index_en.htm>
Some information on law and policy developments can be gleaned from the annual *General Report on the Activities of the European Union*.

European Current Law and *European Current Law Yearbook* (Sweet & Maxwell)
A major part of these two publications consists of summaries of the latest legislative developments and case decisions, arranged under broad subject headings. The individual issues of *European Current Law* are cumulated into the *Yearbook*.

Lawtel EU (subscriber-only service)
This comprehensive service includes the text of the EU treaties with article by article links between the versions, daily updates of proposed EU legislation, details of the latest competition law and merger decisions from notification through to final decision, digests of European Court of Justice and Court of First Instance decisions translated into English within twenty-four hours of the judgment being given, and before the official versions are available. Archives of all these areas of law go back into the late 1990s at least.

9.7.5   General index to law reports

See *LawCite*, 'Citation Service', at section 9.9.2, below.

9.8   COUNCIL OF EUROPE

9.8.1   Treaties and conventions

Is it in force?

Council of Europe: complete list of treaties:
<http://conventions.coe.int/Treaty/Commun/ListeTraites.asp?CM=8&CL=ENG>
For status information, click on the title of the particular treaty required and select from the list of links displayed.

Citation of treaties and conventions in UK cases

JustCite (subscriber-only service)
Citation module devised by *Justis* in which can search to find where in UK case law a small selection of Council of Europe conventions have been cited. The rest of the module comprises citations to the judicial consideration of EU legislation and domestic UK law.

Is it in force and has it been amended?

In relation to the European Convention on Human Rights only, the *Yearbook of the Convention on Human Rights* (Martinus Nijhoff, 1955–) includes in part 1 information on the Convention including summaries of developments in the reform procedure.

9.8.2   Case law

Progress of cases

European Court of Human Rights:
<http://www.echr.coe.int/echr/Homepage_EN>

Home page with links to latest news and pending cases:
<http://www.echr.coe.int/ECHR/EN/Header/Pending+Cases/Pending+cases/
Calendar+of+scheduled+hearings>

9.8.3   General updating services

Yearbook of the European Convention on Human Rights (Martinus Nijhoff, 1955–)
The four parts which usually appear in the *Yearbook* (the fourth part does not appear every year) contain a wealth of updating material. Part 2 includes short summaries of cases decided by the Court, and part 4 summaries of national court decisions concerning the Convention.

One Crown Office Row (free):
<http://www.1cor.com/resources-introduction>
Amongst a variety of resources on this very popular website is a free Human Rights and Public Law email alerter service to new decisions on human rights issues decided by the European Court of Human Rights and domestic courts in the United Kingdom. In 2010 a free UK Human Rights Blog was launched. The services are compiled by a number of staff including Rosalind English, Chambers Academic, who also prepares material for the *Lawtel Human Rights* service.

Human Rights Alerter (Sweet & Maxwell)
Issued ten times a year, this journal provides digests of European Court of Human Rights cases and domestic UK decisions. Cases are printed under practice areas and each issue includes a table enabling the quick location of cases relating to specific articles of the Convention.

Lawtel Human Rights (subscriber-only service)
Weekly email bulletin, issued as part of the range of services provided by this database, highlighting recent European Court of Human Rights judgments. Includes comments on domestic and European Court of Human Rights cases.

9.8.4   Application and interpretation of European Court of Human Rights law by national courts

Full-text sources

Human Rights Law Reports – UK Cases (Sweet & Maxwell)

Butterworths Human Rights Cases (LexisNexis Butterworths)
Publishes a selection of the most significant human rights cases from international tribunals, including the European Court of Human Rights, and national courts in the United Kingdom. Available in electronic form from 1996 on *Lexis®Library*.

Summaries

Yearbook of the European Convention on Human Rights (Martinus Nijhoff, 1955–)
Part 4 contains summaries of national court decisions concerning the Convention. However, this part of the *Yearbook* is not included every year.

Lawtel Human Rights (subscriber-only service)
Summarises reports of human rights decisions from a wide range of UK courts, including hundreds of unreported cases.

9.8.5   General index to law reports

See *LawCite*, 'Citation Service', at section 9.9.2, below.

9.9   INTERNATIONAL LAW

9.9.1   Treaties and conventions

Progress of legislation

Travaux préparatoires contain the drafting and negotiation details leading to a treaty and may be used as an aid to interpretation. They are not easy to trace.

If the United Nations has been involved, through the sponsorship of a Conference or the development of a UN instrument, some may be identified using the free to use Official Document System of the United Nations:
<http://www.un.org/en/documents/ods>

The database contains details of all UN documents from 1993 onwards, and is vast. So, prior to attempting to search the database, it is important to have as much detail about the title or subject of the materials sought.

Alternatively, if a treaty secretariat was set up or the treaty was sponsored by a particular international organisation, trace those websites using Google and search them.

The *International Law Commission Yearbook* and the ILC's website both carry details of drafts of articles and conventions in progress. On the website look under the heading 'Texts, instruments and final reports':
<http://www.un.org/law/ilc>

For further information on searching for travaux préparatoires, see the free guide by Jonathan Prater on the Globalex website:
<http://www.nyulawglobal.org/globalex/Travaux_Preparatoires1.htm>

Is it in force?

All the sites mentioned below are free to use.

ICSID Database of Bilateral Investment Treaties:
<https://icsid.worldbank.org/ICSID/FrontServlet?requestType=ICSIDPublicationsRH&actionVal=ViewBilateral&reqFrom=Main>
Lists bilateral investment treaties made under its auspices providing the date of signature and the date of entry into force. The list can be searched by country, date of treaty and the parties. The full text is not available on this site.

UNCTAD (United Nations Conference on Trade and Development):
<http://www.unctadxi.org/templates/DocSearch.aspx?id=779>
Lists bilateral treaties made under its auspices providing the date of signature and the date of entry into force. The list can be searched by the name of a single country or by the names of both parties. The full text is not available on this site.

UNCTAD (United Nations Conference on Trade and Development):
<http://unctad.org/en/Pages/DIAE/International%20Investment%20Agreements%20%28IIA%29/Country-specific-Lists-of-DTTs.aspx>
Lists details of double taxation treaties concluded by 186 economies (including the United Kingdom) as at 1 June 2012. Searchable only by the name of the country. Provides details of the partners, the type of taxation treaty and the date of entry into force. The full text is not available on this site.

Status of Multilateral Treaties Deposited with the Secretary General (MTDSG):
<http://treaties.un.org/Pages/ParticipationStatus.aspx>
Searchable lists of over 500 multilateral treaties detailing signatures, ratifications, declarations and reservations.

United Nations Commission on International Trade Law (UNCITRAL):
<http://www.uncitral.org/uncitral/en/uncitral_texts.html>
Links to treaties and rules arranged under subject headings. Click on the link to a particular treaty and a further link leads to status information.

United Nations Division for Ocean Affairs and the Law of the Sea:
<http://www.un.org/Depts/los/convention_agreements/convention_agreements.htm>
Authoritative status information on the Law of the Sea convention.

United Nations Environment Programme:
<http://www.ecolex.org/start.php>
Searchable database of over 500 environmental treaties. In the results list click the particular treaty title, scroll down to click 'Parties', to access status information.

Hague Conference on Private International Law:
<http://www.hcch.net/index_en.php?act=conventions.listing>
Attached to the text of each of the forty-plus conventions drafted by the Conference (on family, children, international legal co-operation and litigation, commercial and financial law) is full information of the status: signatures, ratifications, declarations, reservations, entry into force.
A simplified chart of signatures and ratifications is given at:
<http://www.hcch.net/index_en.php?act=text.display&tid=25>

A chart of the seventy-two member countries of the Hague Conference shows the status of each country in relation to the Hague treaties:
<http://www.hcch.net/index_en.php?act=states.listing>

International Committee of the Red Cross:
<http://www.icrc.org/ihl>
Database detailing the implementation and status of over 100 treaties and conventions in the field of international humanitarian law.

International Institute for the Unification of Private Law (UNIDROIT):
<http://www.unidroit.org/english/implement/i-main.htm>
Details status of its conventions: signatures, ratifications, declarations and reservations.

International Labour Organization:
<http://www.ilo.org/global/standards/lang--en/index.htm>
Links at right side of screen to information on the ratification of ILO Conventions and Recommendations.

International Maritime Organization:
<http://www.imo.org/About/Conventions/Pages/Home.aspx>
Links to status information on IMO conventions at left side of screen.

World Intellectual Property Organization:
<http://www.wipo.int/treaties/en>
Text of the twenty-four treaties administered by WIPO with status information attached to each.

Is it in force and has it been amended?

Electronic Information System for International Law (EISIL) (free):
<http://www.eisil.org>
Although not specifically an updating service, this once authoritative website developed by the American Society of International Law appears not to be kept up to date. Significant treaties and conventions are arranged under subject headings. The 'More information' links under each entry lead to information on entry into force, signature dates and amendments.

FLARE Index to Treaties (FIT) (free):
<http://193.62.18.232/dbtw-wpd/textbase/treatysearch.htm>
Although not specifically an updating service, this website hosted at the Institute of Advanced Legal Studies, University of London, is a searchable index of over 2,000 significant multilateral treaties and some bilateral treaties concluded since 1353. Where an authoritative website provides updating information on a treaty or convention the index record includes a link.

9.9.2   Case law

Progress of cases

International Court of Justice (free):
<http://www.icj-cij.org/homepage/index.php?lang=en>
Details of latest cases and press releases.

International Criminal Court (free):
<http://www2.icc-cpi.int/Menus/ICC/Situations+and+Cases>
Links to progress on cases and press releases.

Permanent Court of Arbitration (free):
<http://www.pca-cpa.org/showpage.asp?pag_id=1029>
Lists of pending and past cases.

Project on International Courts and Tribunals (free):
<http://www.pict-pcti.org>
Aims to be a central resource on the work and operation of over twenty international courts and tribunals. Includes news of latest decisions as well as results of more academic, comparative research into the relationship between the institutions and their procedural rules, etc. However, the website appears to be updated only sporadically.

ITA (free):
<http://italaw.com>
Run by Professor Andrew Newcombe of the University of Victoria Law Faculty, investment treaty arbitration (ita) provides information and links to the full text of recent awards, decisions and orders. The full text of materials is not available on this site but as a portal to others it is very useful.

Oxford Reports on International Law (subscriber-only)
An ambitious project, bringing together full text reports of cases from a wide range of international courts, tribunals, domestic courts and ad hoc tribunals. The cases are allocated to one of five modules according to subject matter. Each case will be accompanied by commentary and analysis. A feature of the service is the rapid posting of a skeleton headnote while the full-text report is prepared.

Citation service

LawCite (free):
<http://www.austlii.edu.au/lawcite>
Part of the Australian Legal Information Institute website, it indexes over 18,000 law reports and journals which are included within the documents of the legal institutes and other organisations that are part of the Free Access to Law Movement – the United Kingdom is included through *BAILII*. Easy to use and search this vast database.

JustCite (subscriber-only service)
Citation module devised by *Justis* provides searching of *International Law Reports* (1919–) for the citation of legislation and case law. The majority of the rest of the module is a citator service for EU and UK domestic law.

9.9.3   General updating services on legislation and cases

International Law in Brief (members only):
<http://www.asil.org/electronic-publications.cfm#ilib>
The American Society of International Law (ASIL) *International Law in Brief* is an email alert to members containing analytical abstracts of and links to significant primary documents relating to contemporary developments in international.

ASIL Insights (free):
<http://www.asil.org/insights.cfm>
Provides 'brief, balanced accounts of the international law issues' in the news. An archive of articles back to 1996 is available on the website. On the same website is the American Society of International Law (ASIL) *International Law in Brief* providing short, balanced accounts and analyses of significant legal developments and newsworthy events involving international law:
<http://www.asil.org/ilibmenu.cfm>
Items are fully referenced and footnoted. An archive of articles back to 1998 is available on the website.

9.9.4   General citator service for legislation, cases and other materials

Oxford Law Citator (free add-on to all subscriber-only online services from Oxford University Press)
This powerful service links together a number of Oxford Law Online products covering international law, including *Oxford Reports on International Law*, *Investment Claims* and the online version of the *Encyclopedia of Public International Law*. It links references and citations between judicial and arbitral decisions, treaties and conventions, domestic legislation, institutional rules and other legal instruments, books and journal articles included within the online services.

9.10   UNITED KINGDOM AND INTERNATIONAL LAW

9.10.1   Treaties and agreements

Is it in force?

United Kingdom Foreign and Commonwealth Office (free):
<http://www.fco.gov.uk/en/about-us/publications-and-documents/treaties/publication>
Unfortunately there is no public register or index to the status of treaties to which the United Kingdom is party. Contact the Treaty Information Section's Treaty Enquiry Service:
<http://www.fco.gov.uk/en/about-us/publications-and-documents/treaties/enquiries-service>
Note that the content of these two FCO pages is due to move to a new website in 2013:
<http://www.gov.uk/fco>

9.10.2   General updating service

With the discontinuation of the *Bulletin of International Legal Developments* in July 2009 there is no general updating service.

CHAPTER 10

COMMENTARY ON THE LAW

10.1   INTRODUCTION

Commentary on the law may be found in the following sources:

- practitioner works, including specialist encyclopedias;

- student textbooks – the standard works will be known to practitioners already. Since at the back of *Current Law Monthly Digest* is a list of the latest publications and most university law library catalogues are available to search for free on the internet, these publications are not featured greatly here;

- periodicals or journals – issued at regular and frequent intervals carrying news of the latest legal developments, descriptive or analytical articles, notes of cases and digests;

- research literature – not dealt with here as it is rarely used by practitioners;

- dictionaries – see Chapter 8;

- government publications – see Chapters 11 and 12;

- social media services – a very modern method of researching, but one which is continually increasing in its use and technical sophistication. Questions have been raised regarding their authority, but these may be balanced by advantages such as speed, access and accountability;

- competitor intelligence – many law firms and chambers produce their own views on the law (newsletters, client updates, blog posts, etc), which may provide the reader with a unique and rich commentary on a particular topic;

- asking experts – both *Lexis®Library* and *PLC* now offer access to editorial content teams, and the opportunity to pose questions on the law, to users with particular types of subscription.

Commentary helps to explain and illuminate the law and may be used to support legal argument and actions. When collecting information from commentary the three questions posed at the beginning of Chapter 3 should be put to each item: is the commentary authoritative, accurate and up to date?

Ask yourself: which types of commentary listed above will be relevant to the particular research problem to hand?

For the reasons outlined in the list above, this chapter focuses most on just one form: law journals.

Thousands of law journals are published in the English language. It is worth spending a moment to consider the different types available, for some of the publications and databases which index them and are mentioned below focus on particular types of law journal and not others. To ensure your search for journal commentary is thorough you may need to look at several different indexes.

Five types of law journal may be identified:

- academic interest, aimed at law students and lecturers, carrying lengthy analytical articles on the law, eg *Cambridge Law Journal, Law Quarterly Review, Modern Law Review*;

- practitioners' interest, aimed at solicitors and barristers, carrying a wide range of short articles on both the law, staffing, office management, marketing and promotion, the application of IT to legal practice, eg *Solicitors' Journal, New Law Journal, The Gazette* – some now available on the internet;

- specialist journals covering particular practice areas, primarily aimed at practitioners, containing a mix of articles, case notes and comment on the latest legal developments, eg *Criminal Law Review, Journal of Business Law, Family Law, Civil Justice Quarterly*;

- newsletters, containing up-to-the-minute information and comment on a closely defined practice area, mainly of interest to solicitors and barristers, eg *Business Law Brief, Simon's Tax Intelligence*;

- law journals published abroad, usually from other common law jurisdictions such as the United States, Canada, Australia and New Zealand.

So, given the research problem before you, which type of journal or journals should be searched?

When you have identified information you require, if it is not available within your firm or chambers go to Chapter 13 to identify organisations and services which will enable you to obtain the full-text of the document.

Finally, abbreviations for publications can be converted into their full title by using any of the following:

- Cardiff Index to Legal Abbreviations (free):
  <http://www.legalabbrevs.cardiff.ac.uk>
  Includes over 17,000 abbreviations to over 10,000 law publications worldwide. Can search from abbreviation to title and vice-versa. Also lists the preferred citation where it has been stipulated by the publisher.

- Raistrick, D, *Index to legal citations and abbreviations* (Sweet & Maxwell, 3rd edn, 2008).

- *Osborn's concise law dictionary* (Sweet & Maxwell, 12th edn, 2013).

- The list given in Appendix 1.2.

10.2   CROSS-JURISDICTIONAL

LawCite (free):
<http://www.austlii.edu.au/lawcite>
Part of the Australian Legal Information Institute (AustLII) website, it indexes over 18,000 law reports and journals published across the world, which are included within the documents on the websites of legal institutes and other organisations that are part of the Free Access to Law Movement – the United Kingdom is included through *BAILII*. It is easy to use and search this vast database.

HeinOnline (subscriber-only service)
Nearly 50 million pages of law information are held in this database. The contents are reproduced as pdfs, which means pages appear on screen as they do in the print version. A large part of the database reproduces law journals published in a very wide range of jurisdictions, including many from the United Kingdom. The strength of the database is its archive, for it usually includes issues from the first, through to about a couple of years ago, some right up to the present day.

Also see *Index to Legal Periodicals* and *Index to Foreign Legal Periodicals* at section 10.6, below.

10.3   UNITED KINGDOM

10.3.1   Law publications

Current Law Monthly Digest and *Current Law Yearbook* (Sweet & Maxwell)
Under each subject heading bibliographical details are given of a selection of articles drawn from the *Legal Journals Index* database on *Westlaw UK*. The summaries which appear on *Westlaw UK* are omitted. Towards the back of each *Yearbook* is a cumulated list of all the articles selected that year arranged under the same subject headings.

JustCite (subscriber-only service)
Indexes over 100 law and law-related journals published within and outside the United Kingdom carrying English language articles. Although the oldest indexed article dates from 1980 the majority of indexing commences with issues published from 2000 onwards. *Justis* does not hold the full text of any articles within its modules, but if the user subscribes to other commercial services, it is possible to follow links from the index entry to the full-text of the article.

Lawtel (subscriber-only service)

The Articles Index contains summaries of articles which appeared in about 100 specialist and general legal publications, though the accent is on practitioner rather than academic titles. The indexing of titles commences in the late 1990s, though some have been indexed only within the last few years. The full text of articles can be delivered by fax within an hour of the request being made through the online request service.

Lexis®Library (subscriber-only service)

The Journals library contains summaries of articles some from 1995 onwards, though not all titles were indexed from that date, drawn from over 500 UK and overseas journals. The list comprises a mixture of practitioner and academic titles. Over 200 journals (some not indexed in the service) are available in full text. The list of journals to which each subscriber has access will vary according to the details of the package agreed with the database provider. A disadvantage of a *Lexis®Library* journals search is that the results can contain references to articles where the keywords searched for are just referred to in passing, and not central to the theme of the article. This is because where the journal is not indexed, the search software finds every mention of the keywords in the full text of the article, whether significant or not.

Westlaw UK (subscriber-only service)

See at section 10.4.1, below. In contrast with *Lexis®Library*, *Westlaw UK* searches its comprehensive index of articles, drawn from over 1,000 journals. Each entry has keywords assigned summarising the contents of the article, so the results of a search are more closely focused. In addition to searching for articles in the Journals library, *Westlaw UK* provides quick links at the left side of the screen in the UK Legislation and Cases libraries. When the text of a legislative provision or the text of a case is displayed on the screen, if a relevant article is available in the database, a link appears at the bottom of the list at the left of the screen.

In addition to the general databases and indexes a number of specialist electronic publishers provide access to their own journals. These include:

Family Law Online (subscriber-only service)

Full text of journals published by Family Law – dates held vary according to each title. Search and browse options available.

Practical Law Company (PLC) (subscriber-only service)

In addition to its 'know-how' service (standard forms, precedents and checklists) it provides access to its own journals which focus mainly on company law in both United Kingdom and cross-border (comparative law) practice areas.

10.3.2 Newspapers

There is a range of newspaper databases, those mentioned in connection with business information in particular appear at section 14.3, below. However, lawyers sometimes need to obtain facsimiles of newspapers, rather than news formatted the way a particular database handles it.

The most comprehensive newspaper collection in the United Kingdom is that run by the British Library (BL). Most are held at Colindale in north London, but some have been digitised and are available in electronic form:

<http://www.bl.uk/welcome/newspapers.html>
The BL has major collections of British and overseas newspapers. Either a Newspaper Reader Pass or a BL photographic Reader Pass is required to gain access.

The British Newspapers 1800–1900 database (subscriber-only):
<http://go.ggimg.com/blcsGoAway>
Reproduces two million pages from forty-nine national and local newspaper titles. It is now only available through local public libraries. It is searched using sophisticated techniques similar to those available online via *Lexis®Library* and *Westlaw UK* (see Appendix 4).

Local authority history/records/archives collections often maintain indexes to local newspapers and may have archive sets of the original newspapers in question.

Other libraries, public and some universities, throughout the United Kingdom maintain collections of newspapers, both national and local. Conditions of access vary, especially amongst university libraries, and must be checked before setting out.

Here is a selection of public libraries:

Belfast – Central Library:
<http://www.ni-libraries.net/libraries/newspaper-library>

Cardiff – Central Library:
<http://www.cardiff.gov.uk/content.asp?nav=2868,2970&parent_directory_id=2865&Leisure>

Glasgow – Mitchell Library:
<http://libcat.csglasgow.org>

Leeds – Leeds Reference Library:
<http://www.leeds.gov.uk/leisure/Pages/Libraries.aspx>

Liverpool – William Brown Street Library:
<http://www.liverpool.gov.uk/libraries-and-archives>

Manchester – Central Library:
<http://www.manchester.gov.uk/info/500138/central_library>

Most newspapers keep archives but often the contents do not extend back very far in time. Contact details may be found in press directories such as *Willings Press Guide* (Willings Press, published annually, available in print only, see <http://www.cision.com/uk/products-and-services/print-monitoring/willings>) and *Benn's Media* (Cision UK Ltd, published annually, print only). Most large public libraries will stock one or both of these publications.

Many newspapers historically allowed online access to a limited archive, with older articles having to be paid for. This has changed. Some newspapers now charge for all current and archive information.

10.4   EUROPEAN UNION

10.4.1   Sources focusing on law alone

European Current Law and *European Current Law Yearbook* (Sweet & Maxwell)
Journal articles are listed and summarised briefly under broad subject headings. New books are listed separately. The lists of journal articles and books are both carried over into the *Yearbook*.

Current Law Monthly Digest and *Current Law Yearbook* (Sweet & Maxwell)
In *Current Law Monthly Digest* journal articles are listed (but not summarised) under broad subject headings. The lists are not carried over in the *Yearbook*. New books are listed at the back of each monthly issue but not carried over into the *Yearbook*.

European Law Review (Sweet & Maxwell)
Published six times a year, it focuses on European integration and the Council of Europe, with lengthy articles on recent developments which may appeal more to the academic than the practitioner.

Lawtel EU (subscriber-only service)
The Articles Index contains summaries of both substantive law and practice articles published in the leading general and specialist European journals. References to legislation and cases within each summary are linked those materials elsewhere in the database. The full text of articles can be delivered by fax within an hour through the Articles Express service. Elsewhere in the database is access to press releases issued by the EU institutions.

Lawtel UK (subscriber-only service)
The Articles Index contains summaries of articles which appeared in more than a dozen EU law journals, mostly from January 1999 onwards. The full text of articles can be delivered by fax within an hour of the request being made through the online request service.

Lexis®Library (subscriber-only service)
Journals Index Plus contains summaries of articles from over 500 UK and overseas journals, though the accent is more on UK and US material than EU titles. Over 90 UK titles and nearly 200 overseas titles are available in full text. The list of journals to which each subscriber has access may vary according to the details of the package agreed with the database provider. A disadvantage of a *Lexis®Library* journals search is that the results can contain references to articles where the keywords searched for are just referred to in passing, and not central to the theme of the article. This is because where the journal is not indexed, the search software finds every mention of the keywords in the full text of the article, whether significant or not.

Westlaw UK (subscriber-only service)
The Journals library is an amalgam of two databases (a journals index and the full text of articles) and is probably the most comprehensive law database in the United Kingdom on which to search for journal commentary. The two databases are seamlessly combined. Since 1986 *Legal Journals Index* has provided summaries of articles appearing in over 1,000 English language law journals, including over eighty published in EU countries. Both practitioner and academic journals are represented in the database. Links are provided within the summaries to the full text of cited legislation and case law. The database is complemented by access to the full text of about one hundred journals published by Sweet & Maxwell and

a number of other major law publishers with whom the company has negotiated licences to display their publications.

In addition to searching for articles in the Journals library, *Westlaw UK* provides quick links at the left side of the screen in the EU Legislation and Cases libraries. When the text of a legislative provision or the text of a case is displayed on the screen, if a relevant article is available in the database, a link appears at the bottom of the list at the left of the screen.

10.4.2   General sources

European Sources Online (subscriber-only service)
Possibly the premier indexing service for publications and commentary on the European Union published by the European Union itself and other international organisations, national governments, think tanks and stakeholder organisations. Includes bibliographic records to key academic textbooks and periodical articles (such as *The Economist*). Updated daily. Fully searchable by subject, author, title, issuing body and type of publication. Bear in mind that this database covers the entire range of EU activities, not just law.

ECLAS, the Commission library's union catalogue (free):
<http://ec.europa.eu/libraries/doc/catalogues/index_en.htm>
The catalogue includes the holdings of the European Commission's central library and twenty-five specialised libraries and information centres. Although access, loans and copying services are available only to EC officials, searching the catalogue may uncover material not found in other sources. EU publications may be consulted at European Documentation Centres (EDC), located across all EU member states (see section 13.4.4, below).

10.5   EUROPEAN HUMAN RIGHTS

Yearbook of the European Convention on Human Rights (Martinus Nijhoff, 1955–)
Appendix A is a lengthy bibliography of books and articles acquired and catalogued by the Library of the European Court of Human Rights during the year in question, and must rate as one of the most comprehensive lists available. Many large university law libraries subscribe to this publication and details of how to gain access are given at section 13.4.2, below.

Portal to legal sites and resources in the United Kingdom (free):
<http://www.venables.co.uk/sitesh.htm#humanrights>
Under the human rights heading are listed a range of organisations which provide free commentary on human rights issues. Notable amongst them is One Crown Office Row – see below.

One Crown Office Row (free):
<http://www.1cor.com/resources-introduction>
Amongst a variety of resources on this very popular website is a free Human Rights and Public Law email alerter service to new decisions on human rights issues decided by the European Court of Human Rights and domestic courts in the United Kingdom. In 2010 a free UK Human Rights Blog was launched. The services are compiled by a number of staff including Rosalind English, Chambers Academic, who also prepares material for the *Lawtel Human Rights* service.

Lawtel Human Rights (subscriber-only service)
Two different services are provided: specialist articles on the European Convention on Human Rights and judgments of the European Court of Human Rights, written by Rosalind English, a chambers academic attached to one of the leading human rights law chambers in London (see entry immediately above); summaries of journal articles on human rights law drawn from over 50 leading journals and specialist titles. The full text of the articles can be obtained by fax within an hour through other services within the database.

10.6   INTERNATIONAL LAW

Index to Legal Periodicals (HW Wilson)
First published in 1908 and issued eleven times a year this American publication indexes over 750 English language academic and practitioner law journals from across the world and is valuable on three counts: tracing articles about overseas law; comparative legal research, when seeking information on the law across several jurisdictions; and overseas writing about UK law. The print version carries four indexes: subject, author, a table of cases and table of statutes. Many university law libraries in the United Kingdom hold this publication, though some will have stopped the print subscription in favour of online access, which is available to subscribers only.

In December 2012 *Lexis®Library* announced that HW Wilson had withdrawn the licence to display the *Index to Legal Periodicals* on the database. The database was available within the *Westlaw International* Library but was subsequently withdrawn. The owners of Westlaw hope to re-instate access to the *Index* during 2013. It is assumed that the *Index* will re-appear in the *Westlaw International* library, which is accessed as follows:

> Click tab 'Services' towards top right of screen
> Click tab 'Westlaw International' and continue clicking this tab on subsequent screens until the International Directory is reached
> In 'Search for a database' box (left-hand side of screen) type ILP and click Go
> In the search screen which appears, either:
> – type in the search box the keywords you wish to use
> – or click the tab 'Terms and connectors' and construct a search using the principles set out in Appendix 4.

Index to Foreign Legal Periodicals (University of California Press for the American Association of Law Libraries)
Founded in 1960, this is the finest multi-lingual index to articles appearing in over 470 law journals published worldwide. It is published quarterly and each issue indexes over 2,600 articles. An online version indexing entries from 1985 onwards is available through William S Hein & Co, see: <http://www.law.berkeley.edu/library/iflp>

Public International Law – a current bibliography of books and articles (Springer-Verlag)
Semi-annual publication started in 1975 and compiled by the Max Planck Institute for Comparative Public and International Law. Indexes over 1,000 journals, yearbooks, etc with the book entries compiled from the acquisitions lists of the world-renowned Max-Planck Institute library. Available only in print form.

Lexis®Library (subscriber-only service)

Journals Index Plus contains summaries of articles from over 500 UK and overseas journals. Over ninety UK titles and nearly 200 overseas titles are available in full text. Whilst not as focused on international law as the services described above, useful material can be retrieved.

Westlaw UK (subscriber-only service)

Similarly to *Lexis®Library*, *Westlaw UK* provides access to hundreds of full-text US and Canadian journals, gathered in a library called 'Journal & Law Reviews'. To access a search screen for this part of the database:

> Click tab 'Services' towards top right of screen
> Click tab 'Westlaw International' and continue clicking this tab on subsequent screens until the International Directory is reached
> In 'Search for a database' box (left-hand side of screen) type JLR and click Go
> In the search screen which appears, either:
> – type in the search box the keywords you wish to use
> – or click the tab 'Terms and connectors' and construct a search using the principles set out in Appendix 4.

10.7 HOW TO CITE BOOKS AND JOURNAL ARTICLES

10.7.1 Books

OSCOLA (see section 17.4.3, below) makes detailed recommendations of which just one example is given here:

> Author | *Title* (additional information such as series title | edition | publisher | place | date) | page

Example:

> JH Baker, *An Introduction to English Legal History* (4th edn Butterworths, London 2002) 419–21

However, many publishers adopt a different format which makes compiling lists of authors in alphabetical order much simpler:

> Baker, JH, *An Introduction to English Legal History* (Butterworths, 4th edn, 2002) 419–21

Whichever scheme is adopted, be consistent.

10.7.2 Journal articles

OSCOLA (see section 17.4.3, below) recommends the following:

> Author, | 'title of article' | (date) | volume number, | journal abbreviation | first page number

Example:

> Andrew Ashworth, 'Social Control and Anti-Social Behaviour: the subversion of human rights' (2004) 120 LQR 263

There is a major criticism to be made of this scheme – it is that the abbreviation for a journal is an imprecise location guide, for some abbreviations. CLJ for example, can be applied to several different journals: *Cambridge Law Journal, Company Law Journal, Criminal Law Journal,* in UK practice, and overseas: *Criminal Law Journal* (Australia), *Criminal Law Journal* (India), *Calcutta Law Journal, Ceylon Law Journal, Canada Law Journal, Chicago Law Journal,* etc.

Some publishers adopt a different scheme and also reverse the order of author's family name and forename for the reason set out above for books:

> Ashworth, A, 'Social Control and Anti-Social Behaviour: the subversion of human rights' (2004) 120 *Law Quarterly Review* 263

Again, whichever scheme is adopted, be consistent.

CHAPTER 11

PRE-LEGISLATIVE PROPOSALS

11.1   UNITED KINGDOM

This section is about the various documents which may be issued by branches of government and are instrumental in creating and moulding the content of legislation before it is laid before Parliament at Westminster. Practitioners are most likely to need these materials when undertaking *Pepper v Hart* research described at section 8.2.2, above, but they are sometimes cited in court in other circumstances as well.

In contrast with most other chapters of this book the focus is on one jurisdiction only: Parliament at Westminster. For Scotland, Wales and Northern Ireland any pre-legislative documents which are available are likely to be located on the relevant Parliament or Assembly website, or the websites of the Scottish Government, Welsh Assembly Government or Northern Ireland Executive.

The Westminster publications to be covered here are:

- Law Commission documents;
- Royal Commission reports and other associated publications;
- other official inquiry reports;
- Consultation papers (Green Papers) and Government policy documents (White Papers);
- Select Committee reports on draft Bills – the draft Bills themselves are featured at section 9.2.1, above.

As noted at section 8.2.2, above, references to these publications may have arisen from researching sources such as *Current Law Statutes*, *Hansard*, textbooks, journal articles or even practitioner works.

11.1.1   Law Commission publications

The Law Commission is a permanent body whose purpose, according to the founding Act, is:

> to take and keep under review all the law ... with a view to its systematic development and reform, including in particular the codification of such law, the elimination of anomalies, the repeal of obsolete and unnecessary enactments, ... and generally the simplification and modernisation of the law. (Law Commission Act 1965, s 3)

It reports the results of its investigations and proposals in two stages, as Consultation Papers and as Reports.

Law Commission Consultation Papers

Consultation Papers (up to the end of 1990 referred to as Working Papers) provide a detailed statement of the present law on a topic, an account of the criticisms and supposed defects of the law and a statement of the options for change. The Law Commission normally states its preferred option. The Papers are widely circulated for discussion and comment. These publications are of great value because they summarise the law, analyse it and give options for change.

A full list of Consultation Papers published from 1996 onwards, displayed in alphabetical order by title, is available on the Commission's website:
<http://lawcommission.justice.gov.uk/publications.htm>
The page gives details of where pre-1996 consultation papers are available.

BAILII:
<http://www.bailii.org/ew/other/EWLC>

Official-documents.gov.uk website run by The National Archives:
<http://www.official-documents.gov.uk>

University libraries serving a law school will usually have a full or selected collection of Law Commission Consultation Papers in print form to support teaching and research. See Chapter 13 on these and other sources of assistance.

Consultation Papers are arranged in a running number sequence and frequently lawyers use the number as a short-hand way of to referring to a particular paper, for example: Law Comm. C.P. 215 or just LC CP 215. OSCOLA recommends that the citation of Law Commission Consultation Papers should be similar to that for Reports (see 'Law Commission Reports', below), which would be:

> Law Commission, | *Title* | (Law Com | CP No | nnn, | year)

Example:

> Law Commission, *Conspiracy and Attempts* (Law Com CP No 183, 2007)

Law Commission Reports

Following consideration of the views expressed on the Consultation Paper, a final report is produced which may contain a draft Bill.

A chronological list of Reports from 1996 onwards, with links to the full text of each, is available on the Law Commission's website:
<http://lawcommission.justice.gov.uk/publications.htm>

As with Law Commission Consultation papers (above), earlier reports are available either on *BAILII* or *Official-documents.gov.uk*.

University libraries serving a law school will usually have a full or selected collection of Law Commission Reports in print form to support teaching and research. See Chapter 13 on these and other sources of assistance.

Some lawyers use shorthand to refer to a Law Commission Report, as in Law Comm. Rept. 99 or even just LC Rep 99. OSCOLA recommends the following way of referring to a Law Commission Report:

Law Commission, | *Title* | (Law Com | No | nnn, | year)

Example:

Law Commission, *Evidence of Bad Character in Criminal Proceedings* (Law Com No 273, 2001)

The latest edition of OSCOLA states that the Command Paper reference need not be given.

The Law Commission publishes a number of other documents based on its investigations not within the Consultation Papers and Report series. They are available via links at:
<http://lawcommission.justice.gov.uk/publications.htm>

11.1.2 Royal Commissions

These prestigious, investigative bodies are set up under Royal Warrant to examine a topic of public concern where legislation seems desirable. After issuing its report the Royal Commission is disbanded. Very few Royal Commissions have been set up in the last fifteen years. Their Reports set out recommendations for change. In addition, some Royal Commissions have also published detailed, supporting research studies.

The Reports of Royal Commissions are published as part of a large group of official publications called Command Papers, that is, documents which originate outside Parliament but are presented to Parliament 'by command of Her Majesty', usually the Minister responsible for setting up the particular Royal Commission in the first place.

The first Command Paper was published in 1833 and about 300–400 are issued every year now. Each Command Paper carries a unique reference number, preceded by an abbreviation for the word

'Command'. The form of the abbreviation has changed after approximately every 9,000th paper is issued. At present the 6th series is being published with the prefix Cm, as in the example Cm 5678.

One of the quickest and most precise ways of trying to trace a copy of a Command Paper is to use the unique Cm reference for the particular paper you require and search sources such as the freely available web catalogues of large universities with a law library – see section 13.4.2, below on these and other sources of assistance.

Alternatively, try the following.

Official-documents.gov.uk:
<http://www.official-documents.gov.uk/menu/browseDocuments.htm>
This site run by The National Archives, lists all Command Papers from 17 May 2005 to the present with an archive of many back to 1993. There are links to the full text of each.

TSO (The Stationery Office) Official Documents Archive:
<http://www.archive.official-documents.co.uk/index.html>
The Archive is in two parts: one includes information about Command Papers published between 1994 and 2001, the other 2002 to April 2005. Make sure you select the correct part of the site to search. It includes only a selection issued during the two time periods, with links to those available on government sites.

TSO (The Stationery Office) Parliamentary and Legal Bookshop:
<http://www.tsoshop.co.uk/parliament/bookstore.asp>
The government publishers has a website which can be used to search for Command Papers in print to buy or just to obtain full details before trying other sources for the text. TSO (The Stationery Office) also issues annual catalogues in print form – many large public libraries and university libraries will collect them. The print catalogues are perhaps easier to browse than the TSO website when looking for a publication with the minimum of information to hand about the Command Paper number, date and title.

The University of Southampton web catalogue:
<http://www-lib.soton.ac.uk>
For several decades the University of Southampton was at the forefront in making access to official information easier. As part of its work the BOPCRIS project created detailed catalogue records for a selection of Parliamentary papers between 1801 and 1995. Command Papers were included in this work. Scroll down the page to the simple heading: BOPCRIS Ford Collection:
<http://www.southampton.ac.uk/library/ldu/projects.html#Ford>

OSCOLA (see section 17.4.3, below) recommends that Command Papers should be cited:

> Name of department or body producing the paper, | *Title* | (Cm | nnnn, | year)

Example:

> Secretary of State for Health, *Government Response to the House of Commons Health Committee Report on the Provision of Allergy Services* (Cm 6433, 2005)

11.1.3   Other inquiry reports

Most reports of government inquiries, whether Reports of Departmental Committees set up to review a matter of public concern, or reports of tribunals or commissions of inquiry are published as Command Papers. See section 11.1.2, above, on how to track down copies.

11.1.4   Government consultation papers and policy documents

Green Papers

The popular term for government consultation papers derives from the colour of the cover of the first one issued in 1967. Do not use the term 'Green Paper' when searching for them as the term does not usually appear in the title of the paper or in catalogues.

Green Papers are intended to stimulate public debate on an issue. An increasing number are issued as Command Papers, so may be traceable by the routes suggested at section 11.1.2, above. The remainder will have been published either by TSO (The Stationery Office) as a non-Parliamentary paper or by the government department responsible for drawing up the paper.

If published by TSO and still in print they will be traceable through the TSO Parliamentary and Legal Bookshop, see section 11.1.2, above. If not still in print then try your local university library or city centre public library – see section 13.4.2, below.

If published by the government department then the best place to start a search for them will be on the website of the government responsible. This is where a Google search can turn up trumps. Either:

- type in a few words from the title. You may be fortunate and get some hits, but make sure the document you find is located on an official government website and is not a summary of the contents on an unofficial website. The summary may not be a reliable source to use; or

- search on the name of the government department to find its website. Finding a particular document on a very large departmental website can be difficult, but some sites have search boxes which may help to retrieve the particular document you seek.

A more structured approach to finding the website of a government department is to use the official portal to the entire government service, Gov.uk:
<http://www.direct.gov.uk/en/index.htm>

Some government departments carry web archives of their publications from past years, even though the print copies are no longer available, so watch out for links to the departmental archives

If the paper is not in print and not on the departmental website, try the University of Southampton website. Alternatively, try one of the sources mentioned in Chapter 13.

White Papers

The popular term for a wide range of government publications, including government policy documents, derives from the colour of the cover of the first one issued in 1832. Do not use the term 'White Paper' when searching for them as the term does not usually appear in the title of the paper or in catalogues.

White Papers set out government policy on an issue. If legislation is intended to bring the policy into effect, the content of the Bill will be foreshadowed. White Papers are issued as Command Papers so may be traceable by the routes suggested at section 11.1.2, above.

11.1.5   Select Committee reports on draft Bills

Select Committees are composed of members selected by the House of Commons or the House of Lords who are best qualified for the specialised, essentially investigative work of the Committee. There is a large number of select Committees each examining an aspect of public life, such as the Communities and Local Government Committee or the Transport Committee. Since 1997 draft Bills, created by Government departments, have been submitted to Parliament for pre-legislative scrutiny by appropriate Select Committees. Most Draft Bills are examined either by Select Committees in the Commons or Lords or by a joint committee of both Houses. In practice, Select Committees have taken a middle course between challenging the principle of the Bill and applying the detailed scrutiny of each clause undertaken by the Public Bill Committee when the Bill is submitted formally to Parliament. The Reports of the Select Committees comment on the policy of the Bill and suggest improvements, and are published by TSO (The Stationery Office) as either House of Commons or House of Lords Papers.

For draft Bills going through the scrutiny process in this session and those of past sessions back to 2002–2003 there are links to the relevant Parliamentary Papers for each Bill from:
<http://www.parliament.uk/business/bills_and_legislation/draft_bills.cfm>

Before that time use the sources noted at section 11.1.2, above; either search on the title of the draft Bill or within listings or collections of House of Commons or House of Lords Papers.

OSCOLA recommends the following method of citing Select Committee reports:

> Name of Committee, | *Title of report* | (abbreviation for House responsible | session, | paper number – volume number)

Examples:

> Transport Select Committee, *Report on the draft Local Transport Bill* (HC 2006–2007 692)

> Science and Technology Committee, *Personal Internet Security* (HL 2006–2007 165)

> Joint Committee on the Draft Bribery Bill, *First Report* (2008–2009, HL 115, HC 430-I)

11.2   EUROPEAN UNION

European Union: A Guide to Tracing Working Documents, Patrick Overy (free):
<http://www.nyulawglobal.org/globalex/European_Union_Travaux_Preparatoires1.htm>
This well researched and authoritative guide (Patrick Overy is based at Exeter University and has an international reputation within the field of EU research and documentation) describes the working documents of each of the European institutions (Commission, Parliament and Council) with links to where they are freely available. A section towards the end of the guide covers access to institutional registers of documents and online collections. This is both a 'how to research' and 'where to find it' guide.

11.3   EUROPEAN HUMAN RIGHTS

Travaux préparatoires of the Convention (free):
<http://www.echr.coe.int/Library/COLENTravauxprep.html>
These travaux préparatoires contain the various documents that were produced during the drafting of the Convention and its first Protocol, reports of discussions in the Assembly and its Committee on Legal and Administrative Questions and in the Committee of Ministers and certain of its committees of experts. This official website provides access to the documents held by the Council of Europe Registry. A collected edition in print format was published between 1975 and 1985 by Martinus Nijhoff and is referenced at the bottom of the web page. Most of the larger UK university law libraries will have a set.

11.4   INTERNATIONAL

Travaux préparatoires, meaning literally 'preparatory works', contain the negotiating or drafting history of international treaties and agreements. They can be notoriously difficult to trace but the free guide listed below provides a detailed and admirable approach to researching these documents.

À la Recherche des Travaux Préparatoires: an approach to researching the drafting history of international agreements, Jonathan Pratter (free):
<http://www.nyulawglobal.org/globalex/Travaux_Preparatoires1.htm>
Part of the highly respected New York School of Law set of web guides to international research. The web address given above leads to the latest update of the guide.

CHAPTER 12

OTHER OFFICIAL INFORMATION

12.1   UNITED KINGDOM

The publishing output of the UK Government is huge. Chapters 5, 9 and 11 include references to legislation, Parliamentary publications and the publications of a few advisory bodies outside Parliament. Tracking down other official materials can be difficult because, whilst TSO (The Stationery Office) is the government publisher, many government departments and quangos (such as the Health and Safety Executive or the Equality and Human Rights Commission (EHRC)) publish direct to the public and not through TSO.

So, try these routes: search for a website, use subject-specific encyclopedias, *Knight's Local Government Reports* or a comprehensive catalogue.

To search for a departmental or quango website there are two routes: Gov.uk or Google.

Gov.uk:
<http://www.direct.gov.uk/en/index.htm>
The official web portal to UK Government includes an A–Z directory of central government – link at the bottom of the home page

Note: The devolved administrations in Scotland, Wales and Northern Ireland have websites that provide links to their respective departments and agencies but do not perform quite the same role as Gov.uk for the United Kingdom.

Google:
<http://www.google.co.uk>
A very effective way of tracing hard to locate websites – type in the name of the organisation or even the title of the document, and Google sometimes returns with locations it would have taken some time to trace otherwise. It can be very useful for tracing official publications buried deeply within government websites. But, take care, for the results from a Google search for an official document will also retrieve unofficial versions or commentary or the views of a pressure group as well. Read or re-read the limitations on Google searching in section 3.2.1, above.

Subject-specific encyclopedia

Many practitioner works, especially the looseleaf encyclopedias, include a variety of hard-to-find official and unofficial publications, such as codes of practice, government departmental circulars and technical memoranda.

Knight's Local Government Reports

First published in 1903 and up to 1990 this publication included the full text of a large selection of government circulars and memoranda relating to the work of local authorities. The government departments whose circulars were reproduced were responsible for agriculture, consumer protection, education, the emergency services, the environment, health, housing, local government finance and administration, social services, town planning and trading standards.

Comprehensive catalogue

A more structured way of searching for official publications is to use either a comprehensive printed catalogue or a subscriber-only database.

Catalogue of British Official Publications Not Published by the Stationery Office (Chadwyck-Healey)

This is a print catalogue started in 1980, published bi-monthly with annual accumulations. It combines entries from the TSO (The Stationery Office) catalogue with those from over 2,000 official bodies. Many university libraries will have a subscription to this – see section 13.4.2, below on using these libraries. The catalogue arranges entries alphabetically under issuing bodies which are themselves in alphabetical order, except in those cases where they are entered under their parent body. There are several indexes giving access to the entries and it is necessary to use these to be sure of finding the section required. It appears to have ceased in the early 21st century and was replaced by the online subscriber-only service: UKOP (see below).

In 1989 an online version of the *Catalogue* now called UKOP was commenced, including all the material back to 1980:

<http://www.ukop.co.uk>

It is now published by TSO (The Stationery Office) and is a subscriber-only database. UKOP comprehensively catalogues the same material as the *Catalogue*, above, but makes searching for documents easier and contains links to the full text of publications both on the internet and permanently archived within the database. It is an important source for the full text of the following hard-to-trace material: press releases, circular letters, factsheets, guidance notes, consultation papers, inspection and inquiry reports. The database is updated daily on weekdays.

Some of the most frequently required yet most difficult to trace materials are government circulars and memoranda. If the above routes fail to uncover a source try the main library of the government department concerned. Usually it holds a comprehensive set of publications issued by the department. Use the *Civil Service Yearbook* or one of the directories to Whitehall and the civil service described at section 15.1, below, to trace contact details for the enquiry point.

Further sources of government publications on the web are described at section 11.1, above, especially archives going back into the 1990s. Bear in mind that it is rare to find web versions of government publications issued before the advent of the internet and digitisation technology – there have not been retrospective projects to digitise pre-1990s publications for the web. So, researchers will need to rely on traditional, paper-based collections.

12.2   EUROPEAN UNION

The Europa website, the official website of the European Union, is huge. The search facility on the site is not very reliable or helpful. It may be more effective to use a Google-style search engine for the site at:
<http://searcheuropa.eu>

In contrast to the lack of digitised versions of out of print UK official publications (see section 12.1, above) the EU Bookshop launched its EU Digital Library of 14 million pages of out of print EU publications from 1952 onwards, free to search and use, see:
<http://bookshop.europa.eu/eubookshop/index.action?request_locale=EN>

Here are details of several reliable guides to the publishing output of the European Union.

European Union legal materials: an infrequent user's guide, Duncan E. Alford (free):
<http://www.nyulawglobal.org/Globalex/European_Union1.htm>
Specifically aimed at the infrequent user of EU publications, this guide which is part of the highly regarded New York University School of Law website, provides 'how to' and where to find it' advice. A section on research guides at the end of the document provides details of more detailed guides suitable for the experienced researcher.

European Union law: an integrated guide to electronic and print research, Marylin J. Raisch (free):
<http://www.llrx.com/features/eulaw2.htm>
A descriptive guide similar to Alford's, above, but with the advantage of illustrations of web pages and more detailed 'how to' instructions.

European Information Association Guides:
<http://www.eia.org.uk/publications.php>
The Association's guides of most use to lawyers are the 94-page *European Information: a guide to official sources* and the series of 'How to' guides on finding and using information in particular EU documents such as directives, case law and the national implementation of EU measures. A compendium of the guides is free to download or print.

12.3   INTERNATIONAL

ASIL Guide to electronic resources for international law (free):
<http://www.asil.org/erg>
The American Society of International Law has developed a well researched and presented website of guides to electronic resources freely available the international legal researchers across the world. Each of the guides is critically revised and updated every six months and provides an excellent starting point in developing a research strategy to find international legal materials.

GlobaLex guides to international legal research (free):
<http://www.nyulawglobal.org/Globalex/#>
New York University School of Law has developed a website carrying well researched and frequently updated guides to research in a wide range of international law practice areas. Some of the authors are lawyers practising in the field, others are law librarians. Many of the sources described are freely available. Highly recommended.

UN Documents (free):

<http://www.un.org/en/documents/index.shtml>

The United Nations and a vast number of UN-related organisations publish thousands of documents annually. This website is the gateway to their publishing output, a considerable amount of which is available free on the web. An important aspect of researching UN documentation is that documents may be amended as discussions and negotiations move on so it is important to check whether the information found matches what is sought. A number of well researched and presented guides is available free to assist researchers correctly identify where in the vast web of UN sites the information sought is located. Here are the best:

ASIL Guide to electronic resources for international law – United Nations (free):

<http://www.asil.org/erg/?page=un>

Detailed and regularly updated guide to a selection of the most important official websites carrying information on and documentation produced by the United Nations and related organisations. Partly a 'how to' guide but mainly a 'where to find it' source.

EISIL – Electronic Information System for International Law (free):

<http://www.eisil.org/index.php?sid=276443096&cat=40&t=sub_pages>

Part of the American Society of International Law website, providing lists of web links to key documents, particular UN organisations and resource guides. Essentially a 'where to find it' portal to UN websites. The site appears not to have been updated recently.

Researching the United Nations: Finding the Organization's Internal Resource Trails, Linda Tashbook (free):

<http://www.nyulawglobal.org/globalex/United_Nations_Research1.htm>

Part of the respected Globalex legal research website (see above). Written by an attorney who is also a professionally qualified law librarian, this guide describes 'how to' research UN materials and includes links to 'where to find it'.

UN Documentation: Research Guide (free):

<http://www.un.org/Depts/dhl/resguide>

Not so much a guide on 'where to find it' but more a description of the different types of documents and how to work with them.

The United Nations has set up a network of agreements with national and university libraries throughout the world, for them to receive copies of most UN documents and allow public access to them. There are ten UN depository libraries in the United Kingdom and they are listed at:

<http://www.un.org/depts/dhl/deplib/countries/uk.htm>

UN depository collections are displayed to common standards. The London School of Economics Library produces a very clear, free guide to what is held, how it is arranged and how to research their collection. Since it is updated annually and each revision bears a new web address, so follow the link at the bottom of this web page:

<http://www2.lse.ac.uk/library/collections/govtpub/un/UNlibrary.aspx>

CHAPTER 13

WHERE TO FIND LEGAL INFORMATION NOT AVAILABLE WITHIN YOUR FIRM OR CHAMBERS

13.1   ENGLAND AND WALES

13.1.1   If you are a solicitor

The Law Society Library:
<http://www.lawsociety.org.uk/advice/library-services>
The Law Society has one of the finest law libraries in the United Kingdom focused on the needs of practitioners. Solicitor members of the Law Society of England and Wales may visit in person or phone, fax, or email legal information enquiries to the team of experienced law librarians who will look for the information needed. The website contains further information regarding opening hours and contact details. A Library Service Review took place in 2012 and may result in changes to some of the library's services. The library has exceptional collections of past editions of practice works going back over 150 years. It also retains every volume published of the standard law library titles: the *Halsbury's* publications, *Encyclopedia of Forms and Precedents*, *Atkins Court Forms*, the *White Book* and the *Green Book*.

Links to pages on which to search the library catalogue are not easy to find on a rather cluttered screen at: <http://uk1.lexisnexis.com/LawSocietyLibrary/HomePage.aspx>

Here is where they lead:

- For books:
  <http://uk1.lexisnexis.com/LawSocietyLibrary/Search/DetailedSearch.aspx?zone=Books>

- For journals and law reports:
  <http://uk1.lexisnexis.com/LawSocietyLibrary/Search/DetailedSearch.aspx?zone=JournalAndLawReportTitles>

The library provides a document delivery service (Lawdocs) copying from the huge collection of books, journals and law reports. Copies can be emailed, faxed or posted. Charges vary according to the type of material copied. Non-members may use the service at an additional charge.

13.1.2   If you are a barrister

Each of the four Inns has a magnificent library containing publications for the practitioner, featuring comprehensive collections for the 'home' jurisdiction and also a selection of other jurisdictions and specialising in particular practice areas. They all offer enquiry services by phone, email and in person, and provide access to a range of databases and other services. Documents (subject to copyright) can be sent by fax, post or email to members of the particular Inn working in private practice outside London, or a member of any Inn when the material is not held by their own library. Barrister, judicial and student members of any of the Inns may use any of the libraries. Below is the website address for each of the Inns libraries, with an indication of the specialisations of the collections:

Gray's Inn:
<http://www.graysinn.info/index.php/library-archives>
Specialises in international law, human rights both within the United Kingdom and from wider European and international perspectives. Also the law of Northern Ireland.

Inner Temple:
<http://www.innertemplelibrary.org.uk/welcome.htm>
Apart from a 70,000 volume collection on English law, specialises in Scottish and Commonwealth jurisdictions, especially Canada, Caribbean, Hong Kong and the Indian sub-continent.

Lincoln's Inn:
<http://www.lincolnsinn.org.uk/index.php/library>
Specialises in Commonwealth legislation and law reports, especially Australia, New Zealand, Malaysia, Singapore and Brunei, Africa, Sri Lanka and the Pacific. Also in the law of the Channel Islands and Isle of Man. Noted for its extensive collections of Parliamentary materials including: Parliamentary Papers from 1801 onwards, House of Commons Standing Committee debates from 1983/84 onwards. The English law collection features House of Lords and Privy Council printed cases and appeal documents, which are deposited annually. Chancery practice materials are a speciality.

Middle Temple:
<http://www.middletemple.org.uk/library>
Specialises in European Law, both the law of the Community and the relevant law of the member states; a substantial collection of United States law reports, together with Federal and State legislation. In English law the major specialisation is ecclesiastical law – including unreported ecclesiastical court reports.

13.2   SCOTLAND

13.2.1   If you are a member of the WS Society or other local law society

Signet Library:
<http://www.thewssociety.co.uk/index.asp?cat=Library>
Provides a range of document supply and research services to members. Collections include an extensive collection of Scottish legislation, law reports, periodicals and practice works including historic editions back into 19th century, and selections of English, Irish, Northern Irish, European and international law materials. Also provides access to a wide range on CD-ROM and internet databases.

Royal Faculty of Procurators in Glasgow Library:
<http://www.rfpg.org/library:intro>
Claims it is the largest law library in the West of Scotland purchasing every significant Scottish law text as well as English and UK law materials. Staff provide enquiry, research and document delivery services to members. The website includes access to an online catalogue.

Society of Advocates in Aberdeen Library:
<http://www.socofadvocates.com/resources.php>
Despite its name, this is a local law society library for solicitors. The catalogue is available online and there is a lending service for members. Although the library is open limited hours it does boast wireless internet access.

13.2.2   If you are a member of the Faculty of Advocates

The Advocates Library:
<http://www.advocates.org.uk/library/index.html>
The private library of members of the Faculty of Advocates, the Scottish bar. Non-members may access the majority of the collection via services provided by National Library of Scotland. Apart from Scottish law it maintains collections of Commonwealth, Irish and Manx law.

13.3   NORTHERN IRELAND

13.3.1   If you are a solicitor

The Law Society of Northern Ireland Information Services:
<http://www.lawsoc-ni.org>
Access to the Service is available only to members of the Law Society via the Library Services link on the home page. The Service includes access to a comprehensive collection of textbooks, journals, law reports, encyclopaedic works and legislation covering the jurisdictions of Northern Ireland, Republic of Ireland, Great Britain and European Union and major online databases, the internet and CD-ROMS.

13.3.2 If you are a member of the Bar of Northern Ireland

Bar Library, Belfast:

<http://www.barlibrary.com>

Staff provide enquiry and research services to members. A particular feature is BLAG, The Bar Library Authority Gathering Service. Members may submit their list of authorities and bundles in person, by phone or by email. Library staff source, collate and deliver the case law to members and aim to do this within twenty-four hours of receiving the list. The library's collections comprise some 60,000 volumes including all Northern Ireland legislation, UK primary legislation and some Irish and European legislation. It also holds Northern Irish, English, Scottish and Irish case law. All unreported judgments of the Northern Ireland High Courts are received. Extensive textbook, practitioner and journal collections are available. The standard commercial databases are available to members and a database of Northern Ireland law: OLIB.

13.4   OTHER, FREE SOURCES

13.4.1   Google Scholar

<http://scholar.google.co.uk>

This is a specialised search engine within the Google community. It allows users to cross-search a range of databases and websites, including academic journals and books held in electronic form and the catalogue records of some universities and public bodies. It covers a wide range of disciplines, including law.

There are two major criticisms of Google Scholar:

- it does not reveal its sources, so it is difficult to know what it has searched and what must be searched by other routes;

- search results may include links to materials and databases which require a subscription, so leaving other users with a dead-end.

The contents of Google Scholar have a bias towards American publications but some UK material features. Some publishers, including Oxford University Press and Sweet & Maxwell, have allowed access to the full text of a selection of law books. Others, such as LexisNexis and Bloomsbury Professional (formerly Tottel Publishing), provide only catalogue entries and/or summaries of the contents. Overall, the database is a hotch-potch of sources (journal articles, books, catalogue records, theses) which makes sorting through the results for 'nuggets of gold' a time-consuming process. However, worth a dip if the major law databases are not available and the other sources mentioned in this chapter draw a blank.

13.4.2   Finding and using your nearest university or college law collection

UK Centre for Legal Education, directory of legal education in the United Kingdom:

<http://www.ukcle.ac.uk/students/directory>

The UK Centre for Legal Education closed on 31 July 2011. Its website has been archived and includes a directory of legal education in the United Kingdom, which still has value. Each entry includes a link to the website of a university or college law school. Usually it does not take too much effort to navigate from the law school to the web pages of the library of the university or college. Many university and college libraries make their library catalogues freely available online to search. There are often associated web pages providing details of how to gain access to the library to read and, within copyright law, photocopy material. Some universities and colleges permit members of the public to use the collections for reference only for a few hours, merely on the production of some form of proof of identity. Other libraries have much more restricted entry criteria. It may be worth identifying where your local university or college law library is located and making enquiries about using the collections. Some libraries have corporate external borrower schemes where, for an annual fee, your firm or chambers may be able to borrow certain classes of books from the library, but usually not the heavily in-demand student textbooks.

Access to the university or college computer network and the law databases it contains is available only to staff and students of the university or college. Software and database providers forbid through licence and contract conditions universities and colleges making these services available to non-members.

COPAC:
<http://www.copac.ac.uk>
COPAC is a freely available library catalogue, giving access to the merged online catalogues of many major UK and Irish academic and national libraries, as well as increasing numbers of specialist libraries. The 32 million records, mainly relating to books, include the catalogues of more than twenty of the largest university law libraries in the United Kingdom. Use COPAC to identify books on a topic or trace which library has a copy of an obscure title. The service is quick and easy to use. Unlike Google Scholar none of the results of a search provide the full text of a book, but COPAC does indicate where the item is held. Once you have found a location, search the particular law library's web pages to see if and how personal access may be gained.

13.4.3   Public libraries

The public libraries in many city centres usually collect a range of law books and may have sets of statutes, some practitioner works (particularly on employment, family, social security, social welfare and housing), even in some cases extending to a set of one or more of the *Halsbury's* publications. It may be worth checking out the reference library or information service. In addition, the local history or local studies collections may have collected copies of local and private Acts relating to the local authority, public bodies and private estates in the area.

13.4.4   EU information

European Documentation Centres:
<http://europa.eu/europedirect/meet_us/directory/index_en.htm>
In 1963 the European Union set up a network of documentation and information centres which contain official publications and documents by and about the institutions of the European Union. They are intended to be used by university and research institute staff as well as members of the public. EDCs maintain a comprehensive collection of EU official publications and EDC staff have access to official databases (some of which for law are available online via *Lexis®Library* and *Westlaw UK*). Before contacting an EDC it would be worth verifying exactly what you seek by using ECLAS, the Commission library's union catalogue, see section 10.4.2, above. Designated 'Information Centres' offer a more restricted service. A location map for both EDCs and Information Centres is available at:
<http://europa.eu/europedirect/meet_us/interactive_map/index_en.htm>

Europe Direct:
<http://ec.europa.eu/europedirect/index_en.htm>
A general information and advice service run by the European Commission.

Enterprise Europe:
<http://portal.enterprise-europe-network.ec.europa.eu>
A network of contact points providing information and advice to EU companies on EU matters, in particular small and medium enterprises (SMEs).

SearchEuropa (free):
<http://searcheuropa.eu>
The European Union's official Europa website is vast and sometimes navigating or searching it is daunting and unproductive. An alternative is to use the SearchEuropa engine, a service by the European Journalism Centre for EU4Journalists.eu. It applies Google search software to the Europa website and the results are returned swiftly and effectively. Searches can be restricted to law items only by clicking the radio button on the search form.

13.4.5   Official gazettes

Official gazettes are issued by the governments of many nations and supra-national bodies such as the European Union:
<http://www.ials.sas.ac.uk/flare/flare_fog_unionlist_europe.htm>
They usually contain the authoritative text of treaties, domestic legislation, administrative documents, official notices, parliamentary proceedings and, in a few instances, the reports of the decisions of the courts. The official gazettes of the UK Government (*London Gazette*, *Edinburgh Gazette* and *Belfast Gazette*) are exceptions to the rule, for they carry only official notices – no legislation, case law, or parliamentary debates. However, lawyers sometimes need access to overseas gazettes. The FLARE union list of official gazettes: Europe, allows users to trace which libraries in the United Kingdom have collections for a particular European country and over what period of time. Entries in the list are admirably detailed since many gazettes are issued in several sections, each containing different types of legal information. Many European countries now place the text of recent issues of their gazette on the web and, helpfully, each entry in the list includes a link to the web version of a gazette.

13.4.6   Use your firm or chambers librarian

If you have a firm or chambers librarian make use of them. They have contacts with organisations and other librarians which can make finding and obtaining obscure information or publications much easier and successful. Over 800 people worldwide, mostly law librarians but also a few practitioners, are members of a free, online discussion list called lis-law. Every day queries are put to the list and usually within a short time other members have responded with advice and assistance. The discussion list is a 'closed list', meaning that potential members have to formally apply to be accepted and the postings are not available to the public. For more details go to:
<https://www.jiscmail.ac.uk/cgi-bin/webadmin?A0=lis-law>

If you wish you can register to join, either at the website or send an email message containing a 'join' command to the administrative address of the list (found on the website). The message is usually something like this:

        join <list name> <YourFirstName> <YourLastName>

Substitute as appropriate between the brackets.

Usually you will receive a message informing you that you are now a subscriber to that list.

Lis-law and other email discussion forums to improve information exchange are discussed by Jas Breslin, 'Working the net' (2011) 11 *Legal Information Management* 32–34.

British and Irish Association of Law Librarians (BIALL):
<http://www.biall.org.uk>
Membership of BIALL, the professional body for all those who provide or exploit legal literature, brings access to ideas, and information through its quarterly journal: *Legal Information Management*, current awareness through its bi-monthly *Newsletter*, and, through its annual study conference held in June, access to stimulating learning and exchange of ideas at the plenary and parallel sessions, and many law publishers and database providers who have stands in the exhibition hall.

13.5   THREE CHARGED-FOR SERVICES

Sweet and Maxwell's Document Supply Service (DocDel):
<http://www.sweetandmaxwell.co.uk/our-businesses/docdel.aspx>
This 'pay-as-you-go' service will provide photocopies of articles from over 1,000 titles rapidly. Order by email, online or by fax. The site includes access to the full list of titles within the service, together with a list of abbreviations for all the titles – all the abbreviations also appear in the Cardiff Index to Legal Abbreviations:
<http://www.legalabbrevs.cardiff.ac.uk>

Inter-library loan service
Your firm or chambers librarian or information officer may have access to the international inter-library loan network over which he/she may be able to obtain the information you require, subject to copyright. Ask your librarian or information officer about access to this service.

The inter-library loan network is run in the United Kingdom by the British Library and members of the network, which include the vast resources of the British Library itself, all university, college, public, many government and some law firm libraries, will loan or photocopy material to other members for a small charge. Most material can be supplied within a few days. There are links to libraries outside the United Kingdom for overseas publications.

Directory of British and Irish law libraries (British and Irish Association of Law Librarians, 8th edn, 2006 – out of print)
Tracing a law library in the United Kingdom is made simpler by consulting this directory which lists almost 500 law libraries or libraries with significant collections of legal, regulatory and compliance material in the Great Britain. Entries are arranged according to the nations of Great Britain, then by county and finally alphabetically by town. Brief details of each collection and a full range of contact details are provided. Most importantly, information is given on whether the library is open to the public. The directory is not available online.

CHAPTER 14

BUSINESS INFORMATION

The last decade has seen a dramatic increase in the availability of information online. Finding useful information on the internet using search engines like Google has become second nature for many. Nevertheless, caution must be exercised when relying on such information for the same reasons listed at the start of Chapter 3: authority, accuracy and currency.

This chapter discusses some of the free and subscriber-only sources available when researching business information. What an individual must remember is to focus on their particular requirements (and that of their organisation) when examining which provider of information, whether free or paid, suits them best.

14.1   COMPANY ANNUAL RETURNS AND ACCOUNTS

An annual return is a snapshot of general information about a company's directors, registered office address, shareholders and share capital. Every company registered in the United Kingdom must deliver an annual return to Companies House at least once every 12 months.

Company accounts are the financial documents prepared by a company's accountants. They show income, expenditure, assets, liabilities, and profit and loss details. Company accounts are usually incorporated within a company's annual report.

With documents having to be submitted to Companies House (CH), many users will register to use the Companies House Direct (CHD) service, which will provide them with the vast majority of information they need. The downloading of documents is usually charged, whether these are the history of fillings, company reports or mortgage details. Users may often find the CHD service to be a little dated and difficult to navigate, although only being charged for the documents required and the service's official status are obviously positives.

There are now a vast number of providers who use CH data to provide a more aesthetically pleasing presentation for the user. Not only this, but they also flesh out the skeleton content provided by CH with helpful diagrams and content. Searching and current awareness applications with these providers are much enhanced, with the option of additional, bespoke research undertaken by their team of experts (though usually at a cost). As such services are charged at varying prices, users should approach suppliers with clear requirements to ascertain the best fit. The range of suppliers to be approached would probably include Dun and Bradstreet, Perfect Information, Creditsafe, Experian, Jordans and Bureau Van Dijk, to name only a handful.

14.1.1 Free sources

Tracing a company registry

Official Companies Registers:
<http://www.rba.co.uk/sources/registers.htm>
Provides information on official company registers around the world as well as the details of some general sources for finding information on where companies are registered.

UK official company registries

Companies House WebCheck:
<http://wck2.companieshouse.gov.uk/d9ee079b89121ad8ff3e17c7b5ca9aab/wcframe?name=accessCompanyInfo>
Official company-checking service provided by Companies House. Users can search by company name or number and search for current, dissolved, previous or proposed names. Data includes company names, registration number, registered office and date of latest filings. The site does not include access to the documents filed. This is a basic but useful source of information on companies registered in the United Kingdom.

Northern Ireland Companies Registry
As of 1 October 2009 this registry merged with Companies House UK and all information has been incorporated into the database on the website noted above. However, the Northern Ireland Companies Registry still registers companies with a registered office in Northern Ireland.

Isle of Man Companies Registry:
<http://www.gov.im/ded/companies/companiesregistry.xml>
The Isle of Man Companies Registry was moved to a new Department of Economic Development in 2010. Users must register to view documents filed with the Registry and can purchase company documents, check the availability of company names and submit an application to reserve a company name. Search options include company name or company number. This is the only source for information on companies registered in the Isle of Man.

14.1.2 Subscriber-only services

UK official company registry

Companies House Direct:
<http://direct.companieshouse.gov.uk>
Official site for Companies House, which provides access to all documents lodged at Companies House by UK companies and includes information on the date of the incorporation of a company, the directors of the company, the memorandum and articles of association. The site has a 'company search', which includes current and dissolved companies, and a 'directors search'. Prices for document downloads vary according to the material downloaded, and there is a minimum monthly charge for an account.

Billing for Companies House Direct (CHD) searches can be handled in one of two ways: either law firm staff undertake searches themselves and bill the client directly or the law firm engages a company like 7side (<http://www.7side.co.uk>), which provides a secure link into CHD, with log-in information unique to each client. 7side may then issue the firm with an invoice for searches undertaken on the client's behalf. The costs are exactly the same, but the ease of billing such charges (which may otherwise be written-off) creates an extremely valuable service.

Commercial providers

Dun & Bradstreet:
<http://www.dnb.co.uk>
Official site of the well-known company analysts, Dun & Bradstreet, which provides business and credit information on UK and international companies. Two options for searching are provided: basic search, by company name or number and location, and advanced search, which includes more options relating to the company's location. The global commercial database contains more than 210 million business records.

Hemscott:
<http://www.hemscottir.com>
Well known stocks and shares information provider which was acquired by Morning Star in 2008:
<http://www.morningstar.co.uk>

MyICC:
<http://www.myicc.co.uk>
MyICC contains analysis of UK and Irish limited companies. It provides daily updates of the details of directors and company secretaries, full shareholder information and detailed company 'family trees'. The site also offers further European and international information.

OneSource:
<http://www.onesource.com>
OneSource provides detailed information on companies and individuals worldwide, which can be tailored to personal or business requirements. Information provided includes a summary of the company, list of executives and links to news articles on each company. Significantly, OneSource has a larger archive of annual returns and annual reports and accounts than Companies House and makes it one of the best sites to search and download documents.

Perfect Filings:
<http://pioneer.perfectinfo.com>
Contains over 11 million sets of filings on companies worldwide, also providing background information in addition to the official information. Searching can be made on company name with additional search criteria listed on the site; including document type, industry sector and specific date ranges.

Thomson Research:
<http://research.thomsonib.com>
Provides access to critical company information and analysts' research reports. The forecasts and analyses are based upon research reports from over 980 of the world's leading firms and cover more than 30,000 companies worldwide.

Datastream:
<http://online.thomsonreuters.com/datastream>
Datastream is a financial statistical database, covering asset classes, estimates, fundamentals, indices and economic data. The site includes more than 720 million items of data, some updated daily, and much of it offering at least twenty years of statistical history for a company.

Bureau van Dijk:
<http://www.bvdinfo.com/Home.aspx?lang=en-GB>
Bureau Van Dijk provides a number of tailored products which provide business intelligence and company information. Different sources are provided for each country and the user must ascertain which best suits their requirements. For UK and Irish information, the two most widely recognised products are Fame and MintUK. A range of different products for different countries is available to users.

Creditsafe:
<http://www2.creditsafeuk.com>
Access to company reports for companies registered in Europe and the rest of the world.

LexisNexis Business Intelligence:
<http://www.lexisnexis.co.uk/our-solutions/corporate/business-intelligence>
Information provided through both products unique to this service and existing LexisNexis products, such as the *Nexis UK* news services. Utilises information from Hoovers and ICC.

Banking sector only

Bankscope:
<https://bankscope2.bvdep.com/version-20121221/home.serv?product=scope2006>
Bankscope, a further product from Bureau Van Dijk, contains information on 30,000 public and private banks around the world. It combines data from another information provider, Fitch Ratings, and nine other sources, with software for search and analysis.

14.2   COMPANY ANNUAL REPORTS

Annual reports provide statements from the chairman and chief executive of a company about the immediate past performance of the company, its main achievements and the objectives for the year ahead.

The annual report will also give detailed information about a company's business – where it operates, what it does and how it interacts with stakeholders. There are many sources for company annual reports – here is a selection.

14.2.1   Free sources

Annual report information providers

Northcote:
<http://www.northcote.co.uk>
The site can be searched by particular FTSE Index, by sector, alphabetically by company name or through a general search. Registering for the 'My Portfolio' service allows investors to create lists of companies to

track. In addition to annual reports and interim results the site also provides company overviews, which provide details of the FTSE indices on which the company is listed and contact details of the company secretary.

Annual Reports:
<http://www.annualreports.co.uk>
Provides online versions of company annual reports. The site offers a number of options for searching/browsing including: company name or symbol, by the stock exchange on which they are listed, by industry or sector and finally alphabetically by company name.

CAROL:
<http://www.carol.co.uk>
CAROL provides direct links to the financial pages of listed companies in Europe and the United States, with details of company balance sheets, profit and loss statements, financial highlights and annual reports.

Reuters Annual Reports Service:
<http://reutersuk.ar.wilink.com/v5/index.asp?cp_code=P321&>
Contains an index of UK companies which provide annual reports to Reuters. A valuable and unique feature is the free, surface-posting of up to twenty-five annual reports to a user. There are three search routes to annual reports: by alphabetically by company name, by industry sector or by location. A basic but very useful site for finding company annual reports.

Corporate Reports:
<http://www.corporatereports.co.uk>
Former 'pay per view' service which now provides free access to UK company annual reports and accounts. In addition to a quick search, there are also three browsable sectors.

Tracing which library has an annual report

SCoRe, the national UK catalogue of printed company reports:
<http://www.score.ac.uk>
Search Company Reports is a catalogue of printed company reports held in UK libraries. The basic search is by company name although more options are available under the Advanced Search tab. The catalogue does not provide links to reports held in electronic form on the internet – it is only a finding tool to trace which library has a copy of the report in stock.

14.2.2   Subscriber-only services

Official company registry services

Companies House Direct:
<http://direct.companieshouse.gov.uk>
Official site for Companies House, the subscription service enables access to all documents lodged at Companies House by UK Companies and includes information on the date of the companies' incorporation, the directors of the company, the memorandum and articles of association. The site has a Company search, which includes current and dissolved companies and a Directors search. Prices for document downloads will vary dependant on the material being downloaded.

Commercial providers

Thomson Research:
<http://research.thomsonib.com>
Provides critical company information and analysts' research reports. The website provides access to forecasts and analysis based upon research reports from over 980 of the world's leading firms and covering more than 30,000 companies worldwide.

14.3 COMPANY AND MARKET NEWS

All UK listed companies must release through the London Stock Exchange Regulatory News Service (RNS) information that might affect the price of their shares. These disclosures known as Regulatory News Announcements and include details of the company's interim and final results, the share dealings of directors, merger and acquisition information and operational updates. There are number of sources for RNS announcements – here is a selection.

14.3.1 Free sources

Official source

London Stock Exchange:
<http://www.londonstockexchange.com/home/homepage.htm>
The London Stock Exchange regularly publishes RNS announcements on its website. The announcements can be searched by name/code, FTSE index or by industry sector. The site also offers 'Company Profiles' detailing a company's financial performance and financial data. It is important to remember that the London Stock Exchange provides information on only those companies listed with it.

Commercial providers

Investegate (from Financial Express):
<http://www.investegate.co.uk>
Lists announcements from UK quoted companies and, in addition, news and features on companies and particular industry sectors.

UK Company News:
<http://www.companynews.co.uk>
Contains the details of new and recent announcements, a directory of smaller quoted companies (SQC) and a directory of major quoted companies. The content on this site is a little out of date so should only be used if all other searches have failed. An email delivery service is available.

Marketwire:
<http://www.marketwire.com>
Marketwire provides press and regulatory filings from companies across the world but with more UK content that Business Wire – see below. The advanced search feature is better than the equivalent on Business Wire, including the ability to limit your search to a specific stock exchange.

Business Wire:
<http://www.businesswire.com/portal/site/home>
Business Wire provides press releases and regulatory filings from companies across the world, especially the United States and Canada.

14.3.2   Subscriber-only services

Perfect Filings:
<http://pioneer.perfectinfo.com>
See entry under section 14.1.2, above.

14.4   BUSINESS RISK

In addition to a large number of databases providing current awareness regarding specific areas outlined by an individual, there is also now the possibility of targeting or monitoring organisations that may be in financial distress. This may be for an opportunistic purpose, so as to offer legal services to an organisation in financial difficulty or limit risk for a business which is owed money.

14.4.1   Subscriber-only services

Red Flag Alert:
<http://www.redflagalert.com>
This service from accountants Begbies Traynor, allows a user to search over 6 million business records. The benefit of this product is the ability to tailor updates choosing from a range of criteria, as a result of which companies will be 'flagged' on the pre-determined criteria.

Tracker:
<http://www.trackeronline.com>
A service from accountants RMS Tenon, which is similar to Red Flag Alert. Health ratings for organisations are provided on a gold, silver or bronze scale.

14.5   ANALYST REPORTS AND RESEARCH

Analyst reports are produced by investment banks and provide excellent overviews of company and industrial sector performance. Their intended for use by investors, but the information is useful in a wider business context. There are a number of sources for analyst reports – here is a selection.

14.5.1   Free sources

Corporate Information:
<http://www.corporateinformation.com>
Provides access to analyst reports from Wright's Investors Service. Unfortunately, the free information provided comprises only a small part of that on the subscription-only section of the site. Reports on US companies are also included.

14.5.2 Subscriber-only services

OneSource:
<http://www.onesource.com>
An excellent source for analyst reports, which can be searched for by the name of the company analysed, by industry sector, and by the name of the company that produced the report (the brokerage company). The reports are available in full and as a pdf file (ie they will have the same appearance as the print-published item).

Thomson Research:
<http://research.thomsonib.com>
Provides critical company information and analyst research reports, with access to forecasts and analyses based upon research reports from over 980 of the world's leading firms and covering more than 30,000 companies worldwide.

Morning Star:
<http://www.morningstar.co.uk>
A very good source for analysts' reports and independent research.

14.6 SHARE PRICES

The share price of a company is the price of a single share of a particular type of saleable stock of the company. Once the stock is purchased, the owner becomes a shareholder of the company that issued the share. The price is calculated by dividing the market capitalisation of the company by the total number of shares outstanding.

Because shares are bought and sold throughout the working day share prices can fluctuate greatly so it's important to know where to find both the current price and the historical price of shares. There are number of sites that provide the details of share prices, although there may be a charge for 'real time' prices – here is a selection.

14.6.1 Free sources

UK companies only

Hemscott:
<http://www.hemscottir.com>
In addition to its premium services, Hemscott also provides share price data and tools.

Google Finance:
<http://www.google.co.uk/finance>
Very similar to Yahoo Finance (see below), but much improved over recent times. Easy to use, with lengthier historical share price data than that of Yahoo. Access to UK listed company share prices, stock market indexes and the latest financial and business news obtained from a number of internet sources.

Yahoo Finance:
<http://uk.finance.yahoo.com>
Provides access to share prices, stock market indexes and other business news. Links are also available to other international sites providing information. Where historical share prices have been collected they go back five years and are provided as tables as well as basic and interactive charts. Data can be downloaded in MS Excel spreadsheet format.

UK companies and abroad

Bloomberg:
<http://www.Bloomberg.com>
Bloomberg is well known for its subscription services, but this free site provides current share price service for a selection of markets. The site provides searching over news, quote (current share price) and opinion, all of which is relatively basic. There are other browsable indexes.

Reuters:
<http://uk.reuters.com/business/quotes>
This comprehensive site from Reuters provides access to UK and US company share prices, stock market indexes and the latest news and developments collected by Reuters. Where historical share prices have been collected they go back five years and can be manipulated via interactive charts. Charts also contain links to significant news stories that may have affected share prices – a feature that is unique to Reuters, and provides a significant additional service. Unfortunately there are no options to download or export content.

US companies only

Big Charts:
<http://bigcharts.marketwatch.com>
The US site provides free access to interactive charts, quotes, industry analysis, commentary and market has navigation and use is very straightforward.

14.6.2   Subscriber-only services

FT.com:
<http://www.ft.com>
The online version of the markets section of the *Financial Times*, providing equity data from the world's major stock exchanges. Currently, the only search alternatives are by company name or symbol. The site does offer some interactive charting but there are no options for the exporting or downloading content.

Datastream:
<http://online.thomsonreuters.com/datastream>
An extensive database (as above) which may well cost more than most other databases but benefits from a vast amount of information taken from over 200 different countries.

14.7   INTEREST RATES

One of the main interest rates used by lawyers is the London Interbank Offered Rate (LIBOR) which was created in the mid-1980s as a more uniform measure of financial trading than the variety employed

previously. It is used as a reference or benchmark rate in a variety of financial instruments and as a reference rate for currency movements. It is published daily by the British Bankers Association (BBA). More information will be found on their website with links to historic rates for personal use only rather than commercial or business use. Daily rates are provided by BBA on Twitter:
<http://twitter.com/BBALIBOR>

Commercial data providers such as Thomson Reuters, Bloomberg, Quick, Infotec, Class Editori, IDC, Proquote and Telekurs make LIBOR available to their subscribers.

14.8   BUSINESS NEWS

This section features business and company news sources from the United Kingdom, Europe and internationally. In the United Kingdom the market leaders for business and company news would probably be *Nexis UK* and *Factiva*. Once again, the specific requirements of the individual and organisation would dictate which service provider will suit.

14.8.1   Free sources

Reuters:
<http://www.reuters.com>
The Reuters website provides comprehensive coverage of national, regional and international news. Both business and market sections contain a broad amount of information and users who register may create their own tailored information and current awareness.

Google News:
<http://news.google.com>
This is a custom internet newspaper with articles drawn from 4,500 different news sources with the search function of Google. Much like a printed newspaper, the main stories are listed towards the top of the page, or 'above the fold' in newspaper terms. Unlike a newspaper, Google News items only provide the first paragraph of a news item. To read more, users must click on the headline, which links to the story's source website. Google News benefits from RSS feeds, regular or immediate alerts, news archive and personalisation.

14.8.2   Subscriber-only services

FT.com:
<http://www.ft.com/home/uk>
The official website of the *Financial Times*. Searching for articles is free but by registering, a set number of articles per month may be read and more sophisticated services are made available such as news tracking and portfolio building services, with email alerts and RSS feeds. Free registration of the service allows users very basic functionality, but a paid service (at different pricing levels) allow more sophisticated news and content. An outline of this may be seen at:
<http://registration.ft.com/registration/subscription-service/signuppsp?segid=70009>

Factiva.com:
<http://www.factiva.com>
Factiva incorporates material from 35,000 global news and information resources from 200 countries. The site provides comprehensive search facilities, email alerts and professional newsletters.

236 Legal Research: A Practitioner's Handbook

Nexis UK:

<http://www.lexisnexis.com/uk/nexis>

Nexis UK covers not only UK news, but also news from the United States, Europe and Asia. Apart from newspaper sources it includes information from websites, blogs, trade journals and market researchers. The site provides a number of search alternatives including company information only and a more general news search. Like most commercial databases Nexis UK provides services for users to monitor breaking news and be sent email alerts.

14.9   COMPANY DIRECTORIES

Company directories provide information on companies in the United Kingdom but to various levels of detail. A number are freely available on the internet, but only useful for finding basic information about an individual or a small number of companies. More comprehensive data is provided by the subscriber-only services which also include data formatting software for use in mailing list applications (labels, mail merge, etc).

Amongst the print sources listed below *Kelly's* and *Kompass* are well respected, but *Who owns Whom* provides more information including data on subsidiaries and parent companies than both *Kelly's* or *Kompass*.

14.9.1   Print sources

League tables

Key British Enterprises (Gap Books, 2012)
KBE provides information on 50,000 companies, including rankings for the top 5,000. Product and service, geographical, and trade indexes are provided. The publication, researched and collated by Dun & Bradstreet, consists of three volumes of company listings and a fourth volume of cross-referenced indexes and company ranking.

United Kingdom's 5000 largest companies (ELC International, 2011)
Includes lists of the largest companies organised by profit, loss and number of employees. An extensive trade index is arranged by the International Standard Business Code. An alphabetical index provides full contact details for each company including web and email addresses. Useful only to identify the top companies and their competitors in any industrial sector. GAP books acquired ELC International in 2011.

Europe's 15,000 Largest Companies (ELC International, 2012)
Lists for each European country (including the latest members to join the European Union), the top companies ranked by turnover. In addition, there are lists of the 500 largest companies in Europe, ranked by turnover, profits, and number of employees, as well as lists of the 100 largest companies in each major, industrial sector. Valuable for general review of the top companies but lacks the depth of other sources.

General sources

Kelly's Business Directory (Reed Information Services, 112th edn, 1999)
One of the best-known directories for finding details of particular businesses in the United Kingdom. The directory provides several search alternatives: by company and trade name, product, location, postcode or

specific keywords. *Kelly's* and *Kompass* are the authoritative works in this field and should be used in preference to all other works.

Kompass Register (Kompass, 2012)
A well-renowned and detailed classified listing of companies by their products and services, together with a geographical listing of 42,000 UK companies. The title provides information on directors, bankers, share capital, number of employees, products and services. Free online searching is available online for name and address information only at:
<http://www.kompass.com>

Waterlow's Stock Exchange Yearbook 2011 (incorporating Crawford's Directory of City Connections)
An essential source of financial, contact and reference information for the major London Stock Exchange quoted and unquoted companies and their advisers. The book is divided into three chapters: company information (including financial information), details of professional advisers and information on the top 2,000 major unquoted companies.

Company ownership

Who Owns Whom 2012/2013 (Gap Books, 2012)
A unique publication for establishing relationships between companies and company ownership. There are seven regional directories in total, with the one-volume United Kingdom and Ireland publication including over 375,600 entries.

14.9.2   Online sources

Free sources

The Biz:
<http://www.thebiz.co.uk>
The confusingly bare search screen hides a business directory – click the AbouttheBiz link under the search box to find information which will assist you decide whether the site is appropriate for your research needs. It employs Google to draw together web-based information on businesses, ranging from job opportunities to financial returns and business news. So, it restricts searches to free web sources. Worth a try.

Kompass:
<http://www.kompass.co.uk>
The free version of Kompass provides basic details on 2.4 million companies in sixty-six countries. Registration is required to access detailed data. The database may be searched by company name, products and services, trade name or the names of executives.

14.10   INFORMATION ON INDIVIDUALS

Finding information on individuals is important if an organisation is considering providing them with credit. The electoral roll used to be a readily available and good source of information to verify names and addresses, but access is now restricted since it has been made available in two different forms:

- the Edited Register, which excludes details of members of the public who have chosen to opt out of this part of the register, but is available to all commercial publishers;

- the Full Register, which includes the names and addresses of all people but is available to three credit-checking firms only: Call Credit, Equifax, Experian (see 'Subscriber-only services', at section 14.10.2, below).

Sources to trace information about individuals fall into two categories: general business directories which will provide a general idea of the business standing of an individual or organisation and specialised databases on individual consumers and their credit risk. It can also be extremely important for a host of other requirements for organisations.

14.10.1 Print sources

General directory

Who's Who in the City (Wilmington, 2011)
Provides biographies and contact details for over 15,000 city executives and profiles over 4,800 companies. The professional advisers section lists accountants, auditors, brokers and the full range of City advisors to enable the user to see who is working with whom and who the competitors are. A very useful guide to some of the big City names.

14.10.2 Online sources

Free sources

BT directory enquiries:
<http://www.thephonebook.bt.com/publisha.content/en/search/residential/search.publisha>
Online version of the BT phonebook. The site offers a very simple name and location search with results displayed in alphabetical order. Other search options include business name and business type.

Subscriber-only services

192.com:
<http://www.192.com>
192.com alongside BT directory enquiries (see above) is one of the best starting points for any search conducted on individuals. The site offers several search possibilities including a people and business search and electoral roll search. It is easy to use and the search results are easy to navigate. Unfortunately only limited information is provided free and a subscription is required for more.

CreditSafe:
<http://www2.creditsafeuk.com>
Creditsafe Consumer Reports help companies assess the credit-worthiness of potential customers which are other companies. The Consumer Report includes information on the applicant's name, address and any adverse data.

Call Credit:
<http://www.callcredit.co.uk>
Offers a range of services including the evaluation of an individual's credit profile and credit risk.

Experian:
<http://www.experian.co.uk>
Experian, based in Nottingham, is the largest licensed Credit Reference Agency in Britain. It provides services for individuals to obtain their credit score and services to business, of which assessing the credit risk of customers is just a small part. Experian retains credit data for one year only.

Equifax:
<http://www.equifax.co.uk>
Equifax provides similar services to Experian and offers many different subscription services to suit the requirements of users.

CHAPTER 15

INFORMATION ABOUT PEOPLE AND PERSONALITIES CONNNECTED WITH THE LAW

15.1   CENTRAL GOVERNMENT

15.1.1   Print sources

Civil Service Yearbook (Dandy Booksellers, annual)
Unique, comprehensive list of UK central government and executive agencies, and the devolved administrations of Wales, Scotland and Northern Ireland, with details of ministers and senior civil servants and their responsibilities. Departmental staff structure diagrams help trace relevant sections of departments. Clearly presented lists of contacts for general enquiries and freedom of information requests. Indexes to the names of individual officers featured, departments and subjects. Subscription now includes access to a website carrying updates to entries.

Dod's Civil Service Companion (Dod's Parliamentary Communications, annual)
An authoritative guide to the civil service, including information on every Department of State, Non-Ministerial Department, Executive Agency and Non-Departmental Body. Also contains direct contact details of 4,000 Senior Civil Servants with 400 biographies.

15.1.2   Online sources

Free sources

Gov.uk – departments, agencies and public bodies:
<https://www.gov.uk/government/organisations>
A list of central government departments, executive agencies and non-departmental public bodies with a thumbnail description of the responsibilities of each and a link to their website. The old website used to provide an extremely useful list of central government departments, executive agencies and non-departmental public bodies:
<http://www.direct.gov.uk>
It is being replaced with a new website, with departments migrating material in stages until 2014:
<https://www.gov.uk>
It is hoped that the useful information on the old site will eventually re-appear on the new one.

Subscriber-only services

Civil Service Yearbook:
<http://www.dandybooksellers.com/acatalog/Civil_Service_Yearbook_48th_Edition_2011_12_Online_Access.html#aCSYBONLINE24HOUR>
The online version of the *Civil Service Yearbook*, which was closed by the previous publisher, TSO (The Stationery Office), on 30 April 2010, and previously accessible at:
<http://www.civil-service.co.uk>
The new publisher offers short-term access for 24 hours for a single user.

Municipal Yearbook Directory Online:
<http://www.localgov.co.uk/index.cfm?method=directory.home>
Basic contact information is available free but access to the detailed listings of more than 40,000 staff in local and central government and key local government associations is by subscription only. Information contained in the full entries in this directory is not easily available elsewhere.

15.2   PUBLIC BODIES

15.2.1   Print sources

Councils, Committees and Boards: A Handbook of Advisory, Consultative, Executive and Similar Bodies in British Public Life (CBD Research Ltd, 14th edn, 2011)
A regularly updated, A–Z guide to over 1,700 councils, committees, boards, commissions, government agencies, national training organisations, quangos, tribunals and over 200 similar bodies in British public life. The publication provides contact information, details of staffing, membership, terms of reference, objects and/or mission statement, geographical area of competence, details of activities and publications. Local government and other purely local bodies excluded.

Directory of local authorities 2009 (Sweet & Maxwell, annual)
Fully updated every year, this directory contains contact information for every local authority in England, Scotland and Wales and a gazetteer of over 25,000 place names, all cross-referenced to the appropriate authority. Contact details for authorities include email and web addresses where available. Conveyancing fees and charges for each authority are provided. Contact details of other key organisations involved in the conveyancing process include Land Registry offices, principal mortgage lenders and the name of the chief solicitor for every local authority. Also available in CD format.

15.2.2   Online sources

Free sources

BIS Public Bodies Directory 2010:
<http://bis.gov.uk/assets/biscore/corporate/docs/b/11-533-bis-public-bodies-directory-2010.pdf>
This directory from the Department for Business Innovation and Skills was published in March 2011 and provides a comprehensive snapshot of the non-departmental public bodies (NDPB) sponsored by the department at 31 March 2010. The lists include information on staffing, funding and expenditure, and also statistical information on those serving on the boards of NDPBs and similar public bodies. The publication has not been updated.

Civil Service Resources
<http://www.civilservice.gov.uk/about/resources>
Provides information on non-departmental public bodies (NDPB) including annual reports on the sector and more detailed information on individual NDPBs. Copies of the Public Bodies Directory dating back to 1998 are available online.

Subscriber-only services

Municipal Yearbook Directory Online:
<http://www.localgov.co.uk/index.cfm?method=directory.home>
See entry under section 15.1.2, above.

15.3   COURTS

The United Kingdom does not have a single, unified judicial system. The three jurisdictions: England and Wales, Scotland and Northern Ireland operate separately, so it is important to identify the correct resource for the jurisdiction with which research is concerned.

15.3.1   Print sources

Shaw's directory of courts in the United Kingdom (Shaw & Sons Ltd, annual)
Widely considered to be the definitive source of information on HM Courts and related offices. Provides current details of contact names, phone/fax numbers, addresses, DX numbers, court codes, times and sittings of courts. Also includes a numerical index to enable the identification of any court, whether current, abolished or combined by its court code.

15.3.2   Online sources

England and Wales

Administrative Justice and Tribunals Council (AJTC):
<http://ajtc.justice.gov.uk>
Official site of the AJTC includes publications, consultation papers and information on the work of the Council. Site includes a basic search facility.

Administrative Justice and Tribunals Council (AJTC) Welsh Committee:
<http://ajtc.justice.gov.uk/welsh/welsh.htm>
Official site of the AJTC Welsh committee includes publications, consultation papers and information on the work of the Council. Site includes a basic search facility.

Her Majesty's Courts & Tribunals Service:
<http://www.justice.gov.uk/about/hmcts>
Her Majesty's Courts & Tribunals Service (HMCTS) is an executive agency of the Ministry of Justice (MoJ). The site includes a 'find a court form' database, cause list (calendar of forthcoming actions to be heard) and, both under the 'Courts' tab, access to the free XHIBIT database displaying the daily cause lists for Crown Courts and a court finder database.

Scotland

Scottish Courts:
<http://www.scotcourts.gov.uk>
Provides information relating to civil and criminal courts within Scotland, including the Court of Session, the High Court of Justiciary, the Sheriff Courts, District Courts and Justice of the Peace Courts. The site

also includes selected court judgments and, under 'Rules and Practice', an extensive collection of practice notes, forms, fees, rules and guidance notes on the courts.

Administrative Justice and Tribunals Council (AJTC) Scottish Committee:
<http://ajtc.justice.gov.uk/scottish/scottish.htm>
Official site of the AJTC Scottish committee includes publications, consultation papers and information on the work of the Council. Site includes a basic search facility.

Northern Ireland

Northern Ireland Courts and Tribunals Service:
<http://www.courtsni.gov.uk/en-GB/pages/default.aspx>
Official website of the Northern Ireland Courts and Tribunals Service. The site includes under 'About Us' useful court forms, under 'Services' public court lists with contact information, 'Publications' and, under 'Judicial Decisions' judgments, decisions and practice directions. There is a basic search facility and a link to advanced search, which allows users to limit a search by year and the type of information.

15.4   LAW FIRMS

15.4.1   Print sources

Butterworth's Law Directory 2013 (LexisNexis UK, 2012)
This is a primary source of information on the legal profession. Details of UK solicitors, law firms and barristers in private practice, commerce and local government and public authorities are provided. The online version is known as Lawyer Locator.

Chambers UK. A client's guide to the legal profession (Chambers & Partners, annual)
An invaluable and well-respected guide to solicitors and barristers working in over 70 specialist areas of law. The guide presents law firms and barristers by speciality as well as listing the leaders in particular fields and the 'best of the rest' A good starting point for any research into law firms, solicitors and the ranking of barristers.

Legal 500: United Kingdom (Legalease, annual)
The directory to use when looking for information on the top law firms in the United Kingdom. It provides a breakdown of the top 500 law firms by size, region and area of law. Entries are included on merit and the publication is well respected amongst the legal community as providing a fair analysis of a law firm's strengths and weaknesses. Available as an e-book from:
<http://www.legal500.com/assets/pages/ebooks/uk/uk.html>

The Legal 500: Who's who in the law (Legalease, annual)
The companion volume to the Legal 500 UK, this title contains biographies of over 20,000 of the United Kingdom's leading solicitors, barristers and in-house lawyers in an easy to navigate A–Z directory. It is a well-used and excellent resource for anyone looking for the contact details of law firms. A vast number of specific jurisdiction and practice area editions of the Legal 500 series are now also available. Available as an e-book from:
<http://www.legal500.com/assets/pages/ebooks/uk/uk.html>

15.4.2   Online sources

Find a Solicitor:

<http://www.lawsociety.org.uk/find-a-solicitor>

A searchable database for law firms and organisations throughout the United Kingdom and further afield. Search options include firm name, postcode/location, country and area of law. Unfortunately law firms may opt out of this list so it is not comprehensive, but it remains a very good starting point for law firm searches. Organisations listed are those that employ in-house solicitors or other regulated individuals.

Lawyer Locator:

<http://www.lawyerlocator.co.uk>

Online version of the *Butterworth's Law Directory* (see section 15.4.1, above). It is a free site and searches can be made by area of law, town and postcode. There is a similar search screen for barristers. Searching on the site is free and in addition to the usual searching on practice area or geographical location, users may also create an enquiry which will then be forwarded to local law firms. Firms pay a fee to be included within this directory so it should not be relied upon to provide impartial advice, especially in relation to law firm rankings.

Legal 500:

<http://www.legal500.com/assets/pages/ebooks/uk/uk.html>

Provides access to download the e-book version of the *Legal 500 series of directories* (see section 15.4.1, above). A multitude of versions of the *Legal 500* can also be browsed on the site.

Chambers UK:

<http://www.chambersandpartners.com>

Provides the online version of the various Chambers publications (see section 15.4.1, above) including United Kingdom, Europe and Global. Users may search for firm names and individual lawyers by practice area and county (where applicable). The site provides very useful summaries of the business of each law firm with links to rankings.

Welsh Firms of Solicitors on the Web:

<http://www.venables.co.uk/firmwale.htm>

Alphabetical list by firm name with link to the firm's website, prepared by Delia Venables (see section 16.1, below).

Scottish Law Firm Directory:

<http://www.scottishlaw.org.uk/lawfirms>

The Directory is the largest online directory of law firms, legal services and providers of services to the legal profession in Scotland. Scottish law firms are listed by city. Lists of English law firms and major law firms across the world are also listed. There is no search function so it is necessary to scan the list by eye. Users have noted some broken links, so the site may not be maintained up to date.

Scottish Find a Solicitor:

<http://www.lawscot.org.uk/wcm/lssservices/Find_a_Solicitor/Core/directory.aspx>

Provided by the Law Society of Scotland (the professional body for Scottish solicitors), the site allows searching for individuals and firms by name and location.

Scottish Firms of Solicitors on the Web:
<http://www.venables.co.uk/firmscota.htm>
<http://www.venables.co.uk/firmscotk.htm>
Alphabetical list by firm name with link to the firm's website in two parts: A–J and K–Z, prepared by Delia Venables (see section 16.1, below).

Northern Ireland Firms of Solicitors (Law Firms) on the Web
<http://www.venables.co.uk/firmnort.htm>
Alphabetical list by firm name with link to the firm's website, prepared by Delia Venables (see section 16.1, below).

15.5   LAW LIBRARIES

15.5.1   Print sources

Directory of British and Irish Law Libraries (BIALL, 8th edn, 2006)
See section 13.5, above.

15.5.2   Online sources

England

Bodleian Law Library:
<http://www.bodleian.ox.ac.uk/law>
Although the Bodleian Law Library building dates from 1964 it has benefitted from the legal deposit of all law works published in the British Isles over the last several centuries and contains collections of historic and national significance. Holdings cover a wide range of jurisdictions concentrating on the United Kingdom, Commonwealth and the United States. It is also a European Documentation Centre (EDC) meaning that it receives a copy of virtually every EU publication. The website has information on the collection, a series of research guides prepared by library staff especially relating to its extensive foreign law resources. The library catalogue, SOLO, which covers the majority of the library collections of the University of Oxford including the Bodleian Libraries, is available free to search on the web.

Gray's Inn Library:
<http://www.graysinn.info/index.php/library-archives>
Contains information on the library and archives services provide by Gray's Inn. The website includes a link to the library catalogue, descriptions of the library services, electronic sources available at Gray's Inn to barristers and links to external websites. See also section 13.1.2, above.

Inner Temple Library:
<http://www.innertemplelibrary.org.uk/welcome.htm>
The website includes the library catalogue, information on its collections, guides to the services offered by the library to barristers and information on the current awareness blog published by the library. The blog carries a selection of legal news and developments of interest to UK lawyers and law students. Items are collected from a wide range of websites and may be viewed by date or browsed by subject. Each posting includes a link to the full story. In addition there is a link to the Access to Law gateway of annotated links to over 1,400 selected UK, Commonwealth and worldwide legal websites. See also section 13.1.2, above and section 16.1, below.

Institute of Advanced Legal Studies (IALS):
<http://ials.sas.ac.uk>
The Institute of Advanced Legal Studies was founded in 1947. It was conceived and is funded as a national academic institution, attached to the University of London, serving all universities through its national legal research library. Its function is to promote, facilitate and disseminate the results of advanced study and research in the discipline of law, for the benefit of persons and institutions in the United Kingdom and abroad.

The Institute has a world-class collection of over 278,000 volumes and rates as the United Kingdom's national academic law library with strengths in common law, civil law and Roman-Dutch law systems throughout the world and material in western European languages for all jurisdictions. It also possesses extensive collections of international and comparative law. Details of its subscriber-only research services for law firms are provided on the website – see under Quick Links, Document Supply Services. The website provides a huge range of useful legal information.

Law Society Library:
<http://www.lawsociety.org.uk/advice/library-services>
See section 13.1.1, above.

Lincoln's Inn Library:
<http://www.lincolnsinn.org.uk/index.php/library>
Contains information on the library services including a link to the catalogue and contact information. See also section 13.1.2, above.

Middle Temple Library:
<http://www.middletemple.org.uk/library>
Provides information on the library with details of its collections, services and the archive which contains administrative, financial, membership and property records of the Inn since 1501. The library catalogue is available from the Middle Temple homepage:
<http://www.middletemplelibrary.org.uk/MID_homepage/Default.htm>
See also section 13.1.2, above.

School of Oriental and African Studies:
<http://www.soas.ac.uk/library>
Extensive academic law collections on the countries of Africa (excluding Romano-Dutch jurisdictions which are held at the Institute of Advanced Legal Studies), Asia and the Middle East. Material in western, Asian and African languages Especially strong on customary law, Islamic law, Bangladesh, China, India and Pakistan. Site has access to the library catalogue and guides to collections.

Squire Law Library:
<http://www.squire.law.cam.ac.uk>
One of several UK law libraries with collections benefiting from the legal deposit by publishers of law books published in the British Isles. Extensive holdings, covering a wide range of jurisdictions, concentrate on the United Kingdom, with special collections of antiquarian legal history material, historical labour law and legal biographies. The library also includes Commonwealth, North American, French, German international and comparative law collections. The site includes guides to each collection and access to the online catalogue

Wales

Cardiff University Law Library:
<http://www.cardiff.ac.uk/insrv/libraries/law/index.html>
Cardiff University Law Library is the largest law collection in Wales, serving one of the largest law schools in the United Kingdom. Very little Welsh law existed until the National Assembly was founded in 1999, so only a very small part of the collection relates to the law of Wales itself. An adjacent collection, the Salisbury Collection, includes historical Welsh material including Welsh public and private Acts, and medieval Welsh law texts. The website is designed for the use of students of the University rather than members of the public or practitioners so there is very little information describing the extent of the collections.

Scotland

Advocates Library:
<http://www.advocates.org.uk/library/index.html>
See section 13.2.2, above.

University of Edinburgh Law and Europa Library:
<http://www.ed.ac.uk/schools-departments/information-services/services/library-museum-gallery/using-library/lib-locate/law-lib>
The Law and Europa Library is one of the largest academic law libraries in Scotland. The Library has extensive collections of Scottish, UK, international and some foreign law. The website is designed for the use of students of the University rather than members of the public or practitioners so there is very little information describing the extent of the collections

Northern Ireland

Bar Library – Northern Ireland:
<http://www.barlibrary.com>
See section 13.3.2, above.

Queen's University Belfast Library:
<http://www.qub.ac.uk/directorates/InformationServices/TheLibrary>
The largest academic law library in the province serving the oldest law school, where law has been taught for over 150 years. A library catalogue and information on the services provide by the Library are available on the site. Click link on Access to the Library for information on the availability of library services and resources to non-members.

15.6   LEGAL PROFESSIONALS AND THEIR SOCIETIES

15.6.1   Advocates

Advocates are specialist lawyers who can represent clients in the highest courts in the United Kingdom. Advocates practise in Scotland (at the 'Scottish bar') and also in the Supreme Court in London. Advocates are similar to barristers in England and Wales.

The Faculty of Advocates:
<http://www.advocates.org.uk>
Official website of the Faculty of Advocates the website provides the details of the profession, instructing an advocate, becoming an advocate and information on the Advocates Library (see section 13.2.2, above).

The full text of the Guide to Professional Conduct is also available from the website under the tab: The Profession of Advocate.

Society of Solicitor Advocates:
<http://www.solicitoradvocates.org>
Site contains information about the Society, a members directory which can be used to search for a Solicitor Advocate, becoming a solicitor advocate and instructing a solicitor advocate. Site also includes publications produced by the society, information on training courses and links to others advocate sites. The site is not very well presented and the search engine is very basic but otherwise provides some useful information.

Solicitors Association of Higher Court Advocates (SAHCA):
<http://www.sahca.org.uk>
Website of the Solicitors Association of Higher Court Advocates, the site includes information on training and other events run by SAHCA, how to obtain 'higher rights' and publications produced by SAHCA. The site also includes a member's directory, which can be used to search for an advocate, but appears to be focused more on England and Wales than Scotland.

15.6.2   Barristers

A barrister is a member of the elder branch of the two established professions in England and Wales, and Northern Ireland. A qualified barrister automatically gains full rights of audience in the higher courts. All barristers in England and Wales belong to one of the four Inns of Court who are responsible for their admission. The websites of the four Inns libraries are described at sections 13.1.1 and 15.6.2A, above, and carry links to the general parts of the websites of each Inn. The general regulatory body for barristers in England and Wales is the Bar Council, mentioned at 'Online sources', below. In Northern Ireland barristers belong to the Bar of Northern Ireland which is responsible for their admission and discipline. The website of the General Council of the Bar of Northern Ireland is described at 'Online sources', below.

Print sources

Bar Directory (Sweet & Maxwell, annual)
Annually updated official directory of barristers and their chambers in England and Wales. Includes details of over 700 chambers and over 12,000 barristers. It provides a practical guide to finding information on barristers, chambers and their specialist practice areas.
Butterworth's Law Directory (LexisNexis Butterworths, annual)
Includes a section on barristers, full details at 15.4.1 above.

Haver's defining the Bar (Havers' Directories Ltd, annual)
This is the re-formatted edition of the highly successful publication: Havers Companion to the Bar. Published annually it is designed to assist the selection of a suitable specialist advisor or advocate, providing information about their age, education, experience, publications, languages spoken fluently, fees charged and, uniquely, lists of representative cases in which they have appeared. Unique and indispensable. The print publication is associated with the new Havers-Find-a-Barrister online database. (see below).

Law Society's directory of solicitors and barristers (The Law Society, annual)
Although compiled and published by the Law Society this directory includes listings of barristers chambers.

Online sources

England and Wales

Bar Directory:
<http://www.legalhub.co.uk/legalhub/app/appinit>
Online version of the *Bar Directory* (see 'Print sources', above). The Directory may be searched in a number of ways, including specialism, region or name of the barrister or chamber.

Bar Council:
<http://www.barcouncil.org.uk>
The General Council of the Bar (known as the Bar Council) was founded in 1894 to represent the interests of barristers. The site includes guidance on qualifying as a barrister, information on Bar CPD courses and training, chambers vacancies and the full text of the Bar Standards Board Code of Conduct. The site incorporates a basic search facility.

Bar Standards Board:
<http://www.barstandardsboard.org.uk>
Official site of the organisation that regulates the work of barristers in England and Wales. Site contains details on education and training, continuing professional development, complaints and hearings and the details of consultations.

Find a Solicitor:
<http://www.lawsociety.org.uk/find-a-solicitor/?view=solsearch>
Online version of the *Law Society's directory of solicitors and barristers* (see 'Print sources', at section 15.6.8, below). This is a simply constructed and popular database.

Havers-Find-a-Barrister:
<http://www.havers-find-a-barrister.co.uk>
Freely searchable database of 11,000 barristers providing similar details as found in the print publication: *Havers defining the Bar* (see above).

Lexis Nexis Lawyer Locator:
<http://www.lawyerlocator.co.uk>
This site allows users to search by area of law, town, postcode or firm name. Users can also search for barristers or advocates. The site also includes two useful sections on understanding legal issues (articles and checklist) and an A–Z glossary of legal terms.

Northern Ireland

General Council of the Bar of Northern Ireland:
<http://www.barlibrary.com/about-us/the-general-council-of-the-bar-of-northern-ireland>
Official website of the regulatory body for barristers in Northern Ireland. The Bar Council is responsible for the maintenance of the standards, honour and independence of the Bar and, through its Professional Conduct Committee, receives and investigates complaints against members of the Bar in their professional capacity.

Bar Library, Barrister's Directory:
<http://www.barlibrary.com/barristers-directory>
Official site of the Bar Library, a private library servicing all Northern Ireland Barristers. The Barrister's Directory is easy to use by name, year of call or specialism. Brief biographies are attached to each result. but no contact details. Contact details can be obtained only by a firm signing a confidentiality agreement with the Northern Ireland Bar Library to obtain a username and password for access to more data.

15.6.3   Judges

Judges are individuals who have been invested with powers to hear and determine legal disputes. In the United Kingdom judges are chosen from barristers of long standing, but solicitors can be appointed circuit judges.

Judiciary of England and Wales:
<http://www.judiciary.gov.uk>
Website of the judges, magistrates and tribunal members in England and Wales. The site includes under the Media tab: judgments and tribunal decisions, and under the Publications tab: guidance, practice directions and other publications. The 'About the judiciary' section provides key facts about the judiciary including information on the legal year, judicial biographies and a list of members of the judiciary. The site also includes a basic search facility.

Judicial Appointments Commission:
<http://jac.judiciary.gov.uk>
The Judicial Appointments Commission (JAC) is an independent public body that selects candidates for judicial office. The site describes its role, responsibilities, procedures and activities and includes selection exercises, application forms and information on the selection policy.

Judicial College:
<http://www.judiciary.gov.uk/training-support/judicial-college>
The Judicial College replaced the Judicial Studies Board (JSB) in 2011. It is the organisation responsible for training judges in Crown, County and higher courts. The site includes publications produced by the JSB and the Judicial College, information on training and seminars and a list of useful contacts. There is a basic site search.

15.6.4   Law Societies

Law Society of England and Wales:
<http://www.lawsociety.org.uk>
The Law Society represents solicitors in England and Wales, from negotiating with and lobbying the profession's regulators, government and others, to offering training and advice. The website provides information on the role of the Society, the work of its members, including the 'Find a Solicitor' directory of law firms and individual solicitors who have asked to be included (see 'Online sources', at section 15.6.8, below). Information on the training required to become a solicitor, complaints procedures and downloadable copies of publications.

Law Society for Scotland:
<http://www.lawscot.org.uk>
The Law Society of Scotland is the governing body for Scottish solicitors. The site has information on education and training for solicitors practising in Scotland and also includes the Find a Solicitor search, which provides the details of law firms, solicitors and organisations in Scotland. The site also offers details of CPD training, members information and links to other useful sites:
<http://www.lawscot.org.uk/wcm/lssservices/find_a_solicitor/Core/directory.aspx>

Law Society of Northern Ireland:
<http://www.lawsoc-ni.org>
Official website of the Law Society of Northern Ireland including details of firms and solicitors working across the province. The tab: 'Solicitor Directory' allows free searches for a solicitor by surname, a firm by its name, area of specialisation or location.

15.6.5   Legal Executives

Legal executive lawyers are 'authorised persons' undertaking 'reserved legal activities' alongside solicitors and barristers. A legal executive lawyer specialises in the technical aspects of a particular practice area, and has been trained to the same standard as a solicitor.

Chartered Institute of Legal Executives:
<http://www.cilex.org.uk>
The professional body which represents 22,000 trainee and practicing legal executives. The site includes a searchable directory of members and information on the qualifications required to become a legal executive. The CILEX Members Directory is rather buried at:
<http://www.cilex.org.uk/about_cilex_lawyers/cilex_lawyers_directory.aspx>

15.6.6   Magistrates

In England and Wales, magistrates, also known as Justices of the Peace (JPs), deal with either way offences (as the name implies, these are dealt with either by magistrates or by a Judge at the Crown Court) and summary offences (usually less serious offences such as making offers or minor assault). There are approximately 30,000 magistrates sitting in the 330 magistrates' courts throughout England and Wales.

Magistrates' Association:
<http://www.magistrates-association-temp.org.uk>
The Magistrates' Association is the official organisation for magistrates in England and Wales. The site includes consultation responses and publications produced by the association as well as information on becoming a magistrate.

15.6.7   Paralegals

Paralegals are individuals who assist solicitors with their work but do not have the qualified status of a solicitor, barrister or advocate. In the United States, paralegals may be referred to as legal assistants.

Institute of Paralegals:
<http://www.theiop.org>
The Institute sets standards for non-lawyers undertaking legal work. The site includes information on becoming a paralegal, education and training available and information on accredited courses. There is a basic site search facility.

National Association of Licensed Paralegals:
<http://www.nationalparalegals.co.uk>
The official website of the leading body for paralegals in England Wales includes information on courses and the career path of a paralegal. There is a basic site search facility.

Scottish Paralegal Association:
<http://www.scottish-paralegal.org.uk>
The Association represents the interests of paralegals in Scotland and the site includes information on CPD requirements and opportunities, grading, training and education. The site also includes details of paralegal vacancies. There is a basic site search facility.

15.6.8   Solicitors

Solicitors are lawyers who traditionally deal with any legal matter apart from conducting proceedings in court. In the United Kingdom the legal profession is split between solicitors and barristers, and a lawyer will usually only hold one title.

Print sources

England and Wales

Law Society's directory of solicitors and barristers (The Law Society, annual)
The only directory to draw information from the Law Society's own database of solicitors holding a practising certificate. It is published every July with comprehensive listings of solicitors firms, international solicitors and Law Society panels.

Butterworth's Law Directory (LexisNexis Butterworths, annual)
See 'Print sources', at section 15.6.2, above.

Scotland

Scottish Law Directory (LexisNexis Butterworths, annual)
Also known as the 'White Book', this publication includes the latest list of certificated solicitors and is published with the authority of the Law Society of Scotland. It is the most widely used source for anyone seeking information about legal services north of the border. A fees supplement is also available. The entry for each firm notes the categories of work undertaken but there is no index to assist in identifying firms by their work.

Online sources

England and Wales

Find a Solicitor:
<http://www.lawsociety.org.uk/find-a-solicitor/?view=solsearch>
Online version of the *Law Society's Directory of Solicitors and Barristers* (see 'Print sources', above) which includes details of both solicitors and barristers in the United Kingdom who hold a practising certificate and are licensed to practise. The site offers five search options: last name, first name, law firm/organisation, postcode/location and accreditation scheme membership. This is a simply constructed and popular database.

Lexis Nexis Lawyer Locator:
<http://www.lawyerlocator.co.uk>
The database may be searched by area of law, town, postcode or firm name. Users can also search for either barristers or advocates. The site also includes two useful sections on understanding legal issues (articles and checklist) and an A–Z glossary of legal terms.

Scotland

Scottish Law Agents Society:
<http://www.scottishlawagents.org>
The Scottish Law Agents Society (SLAS) promotes the interests of lawyers and solicitors in Scotland. The site includes the details of consultations undertaken by SLAS, information on professional competence courses as well as more general information on courses and training for Scottish solicitors.

Find a Solicitor:
<http://www.lawscot.org.uk/wcm/lssservices/find_a_solicitor/Core/directory.aspx>
This database of the Law Society of Scotland provides details of law firms, solicitors and organisations in Scotland. Solicitors may be searched for under surname, location, postcode and company name.

Northern Ireland

<http://www.lawsoc-ni.org/solicitors-directory>
Database of the Law Society of Northern Ireland searchable for a solicitor by surname, a firm by its name, area of specialisation or location.

15.7 EXPERT WITNESSES

15.7.1 Print sources

UK register of expert witnesses (JS Publications, annual)
This is an intuitive and well-presented publication, which provides the details of expert witnesses in the United Kingdom. The publication is divided into two section a Subject Index, which refers users to the main list of expert witnesses. There are also two additional indexes, one listing the surnames of expert witnesses and the second a list of abbreviations used. Both this publication and the *Expert witness directory* (below) contain only vetted experts. Also available as an online searchable database (see section 15.7.2, below).

Expert witness directory (Sweet & Maxwell, annual)
Annually updated directory containing details of over 2,600 expert witnesses within 1,800 subject areas. The publication lists contact details, qualifications and experience of individual experts and is the best source for tracing an expert witness. Also available online via Sweet & Maxwell's Legal Hub (see section 15.7.2, below).

Law Society of Scotland Directory of Expert Witnesses (W Green, annual)
Performs same function as *Expert witness directory* (above) but for Scotland only.

Irish Bar and Expert Witness Directory (Thomson Round Hall, annual)
Performs same function as *Expert witness directory* (above) but for Ireland and Northern Ireland only.

15.7.2   Online sources

Academy of Experts:
<http://www.academy-experts.org>
The Academy of Experts is a professional body for expert witnesses in the United Kingdom and around the world. The site includes a free to use register of expert witnesses but for a fee a more detailed matching service: 'ExpertSearch' will match an expert/s to client requirements. Guidance for expert witnesses and mediators is also provided, information about training and accreditation and other protocols.

Expert Witness Directory:
<http://www.legalhub.co.uk/legalhub/app/main?ao=o.I08d91280856011db9e0cf7c65c333a4a&ndd=2&rs=&vr=&bctocguid=I369f4260639711dba7e5e11db8d74eba&ststate=S;S&linktype=toc>
The online version of the *Expert witness directory* (see section 15.7.1, above). Provides a comprehensive search of expert witnesses in the United Kingdom. Search options include specialism, name and region. Individual expert witness profiles are very detailed, with contact information, specialisms and experience all clearly presented.

Expert Witness Institute:
<http://www.ewi.org.uk>
Contains information on the work of the Institute including training and events, membership information and links to related organisations. There is also a basic expert finding resource which is searchable by sector, profession and expertise.

Society of Expert Witnesses:
<http://www.sew.org.uk>
The Society aims to promote excellence in the work of expert witnesses. The free to use membership directory search feature is easy to use, precise and provides useful information about the expert.

The Law Society of Scotland – Expert Witnesses Directory:
<http://www.expertwitnessscotland.info>
Online version of the print directory (see section 15.7.1. above). This site is a fine source of information on expert witnesses not only in Scotland, but also in England, Wales and Northern Ireland. There are three ways to search the site: a structured search (which searches across experience, location and expertise); keyword search (subject search) and name search (name of expert). This is a well-presented and intuitive site, which provides a comprehensive search tool for expert witnesses.

UK Register of Expert Witnesses:
<http://www.jspubs.com>
Online version of the UK register of expert witnesses (see section 15.7.1, above). The expert witness search feature is free to use but the names and contact information of individual experts are withheld from the free part of the site and a subscription is required to view them.

CHAPTER 16

PORTALS, GATEWAYS AND MORE

Here is a selection of valuable sources of legal research information which do not fit into the earlier chapters.

16.1   PORTAL WEBSITES

Portal websites or link pages are classified lists of links to websites developed by subject specialists in law or information technology. They are highly subject-specific so are one of the best places to start a web search in law if you have drawn a blank with the commercial databases and websites featured in earlier chapters. The arrangement of links varies from site to site, and some have a search facility built into the page to assist users locate a relevant site. The most popular are as follows.

Legal resources in the United Kingdom and Ireland maintained by Delia Venables:
<http://www.venables.co.uk>
Delia Venables is an independent computer consultant in the legal field. Her pages contain a wealth of information and links and are probably the most comprehensive law portal pages for UK practitioners. The majority of sites featured are free to use.

Access to Law:
<http://www.accesstolaw.com>
Award-winning site of over 1,400 annotated links to free UK and Commonwealth law websites, focusing especially on the needs of the practitioner. Most sites linked to carry free information. Portal selected and annotated by Inner Temple Library staff.

Lawlinks, legal information on the internet:
<http://www.kent.ac.uk/library/subjects/lawlinks>
Developed by law library staff at the University of Kent, this has more of an academic bias to the sites featured, including some which only staff and students at the University of Kent may access. However, the site is more clearly structured than Delia Venables' and includes free European Union, Council of Europe and international law sites, not featured on her portal.

16.2   SEARCHABLE SUBJECT GATEWAY

Unlike the portals described above, which list websites in hierarchies each website link accompanied by a brief descriptions, the subject gateway includes a search engine to find sites in the database which match the subject terms requested by the user. Further, the gateway featured below selects only the best websites for inclusion and provides evaluative descriptions.

The award winning and best subject gateway for law was:

Intute: law:
<http://www.intute.ac.uk/law>
Unfortunately, in July 2011, funding for the maintenance and development of this resource was withdrawn. The site still operates, but since the records then existing have been taken over by the Institute of Advanced Legal Studies, University of London, and incorporated in its Eagle-i database, researchers should use in preference the database described below.

Eagle-i – Electronic Access to Global Legal Information:
<http://ials.sas.ac.uk/eaglei/project/eiproject.htm>
A vast but easily searchable database of law websites. Selection of the 4,500 or more sites in the database has been quality controlled. Each entry carries an evaluative description of its contents. Eagle-i has worldwide coverage and includes records for sites dealing with more than 200 countries (including the United Kingdom) as well as non-governmental international bodies and organisations involved in international law.

16.3   OVERSEAS DOMESTIC LAW

Whilst this book has specifically avoided detail on researching overseas jurisdictions – where do you draw the line? – here is a selection of websites which may assist.

School of Oriental and African Studies – resource guides:
<http://www.soas.ac.uk/library/subjects/law/region>
Extensive array of links to free sources of law and legal information especially useful for Islamic law, Middle East, Asia and Africa.

Institute of Advanced Legal Studies – research guides:
<http://ials.sas.ac.uk/library/guides/guides.htm>
Although devised by an academic institution primarily for its staff and students, the online research guides for a selection of overseas jurisdictions identify and describe the major legal research sources in both print and electronic format.

FLAG – Foreign Law Guide:
<http://193.62.18.232/dbtw-wpd/textbase/collsearch.htm>
A searchable database of the collections of foreign, comparative and international law held in over fifty university libraries, the British Library, the National Library of Wales, the Advocates' Library (Edinburgh) and the four Inns libraries in London. Can search by country or international organisation, by type of legal material (legislation, treaties, court reports, etc) and specify results for libraries in a particular region of the United Kingdom, to identify where print materials are held.

GlobalLex:
<http://www.nyulawglobal.org/Globalex>
Hosted by New York University School of Law this website contains a cornucopia of authoritative guides to researching overseas jurisdictions, international and comparative law.

LLRX.com:
<http://www.llrx.com/legal-research.htm>
A free website run since 1996 by the sole founder and owner: Sabrini Pacifici. Contains hundreds of articles written by well qualified and experienced law librarians, on how to research a wide range of topics. Distinct US bias to some of the material but well worth exploring on foreign law topics, see:
<http://www.llrx.com/category/1050>

Winterton J and Moys EM, *Information Sources in Law* (Bowker-Saur, 2nd edn, 1997)
Whilst largely pre-dating the internet era, this book still has great value. Each of the thirty-one chapters describes a different European jurisdiction ranging alphabetically from Austria to the states of the former Yugoslavia. The information is arranged under common headings: the legal system, methods of legal research, legislation, codes and commentaries, treaties, law reports and judgments, online systems (very out of date in some instances), government publications, law encyclopedias, directories, current information sources and useful addresses. Each chapter is written by a specialist in the legal materials of that country so the descriptions are authoritative, detailed and accurate. Still useful to identify the major law research sources in each jurisdiction.

16.4 INTERNATIONAL AND COMPARATIVE LAW

Specific guides on some of the websites listed below have been featured elsewhere in this book. It is worth exploring these sites to see if there is a guide to finding information within a particular practice area as opposed to a particular jurisdiction.

Institute of Advanced Legal Studies – research guides:
<http://ials.sas.ac.uk/library/guides/guides.htm>
See section 16.3, above.

GlobalLex:
<http://www.nyulawglobal.org/Globalex>
See section 16.3, above.

LLRX.com:
<http://www.llrx.com/legal-research.htm>
See section 16.3, above.

ASIL electronic resource guide:
<http://www.asil.org/erg>
This part of the American Society of International Law website includes a number of free and authoritative guides, designed to be used by students, teachers, practitioners and researchers as a self-guided tour of relevant, quality, up-to-date online resources covering important areas of international law.

PART C

PRESENTING THE RESULTS EFFECTIVELY

Contents

CHAPTER 17

WRITING TO IMPRESS

17.1   WHAT THIS CHAPTER IS ABOUT

The results of legal research are usually presented in the form of a research memorandum or an email, addressed to any member of a law firm or, in a barristers' chambers, a pupil master/mistress who may have requested the research, a legal letter or a report directed to the client. Knowing who the research is for and how that person would like it presented is essential.

The manner in which the results of research are presented (the general layout, use of typeface, headings, paragraphs, the clarity and logic with which the findings are expressed, the consistency and clarity in referencing sources, etc) will influence the view formed by the intended audience of the quality and authority of the work.

This chapter covers three aspects of written presentation:

- writing skills themselves,

- the use of style manuals to create consistency and readability,

- a specific type of style manual: for legal citations.

Good writing skills are a personal attribute. The other two aspects, relating to the use of style manuals, are perhaps matters outside personal control. Some large law firms may have adopted a particular legal style manual published commercially, like the ones described below, or have even developed an in-house manual to provide consistency in the way written work is presented, as a way of promoting best practice and a corporate image to clients, regardless of which practice area or partner is dealing with the issue. But staff in small firms and many chambers will not be aware of, let alone use style manuals to improve consistency and readability of written work.

Much has been published on the development in lawyers of good writing skills. Style manuals are substantial documents the product of much research, consultation and development, usually by committees of interested parties rather than individuals. For these reasons, this chapter merely draws attention to the key sources on all three aspects of presentation and evaluates each publication in turn – it does not reproduce what is within them. The intention behind the evaluative lists which follow is to help you decide which source will best suit your needs or those of your firm or chambers, and then provide sufficient information to enable you trace a copy and assess the publication for yourself.

The use of Latin abbreviations, such as op. cit., in text is a contentious issue. No sides are taken, but in Appendix 1.3 is a list of common textual abbreviations with their meaning.

In one area computer technology is making accurate writing easier – *Lexis®Check* automatically checks citations in legal documents as they are drafted, applying *Lexis®Library* technology to the task. It checks that legislation is in force displaying links into the full text on *Lexis®Library*, that cases have not received negative judicial comment and for both provides links to related material be it other cases, legislation or commentary. This is a powerful tool which makes accurate and reliable citation easier to accomplish, but is available only as a subscription service.

17.2   ADVICE ON GOOD WRITING SKILLS

Publications are organised below in two groups: those more applicable to the trainee or pupil, and those of more appeal to the qualified practitioner, dealing with the topic in greater depth.

17.2.1 Basic guides designed to support trainee or pupil skills development

Higgins, E and Tatham, L, *Successful Legal Writing* (Sweet & Maxwell, 2nd edn, 2011)
Although aimed at LLB and CPE students, and focused on essay and assignment writing, the chapters on how to evaluate research sources, the writing process and writing good English have universal application. Provides step-by-step advice with worked examples. Many activities are scattered throughout the book to reinforce the techniques and tips explained.

Elkington, A et al, *Skills for Lawyers* (College of Law, annual)
Aimed at students following the Legal Practice Course (LPC) run by the College of Law and written by a number of the College's staff. Updated annually. Part I briefly deals with writing and drafting and is largely in the style of bullet point checklists of points to watch. Good as a primer only – no worked examples or activities to undertake.

Webb, J et al, *Lawyers' Skills* (Oxford University Press, annual)
Annually updated guide to support training and learning on the Legal Practice Course (LPC). Chapter 3 deals with legal writing focusing on planning, writing and revising legal letters, memoranda and emails; strategies to improve writing; varying language and style to suit the needs of the reader, and developing a

self-critical approach to the use and development of writing skills. Section on writing emails sets out basic rules and etiquette of using the medium. All the material is clearly presented with case examples, activities and tests to reinforce learning.

Boyle, F et al, *A Practical Guide to Lawyering Skills* (Cavendish, 3rd edn, 2005)
Substantial compendium on lawyers' skills, including written communication, aimed at students following either the Legal Practice Course (LPC) or Bar Professional Training Course (BPTC). Chapter 1 deals with the basic principles of planning to write, using plain English and presentation. Chapter 2 applies writing skills to letters, memoranda, briefs, attendance notes and reports. Many examples of good practice included in the text but no activities or exercises.

17.2.2 More detailed guides of value to trainees, pupils and practitioners

Costanzo, M, *Legal Writing* (Cavendish Publishing, 1993)
Very readable, thorough and user-friendly guide dealing with writing letters, memoranda, briefs to counsel, articles, newsletters and speeches. Does not cover writing formal legal documents such as contracts, agreements or pleadings. Describes the art of writing, techniques to help the writer think through a problem before producing a draft, how to manage paragraphs, how to create and organise sentences, classes of word to avoid, structures and patterns to use to convey legal argument, and ends with a three week structured course to improve writing skills, together with valuable checklists. It is written by a former solicitor who has trained lawyers in private practice in the United Kingdom and overseas.

Perrin, T, *Better Writing for Lawyers* (Law Society of Upper Canada, c1990)
Detailed, yet eminently readable, forensic approach to developing better writing skills aimed at practitioners as well as advanced students. The bulk of the book describes the six stages through which a piece of written work should pass: checking the truth and accuracy of information and ensuring internal consistency, developing a good, logical overall structure for documents, creating clearly structured paragraphs, creating well formed sentences expressing concepts and ideas in an unambiguous manner, choosing the right words for the audience and occasion and, finally, checking for grammar, spelling and punctuation.

17.3 STYLE MANUALS

17.3.1 General style manuals

Many are intended for scholarly writing and publication, but here are two which, with abridgement, could form the basis for the development of a style manual for a law firm.

Ritter, RM, *The Oxford Guide to Style* (Oxford University Press, 2002)
This volume (623 pages) is a revised and enlarged edition of Horace Hart's *Rules for Compositors and Readers at the University Press, Oxford*, also known as *Hart's Rules*. *Hart's Rules* was the first guide of its kind and is still the standard publication. The *Oxford Guide* sets out rules for consistency in the presentation of writing, covering punctuation, use of capital letters, italics, hyphenation, abbreviations and quotations. Chapter 13.2 devotes more than fifteen pages to rules on good written presentation for law and legal references.

University of Chicago Press, *The Chicago Style Manual* (University of Chicago Press, 16th edn, 2010)
This is the US equivalent of the *Oxford Guide to Style* and runs to over 1,000 pages. In addition to advice on the same topics originally aimed at staff of the University of Chicago Press, the book covers grammar and word useage, albeit form an American standpoint. Only a small part of the text: Legal and public documents, is devoted to citing law and official publications and includes sections on Canadian and UK citation practice.

17.3.2 Law style manuals

There are none generally available in the United Kingdom, though the following reference was found in the catalogue of a university library in Scotland:

Sweet & Maxwell Ltd, *Sweet & Maxwell's house style book: the preparation of books for Sweet & Maxwell, W Green* (Sweet & Maxwell, 3rd edn, 1997)

As noted at section 17.1, above, large law firms and many law publishers have compiled in-house (unpublished) style manuals to ensure consistency in the presentation of written information. These manuals contain some information drawn from the general style manuals mentioned above, but focus most advice on the development of a recognisable 'house style' and consistent use layout and law-specific, words and phrases. Indeed, many document creation systems within law firms force staff to use a specified style.

Here are a few examples of the different types of guidance a law style-manual covers:

- Which typeface and font size should be used;

- The width of margins;

- Should text be left or right justified, or both;

- How should itemised lists be laid out – a) or (a) or i) or (i) or 1) or (1) or using bullet points;

- Should headers and footers be used, and if so, what may they contain;

- Should page numbers be used, and if so, where should they be placed and which type face should be used;

- Capitalisation for the names of official bodies: Court of Appeal, but should an initial capital be used in the phrase 'the Court decided'; should it be Government or government;

- Use of singular or plural – 'the government is' or 'the government are';

- Case citations – should they be given every time or only on the first instance a particular case is referred to;

- Hyphenation: trade mark law or trade-mark law;

- Spellings: judgment or judgment; by-law or bye-law;

- Latin abbreviations, words and phrases: ibid, supra, et seq, ratio, obiter, mens rea – should they be used and, if so, should they be in italics or normal typeface;

- Ship's names – in italics or not;

- Abbreviations: for example, (a) should the title of an official document be spelt out in full or may it be abbreviated: Civil Procedure Rules or CPR; (b) schedule or sch; article or art?

17.4   STYLE MANUALS FOR LEGAL CITATIONS

17.4.1   Why use them?

A citation manual provides:

- standards for the structure and content of legal citations – it is a repository of accepted citation practices;

- a writer with guidance, perhaps shortening the time spent writing.

References made in written work to earlier documents are created for two reasons:

- to cite the authority for statements made in the text;

- to make acknowledgements.

Citations should be set out in accordance with generally accepted standards otherwise the reader will have difficulty understanding which document is being referred to and tracing it in a library or database. This will reduce the impact your work will have on readers and cause them to question the authority of your arguments.

Citation style manuals specifically for law probably originated in the United States. The first part of this section describes the three leading US titles. In the United Kingdom interest in these titles may be limited to lawyers in the UK branches of US firms, who may be required to follow practice in the US parent.

The UK manuals are described in the second part of this section. Amongst the US manuals, *The Bluebook* probably influenced the development of the three UK manuals most. The first UK manual was published in the 1950s but it was not until the last fifteen years that more attention was given to this aspect of presenting the results of legal research.

Many UK publishing houses have developed their own in-house citation manuals to assist the development of uniformity in citation practice within their own publications. But it is only now that in the United Kingdom a generally accepted citation manual is beginning to emerge. The Oxford Standard for the Citation of Legal Authorities (OSCOLA) has the tacit support of a number of publishing houses and looks set to become more widely accepted than any previous attempt to document and guide UK citation practice.

17.4.2   US citation manuals

The Bluebook: a uniform system of citation, compiled by the editors of the *Columbia Law Review*, the *Harvard Law Review*, the *University of Pennsylvania Law Review*, and the *Yale Law Journal* (Harvard Law Review Association, 19th edn, 2010)
The first edition was published in 1926 and, significantly, compiled by the editors of the leading US academic law journals. It has an academic tone about it. The standards are set out in three major parts: first, general standards for the citation and style to be used in legal writing; second, specific rules for the citation of cases, statutes, books, periodicals, foreign materials, international materials, etc; finally, a series of tables which detail which particular publication or authority should be used, when more than one is

available, and how to abbreviate it correctly. The main focus of *The Bluebook* is on US citation practice and it has been criticised for not being user-friendly, since it contains over-elaborate and complex rules, lacking uniformity. It is not recommended for use by UK practitioners.

Frustration with *The Bluebook* led to the creation and publication of the following two citation style manuals.

Universal Citation Guide, compiled by the Citation Formats Committee of the American Association of Law Libraries, AALL Publication Series no 68 (WS Hein, 2nd edn, 2004)
Although acknowledging *The Bluebook* as the premier American legal citation manual, this publication by the American Association of Law Libraries seeks 'to assist *courts, law makers* and others who are considering the adoption of a universal citation, with a useable framework upon which to craft their own rules': Preface to 2nd edn, page xiii (emphasis added). It includes rules for referring to judicial decisions, constitutions, statutes, administrative decisions, regulations, court rules and law reviews. It is much shorter than and not as comprehensive as *The Bluebook* but covers most principles basic to the creation of citations for primary sources. Secondary sources are not covered nor are a number of citation-related concerns including writing style, typeface conventions or quotations.

ALWD Citation Manual: a professional system of citation, compiled by the Association of Legal Writing Directors (Aspen, 4th edn, 2010)
Drawn up by a committee of law professors it is now used widely within US law schools and among paralegals. It is designed to be a simpler system of citation for all types of legal material than *The Bluebook*. For example, one of the long overdue changes from *The Bluebook* is that the *ALWD Citation Manual* contains one system for all legal documents, making no distinction between law review articles and other types of writing. It is divided into six parts, with six appendices. The full version of the second edition is available only in print form and runs to over 450 pages. A selection of material is available to view on the ALWD website. The *ALWD Citation Manual* has received a good press offering a more readable and useable alternative to *The Bluebook*:
<http://www.alwd.org/publications/citation_manual.html>

Martin, Peter W, *Introduction to Basic Legal Citation* (available online only, 2012 edn)
<http://www.law.cornell.edu/citation>
Online guide to US citation practice based on both *The Bluebook* and the *ALWD Citation Manual*, available in three different e-book formats only. Primarily aimed at US law students to act as a guide to the two citation manuals aiming to identify the more important points where there is divergence between the two sets of rules.

17.4.3   UK citation manuals

Manual of Legal Citations: *Part 1: The British Isles – Part 2: The British Commonwealth* (University of London, Institute of Advanced Legal Studies, 1959–1960)
The first manual of UK legal citation practice. It was drawn up by academic lawyers under the auspices of the Institute of Advanced Legal Studies, University of London to create generally accepted standards. Although it was a milestone publication its influence did not extend much beyond academic publishing.

French, D, *How to Cite Legal Authorities* (Blackstone Press, 1996)
A single-handed attempt by a legal author and editor, to set out in print 'conventions which are familiar to lawyers in the United Kingdom ... the British Commonwealth and the Republic of Ireland': Preface. It covers how to cite cases, Acts of Parliament, Parliamentary publications such as Hansard, Bills and Command Papers, subordinate legislation, books and articles. It also presents recommendations on typography and the punctuation of citations. Also included are lists of regnal years, abbreviations for the titles of law reports and other publications, and a list of recommended forms of citation for law reports and other publications. However, for the busy practitioner, the mix of historical background relating to a particular form of law publication, such as nominate law reports, followed by recommendations for citation practice and examples of the recommendation applied, can be confusing. The lists of abbreviations for law reports often does not mention the form of citation or abbreviation preferred by the publisher of the law report or law journal and printed in their publication.

Whilst this publication was the product of considerable effort, it is now overshadowed by OSCOLA, developed in the last decade – see below.

OSCOLA (The Oxford Standard for Citation of Legal Authorities):
<http://www.law.ox.ac.uk/publications/oscola.php>
Developed by staff of the Oxford Law Faculty, the latest revision of OSCOLA is available either as a print publication from Hart Publishing or on the internet, free of charge. It is updated every two or three years. Part 1 sets out general notes on good citation practice with many examples, followed by Part 2 providing standards for the citation of UK primary legal sources. The latest revision of Part 2 devotes considerable space to providing guidance on the citation of authorities from the constituent jurisdictions of the United Kingdom, as well as the European Union and the European Court of Human Rights. Part 3 covers the citation of secondary sources of law and Part 4 consists of appendices. Each section of the publication includes the statement of a citation rule followed, in many cases, by an example of the rule employed in practice. It does not cover a number of citation-related concerns including writing style, typeface conventions or quotations. A 'quick reference guide' at the back of the publication is very handy. Standards on 'Citing International Law' were included up to the 2006 revision but do not appear in the latest version. However, there is a link to the 2006 standard on the home page for OSCOLA, under the heading Supporting Materials. Some of the success of the guide probably stems from the award-winning online tutorial 'Citing the law' – see the link from the OSCOLA home page under the heading: Supporting Materials. The tutorial was compiled by a team led by staff from the Law Library of Cardiff University, and contains explanations and exercises on the use of key parts of the Standard. The tutorial may be accessed directly at:
<https://ilrb.cf.ac.uk/citingreferences/oscola/tutorial>

For more on the latest edition of OSCOLA and also its use in conjunction with reference software, such as Endnote and RefWorks, see Meredith, S, 'OSCOLA, a UK standard for legal citation' (2011) 11 *Legal Information Management* 111–114.

PART D

HOW TO GET THE BEST DEAL FROM COMMERCIAL LAW PUBLISHERS

Contents

CHAPTER 18

BUYING LEGAL INFORMATION

18.1   INTRODUCTION

The market served by law publishers is diverse, including the academic community (universities and colleges), practising lawyers, Government and administration at national and local levels, the courts and judiciary, and the general public. Broadly speaking, law publishers fall into three groups: the Government and other official local, national and international bodies; commercial publishers; and, lastly, special interest organisations and professional bodies.

Each of these publishing groups produces a significant number of publications, all of which are of potential use to anyone researching law. However, this chapter focuses solely on the work of commercial law publishers and discusses:

- who the main commercial publishers are;

- how to buy information in print format;

- the challenges and pitfalls of buying online information;

- hints and tips when negotiating with online law information providers.

18.2   WHO ARE THE MAIN COMMERCIAL PUBLISHERS?

Legal publishing in the United Kingdom has been dominated for a time by LexisNexis UK <http://www.lexisnexis.co.uk> and Sweet & Maxwell <http://www.sweetandmaxwell.co.uk>, both of whom provide both paper and online offerings. Recently, however, a further organisation has entered the UK marketplace: the *Practical Law Company* (*PLC*) <http://uk.practicallaw.com>, which provides an online product, but one which has resulted in a significant impact on the legal information accessible within organisations. In March 2013 Thomson Reuters had its planned acquisition of *PLC* approved by the Office of Fair Trading. The effect of such will possibly remain unknown for some time, although immediate changes to *PLC* or swift integration to any other Thomson Reuters services are doubtful.

LexisNexis UK is part of Reed Elsevier, an Anglo-Dutch FTSE-100 publisher and information provider. LN specialises in legal, tax, news and business information and comprises the two imprints: Butterworths and Tolley. It is linked with the online database *Lexis®Library*.

Sweet & Maxwell is a well-established UK publisher, which joined the Canadian Thomson Organisation in 1987, and is now part of the Thomson Reuters group. Its UK group includes W Green in Scotland and Round Hall in Ireland. Sweet & Maxwell is responsible for the electronic database *Westlaw UK*, as well as the *Lawtel*, *LocalawUK*, *Legal Hub* and DocDel services.

PLC was created in 1990 by two fee-earners, Rob Dow and Chris Millerchip, from the law firm Slaughter & May, with the intention of providing a comprehensive legal forms and drafting package. The service now offers practice area specific matters and also benefits from a US arm.

There are a large number of other publishers in this area. A number of years ago it appeared that the majority of legal publications would be produced by Sweet & Maxwell and LexisNexis UK as they purchased a number of smaller organisations. Recently, however, the market has seen a reduction in this strategy. Indeed, the reverse has been the case, with some smaller publishers purchasing the rights to obtain titles from the major providers.

Some of the mid-market publishers worthy of a mention are as follows.

Informa:
<https://www.informalawlibrary.com>
Informa publishes an online i-law product and *Lloyds Law Report*.

Oxford University Press:
<http://ukcatalogue.oup.com/category/academic/law.do#.UPU0HvKtqQs>
Oxford University Press has added a number of professional titles to its catalogue, to accompany its many academic publications (largely through the acquisition of Blackstone Press).

Jordan Publishing:
<http://www.jordanpublishing.co.uk>
Jordan Publishing has moved a number of its print titles online.

Other publishers with legal titles which may be of use include the following.

Bloomsbury Publishing (formerly Tottel):
<http://www.bloomsburyprofessional.com>

City & Financial:
<http://www.cityandfinancial.com/publications>

Hart Publishing:
<http://www.hartpub.co.uk/books>

The Law Society:
<http://bookshop.lawsociety.org.uk/ecom_lawsoc/public/home.jsf>

Legal Action Group:
<http://www.lag.org.uk/Templates/System/Publications.asp?NodeID=88850>

Legalease:
<http://www.legalease.co.uk/component/page,shop.browse/option,com_virtuemart/Itemid,53>

Peer Practice Publishing:
<http://igpweb.igpublish.com/igp/xpl-publishing>

Shaw & Sons:
<http://www.shaws.co.uk>

Spiramus:
<http://www.spiramus.com>

Waterside Press:
<http://www.watersidepress.co.uk>

Wildy, Simmonds & Hill:
<http://www.wildy.com/wildy-simmonds-hill>

Wiley:
<http://eu.wiley.com/WileyCDA/Section/id-351003.html>

Wilmington:
<http://www.wilmington.co.uk/contact/wilmington-publishing-%26-information>

Wolters Kluwer Law and Business (Kluwer Law International):
<http://www.kluwerlaw.com>

In addition to *PLC*, there are also other organisations which publish solely online, with the most well known probably being *Justis*:
<http://www.justis.com>

As outlined in previous chapters, there is a reasonable proportion of free online information available in addition to that provided by the commercial publishers mentioned above. This may be provided on legal websites or blogs, created by law firms and chambers particularly keen to illustrate their expertise with cutting-edge information.

18.3   HOW TO BUY INFORMATION IN PRINT FORMAT

There are, broadly speaking, three main methods to buy print information: directly from the publisher, from a legal bookshop and through a subscription agent. Each has advantages and disadvantages.

18.3.1   Purchasing materials directly from a legal publisher

All publishers have some form of ordering service, whether by phone or, more usually, through a website. This results in fairly minimal contact with customers.

However, large law firms may be able to obtain the services of a dedicated account manager within a publishing house, who is the main point of contact with a legal publisher and can be a useful conduit for any problems you need attended to. Depending on the size of the legal publisher, account managers may also order materials on your behalf and may meet regularly with the customer to discuss any new publications and developments within their area of expertise. Some of the biggest organisations such as City law firms may also be designated a 'Key Account', with the services of a designated account manager and the possibility of dedicated ordering, technical and content help-lines.

Advantages

- it avoids the middle-man bookseller or agent;

- it can make internal administration easier;

- publishers should normally have direct access to their own products and therefore should not be out of stock;

- customers may be provided with more information on titles that are relevant to them and news on product development;

- discounts may be available for large orders or repeat business.

Disadvantages

- if you are an individual lawyer or a small organisation you will have less influence with the publisher than a subscription agent or bookseller. This could mean that pursuing perceived problems is not so easy and could be more time-consuming;

- establishing a good working relationship with a large publishing house is more difficult than with a subscription agent or bookseller;

- the publisher will require that an account is set up sometimes in the form of a pre-payment account for purchases;

- there is usually no opportunity to obtain publications on approval, as may be available through a subscription agent or some booksellers;

- the standard of customer service from legal publishers is considered in the legal information profession to be usually quite poor, despite some progress having been made recently.

18.3.2 Purchasing materials from a legal bookshop

Legal bookshops such as Wildy <http://www.wildy.com>, Blackwells <http://www.blackwells.com> and Hammicks <http://www.hammicks.com> are normally used by law firms or chambers where a large number of purchases are being made, across several subject fields and from many different legal publishing houses.

Advantages

- free catalogues and newsletters are available, some describing forthcoming and new publications in detail;

- orders from a very wide range of publishing houses can be fulfilled;

- staff have subject-specialist skills and expertise and can offer a knowledgeable and personalised service;

- on-approval services may be available to assist law firms and chambers decide whether to purchase a particular title;

- some bookshops offer 'value-added services' such as free courier delivery for materials required urgently;

- overseas publications can be acquired for firms and chambers with the minimum of fuss for the purchaser;

- if the volume of orders is significant, an account manager may be provided by the bookshop;

- significant customers may be offered access to online systems to manage and amend their orders, subscriptions and invoices, together with the possibility of creating and downloading reports on their own accounts;

- bookshops may be more responsive than a publisher to customer suggestions for improvements to service;

- some large bookshops such as Wildy and Hammicks have teams of account managers who visit firms across the country and provide a valuable customer liaison service;

- discounts may be offered for large orders (by value and quantity).

Disadvantages

- an invoice may be issued with each separate purchase making financial control and administration for the customer more time-consuming;

- some of the disadvantages of using a middle-man will apply;

- a publisher will often not discuss one of its products with a firm or individual who usually orders via a bookshop rather than with the publisher.

18.3.3 Purchasing materials from a subscription agent

Subscription agents include the following.

Wildy:
<http://www.wildy.com>

Blackwells:
<http://www.blackwells.com>

Hammicks:
<http://www.hammicks.com>

Swets:
<http://www.swets.com>

EBSCO:
<http://www.ebsco.com>

Prenax:
<http://www.prenax.co.uk>

Advantages

- subscription agents offer a broad range of services, from the management of print and electronic journals to the purchasing of books, looseleafs and other hard copy resources;

- all subscription agents provide a dedicated account manager and customer service representatives who will manage your account;

- a subscription agent saves administration time by providing a single contact for invoicing, payments, claims for the non-supply of serial publications ordered by subscription and any other matters that need to be handled by a customer service team;

- subscription agents may provide access to their online systems, ranging from the functionally rich (Blog and RSS feeds) to the most basic 'view your subscriptions online';

- some subscription agents will carry out book and journal processing, such as adding ownership stamps and labels, and spine labelling of shelf marks for books – see below for a note on 'consolidation';

- discounts may be offered for large orders (by value and quantity).

Disadvantages

- subscription agents may charge a fee for administering looseleaf and journal subscriptions. There are a number of models which a subscription agent may use:

  - the list price of the journal/looseleaf plus an agreed percentage;

  - the list price plus a fee, agreed in advance, usually calculated on the potential spend of the customer over a period.

- it may still be necessary for the customer to deal direct with some publishers of journals and looseleafs since the subscriptions will be in the name of the customer, not the agent;

- some subscription agents may not wish to manage subscriptions for individuals and very small firms since the agent's profit margin is dictated by the volume of orders placed with them by each customer – however, Wildy and Hammicks will run subscriptions on behalf of small firms, individual barristers and solicitors, as well as the large organisations.

Librarians of most large organisations agree that the potential savings that can be made by directing all print and subscription orders to a subscription agent makes the process worthwhile, although it should be noted that there are some added costs (delivery, courier and administration charges). For an individual or a very small organisation using a subscription agent may not be worthwhile. Any organisation considering using a subscription agent should check carefully whether the subscription agent's prices are exactly the same as the publishers or whether they include a mark-up.

The decision to use either an agent, a bookshop or a publisher depends on a number of additional factors, for example, price, the specific requirements of the organisation and the personalities of those whom you may be dealing with. Peer recommendations are often used to assist the final decision.

A relatively new service offered by some subscription agents to law firms is 'consolidation'. With consolidation subscription agents handle most of the administrative tasks related to the purchasing of journals and looseleafs. These tasks include checking-in journal issues, labelling them before they are dispatched to the customer, providing a consolidated dispatch of all items and of course consolidated invoices for all the items supplied. Subscription agents also automatically claim and dispatch missing issues. Quite apart from the benefits of consolidation itself, having a single person contact in the subscription agent's organisation for queries relating to invoices, subscription and online access is considerable. A single, monthly invoice for all subscriptions saves time and administration costs for the customer.

Many university and college libraries have used consolidation for years and now law firms are looking seriously at it because of the savings in time and costs. Unfortunately, consolidation comes at a price and the costs and benefits to a particular customer need to be analysed carefully.

Further, agents also provide a chargeable cataloguing service. This involves the agent cataloguing a customer's purchases, with a further fee for producing reports and updating materials. These services may be useful where the library stock is unfamiliar, updating has fallen behind or even where the exact subscriptions taken are unknown.

18.4 CHALLENGES AND PITFALLS OF BUYING ONLINE INFORMATION

Perhaps the biggest change in the way legal information is purchased and supplied has come with the development of online resources. Many materials that were traditionally only available in print form are now available in electronic format. The move to online publishing has brought a new set of challenges for anyone involved in purchasing. The challenges include:

- the management and administration of online resources;

- absorbing additional costs associated with online products, such as technical support and provision of adequate and appropriate IT systems and networks;

- creating an appropriate balance between hardcopy and online, bearing in mind the needs and preferences of users;

- negotiating a contract and price for online products where, in the majority of cases, these matters are less than transparent.

18.4.1 Management and administration of online resources

Managing online resources can be a time-consuming process, for both content providers and users. Law firms and chambers with an extensive array of online resources and a large number of users across a network may require a full-time member of staff to ensure services are maintained effectively and can be developed successfully as new products are acquired.

Managing such resources is particularly significant at present in law firms. When organisations choose to merge, the consolidation of electronic resources becomes fundamental and can be an extremely difficult undertaking.

In the United Kingdom the online publishing market is dominated by three products: *Lexis®Library*, *Westlaw UK* and *PLC*. *Lexis®Library* and *Westlaw UK* offer broadly similar functionality and content coverage (primary law and commentary), whilst *PLC* provides procedural materials: standard forms, checklists and articles; *PLC* provides content directly to fee-earners within law firms. *Lexis®Library* and *Westlaw UK* offer vaguely similar functionality and content coverage (primary law and commentary), whilst *PLC* has historically provided information, such as standard forms, checklists, drafting notes and articles, direct to fee-earners. However, this is now changing, with all these organisations expanding into different practice areas and jurisdictions, and developing new and exciting technological enhancements. With a number of smaller online suppliers providing highly sought-after information, these resources can be massively useful, although one has to be wary regarding price and choice of products, and choose what best suits the needs of the organisation. Bookshops and subscription agents are not able to sell such products, thus contractual negotiations usually take place with an account manager or representative from a supplier.

18.4.2   Access and other technical issues

The main challenges associated with managing online resources are in relation to access and technical issues. For example, how will lawyers gain access to the online resources? Some suppliers allow access by a process called IP Authentication, whereby each user has a unique IP address on one of the firm's internal servers. 'Tailorability', the option for an individual to amend his or her functionality to use a product (desktop view, alerts, searching, etc), is hindered when using IP authentication, as is tracking specific usage by individual users.

When a user signs on to a resource, the supplier's computer system checks that the address is authorised to obtain access to the resource. This type of system reduces the administrative burden on the firm. Establishing whether access to a particular online resource can be managed in this way and then implementing the process can be time consuming and potentially frustrating. Firewalls, to prevent breaches of computer security, have been known to prevent access to online publications so checks should be made to ensure the firewall will allow access or whether it is possible to add the resource as a 'trusted site'.

Where access is not being managed by IP authentication, organisations need to carefully consider whether they need to create passwords on an individual basis or provide a generic username and password. Naturally, all access should be within the terms of the licence provided by the supplier of the online resource and thought must also be given to the related data protection laws.

18.4.3   Content issues

Very occasionally content will become unavailable to users, either because there is a technical issue or because the content has been moved or removed by the online supplier. All organisations regardless of size will be concerned about this, so it is essential to identify who in the online supplier will inform you when a source has been removed or is unavailable.

If an organisation has subscribed diligently to a source for ten years and then decides to cancel the online subscription, is it still entitled to access the archive? Similarly, if a source ceases publication or a publisher decides to remove the online resource from the market, what are the options for the subscribing organisation? These questions need to be researched with the online supplier before a contract is signed. One aspect which needs to be explored in particular is the contractual position when large sets of information are removed by the database provider mid-contract, as has happened recently and will certainly occur again.

18.4.4   Usage statistics

Usage statistics play an important part in informing subscribers whether use justifies the cost of renewing a subscription. Unfortunately, many online suppliers do not provide use statistics as standard, therefore, when initially considering taking out a subscription check whether use statistics will be made available regularly. Reasonably detailed usage reports can now be obtained from a supplier, which can prove undoubtedly useful. Nevertheless, suppliers can manipulate usage to provide information which prima facie appears that a product is being used excessively when in actual fact this may not be the case. Those individuals managing usage should familiarise themselves with what the statistics actually mean, for example, do they relate to hits on individual pages (and what constitutes a 'hit'), time spent on particular areas or simply entering a particular resource with a username and password?

Many user organisations are looking at either bespoke reporting tools or applications like Research Monitor or OneLog to report on their use of online resources. Some of these tools will also manage access to online resources, so fulfilling two purposes.

18.4.5   Cancelling online subscriptions

While most suppliers allow customers to cancel subscriptions at the end of the term by simply opting not to pay the renewal invoice, other suppliers require advance notice of the intention to cancel a subscription. This information will be detailed in the contract so it is worthwhile checking to see whether the supplier requires thirty days', three months' or six months' notice of your intention to cancel a subscription. Some organisations regularly cancel contracts before the required notice period even if they intend to continue with the subscription. This is so that they are not bound by the contract if there happens to be a fundamental change in circumstances.

18.4.6   Choice between hardcopy and online

The decision whether to take something in hardcopy or online format is not an easy one. In recent years there has been a shift towards more organisations subscribing to online elements only, especially as the use of services becomes more intuitive and users become familiar with new technologies and the benefits associated with using them. However, as pressure on budgets increases there may be a move back towards hardcopy subscriptions in preference to online subscriptions. The majority of organisations purchasing legal information will now have a 'hybrid' model of both electronic and print material. Here are some of the advantages and disadvantages of print and electronic products.

Print – advantages

- The customer pays for ownership for all time, therefore having access to historical information as this is acquired and grows.
- Print subscriptions do not require expensive hardware or software and specialist staff to maintain them.
- Highly portable, to places where there are no computers.
- Indexes compiled through the intellectual input of skilled indexers and editors.
- Do not attract VAT.

Print – disadvantages

- Take up valuable space within an organisation, particularly sets of law reports.
- Need acquisitions and payment systems in place.

- Need cataloguing or some type of system to ensure individual publications can be located with the minimum of delay.

- Require maintenance, eg updating, binding and/or repair.

- Can become lost or mislaid.

- Searching limited to conventional contents and index pages.

- Cannot carry out simultaneous searches across different types of legal material (statutes, cases, practitioner commentary and journals).

- Often considered by technophiles to be simply old-fashioned and worthless.

- Many publications become difficult to use when organisations have offices scattered in different locations.

- Not particularly portable.

Electronic – advantages

- Access available anywhere on the firm's network and even from anywhere in the world, so long as appropriate communications technology has been purchased and set up.

- Accessible 24/7 not just when the library is open.

- Many and more sophisticated ways of searching each database as compared with a conventional print index.

- Can carry out simultaneous searches across different types of legal material (statutes, cases, practitioner commentary and journals).

- Updating carried out for the customer.

- Parts do not become mislaid or lost like print publications.

- Easy to forward items to colleagues or clients and create links between materials.

- Can tailor the core materials to the needs of a particular practice team or office.

Electronic – disadvantages

- The subscription pays for access to an electronic product but only for the duration of the subscription.

- Commercial database providers may alter the terms or cost of access making it unfavourable for the firm to continue to subscribe.

- The licences which commercial database providers negotiate with other publishers to display material are re-negotiated at intervals. If the negotiations are unsuccessful, a particular title or publisher's products will suddenly disappear from the database.

- Whilst many databases now provide pdf versions of statutes and law reports which are accepted in court, some materials are not in litigation-approved format, and firms may need to fall back on print versions.

- Some databases do not have indexes compiled through the intellectual input of skilled indexers and editors, but searches merely retrieve every occurrence of the word or phrase requested and the user may be inundated with a mass of unsorted and barely relevant material.

- 'Cherry picking' particular sources or practice areas from one provider will often prove more expensive, thus organisations may end up with material they will rarely or never use.

- Electronic resources are virtually always more expensive than the paper equivalent.

- Attracts VAT.

A choice must be made between the flexibility and speed of online searching and the cost incurred.

There is also a misconception that all materials available in hardcopy are available online. This simply is not the case. Whilst online law suppliers are putting more content into their products there are still some significant gaps in coverage, particularly amongst the secondary sources of law, such as practitioner works and commentary.

18.5   HINTS AND TIPS WHEN NEGOTIATING WITH ONLINE LAW INFORMATION PROVIDERS

Negotiating with providers is certainly a skill in itself and surprisingly an experience which a number of people fear. The skill can be developed extensively as experience is gained, although the information which follows will hopefully be of assistance. Having professional contacts at similar organisations to discuss processes with may prove helpful, although obviously confidentiality of both contracts and discussions must be upheld. If further reading is required, there are specific publications written in this area.

18.5.1   Product trials

Negotiate a product trial before you buy. Suppliers will jump at the opportunity to demonstrate and gather feedback on their product and, if negotiations go well, they may even start a subscription from the date the trial ended. A trial is also a good opportunity to demonstrate to both you and the supplier how many individual members of staff will be interested in using the product. If you ask for a trial for ten individuals and only five people use it, this information can be used as a basis for negotiating a more appropriate subscription.

If you decide to take a trial before purchasing a product ensure the trial period is substantial and perhaps longer than that usually offered by a supplier. Ensure there is enough time for you and your staff to review the strengths and weaknesses of the product, especially where a large number of users are involved or they are based in a number of different offices or locations.

If a trial is not available for a product, ask yourself: why? There may be legitimate reasons for this, but largely the proof is in the pudding.

18.5.2   Know the product

Evaluate the strengths and weaknesses of the product. By using a tool like Research Monitor or OneLog it should be possible to see which sources within an online resource are being used most and perhaps significantly which sources are scarcely or not being used. Alternatively, if you regularly use an online publication make a note of the parts you find most useful, and ask colleagues who use it to complete a log or brief questionnaire on their use, what they like about it and, perhaps more importantly, what they do not like about it. Then, when discussions with the supplier begin, the good and less good points of the product can be highlighted to the supplier.

18.5.3 Know other products

Before negotiating, try to know as much as you can about rival products. This will increase your knowledge of whether or not a particular product is essential, whatever the cost. Product trials may also be run simultaneously in the hope that one product may prove vastly more beneficial to an organisation, but be aware that, first, there is no single product which offers everything nor, second, no two products are identical.

18.5.4 Know your contact

Make time to meet the account manager of the supplier as often as possible; quarterly is often the most appropriate. Get to know your contact at the supplier through these account meetings so that negotiations are more enjoyable and potentially more constructive.

18.5.5 Be transparent

Be transparent about what your organisation is doing and what it hopes to achieve from any negotiations then, hopefully, the supplier will be too. If your organisation can only afford an increase in the subscription charge of 3% or is looking to make cost savings of 10%, say so up front. The conversation should then be focused on how to get there without too much difficulty.

18.5.6 Consider any contract carefully

Do not enter into an agreement with a supplier of legal information without analysing the contract provided. Review it carefully to ensure you will be getting the most from the agreement and that the contract takes account of potential changes to the way you do business. Where possible, the contract's terms and conditions should be checked by a procurement team or legal professional. Ensure that the contract is not unnecessarily restrictive or too open to alternative interpretation. Check carefully the definition of 'authorised user' or 'benefiting group', since the cost of the product may vary significantly depending on the number of users and the projected level of usage.

APPENDICES

Contents

APPENDIX 1

LISTS OF ABBREVIATIONS

The following lists include a selection of the most common abbreviations which lawyers, librarians, information officers or researchers may come across when undertaking legal research. They focus on abbreviations found in the UK for:

- Acts;
- the titles of publications (mainly law reports and journals);
- 'textual devices' – mainly Latin abbreviations.

For more comprehensive listings consult the following.

For law reports and law journals only

- Cardiff Index to Legal Abbreviations
  <http://www.legalabbrevs.cardiff.ac.uk/>
- *Osborn's Concise Law Dictionary* (Sweet & Maxwell, 10th edn, 2005)

For EU abbreviations specifically

- *Eurojargon: a dictionary of European Union acronyms, abbreviations and terminology* (European Information Services, 7th edn, 2004)

Comprehensively

The classic index to both abbreviations and acronyms for publications, organisations and legal personalities is:

- Raistrick, D, *Index to Legal Citations and Abbreviations* (Sweet & Maxwell, 3rd edn, 2008)

In four looseleaf volumes, covering more jurisdictions than Raistrick, but restricted to publication abbreviations only:

- Kavass Igor I, and Prince, Mary M, *World dictionary of legal abbreviations* (William S Hein, 1991–)

Appendix 1.1 – Abbreviations for Acts

AccJA 1999	Access to Justice Act 1999
AEA 1925, 1971	Administration of Estates Act
AJA 1920, 1925, 1956, 1960, 1964, 1965, 1969, 1970, 1973, 1977, 1982, 1985	Administration of Justice Act
BExA 1882	Bills of Exchange Act 1882
BNA 1948, 1958, 1964, 1965, 1981	British Nationality Act
CA 1968	Countryside Act 1968
CA various dates	Companies Act
CA 1972, 1989, 2004	Children Act
CAA 1968, 1990	Capital Allowances Act
CCA 1974, 2006	Consumer Credit Act
CCA 1984	County Courts Act 1984
CCR 1981	County Court Rules 1981
CDA 1998	Crime and Disorder Act 1998
CDA 1971	Criminal Damage Act 1971
CDPA 1988	Copyright, Designs and Patents Act 1988
CD&PA 1988	Copyright, Designs and Patents Act 1988
Ch A 1989	Children Act 1989
CJA 1925, 1948, 1961, 1967, 1972, 1982, 1987, 1988, 1991, 1993, 2003	Criminal Justice Act
CJCSA 2000	Criminal Justice and Court Services Act 2000
CJ&CSA 2000	Criminal Justice and Court Services Act 2000
CJIA 2008	Criminal Justice and Immigration Act 2008
CJ&IA 2008	Criminal Justice and Immigration Act 2008
CJPA 2001	Criminal Justice and Police Act 2001
CJ&PA 2001	Criminal Justice and Police Act 2001
CJPOA 1994	Criminal Justice and Public Order Act 1994
CJ&POA 1994	Criminal Justice and Public Order Act 1994
CLA 1826, 1967, 1977	Criminal Law Act
CLSA 1990	Courts and Legal Services Act 1990
C&LSA 1990	Courts and Legal Services Act 1990
CoA 1985, 1989, 2006	Companies Act
Cos A 1985, 1989, 2006	Companies Act
CPA 1947	Crown Proceedings Act 1947
CPA 1965	Compulsory Purchase Act 1965
CPA 1974	Control of Pollution Act 1974
CPA 1987	Consumer Protection Act 1987
CPR	Civil Procedure Rules 1998
CP (Am) R 2000	Civil Procedure (Amendment) Rules 2000
CPIA 1996	Criminal Procedure and Investigations Act 1996
CP&IA 1996	Criminal Procedure and Investigations Act 1996
CRWA 2000	Countryside and Rights of Way Act 2000
C&RWA 2000	Countryside and Rights of Way Act 2000
CSA 1991, 1995	Child Support Act
CSCDA 1960	Caravan Sites and Control of Development Act 1960
CS&CDA 1960	Caravan Sites and Control of Development Act 1960
CSDPA 1970	Chronically Sick and Disabled Persons Act 1970
CS&DPA 1970	Chronically Sick and Disabled Persons Act 1970
CSPSSA 2000	Child Support, Pensions and Social Security Act 2000
CSP&SSA 2000	Child Support, Pensions and Social Security Act 2000
CYPA 1933, 1963, 1969	Children and Young Persons Act

C&YPA 1933, 1963, 1969	Children and Young Persons Act
DDA 1989, 1991	Dangerous Dogs Act
DDA 1995, 2001	Disability Discrimination 1995, 2001
DPA 1998	Data Protection Act 1998
DPMCA 1978	Domestic Proceedings and Magistrates' Court Act 1978
DP&MCA 1978	Domestic Proceedings and Magistrates' Court Act 1978
EA 1988, 1989, 1990, 2002	Employment Act
ECA 1972	European Communities Act 1972
EPA 1964	Emergency Powers Act 1964
EPA 1990	Environmental Protection Act 1990
EPA 1970	Equal Pay Act 1970
EP(C)A 1978	Employment Protection (Consolidation) Act 1978
ERA 1999, 2004	Employment Relations Act
ERA 1996	Employment Rights Act 1996
ER(DR)A 1998	Employment Rights (Dispute Resolution) Act 1998
FA numerous dates	Finance Act
FIA 2000	Freedom of Information Act 2000
FLA 1986, 1996	Family Law Act
FLRA 1969, 1987	Family Law Reform Act
FoIA 2000	Freedom of Information Act 2000
FSA 1955, 1971, 1974, 1984, 1992	Friendly Societies Act
FSA 1986	Financial Services Act 1986
FSMA 2000	Financial Services and Markets Act 2000
FS&MA 2000	Financial Services and Markets Act 2000
GLAA 1999, 2007	Greater London Authority Act
GOWA 1998, 2006	Government of Wales Act
HA 1957	Homicide Act 1957
HA 1980	Highways Act 1980
HA 1985, 1996, 2004	Housing Act
HA 1999, 2006	Health Act
HBCA 1984	Housing and Building Control Act 1984
H&BCA 1984	Housing and Building Control Act 1984
HFEA 1990, 2008	Human Fertilisation and Embryology Act
HF&EA 1990, 2008	Human Fertilisation and Embryology Act
HPA 1986	Housing and Planning Act 1986
H&PA 1986	Housing and Planning Act 1986
HRA 1998	Human Rights Act 1998
HSCA 2001, 2008	Health and Social Care Act
H&SCA 2001, 2008	Health and Social Care Act
HSC(CHS)A 2003	Health and Social Care (Community Health and Standards) Act 2003
H&SC(CHS)A 2003	Health and Social Care (Community Health and Standards) Act 2003
HSPHA 1968	Health Services and Public Health Act 1984
HS&PHA 1968	Health Services and Public Health Act 1984
H&SCA 2001, 2008	Health and Social Care Act
H&SC(CHS)A 2003	Health and Social Care (Community Health and Standards) Act 2003
HSSA 1984	Health and Social Security Act 1984
H&SSA 1984	Health and Social Security Act 1984
HSWA 1974	Health and Safety and Work Act 1974
H&SWA 1974	Health and Safety and Work Act 1974
HTA 2004	Human Tissue Act 2004

IA 1985, 1986, 1994, 2000	Insolvency Act
IAA 1999	Immigration and Asylum Act 1999
I&AA 1999	Immigration and Asylum Act 1999
IANA 2006	Immigration, Asylum and Nationality Act 2006
IA&NA 2006	Immigration, Asylum and Nationality Act 2006
ICA 2006	Identity Cards Act 2006
ICTA 1988	Income and Corporation Taxes Act 1988
Ins A 1985, 1986, 1994, 2000	Insolvency Act
ITA 2007	Income Tax Act 2007
ITEPA 2003	Income Tax (Earnings and Pensions) Act 2003
ITTOIA 2005	Income Tax (Trading and Other Income) Act 2005
JA 1825, 1974	Juries Act
JA 1873	Judicature Act 1873
LA 1872, 1902, 2003	Licensing Act
LA 1980	Limitation Act 1980
LCA 1961, 1973	Land Compensation Act
LCA 1972	Land Charges Act 1972
LGA 1888, 1894, 1929, 1948, 1958, 1966, 1972, 1974, 1978, 1985, 1986, 1988, 1992, 1999, 2003	Local Government Act
LGA 1963	London Government Act 1963
LGHA 1989	Local Government and Housing Act 1989
LG&HA 1989	Local Government and Housing Act 1989
LGPLA 1980	Local Government, Planning and Land Act 1980
LGP&LA 1980	Local Government, Planning and Land Act 1980
LLCA 1975	Local Land Charges Act 1975
LLPA 2000	Limited Liability Partnerships Act 2000
LPA 1925, 1969	Law of Property Act
LP (Misc Provs) A 1989, 1994	Law of Property (Miscellaneous Provisions) Act
LRA 1886, 1997, 2002	Land Registration Act
LRA 1967, 1979	Leasehold Reform Act
LRHUDA 1993	Leasehold, Reform, Housing and Urban Development Act 1993
LRH&UDA 1993	Leasehold, Reform, Housing and Urban Development Act 1993
LR (Misc Provs) A 1934, 1970	Law Reform (Miscellaneous Provisions) Act
LTA 1709, 1730, 1851, 1927, 1954, 1985, 1987, 1988	Landlord and Tenant Act
L&TA 1709, 1730, 1851, 1927, 1954, 1985, 1987, 1988	Landlord and Tenant Act
MA 1939, 1949, 1983, 1994	Marriage Act
MA 1967	Misrepresentation Act 1967
MCA 1965, 1973	Matrimonial Causes Act
MCA 1980	Magistrates' Courts Act 1980
Mat CA 1965, 1973	Matrimonial Causes Act
MDA 1971	Misuse of Drugs Act 1971
MHA 1959, 1983, 2007	Mental Health Act
MHA 1975, 1983	Mobile Homes Act
MIA 1906	Marine Insurance Act 1906
MOA 1950, 1958, 1968	Maintenance Orders Act
MoDA 1971	Misuse of Drugs Act 1971
MSA 1988, 1995	Merchant Shipping Act
NERCA 2006	Natural Environment and Rural Communities Act 2006
NE&RCA 2006	Natural Environment and Rural Communities Act 2006

NHA 1980, 1983, 1997, 2002	National Heritage Act
NHSA 1946, 1977, 2006	National Health Service Act
NHSCPA 2006	National Health Service (Consequential Provisions) Act 2006
NHSWA 2006	National Health Service (Wales) Act 2006
NIA 1947, 1962, 1974, 1998, 2000, 2006	Northern Ireland Act
NIA 1965, 1974	National Insurance Act
NICA 2002, 2006, 2008	National Health Contributions Act
NMWA 1998	National Minimum Wage Act 1998
NPACA 1949	National Parks and Access to the Countryside Act 1949
NP&ACA 1949	National Parks and Access to the Countryside Act 1949
NTA 1907, 1937, 1939, 1953, 1971	National Trust Act
OaPA 1861	Offences against the Person Act 1861
OLA 1957, 1984	Occupiers' Liability Act
OPA 1861	Offences against the Person Act 1861
OPA 1959, 1964	Obscene Publications Act
OSRPA 1963	Offices, Shops and Railway Premises Act 1963
OS&RPA 1963	Offices, Shops and Railway Premises Act 1963
PA 1890	Partnership Act 1890
PA 1949, 1957, 1977, 2004	Patents Act
PA 1964, 1976, 1996, 1997	Police Act
PA 1995, 2004, 2007	Pensions Act
PAA 1964	Perpetuities and Accumulations Act 1964
P&AA 1964	Perpetuities and Accumulations Act 1964
PACE 1984	Police and Criminal Evidence Act 1984
PACEA 1984	Police and Criminal Evidence Act 1984
P&CEA 1984	Police and Criminal Evidence Act 1984
PCA 1991	Planning and Compensation Act 1991
PCA 1995, 2002	Proceeds of Crime Act
P&CA 1991	Planning and Compensation Act 1991
PCC(S)A 2000	Powers of the Criminal Courts (Sentencing) Act 2000
PCPA 2004	Planning and Compulsory Purchase Act 2004
P&CPA 2004	Planning and Compulsory Purchase Act 2004
PDMA 1985	Patents, Designs and Marks Act 1986
PD&MA 1985	Patents, Designs and Marks Act 1986
PHA 1875, 1925, 1936, 1961	Public Health Act
POA 1936, 1963, 1986	Public Order Act
RA 1974, 1977	Rent Act
RIPA 2000	Regulation of Investigatory Powers Act 2000
RoLA 1959	Rights of Light Act 1959
RoPA 1867, 1981, 1983, 1985, 1989, 1991, 1993, 2000	Representation of the People Act
RoWA 1990	Rights of Way Act 1990
RPA 1867, 1981, 1983, 1985, 1989, 1991, 1993, 2000	Representation of the People Act
RRA 1976	Race Relations Act 1976
RR(A)A 2000	Race Relations (Amendment) Act 2000
RTA 1930, 1960, 1974, 1988, 1991	Road Traffic Act
RTOA 1987	Road Traffic Offenders Act 1987
RTRA 1984	Road Traffic Regulation Act 1984
SCA 1981	Supreme Court Act 1981
SEA 1986	Single European Act 1986 (European Community)

SENDA 2001	Special Educational Needs and Disability Act 2001
SGA 1979	Sale of Goods Act 1979
SGSA 1982	Supply of Goods and Services Act 1982
SG(IT)A 1973	Supply of Goods (Implied Terms) Act 1973
SLA 1882, 1925	Settled Land Act
SLRA 1893, 1948, 1950, 1958	Statute Law Revision Act
SL(R)A numerous dates	Statute Law (Repeals) Act
SOA 1956, 1967, 1985, 1993, 2002	Sexual Offences Act
SO(Am)A 1976, 1992, 2000	Sexual Offences (Amendment) Act
SOCPA 2005	Serious Organised Crime and Police Act 2005
SoGA 1979	Sale of Goods Act 1979
SoG(IT)A 1973	Supply of Goods (Implied Terms) Act 1973
SSA 1973, 1979, 1980, 1981, 1985, 1986, 1988, 1989, 1990, 1993, 1998	Social Security Act
SSAA 1992	Social Security Administration Act 1992
SSCBA 1992	Social Security Contributions and Benefits Act 1992
SS(CP)A 1992	Social Security (Consequential Provisions) Act 1992
SSFA 2001	Social Security Fraud Act 2001
TA 1925, 2000	Trustee Act
TA 1968, 1978	Theft Act
TCEA 2007	Tribunals, Courts and Enforcement Act 2007
TCGA 1992	Taxation of Chargeable Gains Act 1992
TCPA 1954, 1959, 1990	Town and Country Planning Act
T&CPA 1954, 1959, 1990	Town and Country Planning Act
TDA1968	Trade Descriptions Act 1968
Th A 1968, 1978	Theft Act
TIA 1992	Tribunals and Inquiries Act 1992
T&IA 1992	Tribunals and Inquiries Act 1992
TMA 1970	Taxes Management Act 1970
TULR(C)A 1992	Trade Union and Labour Relations (Consolidation) Act 1992
TUPE	Transfer of Undertakings (Protection of Employment) Regulations, SI 1981/1794
TURERA 1993	Trade Union Reform and Employment Rights Act 1993
UCTA 1977	Unfair Contract Terms Act 1977
UDHR	Universal Declaration of Human Rights
USGSA 1971	Unsolicited Goods and Services Act 1971
USG&SA 1971	Unsolicited Goods and Services Act 1971
UNCRC	United Nations Convention on the Rights of the Child, 1989
VCRA 2006	Violent Crime Reduction Act 2006
WA 1837, 1963, 1968	Wills Act
WMA 1824, 1985	Weights and Measures Act
W&MA 1824, 1985	Weights and Measures Act
W&M&cA 1976	Weights and Measures etc Act 1976
WRPA 1999	Welfare Reform and Pensions Act 1999
WR&PA 1999	Welfare Reform and Pensions Act 1999
YJCEA 1999	Youth Justice and Criminal Evidence Act 1999
YJ&CEA 1999	Youth Justice and Criminal Evidence Act 1999

Appendix 1.2 – Abbreviations for publications

Note: All punctuation and spaces between words have been stripped out.

Where the abbreviation and full title of a publication are the same or similar, no entry has been created.

Abbreviations are given in letter-by-letter filing order, ignoring upper and lower case. An ampersand (&) is ignored but the abbreviation files after any abbreviations with the same letters but without an ampersand. Examples:

AA
A&A
Ab
AB&C
A&Z
AZ&C

AA&L	Art Antiquity and Law
AB	Advising Business
A&ADR Rev	Arbitration and ADR Review
A&B	Accounting & Business
A&BR	Accounting & Business Research
ABTBull	Association of Banking Teachers Bulletin
AC	Law Reports, Appeal Cases
ACD	Administrative Court Digest
ACLRev	Asian Commercial Law Review
Ad&Fos	Adoption and Fostering
ADIL	Annual Digest of International Law
Ad&MarLL	Advertising and Marketing Law Letter
Ad&MarL&P	Advertising and Marketing Law & Practice
AdminLR	Administrative Law Reports
ADRLJ	Arbitration and Dispute Resolution Law Journal
ADRLN	Arbitration and Dispute Resolution Newsletter
AELN	Alliance Environmental Law News
AER	All England Law Reports
AFI	Asset Finance International
AgriLaw	Agricultural Law
AIAJ	Asian International Arbitration Journal
AIBRev	Allied Irish Banks Review
AIDA PIB	AIDA Pollution Insurance Bulletin
AIIJ	Australian Insurance Institute Journal
AI&L	Artificial Intelligence and Law
AIR	Asia Insurance Review
AJICL	African Journal of International and Comparative Law
ALER	American Law and Economic Review
AllER	All England Law Reports
AllER(Comm)	All England Law Reports Commercial Cases
AllER(EC)	All England Law Reports European Cases
AllERRev	All England Law Reports Annual Review
ALMBrief	Association of Lloyd's Members Brief
ALMNews	Association of Lloyd's Members News

ALQ	Arab Law Quarterly
AmexBR	Amex Bank Review
Anglo-AmLR	Anglo-American Law Review
APJEL	Asia Pacific Journal of Environmental Law
APJHRL	Asia-Pacific Journal on Human Rights and the Law
APLR	Asia Pacific Law Review
AppCD	Appeal Commissioners Decision
AppComp&CommL	Applied Computer and Communications Law
ArbInt	Arbitration International
ArbLM	Arbitration Law Monthly
ArchNews	Archbold News
ArchRev	Archbold Review
ASA Bull	ASA Bulletin
A&SL	Air & Space Law
ASLR	Aberdeen Student Law Review
ATC	Annotated Tax Cases
AviationIR	Aviation Insurance Report
AVMAM&LJ	Action for Victims of Medical Accidents Medical and Legal Journal
BAILII	British and Irish Legal Information Institute
BAJ	British Actuarial Journal
BankersMag	Bankers Magazine
BankLaw	Bankers' Law
BankLR	Banking Law Reports
BB&FLR	Butterworths Banking & Financial Law Review
BCC	British Company Cases
B&C Int	Benefits & Compensation International
BCLC	Butterworths Company Law Cases
BenFile	Benfits File
BEQB	Bank of England Quarterly Bulletin
BFIT	Bulletin for International Taxation
B&FT	Banking & Financial Training
BHRC	Butterworths Human Rights Cases
BIFD	Bulletin for International Fiscal Documentation
BILAJ	British Insurance Law Association Journal
BiletaNews	BILETA Newsletter
BIre	Banking Ireland
BJIB&FL	Butterworths Journal of Banking & Financial Law
BLE	Business Law Europe
BLGR	Butterworths local Government Reports
BLR	Building Law Reports
BMCR	Butterworths Merger Control Review
BM&IA	Broker's Monthly & Insurance Advisor
BMLR	Butterworths Medico-Legal Reports
BNews	Business News
BOF	Back Office Focus
BPILS	Butterworths Personal Injury Litigation
BPIR	Bankruptcy and Personal Insolvency Reports
BPL	British Pension Lawyer
BracLJ	Bracton Law Journal
BractonLJ	Bracton Law Journal
BritJCriminol	British Journal of Criminology
BritJLaw&Soc	British Journal of Law and Society
BritYBIntL	British Yearbook of International Law
BS	Balance Sheet
BSLR	Bio-Science Law Review

BT	Banking Technology
BTC	British Tax Cases
BTR	British Tax Review
BuildLM	Building Law Monthly
BullMedE	Bulletin of Medical Ethics
BusIns	Business Insurance
BusLB	Business Law Bulletin
BusLI	Business Law International
BusLR	Business Law Review
BusLRev	Business Law Review
BusRisk	Business Risk
BusTP	Business Tax Planning
BusyP	Busy Practitioner
ButtC&EEBLB	Butterworths Central and East European Business Law Bulletin
BVC	British Value Added Tax Reporter
BW	Banking World
BYBIL	British Yearbook of International Year
C	Command Paper (issued between 1870 and 1899)
CA	Certified Accountant
CAMag	Chartered Accountant Magazine
CambrianLR	Cambrian Law Review
CanIns	Canadian Insurance
CanJLI	Canadian Journal of Life Insurance
CapTax	Capital Taxes
CBank	Central Banking
CBQ	Criminal Bar Quarterly
CBSIJour	Chartered Building Societies Institute Journal
CC	Corporate Cover
CCA	Cargo Claims Analyst
C&CC	Consumer & Commercial Law Contracts
CCF	Child Care Forum
CCL	Commercial Conflict of Laws
CCLaw	Current Criminal Law
CCLR	Community Care Law Reports
CCLR	Consumer Credit Law Reports
CCLRep	Community Care Law Reports
CCLRev	Carbon & Climate Law Review
CCN	Civil Costs Newletter
CCR	Chambers Client Report
Cd	Command Paper (issued between 1900 and 1918)
CDFN	Clinical Disputes Forum
CE	Central European
CEC	European Community Cases
CETS	Council of Europe Treaty Series
C&EEBLB	Central and East European Business Law Bulletin
C&EL	Construction & Engineering Law
CF	Corporate Finance
CFILR	Company Financial and Insolvency Law Review
C&FL	Credit and Finance Law
CFLQ	Child and Family Law Quarterly
C&FLU	Child & Family Law Update
CG	Corporate Governance
CGTB	Capital Gains Tax Brief
Ch	Law Reports, Chancery Division
CharitiesM	Charities Management

CharityF	Charity Finance
ChartI	Charter-Party International
CHRLD	Commonwealth Human Rights Law Digest
CICReps	Captive Insurance Company Reports
CICRev	Captive Insurance Company Review
CIIJour	Chartered Insurance Institute Journal
CIL	Contemporary Issues in Law
CIPAJ	Chartered Institute of Patent agents Journal
CivLit	Civil Litigation
CivPB	Civil Practice Bulletin
CICReps	Captive Insurance Company Reports
CJ	Contract Journal
CJEurope	Criminal Justice Europe
CJICL	Cambridge Journal of International and Comparative Law
CJQ	Civil Justice Quarterly
CJRB	Commercial Judicial Review Bulletin
CL	Commercial Lawyer
CL	Company Lawyer
CL	Current Law Monthly Digest
CLB	Commonwealth Law Bulletin
CLC	Commercial Law Cases
CLD	Company Lawyer Digest
CLE	Commercial Laws of Europe
CLEANewsletter	Commonwealth Legal Education Association Newsletter
CLI	Commodity Law International
CLInt	Competition Law International
CLJ	Cambridge Law Journal
CL&J	Criminal Law & Justice Weekly
CLL	Corporate Legal Letter
CLLRev	Commercial Liability Law Review
CLM	Company Law Monitor
CLMD	Current Law Monthly Digest
CLN	Construction Law Newsletter
CLOS	Criminal Law Online Service
CLP	Current Legal Problems
CL&P	Company Law & Practice
CL&PR	Charity Law & Practice Review
CLPract	Commercial Law Practitioner
CLS	Current Law Statutes
CLSA	Current Law Statutes Annotated
CLSR	Computer Law & Security Report
CLSRev	Computer Law & Security Review
CLW	Current Law Week
CLWR	Common Law World Review
CLWRev	Common Law World Review
CLY	Current Law Yearbook
Cm	Command Paper (issued since 1986)
CM	Compliance Monitor
CMIR	Continuous Mortality Investigation Reports
CMLJ	Capital Markets Law Journal
CMLNU	Council of Mortgage Lenders News Update
CMLR	Common Market Law Reports
CMLR(AR)	Common Market Law Reports Anti-trust Reports
CMLRev	Common Market Law Review
Cmd	Command Paper (issued between 1919 and 1956)
Cmnd	Command Paper (issued between 1956 and 1986)

CN	Construction Newsletter
CoAcc	Company Accountant
COB	Compliance Officer Bulletin
COD	Crown Office Digest
CoAcc	Company Accountant
COIT	Central Office of Industrial Tribunals
CoLaw	Company Lawyer
CoLDig	Company Law Digest
CoLJ	Commercial Litigation Journal
CoLN	Company Law Newsletter
ComJudJ	Commonwealth Judicial Journal
ComLawyer	Commercial Lawyer
ComLL	Commonwealth Law Librarian
CommInt	Communications International
CommLaw	Commercial Lawyer
CommLeases	Commercial Leases
CommLJ	Competition Law Journal
CommProp	Commercial Property
CommsL	Communications Law
CommsLaw	Communications Law
CompLaw	Company Lawyer
CompLawEC	Competition Law in the European Communities
CompLI	Competition Law Insight
CompLJ	Competition Law Journal
CompLM	Competition Law Monitor
CompLRev	Competition Law Review
CommProp	Commercial Property
Comps&Law	Computers & Law
CommsL	Communications Law
ConLD	Construction Law Digest
ConLR	Construction Law Reports
ConsLaw	Consumer Law
ConsLI	Construction Law International
ConsLToday	Consumer Law Today
Cons&MarLaw	Consumer and Marketing Law
ConstLJ	Construction Law Journal
ConstRef	Constitutional Reform
ConsumerC	Consumer Credit
ConsumLJ	Consumer Law Journal
Conv	Conveyancer and Property Lawyer
Converg	Convergence
CorpBrief	Corporate Briefing
CorpC	Corporate Counsel
CostsLR	Costs Law Reports
CovLJ	Coventry Law Journal
CPCUJour	Chartered Property and Casualty Underwriters Journal
CPDPapers	Criminal Law Week – Extended Papers
CPLJ	Conveyancing and Property Law Journal
CPLR	Civil Practice Law Reports
CPN	Civil Procedure News
CP&P	Civil Practice & Procedure
CPRep	Civil Procedure Reports
CPRev	Consumer Policy Review
CrAppR	Criminal Appeal Reports
CrAppR(S)	Criminal Appeal Reports (Sentencing)
CR&I	Corporate Rescue and Insolvency

CrimLaw	Criminal Lawyer
CrimLB	Criminal Law Bulletin
CrimLF	Criminal Law Forum
CrimLJ	Criminal Law Journal
CrimLN	Criminal Law News
CrimLR	Criminal Law Review
CrimLW	Criminal Law Week
CRisk	Clinical Risk
CRNI	Competition and Regulation in Network Industries
C&R	Compliance & Risk
CS	Corporate Solutions
CSBull	Credit Suisse Bulletin
CSLR	Cambridge Student Law Review
CSP	Current Sentencing Practice
CSR	Company Secretary's Review
CSR&EM	Corporate Social Responsibility and Environmental Management
CSW	Chartered Surveyor Weekly
CT&EPQ	Capital Taxes and Estate Planning Quarterly
CTLR	Computer and Telecommunications Law Review
CTNews&Reps	Capital Taxes News & Reports
CTP	Capital Tax Planning
CTR	Corporate Tax Review
CW	Copyright World
CYELS	Cambridge Yearbook of European Legal Studies
D	Session Cases, 2nd series (Dunlop)
DCJ	Defense Counsel Journal
DD&RM	Due Diligence & Risk Management
DEJ	Digital Evidence Journal
DenningLJ	Denning Law Journal
DE&ESLR	Digital Evidence and Electronic Signature Law Review
DeVoilITI	De Voil Indirect Tax Intelligence
DFI	Derivatives & Financial Instruments
DL	Daily List
DLi	DLi University College Galway Law Graduates Association Gazette
DLR	Discrimination Law Reports
DLR	Dominion Law Reports
DNQ	Domain Names Quarterly
DNVBCU	DNV Bulk Carrier Update
D&P	Development & Planning
DPI	Data Protection Ireland
DPL&P	Data Protection Law & Policy
DP&PP	Data Protection and Privacy Practice
DPQ	Data Protection Quarterly
DULJ	Dublin University Law Journal
EAF	European Accounting Focus
EB&FLJ	European Banking & Financial Law
EBJ	Employee Benefits Journal
EBL	Electronic Business Law
EBLR	Electronic Business Law Reports
EBLRev	European Business Law Review
EBM	European Business Monitor
EBMag	Environment Business Magazine
EBOR	European Business Organization Law Review
ECA	Elderly Client Adviser

EcAff	Economic Affairs
ECC	European Commercial Cases
EccLJ	Ecclesiastical Law Journal
ECCPN	European Commission Competition Policy Newsletter
ECDR	European Copyright and Design Reports
ECEM	EC Energy Monthly
ECFLM	EC Food Law Monthly
ECFR	European Company & Financial Law Review
ECJ	Environmental Claims Journal
ECL	European Corporate Lawyer
ECLaw	European Company Lawyer
ECL&P	E-Commerce Law & Policy
ECLR	European Competition Law Review
ECLRep	E-Commerce Law Reports
ECLRev	Electronic Communications Law Review
ECLReview	European Constitutional Law Review
EcoM&A	Eco-Management & Auditing
ECPR	EC Packaging Report
ECR	European Court Reports
EcRev	Economic Review
ECR-SC	European Court Reports – Reports of European Staff Cases
ECTJ	EC Tax Journal
ECTR	EC Tax Review
EdCR	Education Case Reports
EDD&RM	Environmental Due Diligence & Risk Management
EDILR	Electronic Data Interchange Law Review
EdinLR	Edinburgh Law Review
EdLaw	Education Law Journal
EdLM	Education Law Monitor
EEBL	East European Business Law
EEELR	European Energy and Environmental Law Review
EEFN	East European Forum Newsletter
EEIR	East European Insurance Report
EELR	European Environmental Law Review
EFARev	European Foreign Affairs Law Review
EFFLR	European Food and Feed Law Review
EFP	Encyclopedia of Forms and Precedents
EFPL&P	E-Finance & Payments Law & Policy
EFSL	European Financial Services Law
EG	Estates Gazette
EGCS	Estates Gazette Case Summaries
EGD	Estates Gazette Digest of Cases
EGDC	Estates Gazette Digest of Cases
EGLR	Estates Gazette Law Reports
EHLR	Environmental Health Law Reports
EHRLR	European Human Rights Law Review
EHRR	European Human Rights Reports
EIB	Environment Information Bulletin
EIM	European Insurance Market
EIPR	European Intellectual Property Review
EIRR	European Industrial Relations Review
EIS	European Insurance Strategies
EJC	European Journal of Criminology
EJCL	Electronic Journal of Comparative Law
EJEL&P	European Journal for Education Law & Policy
EJHL	European Journal of Health Law

EJIL	European Journal of International Law
EJLE	European Journal of Legal Education
EJL&E	European Journal of Law & Economics
EJLR	European Journal of Law Reform
EJLT	European Journal of Law and Technology
EJML	European Journal of Migration and Law
EJRB	Environmental Judicial Review Bulletin
EJRR	European Journal of Risk Regulation
EJSL	European Journal of Social Law
EJSS	European Journal of Social Security
EL	Equitable Lawyer
E&L	Education and the Law
ELABriefing	Employment Lawyers Association Briefing
E-LawRev	E-Law Review
ELB	Environment Law Brief
ELD	European Law Digest
EldLJ	Elder Law Journal
ELF	Elder Law & Finance
ELJ	European Law Journal
ELLJ	European Labour Law Journal
ELLR	Environmental Liability Law Review
ELM	Environmental Law & Management
ELN	Environmental Law Newsletter
EL&PD	European Life & Pensions Digest
ELR	Education Law Reports
ELR	Environmental Law Review
ELR	European Law Review
ELRev	European Law Review
ELRI	Employment Law Review – Ireland
EM	European Mergers
EMI	Emerging Markets Investors
EMISELS	EMIS E-Law Service
EMLR	Entertainment and Media Law Reports
EmpLaw	Employers' Law
EmpLB	Employment Law Bulletin
EmpLBrief	Employment Law Briefing
EmpLit	Employment Litigation
EmpLJ	Employment Law Journal
EmpL&L	Employment Law & Litigation
EmpL&LU	Employment Law & Litigation Updates
EmpLN	Employment Law Newsletter
EmployL	Employer's Law
EncCSP	Encyclopedia of Current Sentencing Practice
EncFSL	Encyclopedia of Financial Services
EncITL	Encyclopedia of Information Technology Law
EncPL&P	Encyclopedia of Planning Law & Practice
ENPR	European National Patent Reports
EntLaw	Entertainment Law
EntLR	Entertainment Law Review
EntLRev	Entertainment Law Review
EnvIB	Environment in Business
EnvLaw	Environmental Law
EnvLB	Environmental Law Bulletin
EnvLiability	Environmental Liability
EnvLM	Environmental Law Monthly
EnvLN	Environmental Law Newsletter

EnvLR	Environmental Law Reports
EnvLRev	Environmental Law Review
EnvLM	Envirmental Law Monthly
EnvMan	Environmental Manager
EnvLN	Environmental Law Newsletter
EnvLR	Environmental Law Reports
EnvRisk	Environmental Risk
EOR	Equal Opportunities Review
EORDig	Equal Opportunities Review and Discrimination Case Law Digest
E&P	International Journal of Evidence and Proof
EPEF	Economic Policy: A European Forum
EPG	Environmental Policy and Governance
EPIS	EMIS Personal Injury Service
EPL	European Public Law
EP&L	Environmental Policy and Law
EPLCBrief	European Pharma Law Centre Brief
EPLI	Education, Public Law and the Individual
EPOR	European Patent Office Reports
EPPPLR	European Public Private Partnership Law Review
EPS	EMIS Property Service
ER	English Reports
ERCL	European Review of Contract Law
ERPL	European Review of Public Law
ESLJ	E-Signature Law Journal
E&SLJ	Entertainment and Sports Law Journal
EStAL	European State Aid Law Quarterly
ET	Estates Times
ETMR	European Trade Marks Reports
ETS	European Treaty Series (Council of Europe)
EUBriefNotes	EU Briefing Notes
EuCLR	European Criminal Law Review
EuLF	European Legal Forum
EuLR	European Law Reports
EurAccess	European Access
EurCounsel	European Counsel
EurJCrimeCrLCrJ	European Journal of Crime, Criminal Law and Criminal Justice
EurLRev	European Law Review
EuroCJ	European Competition Journal
EuroCL	European Current Law
EuroEnv	European Environment
EuroLaw	European Lawyer
EuroLB	European Legal Business
EUNews	European Union News
EuroTax	European Taxation
EuroTL	European Transport Law
EuroTS	European Tax Service
EWCACiv	England and Wales, Court of Appeal (Civil Division)
EWCACrim	England and Wales, Court of Appeal (Criminal Division)
EWCB	European Works Councils Bulletin
EWHC(Admin)	England and Wales, High Court (Administrative Court)
EWHC(Admlty)	England and Wales, High Court (Admiralty Court)
EWHC(Ch)	England and Wales, High Court (Chancery Division)
EWHC(Comm)	England and Wales, High Court (Commercial Court)
EWHC(Fam)	England and Wales, High Court (Family Division)
EWHC(Pat)	England and Wales, High Court (Patents Court)
EWHC(QB)	England and Wales, High Court (Queen's Bench Division)

EWHC(TCC)	England and Wales, High Court (Technology and Construction Court)
Exp	Experiodica
F	Session Cases, 5th series (Fraser)
FA	Financial Advisor
Fam	Law Reports, Family Division
FamLaw	Family Law
FamLawB	Family Law Bulletin
FamLB	Family Law Bulletin
FamLJ	Family Law Journal
FamLR	Family Law Reports
FamLR	Green's Family Law Reports
FamLRep	Family Law Reports
FamM	Family Matters
FamMed	Family Mediation
FarmTB	Farm Tax Brief
FarmT&F	Farm Tax & Finance
F&CL	Finance & Credit Law
FCR	Family Court Reporter
F&D	Finance & Development
FD&DIB	Food, Drinks & Drugs Industry Bulletin
F&DIB	Food & Drinks Industry Bulletin
F&DLM	Food & Drink Law Monthly
F&DLR	Futures & Derivatives Law Review
FemLS	Feminist Legal Studies
FI	Fraud Intelligence
FinCon	Finance Confidential
FinLR	Financial Law Reports
FITAR	Financial Instruments Tax & Accounting
FL	Family Law
FLN	Family Law Newsletter
FLR	Family Law Reports
FLT	Family Law Today
FM	Financial Management
FOI	Freedom of Information
Food&DrugsIB	Food & Drugs Industry Bulletin
FoodLM	Food Law Monthly
FPB	Four Pillars Bulletin
FR	Financial Regulator
FRBNYQR	Federal Reserve Bank of New York Quarterly Review
FR&FN	Financial Reinsurance & Futures Newsletter
FRI	Financial Regulation International
FRN	Financial Reinsurance Newsletter
FRR	Financial Regulation Report
FSB	Financial Services Brief
FSBull	Financial Services Bulletin
FSLJ	Financial Services Law Journal
FSLL	Financial Services Law Letter
FSR	Fleet Street Law Reports
FTI	Financial Technology Insight
FTLR	Financial Times Law Reports
GAR	Global Arbitration Review
GC	Global Crime
GCLR	Global Competition Litigation Review
GCR	Global Competition Review

GenIns	General Insurance
GL&B	Global Law & Business
GILSI	Gazette Incorporated Law Society of Ireland
GLJ	Guernsey Law Journal
GLSI	Gazette of the Law Society of Ireland
GoJIL	Gottingen Journal of International Law
GPRIIP	Geneva Papers on Risk Management & Insurance Issues & Practice
GPRIT	Geneva Papers on Risk & Insurance: Theory
GR	Global Reinsurance
GRA	Global Re Analysis
GTB	Global Telecoms Business
GT&CJ	Global Trade and Customs Journal
GWD	Green's Weekly Digest
HaldaneSELB	Haldane Society Employment Law Bulletin
HALL	Health & Law Letter
HCLM	High Court Litigation Manual
HCP	House of Commons Paper
HCWIB	House of Commons Weekly Information Bulletin
HealthLaw	Health Law for Healthcare Professionals
HertLJ	Hertfordshire Law Journal
HJRL	Hague Journal of the Rule of Law
HKLJ	Hong Kong Law Journal
HKLR	Hong Kong Law Reports
HLJ	Hibernian Law Journal
HLM	Housing Law Monitor
HLR	Housing Law Reports
HoldLR	Holdsworth Law Review
HongKongLJ	Hong Kong Law Journal
HongKongLR	Hong Kong Law Reports
HousLR	Green's Housing Law Reports
HowardJ	Howard Journal of Criminal Justice
HPLR	Housing & Property Law Review
HR	Human Rights
HRA	Human Rights Alerter
HR&ILD	Human Rights & International Legal Discourse
HR&UKP	Human Rights & UK Practice
HRCD	Human Rights Case Digest
HRLRev	Human Rights Law Review
HRLR	Human Rights Law Reports
HRLR	Human Rights Law Review
HRU	Human Rights Updater
HS	Hazardous Substances
HSatW	Health and Safety at Work
HSI	Halsbury's Statutory Instruments
H&SB	Health and Safety Bulletin
HSIB	Health & Safety Information Bulletin
H&SIB	Health & Safety Information Bulletin
H&SL	Health & Safety Law
H&SM	Health & Safety Monitor
H&SR	Health & Safety Review
H&SW	Health & Safety at Work
HullCA	Hull Claims Analysis
IALSBull	Institute of Advanced Legal Studies Bulletin
IANL	Immigration, Asylum and Nationality Law

IANL	Journal of Immigration, Asylum and Nationality Law
IBFL	International Banking and Financial Law
IBISRep	International Benefits Information Service Report
IBISRev	International Benefits Information Service Review
IBL	International Banking Law
IBL	International Business Lawyer
IBLJ	International Business Law Journal
IBLQ	Irish Business Law Quarterly
IBN	International Bar News
IBR	Irish Banking Review
IBull	Interrights Bulletin
IC	Investors Chronicle
ICCLJ	International and Comparative Corporate Law Journal
ICCLR	International Company and Commercial Law Review
ICJR	International Court of Justice Law Reports
ICJRep	International Court of Justice Law Reports
ICJRev	International Commission of Jurists Review
ICL	International Corporate Law
ICLB	International Corporate Law Bulletin
ICLit	International Commercial Litigation
ICLJ	Irish Criminal Law Journal
ICLMD	Irish Current Law Monthly Digest
ICLQ	International and Comparative Law Quarterly
ICLR	International Construction Law Review
ICLRev	International Construction Law Review
ICLSA	Irish Current Law Statutes Annotated
ICR	Industrial Cases Reports
ICR	Industrial Court Reports
I&CTL	Information & Communications Technology Law
IDPL	International Data Privacy Law
IDSBrief	IDS Brief Employment law & Practice
IDSDW	IDS Diversity at Work
IDSEmpE	IDS Employment Europe
IDSEmpEmpLBrief	IDS Employment Law Brief
IDSEuroR	IDS European Report
IDSPB	IDS Pensions Bulletin
IDSPLR	IDS Pensions Law Reports
IDSPSB	IDS Pensions Service Bulletin
IELJ	Irish Employment Law Journal
IELR	International Energy Law Review
IELTR	International Energy Law & Taxation Review
IFARev	Independent Financial Adviser Review
IFL	International Family Law
IFLR	International Financial Law Review
IFLRev	International Financial Law Review
IFOSSLR	International Free and Open Source Software Law Review
IHL	In-House Lawyer
IHP	In-House Perspective
IHRLR	Irish Human Rights Law Review
IHRR	International Human Rights Reports
IIBMag	Institute of Insurance Brokers Magazine
IIC	International Review of Intellectual Property and Competition Law
IIC	International Review of Industrial Property and Copyright Law
IIEL	Immigration and International Employment Law
III	Insurance Industry International
IILR	Irish Insurance Law Review

IILRev	International Internet Law Review
IIPLQ	Irish Intellectual Property Law Quarterly
IIPR	Irish Intellectual Property Review
IIR	International Insolvency Review
IIU	Insurance Issues Update
IJ	Irish Jurist
IJBL	International Journal of Biosciences and the Law
IJCL	International Journal of Constitutional Law
IJCLE	International Journal of Clinical Legal Education
IJCLP	International Journal of Communications Law and Policy
IJCP	International Journal of Cultural Property
IJDG	International Journal of Disclosure and Governance
IJDL	International Journal of Discrimination and the Law
IJECL	International Journal of Estuarine and Coastal Law
IJECL&P	International Journal of Electronic Commerce Law & Practice
IJEL	Irish Journal of European Law
IJFDL	International Journal of Franchising and Distribution Law
IJFL	Irish Journal of Family Law
IJFL	International Journal of Franchising Law
IJHR	International Journal of Human Rights
IJIL	International Journal of Insurance Law
IJLBE	International Journal of the Built Environment
IJLCJ	International Journal of Law Crime and Justice
IJL&IT	International Journal of Law & Information Technology
IJLP	International Journal of the Legal Profession
IJLS	Irish Journal of Legal Studies
IJMCL	International Journal of Marine and Coastal Law
IJNL	International Journal of Nuclear Law
IJOSL	International Journal of Shipping Law
IJPL	International Journal of Private Law
IJPL&P	International Journal of Public Law and Policy
IJRL	International Journal of Refugee Law
IJRL&P	International Journal of Regulatory Law & Practice
IJSL	International Journal for the Semiotics of Law
IJT	Irish Journal of Taxation
IJTJ	International Journal of Transitional Justice
IK	Inside Knowledge
ILD	Immigration Law Digest
ILFM	International Law Firm Management
ILJ	Industrial Law Journal
ILP	International Legal Practitioner
IL&P	Immigration Law and Practice
IL&P	Insolvency Law & Practice
ILPr	International Litigation Procedure
ILQ	International Law Quarterly Review
ILR	International Law Reports
ILRM	Irish Law Reports Monthly
IL&S	Islamic Law and Society
ILT	Irish Law Times
ILTR	Irish Law Times Reports
IM&E	Insurance: Mathematics and Economics
IML	International Maritime Law
IML	International Media Law
ImmAR	Immigration Appeal Reports
InComp	In Competition
IndLJ	Industrial Law Journal

IndLR	Independent Law Review
IndSol	Independent Solicitor
IndTR	Industrial Tribunal Reports
IndTribR	Industrial Tribunal Reports
IndustLRev	Industrial Law Review
Info&CommTechL	Information and Communications Technology Law
InfoTLR	Information Technology Law Reports
InHouseL	In-House Lawyer
INL	Internet Newsletter for Lawyers
INLP	Immigration and Nationality Law and Practice
I&NL&P	Immigration and Nationality Law and Practice
INLR	Immigration and Nationality Law Reports
InsAge	Insurance Age
InsInt	Insurance International
InsL&C	Insurance Law and Claims
InsLJ	Insurance Law Journal
InsLM	Insurance Law Monthly
InsL&P	Insurance Law and Practice
InsolvB	Insolvency Bulletin
InsolvInt	Insolvency Intelligence
InsolvL	Insolvency Lawyer
InsolvL&P	Insolvency Litigation and Practice
InsolvP	Insolvency Practitioner
INSOLW	INSOL World
Ins&ReinsLawInt	Insurance and Reinsurance Law International
IntAcc	International Accountant
IntALR	International Arbitration Law Review
IntBankL	International Banking Law
IntBroker	International Broker
IntCLR	International Criminal Law Review
IntCLRev	International Community Law Review
IntCompLQ	International and Comparative Law Quarterly
IntCR	International Corporate Rescue
IntILR	International Insurance Law Review
IntIR	International Insurance Report
IntJCompLLIR	International Journal of Comparative Labour Law & Industrial Relations
IntJCriminol	International Journal of Criminology and Penology
IntJFL	International Journal of Franchising Law
IntJIPM	International Journal of Intellectual Property Management
IntJLaw&Fam	International Journal of Law & the Family
IntJLaw&Fam	International journal of Law, Policy and the Family
IntJSocL	International Journal of the Sociology of Law
IntJLC	International Journal of Law in Context
IntJLPF	International Journal of Law, Policy and the Family
IntlRevLComputers&Tech	International Review of Law, Computers and Technology
IntML	International Maritime Law
IntRel	International Relations
IntRevLaw&Econ	International Review of Law & Economics
IntTLR	International Trade Law & Regulation
InvMan	Investment Management
IOLR	International Organizations Law Review
IP	International Peacekeeping
IP	International Property
IPBus	Intellectual Property Business
IPBRev	Intellectual Property in Business Review
IPD	Intellectual Property Decisions

I&PE	Investment & Pensions Europe
IPELJ	Irish Planning and Environmental Law Journal
IP&ITLaw	Intellectual Property & Information Technology Law
IP&ITLU	Intellectual Property & Information Technology Law Updates
IPL	International Pensions Lawyer
IPLaw	Intellectual Property Lawyer
IPM	Intellectual Property Magazine
IPNews	Intellectual Property Newsletter
IPQ	Intellectual Property Quarterly
IPRevBrief	Intellectual Property in Business Briefing
IProp	Intellectual Property
IP&T	Butterworths Intellectual Property and Technology Cases
IP&T	Intellectual Property and Technology
IR	Irish Reports
IrBL	Irish Business Law
I&RI	Insolvency and Restructuring International
IRLA	Insurance and Reinsurance Law Alert
IRLB	Industrial Relations Law Bulletin
I&RLB	Insurance & Reinsurance Law Briefing
IRLCT	International Review of Law Computers & Technology
IRLIB	Industrial Relations Legal Information Bulletin
IRLN	Insurance and Reinsurance Law Newsletter
IrLR	Irish Law Review
IRLR	Industrial Relations Law Reports
IRN	Industrial Relations News
IRRR	Industrial Relations Review and Report
IRSEmpLaw	IRS Employment Law
IRSEmpLB	IRS Employment Law Bulletin
IRSEmpRev	IRS Employment Review
IRSEmpTrends	IRS Employment Trends
IRSEuroEmpRev	IRS European Employment Review
IRSR	Insurance and Reinsurance Solvency Report
IRTB	Inland Revenue Tax Bulletin
IRTL	Irish Road Traffic Law
IrTR	Irish Tax Review
IRV	International Review of Victimology
ISB	Insurance Systems Bulletin
ISBAL&RR	ISBA Legislative & Regulatory Review
ISI	Insurance Systems International
ISLJ	International Sports Law Journal
ISLR	International Sports Law Review
ISLRev	Irish Student Law Review
ISR	International Securitisation Report
IT&CLJ	Information Technology & Communications Law Journal
IT&CLR	IT and Communications Law Reports
IT&CommNews	Information Technology and Communications Newsletter
ITELR	International Trust and Estate Law Reports
ITI	Information Technology in Insurance
ITLJ	International Travel Law Journal
ITPJ	International Transfer Pricing Journal
ITLQ	International Trade Law Quarterly
ITLR	International Technology Law Review
ITLRep	International Tax Law Reports
ITPJ	International Transfer Pricing Journal
ITR	Industrial Tribunal Reports
ITRep	International Tax Report

ITRev	International Tax Review
ITLT	IT Law Today
IVM	International VAT Monitor
IYLCT	International Yearbook of Law, Computers and Technology
JACL	Journal of Armed Conflict Law
JAfrL	Journal of African Law
JAL	Journal of African law
JAMN	Journal of ADR, Mediation and Negotiation
JBL	Journal of Business Law
JBR	Journal of Banking Regulation
JBusL	Journal of Business Law
JC	Justiciary Cases
JCCL	Journal of Community Care Law
JCCLaw	Journal of Commonwealth Criminal Law
JCIArb	Arbitration: Journal of the Chartered Institute of Arbitrators
JCivLib	Journal of Civil Liberties
JCL	Journal of Child Law
JCL	Journal of Criminal Law
JCL&E	Journal of Competition Law & Economics
JCLLE	Journal of Commonwealth Law and Legal Education
JCLP	OECD Journal of Competition Law & Policy
JCLS	Journal of Corporate Law Studies
JComMarSt	Journal of Common Market Studies
JCP	Journal of Consumer Policy
JCPP	Journal of Civil Practice and Procedure
JCrimL	Journal of Criminal Law
JC&SL	Journal of Conflict and Security Law
JECL&P	Journal of Electronic Commerce Law & Practice
JECL&Pract	Journal of European Competition Law & Practice
JEEPL	Journal of European Environmental & Planning Law
JELP	Journal of Employment Law & Practice
JELS	Journal of Empirical Legal Studies
JEn&NatResL	Journal of Energy & Natural Resources Law
JEnvL	Journal of Environment Law
JEPP	Journal of European Public Policy
JERL	Journal of Energy & Natural Resources Law
JerseyLR	Jersey Law Review
JFC	Journal of Financial Crime
JFRC	Journal of Financial Regulation and Compliance
JFR&C	Journal of Financial Regulation and Compliance
JFSM	Journal of Financial Services Marketing
JGLR	Jersey and Guernsey Law Review
JHL	Journal of Housing Law
JHRE	Journal of Human Rights and the Environment
JIA	Journal of the Institute of Actuaries
JIANL	Journal of Immigration Asylum and Nationality Law
JIBLaw	Journal of International Biotechnology Law
JIBL	Journal of International Banking Law
JIBLR	Journal of International Banking Law and Regulation
JIBR	Journal of International Banking Regulation
JICJ	Journal of International Criminal justice
JICL	Journal of International Commercial Law
JICLT	Journal of International Commercial Law and Technology
JICM	Journal of the Institute of Credit Management
JIDS	Journal of International Dispute Settlement

JIEL	Journal of International Economic Law
JIFDL	Journal of International Franchising & Distribution Law
JIFM	Journal of International Financial Markets
JIL&C	Journal of Islamic Law and Culture
JILT	Journal of International Law & Technology
JIMF	Journal of International Money and Finance
JIML	Journal of International Maritime Law
JIntArb	Journal of International Arbitration
JIntP	Journal of International Trust and Corporate Planning
JIPLP	Journal of Intellectual Property Law & Practice
JITL&P	Journal of International Trade Law & Policy
JITTCP	Journal of International Tax, Trust and Corporate Planning
JJ	Justice Journal
JLaw&Soc	Journal of Law and Society
JLegHist	Journal of Legal History
JLE&O	Journal of Law, Economics & Organization
JLGL	Journal of Local Government Law
JLM&E	Journal of Law Medicine and Ethics
JLR	Jamaica Law Reports
JLS	Journal of Legislative Studies
JLS	Journal of the Law Society of Scotland
JLSS	Journal of the Law Society of Scotland
JMCB	Journal of Money, Credit and Banking
JMDDU	Journal of the Medical and Dental Defence Unions
JMDU	Journal of the MDU
JMDU	Journal of the Medical Defence Union
JMHL	Journal of Mental Health Law
JML	Journal of Media Law
JML&P	Journal of Media Law & Practice
JMLC	Journal of Money Laundering and Control
JNI	Journal of Network Industries
JO&R	Journal of Obligations and Remedies
JOR	Journal of Obligations and Remedies
JourGM	Journal of General Management
JP	Justice of the Peace
JP	Justice of the Peace & Local Government Review
JPILaw	Journal of Personal Injury Law
JPIL	Journal of Personal Injury Litigation
JPL	Journal of Planning & Environment Law
JPL	Journal of Planning and Property Law
JPL	Journal of Planning Law
JPlan&EnvironL	Journal of Planning and Environment Law
JPM	Journal of Pensions Management
JPM&M	Journal of Pensions Management & Marketing
JPN	Justice of the Peace Newspaper
JPN	Justice of the Peace and Local Government Law
JPRep	Justice of the Peace Reports
JPrivIntL	Journal of Private International Law
JPropFin	Journal of Property Finance
JR	Judicial Review
JR&I	Journal of Risk and Insurance
JRLS	Jerusalem Review of Legal Studies
JRS	Journal of Refugee Studies
JSBJ	Judicial Studies Board Journal
JSF	Journal of the Society of Fellows
JSIJ	Judicial Studies Institute Journal

JSocWel&FamL	Journal of Social Welfare and Family Law
JSocWelL	Journal of Social Welfare and Family Law
JSPTL	Journal of the Society of Public Teachers of Law
JSSL	Journal of Social Security Law
JSWL	Journal of Social Welfare Law
JTCP	Journal of International Trust & Corporate Planning
JuridRev	Juridical Review
Juris	Jurisprudence
JurRev	Juridical Review
JWBL	Journal of Welfare Benefits Law
JWEL&B	Journal of World Energy Law & Business
JWIP	Journal of World Intellectual Property
JWL	Journal of Water Law
JWorldTr	Journal of World Trade
JWorldTrL	Journal of World Trade Law
JWorldTradeL	Journal of World Trade Law
JWT	Journal of World Trade
JWTL	Journal of World Trade Law
KB	Law Reports, King's Bench
KCLJ	King's College Law Journal
Kemp&Kemp	Kemp & Kemp, The Quantum of Damages
KHRPLR	Kurdish Human Rights Project Law Review
KIMLegal	Knowledge and Information Management
KingstonLR	Kingston Law Review
KIR	Knight's Industrial Law Reports
KILR	Knight's Industrial Law Reports
KLGR	Knight's Local Government Law Reports
KLJ	King's Law Journal
LAG Bull	Legal Action Group Bulletin
LAL	Local Authority Law
Law&Crit	Law and Critique
LawforBus	Law for Business
LawinEur	Lawyers in Europe
LawJ	Law Journal
LawJ	Law Journal Reports
LawJour	Law Journal
LawJour	Law Journal Reports
Law&Just	Law and Justice
LawLib	Law Librarian
LawMag	Law Magazine
Law&Phil	Law & Philosophy
Law&Pol	Law and Policy
Law&TaxR	Law and Tax Review
LawTeach	Law Teacher
LBEB	Lloyds Bank Economic Bulletin
LBR	Law Business Review
LC	Scottish Land Court Reports
LC&AI	Law, Computers & Artificial Intelligence
LCB	Legal Compliance Bulletin
LCCD	Law Commission Consultation Document
LCNews	Law Centres News
LCRep	Law Commission Report
LCWP	Law Commission Working Paper
LD	Legal Director

LD'I	Lettre D'Information
LE	Lawyers' Europe
Leg	Legisprudence
LegalBus	Legal Business
LegalIEI	Legal Issues of Economic Integration
LegalM	Legal Marketing
LegalTJ	Legal Technology Journal
LegalM	Legal Marketing
LegalTJ	Legal Technology Journal
LEx	Legal Executive
LF	Litigation Funding
L&FMR	Law & Financial Markets Review
LGC	Local Government Chronicle
LGCLaw&Admin	Local Government Chronicle Law & Administration
LGD	Law, Social Justice and Global Development
LGI	Law Gazette International
LG&L	Local Government and Law
LGLR	Local Government Review Reports
LGLRep	Local Government Law Reports
LGR	Local Government Reports
LGRev	Local Government Review Reports
LGRev	Local Government Review
LGRRep	Local Government Review Reports
L&H	Law & Humanities
LIEI	Legal Issues of Economic Integration
LII	Life Insurance International
LIM	Legal Information Management
LinkAWS	Link Association of Women Solicitors
LIT	Law, Innovation and Technology
Lit	Litigation
LitL	Litigation Letter
LiverpoolLR	Liverpool Law Review
LJ	Law Journal
LJIL	Leiden Journal of International Law
LLID	Lloyd's List Insurance Day
LlInsInt	Lloyd's Insurance International
LlLog	Lloyd's Log
LlLR	Lloyds Law Reports
LlMCLQ	Lloyds Maritime and Commercial Law Quarterly
LlNews	Lloyd's of London Newsletter
Lloyd'sRep	Lloyd's Reports
Lloyd'sRepBank	Lloyd's Law Reports Banking
Lloyd'sRepMed	Lloyd's Law Reports Medical
Lloyd'sRpIR	Lloyd's Law Reports Insurance & Reinsurance
Lloyd'sRpPN	Lloyd's Law Reports Professional Negligence
LLR	Licensing Law Reports
LLR	London Law Review
LMCLQ	Lloyd's Maritime and Commercial Law Quarterly
LMELR	Land Management and Environmental Law Report
LMLN	Lloyd's Maritime Law Newsletter
LMN	London Market Newsletter
LN	Law Notes
LNTS	League of Nations Treaty Series
L&P	Law and Practice of International Courts and Tribunals
LPICT	Law & Practice of International Courts and Tribunals
LP&R	Law, Probability & Risk

LQR	Law Quarterly Review
LR	Licensing Review
LR	Law Reports
LR&I	Liability Risk & Insurance
LRLR	Lloyd's Reinsurance Law Reports
LS	Legal Studies
LSG	Law Society's Gazette
LS&P	Law, Science and Policy
LT	Law Times
LTJ	Law Technology Journal
L&TR	Landlord and Tenant Law Reports
L&TRev	Landlord & Tenant Review
L&TReview	Landlord & Tenant Law Review
M	Session Cases, 3rd series (Macpherson)
MA	Management Accounting
MaastrichtJ	Maastricht Journal of European and Comparative Law
MAdvice	Money Advice
MAdvocate	Maritime Advocate
M&AInsRep	Marine & Aviation Insurance Report
ManL	Managerial Law
ManLaw	Managerial Law
MarineIR	Marine Insurance Report
MasonsCLR	Masons Computer Law Reports
MasonsLR	Masons Computer Law Reports
MALQR	Model Arbitration Law Quarterly Reports
MCP	Magistrates' Courts Practice
MDU	Medical Defence Union Journal
MDUJour	Medical Defence Union Journal
MECLR	Middle East Commercial Law Review
MedLegJ	Medico-Legal Journal
MedLInt	Media Law International
MedLit	Medical Litigation
MedLJ	Medico-Legal Journal
MedLMon	Medical Law Monitor
MedLR	Medical Law Reports
MedLRev	Medical Law Review
MedSciLaw	Medicine, Science & the Law
MFG	Mortgage Finance Gazette
MFS	Managing for Success
MIM	Motor Insurance Market
MIP	Managing Intellectual Property
MJ	Municipal Journal
MJLS	Mountbatten Journal of Legal Studies
MLB	Manx Law Bulletin
MLJI	Medico-Legal Journal of Ireland
MLN	Media Lawyer Newsletter
MLR	Modern Law Review
MM	Money Marketing
MMan	Money Management
ModernLR	Modern Law Review
ModernLRev	Modern Law Review
ModLR	Modern Law Review
ModLRev	Modern Law Review
MoneyLB	Money Laundering Bulletin
MortgageM	Mortgage Monthly

MP	Managing Partner
MR	Media Review
MRDB	Monthly Report Deutsche Bundesbank
MRI	Maritime Risk International
MT&F	Matrimonial Tax & Finance
MW	Money Week
MWorld	Media World
NatwestITB	National Westminster Bank International Trade Bulletin
NEGRIE	Newsletter of the European Group of Risk and Insurance Economists
NIC&LLJ	Northern Ireland Conveyancing and Land Law Journal
NIER	National Institute of Economic Review
NILQ	Northern Ireland Law Quarterly
NILR	Northern Ireland Law Reports
NILRev	Netherlands International Law Review
NIrLQ	Northern Ireland Law Quarterly
NIrLR	Northern Ireland Law Reports
NJIL	Nordic Journal of International Law
NLJ	New Law Journal
NLT	Northern Law Today
NottLJ	Nottingham Law Journal
NPC	New Property Cases
NQHR	Netherlands Quarterly of Human Rights
NRGQ	Netherlands Re-insurance Group Quarterly
NSAIL	Non-State Actors and International Law
NWBQR	National Westminster Bank Quarterly
OccPen	Occupational Pensions
OD&IL	Ocean Development and International Law
OGJFI	Open Government: a Journal on Freedom of Information
OGLTR	Oil & Gas Law & Taxation Review
OHR	Occupational Health Review
O&ITRev	Offshore & International Taxation Review
OJ	Official Journal of the European Communities
OJ Annex	Official Journal of the European Communities, Annex
OJ C	Official Journal of the European Communities, C Series
OJ CE	Official Journal of the European Communities, C Series, electronic version
OJ EC	Official Journal of the European Communities
OJ L	Official Journal of the European Communities, L Series
OJLR	Oxford Journal of Law and Religion
OJ S	Official Journal of the European Communities, S Series
OJLS	Oxford Journal of Legal Studies
OLS	One Lime Street
ON	Oftel News
OPLR	Occupational Pensions Law Reports
OR&C	OpRisk & Compliance
OR&R	Operational Risk and Regulation
OSSBull	Office for the Supervision of Solicitors Bulletin
OTPR	Offshore Tax Planning Review
OTR	Offshore Tax Planning Review
OUCLJ	Oxford University Commonwealth Law Journal
OxJLS	Oxford Journal of Legal Studies
P	Law Reports Probate Division
PA	Product Advisor
PABB	Pay and Benefits Bulletin

PAD	Planning Appeal Decisions
Palmer'sCL	Palmer's Company Law
ParlAff	Parliamentary Affairs
PayMag	Pay Magazine
PB	Professional Broking
PC	Law Reports Privy Council Reports
PCB	Private Client Business
PC&L	Psychology, Crime & Law
PCLB	Practitioners' Child Law Bulletin
PCLJ	Practitioners' Child Law Journal
PCP	Private Client Practitioner
PCR	Proceeds of Crime Review
P&CR	Planning and Compensation Reports
P&CR	Property and Compensation Reports
P&CR	Property, Planning and Compensation Reports
P&D	Law Reports Probate and Divorce Cases
P&DP	Privacy & Data Protection
P&EB	Pensions & Employee Benefits
PEBL	Perspectives on European Business Law
PELB	Planning and Environmental Law Bulletin
Pen	Pensions
PenLaw	Pension Lawyer
PenLR	IDS Pensions Law Reports
Penweek	Pensions Week
PenWorld	Pensions World
PersToday	Personnel Today
PF	Property Finance
PF&D	Property Finance and Development
PharmLI	Pharmaceutical Law Insight
PHB	Parliament House Book
PI	Personal Injury (Wiley)
PIComp	Personal Injury Compensation
PIBULJ	Personal Injury Brief Update Law Journal
PIC	Palmer's In Company
P&IInt	P & I International
PIJ	Planning Inspectorate Journal
PILJ	Personal Injury Law Journal
PILMR	Personal Injury Law and Medical Review
PIN	Personal Injury Newsletter
PInjury	Personal Injury (EMIS)
PInt	Portfolio International
PIP	Property in Practice
PIQR	Personal Injuries and Quantum Reports
PL	Public Law
PL&BIN	Privacy Laws & Business International Newsletter
PL&BUKN	Privacy Laws & Business United Kingdom Newsletter
PLB	Property Law Bulletin
PLC	Practical Law for Companies
PLCR	Planning Law Case Reports
PLI	Product Liability International
PLJ	Property Law Journal
PLN	Property Law Newsletter
PLR	Estates Gazette Planning Law Reports
PlSav	Planned Savings
PLT	Professional Liability Today
PLToday	Purchasing Law Today

PLU	Pensions Law Update
PM	Pensions Management
P&MILL	Personal and Medical Injuries Law Letter
PN	Professional Negligence
PN&L	Professional Negligence & Liability
PNLR	Professional Negligence & Liability Reports
P&OJ	Procurement and Outsourcing Journal
PolJ	Police Journal
PolicingT	Policing Today
PostMag	Post Magazine
PP	Professional Pensions
P&P	Practice and Procedure
PP&D	Practical Planning & Development
PPL	Practical Planning Law
PPLR	Public Procurement Law Review
PPM	Professional Practice Management
PR	Property Review
PracLaw	Practical Lawyer
PractToday	Practice Today
PractVAT	Practical VAT
PrisonServJ	Prison Service Journal
ProbatJ	Probation Journal
ProfL	Professional Lawyer
PropLB	Property Law Bulletin
PropS	Property Service
PS	Pensions Systems
PS	Probate Section
P&S	Punishment & Society
PSELJ	Public Sector Employment Law Journal
PSP	Police Station Practice
PST	Pension Scheme Trustee
PT	Pensions Today
PTPR	Personal Tax Planning Review
PTreas	Public Treasurer
PubLawBull	Public Law Bulletin
PublicF	Public Finance
PV	Property Valuer
PW	Patent World
PWeek	Property Week
QA	Quarterly Account
QB	Law Reports Queen's Bench
QMJIP	Queen Mary Journal of Intellectual Property
QR	Quantum Reports
QRTL	Quarterly Review of Tort Law
R	Session Cases, 4th Series (Rettie)
RA	Rating Appeals
RADIC	African Journal of International and Comparative law
RALQ	Receivers, Administrators and Liquidators Quarterly
R&BCP	Renton & Brown's Criminal Procedure
R&BCPL	Renton & Brown's Criminal Procedure Legislation
R&BSO	Renton & Brown's Statutory Offences
RECIEL	Review of European Community and International Environmental Law
RELP	Renewable Energy Law and Policy Review
ReLR	Reinsurance Law Reports

Reins	Reinsurance
RepB	Reparation Bulletin
RepLR	Reparation Law Reports
ResB	Home Office Research Bulletin
RevCEELaw	Review of Central and East European Law
RiskMan	Risk Management
RiskMR	Risk Management Reports
RLEJP	Research in Law and Economics: A Journal of Policy
RLR	Restitution Law Review
RMB	Risk Management Bulletin
RMHL	Review of Mental Health Law
RMR	Reinsurance Market Report
RoadL	Road Law
RoadLaw	Road Law and Road Law Reports
RoadLR	Road Law Reports
ROWBull	Rights of Women Bulletin
RPatCas	Reports of Patent, Design and Trade Mark Cases
RPC	Reports of Patent, Design and Trade Mark Cases
RPDTMC	Reports of Patent, Design and Trade Mark Cases
RPRM	Research Programme of Risk Management
RQ	Reinsurance Quarterly
RR	Revised Reports
RRLR	Rent Review and Lease Renewal
RSI	Reinsurance Security Insider
RTI	Road Traffic Indicator
RTR	Road Traffic Reports
RVR	Rating and Valuation Reporter
RWB	Rights Workers Bulletin
RWLR	Rights of Way Law Review
S	Session Cases, 1st series (Shawl)
SB	Scottish Banker
SBT&F	Small Business Tax & Finance
SC	Session Cases
SC(HL)	Session Cases (House of Lords)
SC(J)	Session Cases (Justiciary Reports)
SCAL&P	Scottish Constitutional and Administrative Law & Practice
SCCR	Scottish Criminal Cases Reports
SCL	Scottish Criminal Law
S&CL	Sports and Character Licensing
SCLR	Scottish Civil Law Reports
SCLRev	Scottish Construction Law Review
SCLT	Social Care Law Today
SCOLAG	Scottish Legal Action Group Bulletin
ScotLT	Scots Law Times
ScotsLT	Scots Law Times
SCP	Supreme Court Practice
SCPNews	Supreme Court Practice News
S&D	Session Cases, 1st series (Shaw & Dunlop)
S&EEBLB	Butterworths Soviet and East European Business Law Bulletin
SEGJ	Law Society Solicitors' European Group Journal
SessCas(6 Ser)	Session Cases, 6th series
SFLL	Scottish Family Law Legislation
SHRJ	Scottish Human Rights Journal
SI	Statutory Instrument
SIR	Space Insurance Report

SJ	Scottish Jurist
SJ	Solicitors Journal
SJLB	Solicitors Journal LawBrief
SLA&P	Sport's Law Administration & Practice
SLB	Sports Law Bulletin
SLCR	Scottish Land Court Reports
SL&F	Sports Law & Finance
SLG	Scottish Law Gazette
S&LJ	Sport and the Law Journal
SLLP	Scottish Licensing Law and Practice
SLA&P	Sports Law Administration Law & Practice
SLPQ	Scottish Law & Practice Quarterly
SLRev	Student Law Review
S&LS	Social & Legal Studies
SLT	Scots Law Times
SLR	Scottish Land Court Reports
SLR	Student Law Review
S&LS	Social & Legal Studies
SLSReporter	Society of Legal Scholars Reporter
SMM	Single Market Monitor
SNews	Sentencing News
SocL	Socialist Lawyer
Sol	Solutions
Sol	The Solicitor
SolicJ	Solicitors Journal
SolJ	Solicitors Journal
SolJo	Solicitors Journal
SPCLR	Scottish Private Client Law Review
SPEL	Scottish Planning and Environmental Law
SPLP	Scottish Planning Law & Practice
SPLR	Scottish Parliament Law Review
SPTLReporter	Society of Public Teachers of Law Reporter
StatLR	Statute Law Review
StatLRev	Statute Law Review
STC	Simon's Tax Cases
STC(SCD)	Simons Tax Cases: Special Commissioners Decisions
S&TI	Shipping & Transport International
STL	Shipping and Trade Law
S&TLI	Shipping & Transport Lawyer International
SWTI	Simon's Weekly Tax Intelligence
TACTReview	The Association of Corporate Trustees Review
TAQ	The Aviation Quarterly
Tax&Inv	Tax and Investment
TaxA	Tax Advisor
TaxB	Tax Briefing
TaxBus	Tax Business
TaxC	Tax Commentary
TaxJ	Tax Journal
TaxPN	Tax Practice Notes
Tax	Taxation
TaxInt	Taxation International
TaxP	Taxation Practitioner
TB	Technical Bulletin
TBSPI	Technical Bulletin of the Society of Practitioners of Insolvency
TC	Tax Cases

TCLR	Technology and Construction Journal
TED	Tenders Electronic Daily, electronic version of OJ S series
TELJ	Technology and Entertainment Law Journal
TEL&P	Tolley's Employment Law & Practice
TEL&TJ	Trusts & Estates Law & Tax Law Journal
TELL	Tolley's Employment Law-Line
TELLN	Tolley's Employment Law-Line
T&EP	Trust & Estates Practitioner
T&ETJ	Trusts and Estates Tax Journal
TFA	Transactions of the Faculty of Actuaries
TheoCrim	Theoretical Criminology
TIA	Troubled Insurer Alert
TIJMCL	The International Journal of Marine and Coastal Law
TimesLR	Times Law Reports
TimesLRep	Times Law Reports
TLJ	Travel Law Journal
TLP	Transport Law & Policy
TL&P	Trust Law & Practice
TLR	Times Law Reports
TLT	Telecoms Law Today
TMIF	Tax Management International Forum
TNIB	Tolley's National Insurance Brief
TOC	Transnational Organized Crime
Tort&InsLJ	Tort and Insurance Law Journal
TortLR	Tort Law Review
TOTR	Tolleys Overseas Tax Reporter
TPA&A	Tolleys Practical Audit & Accounting
TPIAPF	Tax Planning International Asia-Pacific Focus
TPIe-commerce	Tax Planning International e-commerce
TPIEUF	Tax Planning International European Union Focus
TPIIT	Tax Planning International Indirect Taxes
TPIJ	Transfer Pricing International Journal
TPIR	Tax Planning International Review
TPITP	Tax Planning International Transfer Pricing
TPN	Tolleys Practical NIC
TPNN	Tolleys Practical NIC Newsletter
TPNS	Tolleys Practical NIC Service
TPT	Tolleys Practical Tax
TPTN	Tolleys Practical Tax Newsletter
TPTS	Tolleys Practical Tax Service
TPV	Tolleys Practical VAT
TPVN	Tolleys Practical VAT Newsletter
TPVS	Tolleys Practical VAT Service
TQR	Trust Quarterly Review
TR	Taxation Reports
TradL	Trading Law
TransL&P	Transport Law & Policy
TransLT	Transnational Legal Theory
TrentLJ	Trent Law Journal
Tr&Est	Trusts and Estates
Tr&EstLJ	Trusts and Estates Law Journal
TrLaw	Trading Law & Trading Law Reports
TrLR	Trading Law Reports
Tru&ELJ	Trusts & Estates Law Journal
TruLI	Trust Law International
TrustL&P	Trust Law & Practice

T&T	Trusts & Trustees
TTI	Tolleys Tax Investigation
TW	Trademark World
UCELNET	Universities and Colleges Education Law Network
UCLJurisRev	UCL Jurisprudence Review
UKCLR	UK Competition Law Reports
UKHL	United Kingdom House of Lords
UKHRR	United Kingdom Human Rights Reports
UKInsBroker	UK Insurance Broker
UKPC	United Kingdom Privy Council
ULR	Utilities Law Review
UniformLR	Uniform Law Review
UNTS	United Nations Treaty Series
UtilLR	Utilities Law Review
UtilLawRev	Utilities Law Review
UKTS	United Kingdom Treaty Series
V&DR	Value Added Tax and Duties Tribunals Reports
VATTribRep	Value Added Tax Tribunal Reports
VATTR	Value Added Tax Tribunal Reports
VATDig	VAT Digest
VATInt	VAT Intelligence
VATPlan	VAT Planning
V&DR	Value Added Tax and Duties Tribunals Reports
WalesLJ	Wales Law Journal
WB	Welfare Benefits
WComp	World Competition
WCRR	World Communications Regulation Report
WDPR	World Data Protection Report
WebJCLI	Web Journal of Current Legal Issues
WEC&IPR	World e-commerce and IP Report
Wel&FamL&P	Welfare and Family: Law & Practice
WelfRBull	Welfare Rights Bulletin
WFSB	World Fire Statistics Bulletin
WIB	Weekly Information Bulletin (House of Commons Library)
WICR	World Insurance Corporate Report
WIPOJ	WIPO Journal
WIPR	World Intellectual Property Report
WIRep	World Insurance Report
WL	Water Law
WL	Journal of Water Law
WLLR	World Licensing Law Reports
WLR	Weekly Law Reports
WLTB	Woodfall Landlord & Tenant Bulletin
WM	Waste Management
WOGLR	World Online Gambling Law Report
Woodfall	Woodfall: Landlord & Tenant
WorldILR	World Internet Law Report
WorldlawBus	Worldlaw Business
WorldTR	World Trade Review
WPG	World Policy Guide
WQ	Watson's Quarterly
WRTLB	Wilkinson's Road Traffic Law Bulletin
WSLR	World Sport Law Report

WSLRev	Warwick Student Law Review
WTJ	World Tax Journal
WTLR	Wills and Trusts Law Reports
WTR	World Tax Report
YbInt'lEnvL	Yearbook of International Environmental Law
YC&ML	Yearbook of Copyright & Media Law
YEL	Yearbook of European Law
YJ	Youth Justice
YLCT	Yearbook of Law, Computers and Technology
YMEL	Yearbook of Media and Entertainment Law
YSGMag	Young Solicitors Group Magazine

Appendix 1.3 – Abbreviations for textual devices

c.	(Latin: circa), about
cf	(Latin: confer), compare
colloq	colloquial(ly)
corresp	corresponding
d	died
derog	derogatorily
dimin	diminuative
eg	(Latin: exempli gratia) for example
erron	erroneously
esp	especially
etc	(Latin: et cetera) and so on, the rest
et seq, et sq	(Latin: et sequens) and what follows
et seqq, et sqq	(Latin: et sequentes, et sequentia) and those that follow
ff	following pages
fig	figuratively
fl	(Latin: floruit) flourished
foll	followed, following
gen	generally
id	(Latin: idem) the same
i.e.	(Latin: id est) that is
incl	including
infra	(Latin: infra) below, lower down the page
iq	(Latin: idem quod) the same as
irreg	irregular(ly)
lit and fig	literal(ly) and figurative(ly)
neg	negative
obs	obsolete
opp	opposite, opposed
op. cit.	(Latin: opere citato) in the work cited
orig	original(ly)
per	according to
pfx	prefix
pl	plural
poss	possible, possibly
prev	previous
prob	probably
pron	pronounced, pronunciation
QED	(Latin: quod erat demonstrandum) which was to be proved or demonstrated
qv, plural: qvv	(Latin: quod vide) which see
sfx	suffix
sic	(Latin: sic) thus, so
sing	singular

supra	(Latin: supra) above, higher up the page
sv	(Latin: sub verbo) under the word
transl	translation, translating, translated
ult	ultimate
usu	usually
viva voce	(Latin) orally
viz	(Latin: videlicet) namely, that is to say
vulg	vulgar(ly)

APPENDIX 2

WHAT DOES THIS TECHNICAL TERM MEAN?

This glossary includes terms commonly discovered or used in the process of legal research. It covers not only usage in the United Kingdom but also in associated jurisdictions within which UK-based users might need to research (eg the European Union, the United States and within international law). Standard legal terms which may be found in a general dictionary of law have been omitted except in a few instances. Also, where a term has several meanings, usually, only the definitions relating to the process of legal research have been selected for inclusion.

The following were consulted in the preparation of this glossary:

- Beaton, JA, *Scots law terms and expressions* (W Green & Son, 1982).
- Clinch, P, *Using a Law Library* (Oxford University Press, 2nd edn, 2001).
- Curzon, LB, *Dictionary of law* (Longman, 6th edn, 2002).
- Fox, EH (compiler), *The legal research dictionary: from advance sheets to pocket parts* (Legal Information Services (US), 2nd edn, 2006).
- McKie, S, *Legal research: how to find and understand the law* (Cavendish, 1993).
- Garner, BA, *A dictionary of modern legal usage* (Oxford University Press, 2nd edn, 2001).
- Redfield, SE, *Thinking like a lawyer* (Carolina Academic Press, 2002).
- Stott, D, *Legal research* (Cavendish, 2nd edn, 1999).
- Tunkel, V, *Legal research* (Blackstone Press, 1992).

Key
Most entries refer to terms used in the United Kingdom. Where it is necessary to differentiate between nations the following indicators are given at the beginning of the definition:

- EU: definition applicable to use in the European Union.
- Scotland: definition applicable to use in Scotland.
- UK: definition applicable to use in the United Kingdom.
- US: definition applicable to use in the United States.
- Wales: definition applicable to use in Wales.

Where a word or phrase in a definition or explanation is given in italics, an entry for that item (usually in the singular spelling of the word) appears elsewhere in the glossary.

Abridg(e)ment

Usually spelt without -e-. A legal *digest* or *encyclopedia*, referring usually to those published between the late-15th and late-18th centuries

Abstract

(1) UK: summary of a *judgment* or title
(2) US: shortened form of 'abstract of title', that is, the history of a particular piece of land, consisting of a written summary of the documents affecting title

Acronym

Initial letters or parts of a phrase or compound term, eg NATO

Act (as in enactment)

(1) Synonym for *statute*. Usually capitalised as 'Act' to avoid confusion with the noun: act (a process of doing something)
(2) The document resulting from a formal conference of the officials of nations or international bodies

See also *Statute*

Acts and resolves

US: Name of the compiled *session laws* in some states of the United States

Acts of Adjournal

Scotland: made by the High Court of Justiciary and contain rules for regulating procedure in criminal cases in that court, in the sheriff court when dealing with criminal cases, and in the district court. An Act of Adjournal is a *Statutory Instrument*. The Acts are published by *The Stationery Office* and reproduced in *Scots Law Times* and in the *Parliament House Book*

Act of Parliament

UK: a *Bill of Parliament* which has been passed by both Houses of Parliament at Westminster and then received the *Royal Assent*. Acts of Parliament are sometimes collectively known as *'The Statute Book'*

Act of the Scottish Parliament

A *Scottish Parliament Bill* which has been passed by the Scottish Parliament and has received the *Royal Assent*

Acts of Sederunt

Scotland: made by the Court of Session and contain provisions of a legislative kind but most are concerned with the regulation of procedure followed in the Court of Session, in civil cases in the sheriff court and by administrative tribunals. They are *Statutory Instruments* and published by *The Stationery Office* and reproduced in *Scots Law Times* and in the *Parliament House Book*

Administrative code

US: a publication, organised by subject area, containing the permanent, general and current rules in effect as of the date of publication. The subject areas are often called titles. Some administrative codes are *annotated*

Administrative law

Decisions, opinions, rules and other actions that issue from federal and state administrative agencies and the executive branch

Advance annotation service

US: a service consisting of pamphlets published commercially throughout the year, often monthly or bimonthly. The pamphlets update the *statutory code* and the *pocket parts* and contain recent annotations to authority applying or interpreting the law. Also called later case service

Advance code service

See *Advance legislative service*

Advance legislative service
US: a series of pamphlets published commercially throughout the legislative session at periodical intervals (and after the session has ended) with the text of the new session laws. The service updates the *statutory code* and annual *pocket parts*. Also called legislative service, session law service or advance code service

Advance opinions
See *Advance sheets*

Advance reports
See *Advance sheets*

Advance sheets
US: collections of *reported cases* published in soft-cover publications:
(1) legislative advance sheets, see *Advance legislative service*
(2) judicial/administrative advance sheets
Pamphlets of recent *opinions* (or sometimes a group of pages from a looseleaf service) covering one court or a group of courts. Also called advance reports or advance opinions

Advisory opinion
US: term used in three different contexts:
(1) Judicial advisory opinion: a nonbinding *opinion* issued by a court that interprets the law. Issued in response to a request from government officials, often legislators or the chief executive
(2) administrative agency advisory opinion: an *opinion* issued by an administrative agency. The *opinion* often interprets or implements a rule or statute over which the administrative agency has *jurisdiction*
(3) attorney-general advisory opinion, see separate entry

Agenda
(1) plural form of Latin noun: agendum – 'something to be done'
(2) a singular noun meaning 'a list of things to be done' or 'a list of business to be conducted at a meeting'

Agreement
(1) a generic term embracing the widest range of international instruments both written (a *treaty* or *convention*) and oral
(2) specific term referring to a less formal document with a narrower range of subject matter than a *treaty*. There is a tendency to apply the term to bilateral or restricted multilateral treaties. Agreements frequently cover matters of co-operation
(3) specific meaning in connection with agreements in regional integration schemes, where instruments concluded within the framework of the constitutional treaty of the scheme are termed agreements

Amendment
(1) a legislative change in a *statute* or *constitution*, usually by adding provisions not in the original or
(2) the correction of an error or supplying of an omission in process or *pleadings*

American Association of Law Libraries (AALL)
US: professional association founded in 1906 to promote and enhance the value of law libraries to the legal and public communities, to foster the profession of law librarianship, and to provide leadership in the field of legal information. See <http://www.aallnet.org/>

American Digest System
US: indexing classification system created by John West in the late 1800s to access reported *case law*

Amicus brief
US: a document submitted to a court to persuade the court to accept a legal proposition. An amicus brief is submitted to a court by a non-party to the litigation either in support of a party to the litigation or is submitted by a party having an interest in the issue being litigated

Annotation
A note that explains or criticises (usually a *case*), especially to give, in condensed form, some indication of the law as deduced from *cases* and *statutes*, as well as to point out where similar *cases* can be found

Annotated
A publication that provides *annotations* to clarify, explain or interpret text

Annotated Code
US: a code with *annotations* added by editors employed by the publisher. The annotations generally include excerpts of judicial *opinions* that have interpreted the *statute*, relevant secondary authority discussing or analysing the *statute* and other references and research aids. Annotated statutory codes are usually unofficial publications. See also *Administrative code*, *Statutory code*

Annual Abridgement
Volumes published each year recording in summary form changes to the law. In England and Wales the best known example is the set of Annual Abridgment volumes to *Halsbury's Laws of England*

Annual report
Report produced each year on the activities, operations and accomplishments of an official or organisation or other entity during the previous year

Appeal
The transfer of a case from an inferior to a higher tribunal in the hope of reversing or modifying the earlier decision

Appendix
Subsidiary matter at the end of a publication. Appendixes and appendices are both correct, plural forms for appendix

Applied
Used where the court in a case heard in a superior *jurisdiction* has applied the principle of law enunciated in a case by a court of inferior *jurisdiction*, to a new set of facts

Approved
Used where the court has approved the decision of an inferior court in unrelated proceedings, although the decision is not necessary for the disposition of the more recent case

Argument
Act or process of arguing or the art of persuading

Arrangement of clauses/sections
UK: a table at the front of most printings of all but the briefest *Bills* and *Acts*, setting out in order the *parts*, *chapters* and *clauses* (*Bills*) or *sections* (*Acts*) into which the text is divided

Article
A division of a *Statutory Instrument* or of a *journal*

Assembly measure
Wales: a form of primary legislation equivalent to an *Act of Parliament* made at Westminster, but made by the National Assembly for Wales and applying only to Wales. Under Government of Wales Act 2006, Sch 5, Westminster has granted twenty devolved areas or Fields within which the National Assembly for Wales can seek legislative competence (ie the ability) to pass Assembly Measures over certain topics, called Matters. See also *Legislative competence order*

Attorney General opinion
US: an advisory opinion issued by the attorney general which clarifies the meaning of the existing law by interpreting the *case law* or *statute*, or otherwise legal guidance. The advisory opinion has only persuasive authority because it is not the law. Opinions are printed in the annual report of the Attorney General
EU: see *Opinion of the Attorney-General*

Auditor General's report

Scotland: all *Executive Bills* submitted to the Scottish Parliament which contain any provision charging expenditure on the Scottish Consolidated Fund, must contain a report from the Auditor General setting out an opinion on whether the charge is appropriate

Authorised reports

UK: the name given to particular *law reports*, from about 1785 onwards, where the judges assisted the reporter in revising the oral judgments and providing copies of written notes, prior to publication. Also called 'regular reports'. Continued to the present day by the series called the *Law Reports*

Authority

(1) a statement of law used to support a legal proposition or argument
(2) a law book that contains statements of the law
(3) a body exercising powers, eg a local authority
For associated terms of specifically US origin, see also *Primary authority*, *Secondary authority*, *Mandatory authority*, *Persuasive authority*

Authority note/authority table

US: a note or table that identifies the *authority* by which a *rule* was promulgated or the original *session law* from which a *statutory code* was derived

Back cover information

UK: a variety of information printed sideways across the back cover of a *Bill of Parliament* submitted at Westminster

Back sheet information

Scotland: a variety of information printed on the outside back cover of a *Scottish Parliament Bill*

Bar Association periodical

US: a type of legal periodical published by a bar association and intended for use by legal practitioners. Generally contains practical rather than theoretical or academic articles; also reports news of the bar association. Also called bar journal

Bar journal

(1) US: see Bar Association periodical
(2) US: a journal published by the state bar agency that regulates the practice of law in that jurisdiction

Belfast Gazette

Official publication of the UK government in Northern Ireland, first published on 7 June 1921 and every Friday since. Registered as a newspaper, and containing official notices. Published by *The Stationery Office*. See <http://www.belfast-gazette.co.uk/> Its forerunner was the *Dublin Gazette*

Bench memo

(1) US: a short brief submitted by a lawyer to a trial judge, often at the judge's request or
(2) a legal memorandum prepared by an appellate judge's law clerk to help the judge prepare for an participate in oral argument

Bibliography

(1) a list of books or other items referred to in (most usually) a scholarly work. Sometimes printed as an *appendix*
(2) a history or description of books, including authors, editions, etc

Bill

A proposal for *legislation*. Un-enacted *legislation*

Bill tracking

A service that tracks the status of a *bill* or, in US additionally, a resolution. Provides information on its status as the measure moves through the legislative process

Bill of Parliament

UK: a draft version of a proposed *Act of Parliament* – a proposal for legislation

At Westminster: a Bill may be introduced into either the House of Lords or the House of Commons but must successfully pass all stages in both Houses before it can be submitted to the Sovereign for *Royal Assent*. Bills are numbered sequentially in each House of Parliament

In the Scottish Parliament in Edinburgh: a Scottish Parliament Bill is a version of a proposed *Act of the Scottish Parliament* (ASP)

Binding authority

See *Mandatory authority*

Biographical dictionary

See *Dictionaries*

Black Book

See *Blue book (8)*

Blackletter law

Legal principles that are fundamental and well settled – what the law is, as compared with 'public policy' – why the law is or what it ought to be. Term derived from Gothic or Old English type used in antiquated books – black-letter type

Blank bill

US: a *Bill* that has a general title and enacting clause but little or no text or substantive provisions. A blank bill is fled to meet a deadline; the substance is added later

Blue Book

(1) UK: a printed report (as of a Royal Commission) presented to *Parliament* and traditionally bound in soft-bound blue covers. The term has no other significance

(2) UK: popular name for the annual publication: *United Kingdom national accounts*, formerly known as *National income and expenditure*, compiled annually by the Central Statistical Office

(3) UK: name given on the cover of the former Government publication: *Carriage of Dangerous Goods by Sea (The Blue Book)*

(4) US: in some American states, a compilation of *session laws*

(5) US: a volume formerly published to give parallel citation tables for a volume in the *national reporter system*

(6) US: the popular name for the *citation manual: A Uniform System of Citation* (usually written *Bluebook*) because of its blue cover. One of the most widely accepted *citation manuals* for legal writing in the United States. See *Bluebook*

(7) US: a paperback book with a blue cover prepared by the US Congress to explain the various tax legislation that was enacted in a particular legislative session

(8) US: a book that describes the organisation of the federal government or a state government. It provides data on public officials, branches of government, and related legal, political and statistical information. Also called government manual, legislative manual, red book, black book or green book

Bluebook

US: popular name for *A Uniform System of Citation*, the most widely accepted *citation manual* on the compilation of references to publications and databases in legal writing in the United States, so-called because of its blue cover. Sometimes referred to incorrectly as the Blue Book

Book of authority

Name given to a few, older works written between the late-12th and mid-18th centuries, before the system of law reporting was fully developed, which are accepted as reliable statements of the law of their time. Examples include Sir Edward Coke's *Institutes of the Law of England* (1628–1644) and William Blackstone's *Commentaries on the Laws of England* (1765–1769)

Boolean connectors

Logical operators recognised by electronic search software and used to join concepts to make a search more specific (registration AND divorce), widen a search where there are synonyms (road OR highway) or exclude words (murder NOT manslaughter)

Brackets

In the UK in a case citation, where the year is given in square brackets, for example: [1990] 1 WLR 270, it is essential information to find the case. Where the year is given in round brackets, for example: (1985) 85 Cr App Rep 117, the date is not essential, for the case can be found by using the volume number

Brief

(1) UK: a document by which a solicitor instructs a barrister with an abstract of the pleadings and facts as the barrister prepares to appear as an advocate in court
(2) UK: a barrister's authority to appear
(3) US: the written arguments of counsel submitted to the court by a party to litigation to persuade the court to accept a legal proposition advanced by that party
(4) US and UK: an abstract of all the documents affecting the title to real property (known as an abstract of title)

British and Irish Association of Law Librarians (BIALL)

The only professional body in the United Kingdom and Ireland to represent and serve information professionals working with legal information. Formed in 1969 and with members drawn from law firms, chambers, universities, colleges, government departments and private institutions. See <http://www.biall.org.uk>

Brown Book

UK: popular name for Jordans Civil Court Service

Budget Bill

Scotland: a special category of *Scottish Parliament Bill*

Bulletin

See *Register*

By-law or bye-law

Either spelling is acceptable

(1) UK: regulations made by a public corporation or local authority, such as a railway, inland waterway or town, usually under powers conferred on it by a minister of government. A form of *secondary legislation*. Copies of by-laws are obtainable from the public or local authority concerned. Some public libraries, in their local history collections, may keep copies of those for the local authority in whose area they are situated
(2) Scotland: in addition to the above, a descriptive register of all the authority's by-laws should be available
(3) UK and US: rules made by a company or society or provisions of a corporation that are attached to the articles of incorporation

Canon law

Codified law constituted by an ecclesiastical authority for the organisation and governance of a Christian church. Traditionally has referred specifically to the ecclesiastical law governing the Roman Catholic church. *Ecclesiastical law* has a wider remit

Cartwheel

A word association technique, to assist in deriving all possible keywords in preparation for searches of print and electronic databases. See section 1.3, above

Case

(1) a judicial or administrative decision and the accompanying *opinion*
(2) a lawsuit or legal action between two or more parties

Casebook

UK: a law school textbook that covers an area of the law with excerpts of illustrative appellate court *opinions* on a particular subject, sometimes with editorial commentary

Case citation

A shorthand way of referring to where the text of a case may be found. If a case has been reported, throughout the common law legal world the case citation consists of the following elements: the names of parties, the year of the volume in which the report will be found, a volume number (if more than one was published that year), an abbreviation for the title of the publication and the number of the first page of the report, for example: *Watts v Morrow* [1991] 1 WLR 1421. See *brackets* for the convention on the use of square and round brackets. See *neutral citation* for the referencing of cases in the UK since 2001. See Appendix 3 for rules on the citation of cases in litigation

Case citator

See *Citator*

Case history

UK and US: multiple citations to a case as it moved through different levels of courts. The case history includes both the citations to the various *opinions* and the actual disposition by the courts (eg reversed, affirmed). Case citators (in print and electronic form) provide this information. In the UK the most oldest established is *Current Law Case Citator*, now embedded within Westlaw UK

Case law

Three different spellings: caselaw, case law, case-law

Law derived wholly or partially from an adjudication and law derived from ancient customs through the medium of judicial decisions. Law embodied in the decisions of the courts. Contrast with statute or statutory law. Also called common law, judge-made law or unwritten law

Case notes (US term)

See *Notes of decisions*

Casenote

A scholarly essay so restricted in scope that it deals only with a single case

Case reference

Shorthand reference to a case, usually using the first name in the case style or some distinctive name. See Appendix 5

Catalogue

In US spelt catalog

List of items, usually in alphabetical order or some other systematic order, often with a description of each item

Catchword

List of subject terms at the head of a case published in law reports briefly summarising the subject of the decision. The catchwords are compiled by the law reporter and have no official standing with the court. Sometimes referred to as keywords. In US referred to as *Keynote*

Cause

How an action or other proceedings in a civil court is referred to. Synonym for *Case*

Certificate

(1) a document in which a fact is formally attested
(2) a document certifying the status or authorisation of the bearer to act in a specified way
(3) a writing made in one court, by which notice of its proceedings is given to another court, usually by transcript. One example is a court certifying that a question of law has arisen on which a decision of a higher court is required

Chambers case/decision

A case heard and determined in a judges' private chambers, occurring most often in family law cases. As such, the decision may not be reported – see *Law report*

Chapter

(1) UK: each *Act of Parliament* passed at Westminster is numbered sequentially when it receives the Royal Assent, as a chapter of the total legislation of the whole year. Printed below the title of the Act is the word 'Chapter' followed by a number. See *Chapter number*

(2) US: the sequential number given to a statute enacted during a legislative session

(3) UK: a subdivision of a legislative act, comprising a number of sections

(4) UK: the dean and clergy of a cathedral

Chapter number

Part of a shorthand way of referring to an Act, comprising the year and a running number. Acts are numbered sequentially, beginning with 1, throughout the calendar year, in the order in which they receive the Royal Assent. Public General Acts are numbered in Arabic numerals (Chapter 26), Local and Personal Acts are numbered with lower-case roman numerals (Chapter iv). The word 'chapter' is frequently abbreviated to 'c' or 'cap' or 'ch'. The nomenclature derives from medieval times when *Parliament* passed a single Act each year, divided into chapters, each chapter containing new laws on a different topic

Charter

(1) in international law, a particularly formal and solemn instrument, such as the constituent treaty of an international organisation. The term itself has an emotive content that goes back to the Magna Carta of 1215. Well-known recent examples are the Charter of the United Nations of 1945 and the Charter of the Organization of American States of 1952.

(2) in domestic law, the basic legal document or organic law of a municipality or other local government unit. Analogous to a constitution. Also called municipal charter

Church law

See *Canon law*

Circular

See *Government circular*

Citation

(1) an oral or written reference to a legal authority, usually a case or a statute. See also *Citation manual, Parallel citation, Neutral citation*

(2) an official summons directing a person to appear before a court

Citation index

(1) a list of commonly applied abbreviations for the titles of publications with their meaning

(2) a list of publications including book titles or journal article titles, with details of the authors and titles of later publications which have referred back to or cited each work. There is no citation index of this type specifically for UK law publications

Citation manual

A manual or guidebook that prescribes the standard form of citation to be used when citing authorities in legal writing – see Chapter 16. Also called a style manual; see *Bluebook*

Citation of cases

The UK courts have laid down rules for the correct citation of cases before them. See Appendix 3

Citator

A listing of original documents, whether *Acts, Statutory Instruments* or *cases*, with details of references or 'citations' made in later *Acts, Statutory Instruments* or *cases*, to the original documents. Citators provide information on the status of legislation or *case law* – whether it is still 'good law'

Print or online services help lawyers determine whether a specific piece of legislation has been amended, repealed or interpreted by the courts and how a case has been treated by courts subsequently considering them – whether on appeal or as precedents. By a system of codes citators show whether later cases have *applied, approved, considered, doubted, distinguished, explained, extended, followed, not followed, overruled* or referred to a given case (see separate entries in this glossary for the meaning of each of these terms).

In the United Kingdom, the longest established citator service is a series of volumes under the banner: *Current Law [Case or Legislation or Statute] Citator*. Citators have been built into the major UK law databases: Lexis®Library and Westlaw UK

In the United States, the term citator usually refers to listings relating to cases only, of which there are two major services: *Shepard's*, available in print and online through LexisNexis, and *KeyCite*, an online citator available through Westlaw. See *KeyCite, Shepardize, Shepard's*

Cite

(1) to commend
(2) to adduce as precedent or as binding law – to cite a precedent or statute – to give its substance and to indicate where it is to be found. Contrast with 'quote': to repeat someone else's words, enclosing them in quotation marks. In legal writing, a citation usually follows after a quotation

Civil code

See *Napoleonic Code*

Civil law

(1) to a common law practitioner, private law, as opposed to criminal law or administrative law or ecclesiastical law
(2) to a legal historian, the civil law of Rome
(3) to a comparative law specialist within the common-law system, the civil-law tradition in civil code countries, the entire system in nations falling within the civil-law tradition
(4) to a civil-law practitioner, the fundamental content of the legal system, as opposed to public and commercial law – of persons, of things, of obligations
(5) to an ethicist, the law imposed by the state, temporal as opposed to moral law

Civil Procedure Rules (CPR)

A code of rules governing the practice and procedure of the civil courts in England and Wales. They came into effect in 1999 and augmented and replaced most of the provisions of the former High Court Rules (Rules of the Supreme Court 1965 (SI 1965/1776) or RSC) and the former County Court Rules (the County Court Rules 1981 (SI 1981/1687) or CCR)

Classification

A scheme (numerical or subject) used in a digest or code to organise law by subject

Classification table

US: A cross-reference table that shows where session laws have been classified in the statutory code. Also called code classification table, statutory classification table

Clause

A unit within a legal document, and especially in the UK, a *Bill* before *Parliament*. On *Royal Assent* a clause in a *Bill* becomes a *section* within an *Act*

Clean bill

US: A new bill that has been substantially amended from an earlier bill or bills and is substituted for the earlier version

Code

Derives from Justinian's Codex of 534 AD – a collection of legislation. Now applied in several ways:
(1) a systematic arrangement by subject of existing statutes
(2) a systematic consolidation of statutory law
(3) a revision of the whole law, both statutory and *case law*, reducing its principles to a clear and compact statement
Senses (1) and (2) better termed: consolidation. See *Consolidating statute*

Code classification table

See *Classification table*

Codification
(1) the process of systematically arranging and organising by subject the existing statutes and rules of a jurisdiction
(2) the organising of a body of law (such as a penal code) which may include both statutory and *case law*

Code Napoleon
See *Napoleonic Code*

Code of Practice
A statement of accepted good practice intended to provide guidance. A code approved by *Parliament* is referred to as a *statutory code of practice*; a code not legally enforceable in its own right is termed a *voluntary code of practice*

Codex
A variant of code

Codifying _tatute
A statute exhaustively r_stating the whole law on a topic including prior *case law* as well as legislative provisions

Cold starting
Legal research where it is not possible with certainty to identify the particular branch of law involved or identify the sources to turn to first. See Chapters 1–3 for assistance

Collocate
To arrange in place, to set aside

Collate
(1) to compare minutely and critically
(2) to collect and compare for the purpose of arranging accurately
(3) to assemble in a proper order

Colloquium
plural: colloquia
An academic conference or seminar

COM documents
EU: a range of working documents of the European Commission, some setting out the initial text of a proposal for legislation and others later amendments and statements on the proposal. The text of proposals is published eventually in the *Official Journal* 'C' series. Publication as a COM document marks the first public appearance of a proposal

Command paper
Document which originates outside *Parliament* at Westminster and is presented to *Parliament* 'by command of Her Majesty' usually by the Minister responsible. About 300 to 400 a year are presented to *Parliament*

Commencement clause
Found towards the end of a *Bill of Parliament* at Westminster or a *Scottish Parliament Bill* detailing when the legislation will come into force

Commentaries
Collective name for a range of secondary sources of law which explain, review or provide guidance on the law

Commissioners' decisions
A shorthand way of referring to the decisions of the Social Security Commissioners or similar body

Committee print
US: a research publication of a US Congressional committee containing surveys of information, analyses of political and financial issues or statistical data, to be used by legislators for background information. Committee prints may also reprint rules of standing committees, drafts of bills and committee reports

Common law
(1) judge-made law – term developed originally in England
(2) judge-made law as distinguished from the law of equity (q.v.)
(3) distinguished from ecclesiastical law
(4) the law common to a country as a whole as distinguished from laws of local application
(5) distinguished from statutory law

Community law
The directly applicable law of the European Union, based on the treaties and other instruments made by the institutions of the Union

Companion bill
US: a bill introduced in one house of the legislature that is identical or similar to a bill introduced in the other house. This process speeds consideration of the proposed legislation

Comparative law
The study of similarities and differences between the legal systems of different jurisdictions, such as between civil-law and common-law countries

Compendium
A concise summary or abridgment

Compiled laws
See *Statutory code*

Compiled legislative history
US: a legislative history that has already been researched, compiled and published for a particular piece of legislation. Often compiled in-house by law firm library staff

Compiled statute
US: alternative name for a statutory code

Computer-assisted legal research
Legal research performed by searching a fee-based or free online database. Also called online legal research

Conflict of laws
(1) a difference between the laws of different states or countries in a case in which a transaction or occurrence central to the case has a connection to two or more jurisdictions
(2) the body of jurisprudence which undertakes to reconcile differences or to decide what the law is to govern in these situations – the principles of the choice of law. Often referred to as 'conflicts'

Conflicts
See *Conflict of laws*

Connectors
See Boolean connectors

Considered
Used where the court in a case has discussed the decision in another case but has made no adverse criticism of the original decision

Consolidated laws
See *Statutory code*

Consolidating statute
A statute collecting together legislative provisions on a particular topic and embodying them in a single statute, often with minor amendments and drafting improvements

Consolidation Bill
A Public Bill which does not introduce any new law but seeks to tidy up existing legislation by bringing together scattered elements into one Bill. See also *Re-write Act*

Constitution
The basic, fundamental document of a state or nation. It establishes the structure, organisation, functions and powers of the government and the rights of citizens

Continuing legal education
Legal education programmes for practising lawyers. In US also called legal institute

Continuous series (law reports)
Generic name for law report series which were published in lawyers' periodicals or newspapers in the 19th century and in most cases were absorbed into other publications in the mid 20th century. Such titles include: *Law Journal Reports* (LJ), *Law Times Reports* (LT), and *Times Law Reports* (TLR). One series survives: *Justice of the Peace Reports*, which started in 1837

Convention
(1) generic meaning: a term embracing all international agreements. Synonymous with treaty
(2) specific meaning: a term originally applied to bilateral agreements, but in the last hundred years normally open for participation by the international community as a whole, or by a large number of states. Usually the instruments negotiated under the auspices of an international organisation are termed conventions

Copyright
Property rights in literary, musical, artistic, photographic and film works as well as maps and technical drawings. One of the two branches of intellectual property, the other being industrial property

Corpus juris
Latin phrase meaning 'the body of law'. The abbreviated title for the well known US encyclopedia of law: *Corpus Juris Secundum*

Correlation table
US: a cross-reference table in a book, digest or other type of finding tool that shows where the subject matter included in an old chapter, edition, digest or legal encyclopedia is now located in a revised, reclassified or new edition of the work. Also called a parallel transfer table or a table of parallel references

Corrigendum
Note containing the correction of errors made in printing discovered only after the work has been printed

Court
A judicial tribunal that decides matters of fact and/or law in controversies. Also refers to the individual judges or the place where they work

Court reporter
(1) UK: barrister employed to make a transcript of the proceedings of a case
(2) US: court official employed to make a transcript of the proceedings in a case
(3) US: prior to 1900, used to denote a set of books, as in *Supreme Court Reporter*
(4) UK and US: journalist who makes a report of cases for a newspaper

Court reports
See *Reporter*

Cross-references

References contained in a document which direct attention to other parts of the same document or other documents. When undertaking legal research it is advisable to follow up all cross-references to ensure the relationship between them is understood

Cumulative supplement

Material that supplements the material in the main body of a legal publication. It includes the material contained in the previous supplement plus more recent developments which have occurred since the previous supplement was published

Customary law

Practices and beliefs that are a vital and intrinsic part of a social and economic system which are treated as if they are laws. Often handed down generations as unwritten law, though finally collected into a written code

Daily List

Popular name for the *Daily List of Government Publications* issued late afternoon every working day. It provides publishing information for all of *The Stationery Office* (TSO) and some non-TSO official publications issued that day. Includes the official publications not only of *Parliament* at Westminster, but also *Parliament* in Edinburgh, and the Assemblies in Cardiff and Belfast. Up to the middle of May 2009 the list was available in paper form but is now published only on the internet

Debate

US: Equivalent of oral argument; an advocate's spoken presentation to a court supporting or opposing the legal relief at issue

Decision

(1) a judicial determination after consideration of the facts and the law. Also called a ruling or a *judgment*
(2) in the European Union, a form of secondary legislation which may be addressed to member states, individuals, groups of individuals or companies. It is the means by which the European Community implements treaties or regulations

Declaration

Term used for a variety of international instruments, often to indicate to the parties that the document is not legally binding (eg Rio Declaration of 1992). However, some are intended to be legally binding, such as the declarations made under the Statute of the International Court of Justice

Decree

(1) judicial decision given in a court of equity, admiralty, divorce and probate. More widely used now to refer to any court order whether or not the relief granted was equitable in nature
(2) to command by decree

Delegated legislation

See *Secondary legislation*

Delict

A tort, a civil wrong

Departmental Committee

Set up by a Minister of central government at Westminster to carry out investigations into a matter of public concern. Reports are usually published as *Command Papers*

Depository library

A library designated to receive and store copies of specific materials and make those materials available to the public. In the United Kingdom, publishers are legally obliged to send one copy of a new publication to each of the legal deposit libraries within one month of publication. The legal deposit libraries are the British Library, the Bodleian Library at Oxford, Cambridge University Library, the National Library of Scotland, the National Library of Wales and Trinity College Library, Dublin. There are also depository libraries for the publications of the United Nations, see list at
<http://www.un.org/Depts/dhl/deplib/countries/index.html>

For the European Union, see list of European Documentation Centres at
<http://www.europe.org.uk/infolinks/-/ctid/5/>

The UN and EU libraries provide reading facilities for members of the public and others wishing to consult the publications deposited

Descriptive word index
US: a subject index to a digest or to an annotated law report used to locate relevant *opinions*. It indexes both legal issues and fact patterns. Also called a word index

Deskbook
US: a compact, portable law book designed to aid research

Devolution
The passing of the power or authority of one person or body to another

Dictionary
At least five types may be identified:
(1) conventional dictionaries, which provide an explanation of a word or phrase to varying degrees of detail, for example, the *Oxford English Dictionary*. Specialist law dictionaries range from the paperback *Osborn's Concise Law Dictionary* to the multi-volume *Jowitt's Dictionary of English Law*. In Scotland an equivalent of *Jowitt* is *Greens Glossary of Scottish Legal Terms*
(2) judicial dictionaries of words and phrases, which provide details of and quotations from statutes and cases where the courts have considered the meaning of each word or phrase, for example, *Stroud's Judicial Dictionary of Words and Phrases*. In Scotland an equivalent is the *Scottish Contemporary Judicial Dictionary of Words and Phrases*
(3) indexes or lists of legal abbreviations and citations, with explanations of their meaning, for example Donald Raistrick's *Index to Legal Abbreviations and Citations*
(4) biographical dictionaries, providing a 'who is who' or 'who was who' of the legal profession, for example, *Havers' Companion to the Bar* or *Chambers and Partners' Directory*. In Scotland: *Who's Who in Scotland*
(5) in Scotland only: Dictionaries of decisions, the collective name for 18th and 19th century collections of cases arranged by subject, Morison's *Dictionary* being the most well known

Dictum
Short form of obiter dictum. Latin: 'a remark by the way'; 'something said in passing' A statement that a court makes in its decision that is not essential to resolving the legal issue before it, ie it is not essential to the court's decision. The statement is not binding as precedent

Dictum page
See *Pinpoint citation*

Digest
(1) a general summary of actions taken or of the law
(2) a research tool that provides access to reported cases by subject. An example is *The Digest*. Also called a case digest. In US also called a topical digest

Directive
In the European Union, a form of secondary legislation addressed to all member States, laying down an objective to be achieved in a specific time but member States are left to legislate the details of the implementation

Directory
A list of people or organisations
See also *Law directory*

Disapproved
Similar to 'doubted' except that the court has clearly stated that the reasoning in the earlier case is wrong

Dissertation

A report on the aims, execution and findings of an extended piece of research submitted to a degree awarding body in part or complete fulfilment of the regulations for the award, usually at Masters or Doctorate level. Also known as a thesis. In the UK, the British Library provides via the inter-library loan service a thesis request and copying service

Distinguished

Used where the court has decided that it need not follow the decision in a previous case, by which it would otherwise be bound, because of some salient difference between the two cases

Docket number

Number allocated by the court to each case and printed beneath the names of parties to the action in some of the law report publications of the Incorporated Council of Law Reporting, including *Chancery*, *Queen's Bench* and *Weekly Law Reports*. Also known as official court roll number. With the adoption of neutral citations from 2001 onwards, the practice has died out

Doubted

Used where the court has disagreed with the decision in an earlier case but either it was not necessary to overrule the decision or the court had no power to do so

Ecclesiastical law

All laws relating to a church, whether state, divine, natural or societal. Canon law has a more restricted definition

Edinburgh Gazette

Official publication of the UK government in Scotland, first published in 1699, and running continuously from 1793 to the present. Registered as a newspaper and containing official notices. Published by *The Stationery Office* (TSO), see <http://www.edinburgh-gazette.co.uk/>

Emergency Bill

A special category of *Scottish Parliament Bill*

Enabling statute

Any statute conferring powers on executive agencies to carry out various tasks delegated to them

Enacting formula

A short paragraph preceding the first clause of a Bill or section of an Act summarising the legislative authority of *Parliament*. Used in legislation at both Westminster and Edinburgh
US: known as *Enacting words*

Enacting words

US: an enacting clause; the part of a statute stating the legislative authority by which it is made and when it takes effect. In codifications of statutes, the clause may not appear as part of the text of the statute, but in historical or legislative notes
UK: known as *Enacting formula*

Enactment

(1) action or process of making a legislative bill into law
(2) a statute

Encyclopedia

'An elaborate and exhaustive repertory of information on all branches of some particular art or department of knowledge, especially one arranged in alphabetical order' (*Oxford English Dictionary*). See also *Legal encyclopedia*

Endnote

Note printed at the end of an article, chapter or book

Endorsement

Information printed sideways across the back cover of a *Bill of Parliament* at Westminster

The English Reports
Publication in 176 volumes reprinting the most significant court decisions in England and Wales up to 1865. Now available free to use on the CommonLII website <http://www.bailii.org/form/search_ers.html> and as part the *HeinOnline* and *Justis* subscriber-only services

Equity
(1) the body of principles constituting what is fair and right; natural law
(2) the system of law or body of principles originating in the Court of Chancery and superseding the common and statute law when the two conflict
(3) a right, interest or remedy recognisable by a court of equity

Erratum
Note containing the correction of errors made in printing discovered only after the work has been printed

Ex parte
Proceeding involving only one party. Antonym of *inter partes*

Ex rel
Latin: Ex relatione = upon the relation or information of
(1) in some publications containing digests or summaries of personal injury cases (notably *Current Law*) the abbreviation follows the case name and hearing details, to indicate that the information was submitted for publication by counsel or solicitors representing one of the parties to the action, whose name follows after
(2) used in styles of cause by an official body on the application of a private party (the *relator*), that is somehow interested in the matter (as in an action to abate a public nuisance)

Executive Bill
(1) A Public Bill submitted the Scottish Parliament in Edinburgh by a Member of the Scottish Parliament (MSP) acting in his or her capacity as a member of the Scottish Executive
(2) Form of legislation introduced into the Scottish Parliament to give effect to the policy of the Scottish Executive on a particular matter

Executive order
US: a directive order from the chief executive (federal or state) generally directing government officials or administrative agencies to take action

Executive proclamation
See *Executive order*

Exclusive citation
Rule which developed in England and Wales after 1865 that the series the *Law Reports*, should be cited in preference to all other law report publications because of the authority its reports commanded, particularly since the transcripts were checked by the bench before publication. This rule has been enshrined in various Practice Directions and Practice Statements, the most recent being Practice Statement (Supreme Courts: Judgments) [1998] 1 WLR 825

Explained
Used where the court has interpreted the decision in an earlier case and stated what it means

Explanatory memorandum
Attached to the first printing of a Bill. It is a brief description of the contents and objectives of a *Bill of Parliament*, describing the Bill clause by clause in non-technical language. From the late 1990s onwards replaced by an *Explanatory Note*, published separately

Explanatory note
Prepared by the Government Department sponsoring a Public Bill, these notes published separately from the Bill are written in non-technical language and intended to help inform debate and understanding of the Bill. Prior to late 1990s called *Explanatory memorandum*

Extended
Used in similar circumstances to *applied*

Extent clause
Placed towards the end of a Bill detailing the geographical area to which the Bill applies: England, Wales, Scotland, Northern Ireland individually or in any combination, or the United Kingdom as a whole

Extract
In Scots law means a formal copy of a legal document, for example a copy of a decree of court extracted from the court records which can be used by the party to enforce it against the defender

File binder
See *Transfer binder*

Financial memorandum
All Government Bills (Westminster) or Executive Bills (Edinburgh) requiring expenditure must include a financial memorandum, setting out the financial effects with estimates, where possible, of the amount of money involved, and also forecasts of any effects on manpower in the public service, expected as a result of the passing of the Bill

Finding list
US: a cross-reference table within a legal publication, listing a variety of legal documents

Focused problem
The simplest form of a research query, where the information required is clearly expressed as a question: for example, what is the maximum sentence, the period of notice required, the appropriate form

Followed
Used where the court in a case has expressed itself bound by the decision in an earlier case which is by a court of co-ordinate or superior jurisdiction

Following through
The research technique of updating information about a statute or case to identify whether it is still good law

Footnote
Note printed at the foot of a page

Foreign law
(1) law of another country
(2) conflict of laws. The law of another state or foreign country

Foreword
Preface written by someone other than the author

Form book
A collection of model forms or documents for use in both non-litigious and transactional matters, such as contracts, wills, and for litigation, eg court procedure

Formal order
A statement found at the end of a reported case giving the result of the litigation. For example, in a criminal case it might read 'Appeal against conviction allowed' or in a civil action 'Application dismissed'

General act
See *General statute*

General law
See *General statute*

General laws
See *Statutory code*

General series
Name given to a small number of law reports published in the UK which attempt to report cases on points of law of wide interest. The titles include the *Law Reports*, the *Weekly Law Reports* and the *All England Law Reports*

General statute
US: a statute that applies to, or affects, the general public. Also called public law, general act, general law

General statutes
See *Statutory code*

General Statutory Instrument
See *Statutory Instrument*

Government circular
Administrative or technical advice or guidance published by a government department, addressed to other official bodies, such as local authorities or health authorities, to assist them in the application of the law or government policy

Government publication
A publication that is issued by, or whose publication is sanctioned by, the government, a unit of government or government official. Includes both legal and non-legal publications

Great Britain
England, Wales and Scotland comprise Great Britain

Green Book
(1) England and Wales: a publication called *County Court Practice*, which contains statutory provisions, practice directions, forms and commentary
(2) US: see *Blue Book* (8)

Green Paper
'A statement by the Government not of policy determined but of propositions put before the whole nation for discussion' (House of Commons Debate (1966–1967) vol 747, col. 651). So named after the cover of the first such document issued in 1967. A consultation paper or consultative document

Guidance
See *Code of Practice*

Halsbury's
Popular term, lacking clarity, used to refer to one or more of the three publications bearing the name of the Earl of Halsbury, under whose general editorship they were first published: *Halsbury's Laws of England*, *Halsbury's Statutes* and *Halsbury's Statutory Instruments*

Handbook
US: a type of law book that provides a compact, practical overview of the substantive law on a particular legal subject. It often includes statutes and cases, statutory analysis, and analysis of *case law* on the subject. Often issued annually. See also *Hornbook*

Hansard
Popular name for the official reports of proceedings on the floor of the House of Commons and the floor of the House of Lords at Westminster. They take their name from Luke Hansard, printer of the *Journal of the House of Commons* from 1774 to 1828, and his son, Thomas Curson Hansard, printer of *Parliamentary Debates* during the 19th century. The full title is *Official Reports of Parliamentary Debates*. There are two series, one for the House of Commons and one for the House of Lords. Debates on legislation held away from the floor of the House of Commons are reported in *House of Commons Official Report of Public Bill Committees*, formerly called *House of Commons Official Report of Standing Committee Debates*

Harvard Law Review System of Citation
A system of rules for the citation (referencing) of law materials devised in the United States by the Harvard Law Review Association and published as *A Uniform System of Citation*, popularly called the *Bluebook*. For more details see Chapter 16

Harvard system of citation
A system of rules for the citation (referencing) of documents in written work. Employed in all subjects across the world. Also known as the 'name and date system'. Not to be confused with the *Harvard Law Review System of Citation* which is specific to law and most widely used in the United States

Headnote
The UK term for the summary placed at the beginning of a reported case. It is a summary of the facts of the case, the questions of law and finally, after the word 'Held' frequently printed in bold type, the decision of the court. It is compiled by the law reporter and consequently has no official standing with the court. It ought not to be cited in support of a legall argument. The US equivalent is called the *syllabus*

History note
US: a note or record in a statutory code, administrative code or topical law reporter of the chronology of the statute or rule and often also the authority. It is placed after the text of the law. For a statute, the note may include the bill number from which the statute was derived; the effective date of the statute; amendments to the statute and description of how each amendment affected the original session law; citation to session law; and citations to repealed statutes or sections of statutes. Also called historical note, historical comment, amendatory history, administrative history, source note, statutory note

HMSO
Her Majesty's Stationery Office. Following privatisation this small, residual HMSO is still responsible for printing Acts of Parliament. The Comptroller of HMSO is still referred to as the Queen's Printer

Holding
(1) a court's determination of a matter of law pivotal to its decision; a principle drawn from a decision. Also called *ratio decidendi*
(2) a ruling on evidence or other questions presented at trial
(3) legally owned property, especially land or securities

Hornbook
US: a law book containing the rudiments of the law. It generally refers to the series of books published by West (West Hornbook Series). Originally, a first book for the use of children, the pages covered with a thin layer of horn to protect them. See also *Handbook*

Hybrid Bill
A *Public Bill* which may in certain respects affect private rights and is dealt with in *Parliament* by a special procedure

In camera
Latin: camera = chamber; in the chamber, privately
(1) usually refers to proceedings heard in a judge's chambers resulting in a *chambers decision*
(2) a courtroom from which all spectators have been excluded
(3) a judicial action taken when a court is not in session

In chambers
See *In camera*

Index
Plural = indexes rather than indices
Alphabetical list of the topics or other items included in a single book or document or in a series of volumes, usually found at the end of the book, document or series

Indexing publication
A commercially produced index to the contents of tens if not hundreds of periodicals, with references to articles arranged under appropriate subject headings. An example is *Legal Journals Index* (LJI), which is available as part of the Westlaw UK, subscriber-only database

Industrial property
Property rights in patents, inventions, trademarks and industrial designs. One of the two branches of *intellectual property*, the other being *copyright*

In re/en re
Latin = regarding, in the matter of
Used in the style of cause (names of parties) for a judicial proceeding not involving adverse parties but rather involving something, eg an estate: *In re Butler's estate*

Institutional writings
The Scottish equivalent of the books of authority in England and Wales, dating from the mid-17th to the early 19th centuries. Examples include Stair, JD, *Institutions of the Law of Scotland* (1681) and Bell, GJ, *Commentaries on the Mercantile Law of Scotland* (1800)

Intellectual property
Rights protecting commercially valuable products of the human intellect. There are two branches: *industrial property* and *copyright*

Inter-library loan
A national and international network of libraries through which requests for publications and *dissertations* can be satisfied either by the loan of print materials or the provision of digital copies, subject to copyright. All university, college and public libraries in the UK are members of the national scheme. A large number of privately funded libraries (such as those in law firms) are also part of the network

International law
The system of law regulating the interrelationship of sovereign states, and their rights and duties vis-à-vis one another. Also carries a broader meaning including *private international law* or the *conflict of laws*

Inter partes
Proceeding where more than one party is involved. Antonym of *ex parte*

Interpretation
Seeking out the real meaning of legal phraseology. Only staff qualified to provide legal advice, such as solicitors and barristers, should interpret the meaning of the law discovered as a result of the process of legal research

Interpretation clause
Part of an Act which provides that certain words and phrases used in the Act shall have certain meanings

Journal
(1) an official record of the daily proceedings (bills proposed, motions made, votes taken) of a legislature published during the legislative session. Also called a legislative journal
(2) alternative word for *periodical*

Judge-made
Law established by judicial precedent rather than statute
See *Case law*

Judicial decision
See *Decision*

Judicial dictionary
See *Dictionary*

Judicial opinion
See *Judgment*

Judicial reports
See *Reporter*

Judgment
Sometimes written as judgement in non-legal texts
A final decision of a court in defining the rights and obligations of parties. Also called a *decision*. Equivalent in US to 'judicial opinion'

Jump citation
See *Pinpoint citation*

Jurisdiction
(1) a government's general power to exercise authority over all the persons and things in its territory
(2) a court's power to decide a case or issue a decree
(3) a geographical area within which political or judicial authority is exercised
(4) a political or judicial subdivision within such an area

Jurisprudence
(1) the study of the general or fundamental elements of a particular legal system as opposed to its practical and concrete details
(2) the study of legal systems in general
(3) judicial precedents considered collectively
(4) in German literature, the whole of legal knowledge
(5) a system, body or division of law
(6) *case law*

Jus gentium/juris gentium/jure gentium
'The law of nations', meaning international law or Roman law, the body of law dealing with relations between Roman citizens and foreigners

Keycite
US: an online citator available of Westlaw. Allows the researcher to trace the history of a variety of types of authority and find other citing authority; to track pending legislation affecting federal and statue statutes; and monitor the status of cases, statutes and rules

Key numbers
US: an element of the West American Digest System of classification of reported case *opinions*. The *opinions* are organised into digest topics; each digest topic is further subdivided into numerical subdivisions called key numbers. Each key number corresponds to particular point of law. Under each key number *headnotes* corresponding to that particular point of law appear with their case citations. Key numbers are assigned by West editors and are uniform throughout the American Digest System

Keyword
(1) Any term which is legally significant and therefore worthy of being indexed
(2) See *Catchword*

Know-how
Information, practical knowledge, techniques and skill required to achieve a practical end. Law firms have developed databases of 'know-how' including published and in-house generated information and materials to assist business

Landmark decision
A judicial decision that significantly changes existing law

Lapse statute
US: a *statute* which is designed to provide a substitute beneficiary for the deceased legatee in certain situations. A *statute* designed to prevent the lapse of testamentary gifts

Later case service
See *Advance annotation service*

Law dictionary
A law book with definitions of legal words, terms and phrases. The definitions may include citations to cases and other authorities in which the words are defined. Some cover law generally, some cover specific areas. Some provide foreign language equivalents of English law words

Law directory
A list of lawyers, law professors, law firms, judges, arbitrators or others with a variety of personal and professional information included. Some directories provide data on courts and departments of government. For example, for England and Wales, the *Law Society Directory of Solicitors' and Barristers'*. Formerly called the *Law List*, a term still used in the US along with lawyers list

Law French
Anglo-Norman patois used in legal documents and all judicial proceedings from the 1260s to the reign of Edward III (1327–1377), and used in legal literatur_ up to the early 18th century

Law journal
See *Legal periodical*

Law periodical
See *Legal periodical*

Law list
See *Law directory*

Lawnote
US: a scholarly legal essay shorter than an article and restricted in scope to the discussion of a number of cases in a general area of law. Usually written by a law student for publication in a law review. Also called *Note*

Law report
(1) UK: the name given to a single, published decision of the courts: 'an adequate record of a judicial decision on a point of law, in a case heard in open court, for subsequent citation as a precedent' (Moran, CG, *Heralds of the Law* (Stevens, 1948), p13). In the plural, the term 'law reports' refers to the publication(s) containing collections of decisions
(2) US: see *Reporter*
(3) US: legal essays published in *American Law Reports*. The multi-volume set contains lengthy research articles that discuss a leading case and then summarise the case or statutory law regarding the legal issue presented by that case

Law review
(1) a type of legal periodical
(2) US: law reviews are scholarly legal periodicals edited by law students. The articles may be written by law students, law professors, judges and legal practitioners and tend to be long and heavily footnoted; notes and comments (sometimes unsigned) are written by law students. A few examples of student edited law reviews are starting to appear in the UK: the *Mountbatten Journal of Legal Studies* founded in 1997 and edited by students at Southampton Institute was probably the first

Lawyers list
See *Law directory*

Leading case
(1) a judicial precedent that first definitely settled an important rule or principle of law and that has since been often and consistently followed
(2) an important, often the most important, judicial precedent on a particular legal issue
(3) a reported case that determines an issue being litigated

Legal abbreviation
Often, though not exclusively, used to refer specifically to an abbreviation used in a citation. In the UK Donald Raistrick's *Index to Legal Citations and Abbreviations* (Sweet & Maxwell, 3rd edn 2008) is the classic published list of abbreviations for publications, organisations and personalities, providing the meaning of over 34,000 legal acronyms

Legal bibliography
The study of the sources of law and the organisation and publication of law books

Legal encyclopedia
A law book or set of law books containing an exhaustive statement of and/or commentary on the law, usually arranged alphabetically by broad subject. In English law there is one *encyclopedia* which attempts to provide information on the whole extent of the law of England and Wales: *Halsbury's Laws of England*. In Scotland the equivalent is *Laws of Scotland*, also referred to as the *Stair Memorial Encyclopedia*
Other *encyclopedias* provide information on either particular forms of legal publication such as *The Encyclopedia of Forms and Precedents*, or on a specific practice/subject area, such as the *Encyclopedia of Planning Law and Practice*
US: the term cyclopedia is sometimes substituted for encyclopedia

Legal institute
US term: see *Continuing legal education*

Legal journal
See *Legal periodical*

Legal journals index
See *Legal periodicals index*

Legal newsletter
A type of *legal periodical* reporting on a specialised area of law, often published monthly and reporting a variety of news, cases and other developments. Contains brief articles and case summaries

Legal newspaper
A type of *periodical*, published daily, weekly or monthly. In the UK the scope will be national but in US it may be national or local or both. Reports on legal developments and news. It may publish articles on law firms, specific attorneys etc. A UK example is *The Lawyer*

Legal periodical
A regularly issued periodical, including bulletins, journals, law reviews, newsletters and newspapers, that reports on an area of law or on legal developments and trends generally. Five types may be identified: those of primarily academic interest such as *Cambridge Law Journal*; practitioners' periodicals, for example, *Solicitors' Journal*; specialist periodicals covering particular areas of law, for example, *Criminal Law Review*; newsletters, containing topical information and comment on discreet practice areas, for example, *Business Law Brief*; and law periodicals published abroad, particularly in other common law jurisdictions, for example *Harvard Law Journal*. A small number of British law periodicals are published only on the internet, for example, *Journal of Information Law and Technology* (JILT). Also called law periodical

Legal periodical index
An index to articles in legal periodicals on specific subjects, cases and statutes. It may also index material in books and government publications and book reviews. The most comprehensive example covering English language UK and European legal periodicals is the journals index on *Westlaw UK*, formerly known as *Legal Journals Index*. The most comprehensive covering common-law jurisdictions world-wide is *Index to Legal Periodicals*, available in print or electronic form from HW Wilson or on subscription as part of the international materials library of Lexis®Library

Legal research

The process of searching for the law that applies to a specific fact situation or legal issue. Legal research is done in the context of both litigation and transactions (legal, business and personal transactions). The goal is to discover the law that applies to a specific fact situation and that answers a specific legal question

Legal thesaurus

A collection of legal terms, with synonyms and related terms. The thesaurus may also provide definitions, parts of speech and alternative terms and concepts. It is useful for comparing nuances or shades of meaning among legal terms and may also be used by the researcher to expand search terms when consulting indexes and performing online research. Some databases have built-in thesauri; an updated version of Miskin, C, *A Legal Thesaurus* (Legal Information Resources, 3rd edn, 1997) operates behind searches undertaken on Westlaw UK

Legal treatise

A type of book or legal textbook that discusses, explains, analyses or interprets an area of law. It is usually heavily footnoted with multiple types of authority (primary and secondary). It is less detailed and less heavily footnoted than academic legal periodical articles. Legal treatises are useful when beginning research because they give an overview on the law emphasise key cases and applicable statutes and cite to other authority. The term is perhaps more widely used in the United States than the United Kingdom

Legislation

What a legislature has enacted, the whole body of enacted laws

Legislation citator

See *Citator*

Legislative competence order (LCO)

Wales: a new category of legislation, brought about by the Government of Wales Act 2006. They are a type of *Order in Council* which enables the National Assembly for Wales to acquire the power from the UK *Parliament* to legislate in a particular area for Wales. Where the National Assembly has legislative competence it can pass *Assembly Measures* which can do anything that an *Act of Parliament* can do in relation to Wales

Legislative documents

US: documents and publications generated during the legislative process or otherwise authorised by the legislature. These materials include bills, statutes, resolutions, committee reports, committee prints, committee hearings, legislative debate, journal of proceedings and other documents. See also *legislative history*

Legislative history

US: a chronology of events and the publications generated during the legislative process. See also *Compiled legislative history*

Legislature

US: the branch of government that sets policy by enacting statutes. Also called congress, general assembly, general court, legislative assembly

Lexis/Nexis

One of the major online databases in the United States. The UK arm is *Lexis®Library* (formerly *LexisNexis Butterworths*). See also *Computer –assisted legal research*

Lis-law

A UK-based email discussion list service used by over 800 law librarians in all types of organisation worldwide. It is a closed list with the need to register to join. The home page is at <http://www.jiscmail.ac.uk/lists/lis-law.html> Its value lies in members being able to post requests for help in finding information, keeping up to date with developments in the legal information world, and discuss matters of common interest, such as the characteristics, deficiencies and cost of publications or databases

Local and Personal Act
An *Act of Parliament* restricted in application to a particular geographical location or organisation (such as a local authority area, a harbour or port) or a group of individuals. As a draft it would have been called a *Private Bill*

Local law
(1) UK: see *By-law*
(2) US: an act that applies only within a specific geographical area (city, county other type of local unit of government) rather than throughout the entire jurisdiction. A type of *special law*. See also *General law*

Local Statutory Instrument
See *Statutory Instrument*

London Gazette
Official publication of the UK government, first published in the mid-17th century. Registered as a newspaper, and containing official notices. Published by *The Stationery Office*. See <http://www.london-gazette.co.uk/>

Long title
Paragraph near the head of a *Bill* or and *Act* setting out in general terms the purposes of the piece of legislation

Looseleaf service
A lawbook or set of law books published in looseleaf binders for easy updating. The service is updated by inserting and removing individual pages or groups of pages. Looseleaf services are published on a variety of areas of law, mostly regulated industries (banking, employment, tax) as either cumulating services or interfiled services. They provide comprehensive coverage including *primary legislation* and *secondary legislation*, *case law*, commentary and analysis, *citators* and many finding aids. Archived material may be moved to *transfer binders* or transfer books to make room for current material. In the United States, *opinions* published in the service may be reprinted in permanent bound volumes that supersede the individual looseleaf pages
US: see also *Topical reporter*

Magazine
See *Periodical*

Magna Carta/Magna Charta
Latin: 'great charter'. English charter that King John granted the barons in 1215 and confirmed by later monarchs. Generally regarded as one of the great common-law documents and as the foundation of constitutional liberties

Management rules
Scotland: a form of secondary legislation introduced by the Civic Government (Scotland) Act 1982 and employed to regulate the use of land or premises in local authority control. Unlike other forms of secondary legislation there is no external confirming authority. Management rules must be prominently displayed at the entrance to the land or premises to which they apply and copies must also be made available for public inspection

Marginal note
UK: brief note placed to the side of a *section* of an *Act* indicating the scope or subject matter. It is not authoritative as a guide to interpretation because it was not debated as part of the *Bill* and may be misleading

Manual
(1) a practical law book that provides guidance on specific transactions. May include statutes, rules, sample documents and forms, and worksheets. Also called a practice book. See also *Form book*
(2) US: see *Blue Book* (6)

Martial law
The body of rules applied on grounds of necessity by a country's rulers when the civil government has failed or looks as if it might fail to function, the armed forces assuming control purportedly until civil processes and courts can be restored to their lawful places. Applies to both civilian and soldiers

Measure
A shorthand way of referring to a Measure of the General Synod of the Church of England. A form of secondary legislation made by the General Synod under powers given by an enabling section in an *Act of Parliament*

Medico-legal
The application of medical science to law

Medium-neutral citation
See *Neutral citation*

Member's Bill
A *Scottish Parliament Bill* introduced by an individual member of the *Parliament* as opposed to a bill submitted by a member on behalf of the Scottish Executive (an *Executive Bill*) or a Committee of Parliament (a *Committee Bill*)

Memorandum of law
(1) US: see *Brief*
(2) US: a thorough discussion (with authorities) of the law that applies to a specific fact situation. Often used internally (eg in law firm) to evaluate the strength of a legal position

Mercantile courts
Courts hearing commercial law matters – litigation relating to merchants or trading

Military law
The special branch of law that governs military discipline and other rules regarding service in the armed forces

Mind mapping
A technique to aid analysis of a legal problem. See section 1.2.2, above

Model Act/Model Code
US: a proposal for legislation, often comprehensive, drafted by the National Conference of Commissioners on Uniform State laws (NCCUSL), American Law Institute, American Bar Association, or another organisation. A proposal is designated a model act by the NCCUSL when its principal purposes can be substantially achieved even if it is not adopted in its entirety by every state. Model acts promulgated by other organisations are proposed as guideline legislation for the states, which can modify the proposal to suit their own needs. See also *Uniform act*

Modern reports
Generic name for law reports published in England and Wales from 1865 onwards, when the present system of law reporting in that jurisdiction originated. A modern law report would comprise as a minimum: the names of parties, court in which the case was heard, date of hearing and *judgment*, the full text of the judgment, the formal order. The more respected series also include *catchwords*, a *headnote*, the names of counsel, solicitors and the *law reporter*. In Scotland the commencement of *Sessions Cases* in 1821 is frequently taken as the start of modern law reports in that jurisdiction

Moys classification
A special variation of the traditional Dewy Decimal and Library of Congress book classification schemes, first published in 1968 and named after Elizabeth Moys who devised it. It is widely used in academic law libraries in the United Kingdom

Municipal code
US: a subject arrangement of the general and permanent ordinances in effect in the municipality

Municipal law
(1) the law of or relating to a town, city or local governmental unit (as contrasted with county, state or national)
(2) the law of or relating to the internal government of a state or nation (as contrasted with international)

Name and date citation system
See *Harvard system of citation*

Napoleonic Code
Collection of five codes commissioned by Napoleon and published between 1804 and 1811 to codify French law

National Reporter System
System of law reports established in 1879 by the West Publishing Company each 'Reporter' being a set of books containing judicial *opinions* from a geographical area within the United States. The national system of reporters published by West in which the United States is divided into a number of regional reporters and jurisdiction-specific reports. It includes *opinions* of the appellate courts of the states and also the federal reporters published by West. All cases reported in the system are classified by to the West key number system and share other editorial features. See also *Regional reporter*

Neutral citation
A citation that identifies a case without reference to a publication or page number. A typical neutral citation includes the year, jurisdiction, court, and case number assigned by the court, for example: *Chester v Afshar* [2004] UKHL 41. This form of citation provides a uniform method of citation that is independent of both format (print, online) and publisher. In the United Kingdom the scheme began in 2001 (see Appendix 3) and countries throughout the common-law world have adopted similar schemes. Also called vendor-neutral citation, public-domain citation

Newsletter
See *Legal newsletter*

Newspaper law reports
Reports of cases prepared by a barrister and published in a daily newspaper. At one time several UK national newspapers carried law reports but *The Independent* ceased in November 2006 and now only *The Times* carries them

Nominate reports
Name given to more than 500 different publications co_taining law reports appearing between 1571 and 1865, in which collections of cases were published under the name of the individual responsible for compiling them. Selections have been reprinted in the *English Reports* (the most comprehensive set covering cases from 1220 to 1865), the *Revised Reports* (covering cases from 1785 to 1865 only) and the *All England Law Reports Reprint* (covering cases from 1558 to beyond the period ending in 1935)
US: the term *Nominative reporter* is used

Nominative reporter
US: early 18th or 19th century law reports, official or unofficial, named after the individual who compiled or edited the reporters (sometimes the judge himself). Many of these reporters have been numbered to conform to the officiall jurisdictional numbering

Non-parliamentary papers/publications
Publications other than those required for the conduct of the business of *Parliament*. There is a huge range which may be divided into three broad categories: reports, for example, annual reports of government institutions and the reports of investigative bodies; information publications: a wide variety of books, pamphlets, leaflets and periodicals providing public information and advice; publications of government departments not issued through *The Stationery Office* (TSO). To trace a non-parliamentary paper it is important to identify whether it has been published by TSO or by the individual government department concerned, and so on which website it may be published

Not followed
Used where the court in a case has declined to follow the decision in a previous case which is by a court of coordinate jurisdiction

Note
US: a scholarly essay shorter than an article and restricted in scope, usually written by a student for publication in a law review

Noter-up
Part of the service provided by some publishers as part of their law encyclopedia publications. A booklet or series of loose pages published at regular and frequent intervals (often a month) carrying details of recent developments in the law which amend or replace information given in the main volumes of the encyclopedia. The term is used in particular within the *Halsbury's* publications

Numeric system of citation

A system for linking the mention of a publication in the body of the text, with the full reference given in the bibliography or list of references at the end of the document. Each reference is given a number in the order in which it is cited in the text and at the end of the document the full references are listed in numerical order

Nutshell

US: a compact paperback book providing a concise explanation of the law on a particular topic. The (In a) Nutshell series is published by West on over 100 areas of law. Nutshells are written mainly for law students but may also benefit a researcher seeking a basic explanation of the law

Official gazette

A publication of a government or international organisation, often issued daily, containing some or all of the following: the authorised text of new legislation, reports of decisions of the courts, proceedings of the legislature, official notices and administrative directions. For UK examples see *London Gazette*, *Edinburgh Gazette* and *Belfast Gazette*. For the European Union see *Official Journal* and for the United States see *Register* (3)

Obiter dictum

Latin: by the way. An *opinion* expressed by a judge on a matter or point not essential to the decision of the case of the *judgment* in which the *opinion* is part. Although the *opinion* may not be authoritative it may be used to assist the decision of some other case to which it is relevant

Official citation

(1) for Acts passed at Westminster, the shorthand way of referring to an Act, comprising a date and a running number, for example 1976 chapter 26. Acts are numbered sequentially, beginning with 1, throughout the calendar year, in the order in which they receive the Royal Assent. Public General Acts are numbered in arabic numerals (1, 2, 3,). Local and Personal Acts are numbered with lower case roman numerals (i, ii, iii). So the example was the 26th Act to receive the *Royal Assent* in 1976

(2) for Acts of the Scottish Parliament (ASP), the shorthand way of referring to an Act, comprising a date, the letters asp and a running number, for example: 2000 asp 1. Acts of the Scottish Parliament are numbered sequentially, beginning with 1, throughout the calendar year, in the order in which they receive the *Royal Assent*

Official court roll number

See *Docket number*

Official journal

Shorthand way of referring to the official daily publication: *Official Journal of the European Communities*, containing details of community legislation, proceedings of the European Court of Justice and proposals made by the Commissioners. Published in all EU languages and in three series: 'L' (Legislation) including the text of EU legislative acts; 'C' (Communications) including legislative proposals from the Commission and extracts from Court judgments; 'S' (Supplement) including invitations to tender for public works contracts

Official publications

Publication (print or online) published by or under the direction of the government, or the government may designate publication by a private publisher as official. In the United Kingdom some national statistics are published by private publishers and in the United States some states have designated as the official reporter the West regional reporter that publishes the state's *opinions* as the official reporter for the state

Official Report

Title of the publication containing a verbatim report of proceedings in the Scottish Parliament and its committees

Official Reports of Parliamentary Debates

Official title of the publication containing a verbatim report of proceedings in the House of Commons and the House of Lords at Westminster. See *Hansard*

Old Scots Acts

Acts of the Parliaments of Scotland passed before or in 1701

Opinion

(1) UK: term applied to a *judgment* delivered by the Law Lords in the House of Lords or the newly created Supreme Court
(2) US: the document prepared by a judge justifying their *decision* or *judgment*. Technically, the written statement of the court explaining its decision, ie a written explanation by the court of why it took the action it did. Equivalent of *judgment* in the United Kingsom. See *Unpublished opinion*
(3) EU: a form of secondary legislation suggesting a line of action or *opinion* – not legally binding

Opinion of the Advocate-General

Within each individual case report of the European Court of Justice, the opinion states an impartial review of the issues and prior decisions of the Court, with a discussion of the alternative choices available to the Court and the Advocate-General's personal view of what in law should be done. The opinion is printed in front of the *judgment* of the court and after the report for the hearing

Order

(1) a particular type of *Statutory Instrument*
(2) see *Formal order*

Orders in Council

Orders made by the Sovereign when in session with the Privy Council. Usually restricted to actions in wartime and making legislation relating to, for example, the Church of England, universities, the Channel Islands and what remains of the British Colonies. A list of those Orders made since 11 October 2000 is at <http://www.privy-council.org.uk/output/Page473.asp>. Many are published as *Statutory Instruments*; some are published in the *London Gazette*. Those not so published may be obtained from the Privy Council Office

Orders of Council

Orders made by the Privy Council in the Sovereign's absence. See *Orders in Council*

Ordinance/ordnance/ordonnance

(1) a decree made by the UK *Parliament* without the consent of a constituent element (for example, the House of Lords)
(2) a declaration by the Sovereign made without Parliament's consent
(3) a form of primary legislation found in jurisdictions outside the United Kingdom, such as the Channel Islands and Gibraltar
(4) US: an enactment by the local governing body (city council, county board of supervisors etc) concerning a local matter. Ordinances generally deal with local matters such as zoning, parking and traffic. The ordinances of some cities are compiled into a municipal code. Also called municipal statute, municipal ordinance

Overrule

Used where the court in a case which is based on substantially identical facts with an earlier case, has decided that the decision in the earlier case, which was given by a court of inferior jurisdiction in unrelated proceedings, is wrong

Oxford System for the Citation of Legal Authorities (OSCOLA)

See Chapter 16

Pact

A less formal type of *agreement* between nations than a *treaty*

Paragraph

Subdivision of a document, often numbered for reference

Pardon

The excusing of an offence or remission of a punishment. Information on pardons granted was held by the Home Office until the formation of the Ministry of Justice, which is now the responsible government department

Parliament

Supreme legislative body in the United Kingdom based at Westminster. Since 1999 the Scottish Parliament in Edinburgh assumed powers and now legislates for Scotland on most of its internal affairs. Westminster can still make legislation which is effective in Scotland. Also since 1999 the National Assembly for Wales and the Northern Ireland Assembly have received powers from Westminster to make legislation on a limited number of subjects

Parliamentary debates (Official Reports)
The full report of what is said in the House of Commons and the House of Lords at Westminster. Popularly known as *Hansard* after the printer of one of the earliest reports of Parliamentary debates

Parliament House Book
Scotland: looseleaf publication containing primary and secondary legislation relating to Scotland in the areas of private law and court procedure

Parliamentary papers/publications
Publications required for the conduct of the business of *Parliament* at Westminster, including House of Lords papers, Bills and debates, House of Commons papers, Bills and debates, command papers, Acts and Measures of the General Synod of the Church of England

Parallel citation
Multiple sources of publication (and therefore multiple citations) to the same published *judgment* or *opinion*; a cross reference from one publication to another. Each citation shows where the *judgment* or *opinion* is to be found in a specific publication

Parallel transfer table
See *Correlation table*

Parties
The persons or organisations involved in court cases. Individual cases are identified and referred to by the names of parties

Penal statute
A law that defines an offence and prescribes its corresponding fine, penalty or punishment

Pepper & Hart research
The name given to research into the background relating to the passing of a Bill, to assist in the interpretation of the meaning of the statute. The House of Lords' decision in *Pepper v Hart* [1993] AC 593 modified, in certain defined circumstances, the general rule that when interpreting a statute no reference should be made to background materials relating to the passing of an Act, such as drafts of the Bill, reports of committees and Parliamentary debates

Periodical
A publication comprising individual issues, which at predetermined intervals are gathered together to form a volume with a title page and/or an index. Each issue is characterised by a variety of contents: articles, news, notes and digests of information; and a variety of contributors. See *Legal periodical*. Also called journal or magazine

Persuasive authority
Authority that is not mandatory or binding on the court or administrative agency when making its decision; that is not mandatory authority. The tribunal may choose to follow it but is not obligated to follow it. The most frequent example of the use of persuasive authority is the consideration of a UK court of a decision on a similar matter made by a superior court of a Commonwealth country when reaching its own decision

Photocopies
The making of photocopies of legal materials is governed by copyright law – see one of the leading practitioner texts on the topic such as *Copinger and Skone James on Copyright*

Pincite
See *Pinpoint citation*

Pink index
Popular name for the monthly index volumes to the *Law Reports*, named after the colour of their covers

Pinpoint citation
US: a reference to the exact page (or paragraph) of an *opinion* from which a quotation or citation is taken (rather than a reference to the first page of the *opinion*). Also called a dictum page or a jump citation or a pincite

Plagiarism
The act or an instance of copying or stealing another's words or ideas and attributing them as one's own

Pocket part
US: a paper pamphlet supplement to a law book or set of law books that is inserted into the book(s) through a slit in the inside cover (usually the back cover but sometimes the front). The information in the pocket part updates the information in the main volume. Also called a cumulative supplement

Policy memorandum
Scotland: all Executive Bills submitted to the Scottish Parliament must be accompanied by a policy memorandum setting out the policy objectives of the Bill, justifying the approach taken to meet those objectives, detailing the consultation which has taken place, and assessing the overall effect

Popular names
See Appendix 5

Power
(1) legal authorisation
(2) a document giving legal authorisation – often used to identify the *Act* from which a *Statutory Instrument* takes its power or authority

Practice books/manuals
Guides to the practice and procedure in the courts, primarily for the use of practitioners. Examples include *Civil Procedure* and *Civil Court Practice*. See *Manual*

Practice Direction/Note/Statement
Documents published in law reports indicating the views of the judges of the Court of Appeal, or the judges, masters and registrars of the High Court on matters of court practice and procedure. See Appendix 3 for a summary of the practice materials relating directly to legal research

Practicks
An early form of encyclopedia developed in Scotland in the 16th and 17th centuries. Originally compiled for private use, they comprised notes of decisions, abstracts of statutes and other legal materials in an alphabetical subject sequence. Some were published

Practitioners' book
A general term including a range of publications which assist and support the work of solicitors, barristers and advocates in the practice of the law. They include *practice books/manuals* and *precedent books*

Preamble
(1) a paragraph near the head of a *Local and Personal Act* stating the reason for and the expected effects of the legislation
(2) the first part of a *treaty* comprising the names of the Heads of the Contracting Parties and their duly authorised representatives and the motives for concluding the *treaty*

Precedent
(1) a decided case that provides the basis for determining an identical or similar case that may arise later, or a similar question of law
(2) a model form; a pattern for draftsmen. In Scotland called a *Style* (3)

Precedent Book
A collections of forms and documents which have been found valid, effective and useful in the past, and provide lawyers with a general layout and wording accepted as standard. It is frequently used for the preparation of documents in connection with a court action, or in conveyancing. Examples include *Atkin's Court Forms* and *The Encyclopaedia of Forms and Precedents*. In Scotland the equivalent is a *Style book*

Preface
An introductory essay written by the author of the book

Preliminary print

US: the brown paperback official advance sheet pamphlets to US Supreme Court *opinions*

Primary authority

US: the law itself; authority that issues from one of the branches of federal, state or local government as part of its function, or that issues from the constitution (of a country or state) or the charter (of a municipality); legislation enacted in the form of statutes or joint resolutions (by stat and federal legislatures) and ordinances (enacted by municipalities); treaties; decisions and *opinions* issued by adjudicative tribunals (either judicial or administrative); rules issued by administrative agencies or the chief executive; rules of court

Primary legislation

Legislation which, in general, becomes law only after detailed debate and scrutiny within *Parliament* at Westminster or in Edinburgh, culminating in approval by the sovereign

Primary sources of law

Original and authoritative statement_ of the law comprising *legislation* and *case law*

Private Act

(1) a statute passed by *Parliament* at Westminster or the Scottish Parliament in Edinburgh, which enables a person or persons, a public company or corporation, a local authority or similar body to do something or carry on some activity which is for his, her or their constituents' particular interest or benefit. Name distinguishes legislation from a measure enacted as a matter of public policy in which the whole community is interested. A Private Act passed at Westminster is more correctly referred to as a *Local and Personal Act*

(2) US: see *Private law*

Private Bill

A *Bill of Parliament* (whether at Westminster or Edinburgh) which relates to an individual or a small group of people, a public company or corporation or a local authority. At Westminster, if successful a Private Bill will become a *Private Act* (more correctly a *Local and Personal Act*). Not to be confused with a *Private Members' Bill*

Private International Law

International conflict of laws. Not a parallel system of law with public international law, but a part of the private law of each legal systems. Also called international private law

Private law

UK: those areas of law concerned primarily with duties and rights of individuals with which the state is not immediately or directly involved, for example the law of contract

US: a statute that has limited applicability. It applies to or affects a specific group, individual or entity rather than the public at large. A private law is a type of special law. Also called a private act. See also *General statute*

Private Member's Bill

Draft legislation introduced into *Parliament* at Westminster either in the House of Commons by an individual Member of Parliament (MP) or in the Lords, by an individual peer. Not to be confused with a *Private Bill*

Procedural law

In criminal law the steps by which a violator is brought to punishment and in civil law the steps in having a right or duty judicially defined or enforced

Proces-verbal

An instrument that contains a record of certain understandings arrived at by the contracting parties to a treaty or convention

Proclamation

(1) UK: a formal public announcement made by the Sovereign on the advice of the Privy Council. A list of proclamations made at meetings of the Privy Council from 11 October 2000 onwards is at <http://www.privy-council.org.uk/output/Page473.asp> The text of proclamations is available on application to the Privy Council Office and some are printed in the London Gazette

(2) US: a formal public announcement made by the government. See *Executive proclamation*

Protocol

An instrument subsidiary to a treaty and drawn up by the same parties, dealing with either

(1) subsidiary matters (such as the interpretation of particular clauses of the treaty) and known as a Protocol of Signature or,
(2) establishing additional rights and obligations, often signed the same day as the treaty but signed independently and known as an Optional Protocol, or
(3) specific obligations under the general principles of the treaty, or
(4) amending one or more earlier treaties.

In legal research, the term is most commonly employed in its fourth meaning

Provisional order

An order (a form of *Statutory Instrument*) which normally does not take effect until confirmed by *Parliament* at Westminster, issued by a government department and relating, for example to a local government scheme

Public Act

(1) An Act passed by *Parliament* at Westminster applying to the whole population of the UK unless *Parliament* specifically determines otherwise
(2) An Act passed by the Scottish Parliament and having effect within Scotland only
(3) US: see *General statute*

Public Bill

(1) draft legislation of *Parliament* at Westminster relating to matters of public policy introduced by a member of *Parliament*. If introduced by a member of government the bill will be referred to as a *Government Bill*; if it is introduced by a private member of *Parliament* (either an individual MP or an individual peer in the Lords) it is referred to as a 'unofficial Member's Bill', or more familiarly, a '*Private Member's Bill*'. If successful a Public Bill will become a *Public General Act*
(2) draft legislation of the Scottish Parliament relating to matters of public policy introduced by a Member of the Scottish Parliament (MSP). If introduced by a member of the Scottish Executive the bill will be referred to as an *Executive Bill*; if it is introduced by a member of a particular committee of the Parliament or as an individual member of the Scottish Parliament, it is known as a *Committee Bill* or *Member's Bill* respectively. If successful a Public Bill will become an *Act of the Scottish Parliament* (ASP)

Public General Act

An *Act of Parliament* (either Westminster or Edinburgh) which relates to matters of public policy. As a draft it would have been called a *Public Bill*

Public law

(1) constitutional law, criminal law and administrative law taken together
(2) published law
(3) US: see *General statute*

Published opinion

US: an *opinion* directed by the court to be published. Published *opinions* have precedental value. Opinions may be reported although they are directed 'not for publication'. See *Reported opinion, Unpublished opinion*

Queen's Printer's Copy

The copy of an *Act of Parliament* printed and published by the Queen's Printer (currently the Controller of Her Majesty's Stationery Office (HMSO)). The text of the Act is in the form in which it received the *Royal Assent* and is accepted as evidence in courts of law

R

Abbreviation for Rex or Regina, meaning the King or the Queen. Used in the names of parties in a criminal action

Raistrick's Index

Refers to Raistrick, D, *Index to legal Citations and Abbreviations* (Sweet & Maxwell, 3rd edn, 2008) the most comprehensive list of legal abbreviations and acronyms in use in the United Kingdom, Commonwealth and the United States

Ratio decidendi

Latin: 'the reason for deciding'. The principle upon which a case is decided. In the US the term *holding* is often used

Re
Latin: regarding. In the matter of; concerning. For example: re Smith, meaning that Smith is the party on whose application the case is heard

Recommendation
In the European Union, a form of secondary legislation suggesting a line of action or opinion – not legally binding. See also *Opinion*

Red Book
(1) UK: term used to refer to the decennial index volumes of the *Law Reports* owning to the colour of their covers
(2) UK: popular name for Jordans Family Court Practice
(3) US: see *Blue book* (8)

Referred
Used where the court in a case has dealt with the point of law in the an earlier case without comment of any definite character on the latter

Regional reporter
US: a unit of the *National Reporter System*. Each regional reporter includes the appellate opinions from states within a specific region of the country

Register
(1) US: see *Blue book* (8)
(2) US: law directory
(3) US: a daily or weekly or monthly chronological publication of administrative and executive activities and documents of general applicability and legal effect that are required by statute to be published. Registers publish a variety of executive documents

Regnal year
The year beginning with the date of the Sovereign's accession to the throne – for Queen Elizabeth II the regnal year commences on 6 February. Prior to 1963 Acts of Parliament were bound together in volumes according to the regnal year and the citation was used to identify the individual Act, for example: Public Order Act 1936 (1 Edw. 8 & 1 Geo. 6, c.6). From 1963 Acts have been bound in volumes according to the calendar year in which they received the Royal Assent

Regular reports
See *Authorised reports*

Regulation
(1) UK: a type of *Statutory Instrument* (secondary legislation)
(2) EU: a form of secondary legislation addressed to all member states, to be applied in full and directly applicable without the creation of national legislation
(3) US: see *Rule*

Repeal
To rescind or revoke

Report
(1) UK: written account of a proceeding and judicial decision
(2) US: see *Reporter*

Report bulletin
See *Report letter*

Report letter
US: a pamphlet or piece of paper that accompanies the updating pages and filing instructions to a looseleaf service. The report letter summarises the material in the update. It also reports developments occurring since the last update was issued. Also called alert, report bulletin

Report of proceedings
US: refers to the verbatim transcript of any on-the-record proceedings before a judge

Reported opinion
US: an opinion included in a reporter either online or print (official, unofficial, looseleaf service, *topical law reporter*). Although reported it may not have precedental value. See *published opinion, unpublished opinion*

Reporter
(1) UK: the person who reports or edits the cases in any series of law reports
(2) US: see *Reporter of decisions*
(3) US: generally, hardbound publications of opinions of courts or administrative agencies issued serially in approximate chronological order by date of decision. The volumes also may include changes in rules of court and orders of the court. Various editorial features may be added: *headnotes*, synopses. Also called report, laws report, court report, judicial report
(4) US: refers to any single title in the West National Reporter system, reporting, each title reporting cases from a geographical area of the United States

Reporter of decisions
US: an individual who supervises publication of a court's opinions, including adding *headnotes*, table of cases and index. Also called reporter

Reporter's syllabus
See *Headnote*

The Reports
Coke's thirteen volumes that began to appear in 1600. Coke tried to present every previous authority bearing on each case he reported, and thus his work remains the historian's key to the study of medieval *case law*

Reports of Standing Committees of the House
Publication which up to the start of Parliamentary session 2007/2008 published verbatim debates on legislation held away fro the floor of the House of Commons, in Committee. Continued by *House of Commons Official Report of Public Bill Committees*

Resolve/resolution
US: a written proposal that expresses the will or sentiment of the legislature. It is generally used for stating policy or making a declaration

Restatement of the law
US: a summary of the general principles of US law in a selection of subjects, with scholarly and analytical comments. Although it is secondary authority it may be highly persuasive in the United States to courts and is often cited in judicial opinions

Reverse
An appellate court reverses a decision when it overturns what the trial court did below in the same case

Revised statutes
US: current and permanent statutes that have been organised (or reorganised) and re-enacted as law by the legislature. See *Statutory code*

Re-write Act
Name given to a number of Acts of Parliament at Westminster which are not consolidation Acts in the strict sense of the phrase, but share similar features – especially applied to tax law, to re-write the United Kingdom's primary direct tax legislation to make it clearer and easier to use, without changing the law. See also *Consolidation Bill*

Rex/Regina
Rex = the King; Regina = the Queen; abbreviation = R

Roman law
(1) the law of the Roman people
(2) civil law

Round brackets
See *Brackets*

Royal Assent
When a *Bill of Parliament* at Westminster has successfully passed through all stages in both Houses of Parliament or a *Scottish Parliament Bill* has passed all stages, it is presented to the Sovereign to signify assent to the legislation becoming law

Royal Commission
Investigative body set up under Royal Warrant to examine a topic of public concern where legislation seems desirable. Reports are published as *Command Papers*

Rubric
(1) an introductory or explanatory note; a preface
(2) in a statute includes the title and side notes. In the case of the official report of a court case, it means the *headnote*

Rule
(1) UK: a type of *Statutory Instrument* (*secondary legislation*) often concerned with setting out rules for litigation and court business
(2) US: a directive or order of an administrative agency or the chief executive authorised by statute with general applicability and effect. Rules are published chronologically in a register and then the permanent rules in effect at the time of compilation are compiled by subject into an administrative code. Also called regulation

Rules of Court
(1) UK: rules made by an authority, usually *Parliament* at Westminster, governing the practice and procedure of the courts
(2) US: directives of a court governing practice and procedure in the courts of a particular jurisdiction or in a specific court. Some rules of court have broad jurisdictional coverage (eg Federal Rules of Civil Procedure). Some, such as the Federal Riles of Civil Procedure must be approved by the legislature

Ruling
(1) UK: an outcome of a court's decision either on some point of law (such as the admissibility of evidence) or ion the case as a whole
(2) US: see *Decision*

Ruling case
A reported case that determines an issue being litigated. In US also called a leading case

S
Abbreviation for (1) statute, (2) section

Saving clause
Used in a repealing act to preserve rights and claims that would otherwise be lost

Schedules
Found at the end of many *Bills* and *Acts* containing detailed provisions dependent on one or more of the preceding clauses (Bills) or sections (Acts); rather like appendices at the end of a book

Scope note
US: an introductory note that describes the content of an article in a legal publication. It states what is included in the discussion and what is excluded. Often found in legal encyclopedias, digests and annotated law reports

Scottish Parliament Bill
A version of a proposed *Act of the Scottish Parliament*

Scottish Statutory Instrument

A *Statutory Instrument* made by a Minister of the Scottish Executive under powers derived either from an *Act of the Scottish Parliament* or from a pre-devolution Westminster Act

Secondary authority

Authority other than primary authority. A source or statement of the law that does not issue from a branch of government in the exercise of its law-making function. Secondary authority provides an overview and background

Secondary legislation

(1) UK: legislation made by a person (for example, a minister) or a body (for example, a local authority) under authority delegated by *Parliament* (either Westminster or Edinburgh) or an Assembly (Cardiff or Belfast) by a statute. There are four types: *statutory instruments, codes of practice, by-laws* (in England and Wales) and *by-laws and management rules* (in Scotland), and *Measures of the General Synod of the Church of England*. When a statute is repealed, under which *statutory instruments* have been made, all statutory instruments so made are impliedly repealed unless expressly saved. Also known as delegated legislation and as subordinate legislation

(2) US: similar definition but forms include *rules, rules of court, executive orders, executive proclamations, ordinances*. Also known as delegated legislation

Secondary sources of law

See *Secondary authority*

Section

Sub-division of a document or a subdivision of an article in a document, statutory title or code. In particular, the division of an *Act of Parliament* or and *Act of the Scottish Parliament*

Select committee

(1) UK: a committee appointed by a House of *Parliament*, to consider and take evidence on some subject and to report to the House. Most notably they scrutinise government policy and actions. They proceed by taking evidence. Known as select because the members are specifically nominated by the House

(2) US: a committee that studies a particular issue and reports its findings and recommendations. Known as select because of the membership is elected. See also *Special committee*

Session law

US: an individual enactment of the legislature during a legislative session. See also *Session laws*

Session law service

See *Advance legislative service*

Session laws

US: statutes enacted by a legislative body and published in a form identifying them with the term in which the legislative session took place

Shepardize

US: the process of checking whether an earlier decision, upon which reliance is to be placed, is still good law, using Shepard's Citators, now incorporated in the US databases of LexisNexis. See *Shepard's*

Shepard's

US: a citator covering many different types of legal material including opinions, rules, constitutions, ordinances, legal periodicals. It is published both by jurisdiction and by subject. A product of LexisNexis

Short title

(1) UK: the title under which a *Bill* and eventually an *Act* is generally known. On Bills of *Parliament* at Westminster it is given in three places: at the head of the Bill, in a clause of the Bill (usually towards the end) and on the outside of the back cover. For an Act the short title is given only in the first two locations.

On a Scottish Parliament Bill it is given in three places: at the top of the Bill, on the back sheet and in italics in the running header on each page

(2) US: an abbreviated name of a statute. The language of the statute may specify the short title by which the statute may be cited. Not all statutes have short titles

Slip decision
See *Slip opinion*

Slip law
US: an unbound pamphlet (or for some statute a single piece of paper) that contains the text of an individual statute (either public law or private law) enacted by the legislature. The pamphlet is published soon after the statute is enacted and is the first official form of the publication for a newly enacted statute. See also *Advance sheet* (1)

Slip opinion
US: publication of an opinion soon after the opinion has been issued. Slip opinions are usually issued by the court itself, rather than by a private publisher and are identified by the case name, date and docket number. Slip opinions are later reprinted as advance sheets and finally as hardbound reporters. Also called slip sheet, slip decision

Slip sheet
See *Slip opinion*

Socio-legal
Relating to the field of law and society

Source note
See *history note*

Sources of law
(1) the literary source from which we obtain our knowledge of the law, eg a statute book or reports or treatises
(2) the ultimate authority that backs up the law, ie the state
(3) the causes that have brought into existence rules that have subsequently acquired legal force, such as custom, religion, and scientific discussion
(4) the organs through which the state either grants legal recognition to rules previously unauthoritative, or itself creates new law, such as legislation and adjudication

Special act
See *Special law*

Special committee
US: a committee (often without jurisdiction to propose legislation) with members appointed to perform special functions concerning issues that are beyond the jurisdiction of ability of a standing committee. See also *Select committee*

Special law
US: a private law or local act. May also refer to a temporary law. Also called a special statute, special act

Special statute
See *Special law*

Specialist series
Generic name for a large number of law reports which select cases of interest to lawyers working in a discrete practice area. Examples include *Criminal Appeal Reports* and *Property and Compensation Reports*

Speech
A *judgment* in the House of Lords. Derives from the law lords' custom of delivering their pronouncements orally, as Parliamentary speeches

Square brackets
See *Brackets*

Standing committee
UK: a committee of a House of Parliament which proceeds by debate rather than taking evidence – see *Select committee*
US: a permanent committee with jurisdiction over a specific subject matter. It sets policy on that subject matter and may propose legislation

Star pagination/paging
US: page references in an *unofficial reporter* to the corresponding pages in the *official reporter*

Stare decisis
Latin: 'to stand by the things decided'. The doctrine of precedent, under which it is necessary for a court to follow earlier judicial decisions when the same points arise again in litigation. See *Precedent*

Starred decision
A decision of the Social Security Commissioners made since the beginning of 1987 which is of general significance and in the opinion of the Commissioners ought to be published. Before 1987 such decisions bore the suffix KL, standing for Key Law

Stationery Office
See *The Stationery Office*

Status table
US: a table that tracks legislative or judicial actions and provides the current status of a bill or a case

Status entry
Information printed near the head of a Scottish Parliament Bill, following the short title, indicating the version of the Bill to hand, presented in upper-case characters within square brackets

Statute
A legislative act that the state gives the force of law. In the United Kingdom it covers *Acts* and *Statutory Instruments*

Statute Book
Term sometimes used to refer to the whole collection of UK *Acts* of Parliament

Statute citation
Before January 1963 an Act was referenced or cited by the *regnal year*, for example: Public Order Act 1936 (1 Edw. 8 & 1 Geo. 6, c.6). From January 1963 an Act is cited by the calendar year in which it was passed, for example: Human Rights Act 1998 (c.42)

Statute law
(1) law contained in a statute
(2) the system of law and body of principles laid down in statutes, as distinct from the common law

Statutory code
(1) US: single statutory code divided into titles and numbered within titles. The permanent and general statutes of a jurisdiction, classified by subject matters into one code. May be official, unofficial, annotated or un-annotated
(2) US: subject specific statutory codes. Separate codes for each area subject to regulation. Used only for a few states of United States

Statutory code of practice
A statement of accepted good practice intended to provide guidance, which has the approval of *Parliament* or a Secretary of State or a Minister or a body outside *Parliament* depending on the provisions of the Act which required the code to be drawn up. Some statutory codes, such as the Police and Criminal Evidence Act codes, have legal effect and may be used in civil and criminal proceedings. Some codes are published by *The Stationery Office* (TSO), some by the organisation which drew it up (search the organisation's web site). Alternatively, to obtain a code consult a specialist looseleaf encyclopedia covering the practice/subject area. See also *voluntary code of practice*

Statutory Instrument
A government order similar to executive order or agency regulation in the United States

A document consisting of rules, regulations or orders made in exercise of powers conferred by *Parliament* on a government department or other body or persons. Statutory Instruments were introduced by the Statutory Instruments Act 1946 which covers their definition, Parliamentary procedure and publication. A Statutory Instrument falls in the category of *subordinate legislation*. There are two broad classes of Statutory Instrument: general and local. General instruments are published by *The Stationery Office* (TSO). Local instruments often relate to a particular local authority area and are exempt from printing and sale unless the minister concerned requests otherwise. To obtain a local statutory instrument contact the government department which issued it, to see if a copy can be made available

Statutory note
See *History note*

Statutory Rule & Order
A form of secondary legislation which pre-dated the introduction of *Statutory Instruments* by the Statutory Instruments Act, 1946

String citation
US: a list of citations to authorities (usually cases) one after another, to support a legal proposition. Generally there is little or no discussion of the authorities listed

Style
(1) UK: name or title of a person
(2) UK and US: the case name
(3) Scotland: a model form or precedent of a deed or pleading. Equivalent of *precedent* in England and Wales

Style book
A collections of model forms or precedents relating to Scots law. Examples include *Greens Litigation Styles* and *Greens Practice Styles*. The equivalent of precedent books in England and Wales

Style manual
See *Citation manual*

Style of cause
The name of a case

Sub nom
Sub nomine (Latin) = under the name. Abbreviation commonly used to note that a certain case may have involved different parties at an earlier procedural stage

Subordinate legislation
See *Secondary legislation*

Summary judgment
A *judgment* granted on a claim about which there is no genuine issue of material fact and upon which the party moving the claim is entitled to prevail as a matter of law

Supplement
An update to a law book. Supplements are published in various formats: looseleaf pages that are inserted into a looseleaf binder (sometimes replacing other pages that are removed and discarded); separately issued standalone *cumulative supplements* that are either paperback or hardcover
US: pocket parts that are inserted into a slot in the inside back or front cover of a hardbound volume
See also *pocket part, cumulative supplement*

Supra
Latin = as above

Syllabus

US term for the reporter's summary of a judicial opinion, usually placed at the beginning of the reported case. It states each rule of law that the case supposedly involves. They are generally not written by the judges themselves but are added by the court's *Reporter of Decisions* or by a commercial publisher's editors. Consequently the syllabus carries no authority and should not be cited in support of a proposition. The UK equivalent is called the *headnote*

Synopsis

See *Syllabus*

Table of authorities

(1) US: see Authority note/authority table
(2) US: a list of authorities in a brief, including cases, statutes, rules, and other authorities

Table of cases/table of decisions

See *Finding list*

Table of parallel references

See *Correlation table*

Temporary law

A statute of limited duration. An enactment by a legislature that continues for a specific time (that is, does not continue indefinitely as does a permanent law)

Term Reports

Popular name given to law reports of King's Bench cases compiled by Charles Durnford and Edward East and published from 1786 onwards 'within a short time after each term' (Durnford and East, 1786, preface)

Textbook

Book which collects, syntheses and critically evaluates the law. In US also known as a *legal treatise*

The Stationery Office (TSO)

The official UK Government printer

Thesaurus

A list of words or concepts arranged according to their sense. In the United Kingdom the most well known dealing specifically with law terminology is Miskin, C, *A Legal Thesaurus* (Legal Information Resources, 3rd edn, 1997) now out of print. An updated version is used to classify documents in the Westlaw UK database

Theses

See *Dissertation*

Title

(1) name of a statute
(2) US: a broad area of law subject to regulation. Used to organise administrative codes, statutory codes and municipal codes. Titles are broken down into further subdivisions such as chapters and parts
(3) US: major division of a statute

Topic

US: a broad area of law used a s a major unit of organisation in a digest to classify cases. Also called a topic digest. See also *headnote, key number*

Topical digest

See *Digest*

Topical law reporter

US: a reporter that covers a specified area of the law (most reporters publish opinions chronologically within the specific jurisdiction or group of jurisdictions). A looseleaf service is a type of topical reporter

Tort
A civil wrong, the breach of a duty that the law imposes on everyone. It derives from Law French meaning literally wrong or injustice and ultimately from the Latin tortus = twisted or crooked

Transcript
Official copy of the recorded proceedings in a trial or hearing taken down by a court reporter

Transfer binder
A cardboard or plastic binder into which the pages of a looseleaf service are transferred for permanent retention, to make room for new pages in the current binder. Also called a File binder

Transfer book
Mainly used in US: a book into which pages from a looseleaf service are transferred for permanent retention, freeing up space in the current looseleaf binder. The transferred pages are usually advance sheets. A transfer book is similar to a transfer binder except it has a hard cover and a reinforced spine

Travaux préparatoires
The preparatory work of a treaty which may be used as an aid to interpretation. See section 11.1.1

Treatise
See *Legal treatise*

Treaty
An international agreement concluded by States or international organisations in written form and governed by international law. A bilateral treaty is between two parties; a multilateral treaty is between more than two parties

TSO catalogue
Catalogue of *The Stationery Office*, the UK government publisher

Unannotated
US: describes a publication that contains only the text of a statute, rule or other type of legal material without any annotations

Uncodified law
US: describes a statute or rule that is not classified to a code because it is not general or permanent or because it was not in effect at the time the code was published. Also called unconsolidated law

Unconsolidated law
See *Uncodified law*

Unfocused problem
A complex research problem including a mass of raw information in which the lawyer has to recognise and select significant facts to arrive at the legal issues to be the subject of research

Uniform law/Act
US: a proposal for legislation that is drafted and recommended for adoption by the states in order to promote uniformity. See also *Model act*

United Kingdom
England, Wales, Scotland and Northern Ireland comprise the United Kingdom

Unofficial
A publication without government authorisation that designates the publication as official; in other words, a private publication without official sanction

Unpublished opinion

US: an opinion directed by the court not to be published (the court designates the opinion as 'not for publication'). Rules of court of the jurisdiction establish criteria for not publishing an opinion. Opinions originally designated 'not for publication' may be published later on a successful motion filed with the court by counsel. The significance of whether an opinion is published or unpublished is whether the opinion has precedental value and may be cited as authority in documents submitted to the court. See also *Published opinion*

Unreported case

The *transcript* of a case that does not appear in published law reports

v/vs

Abbreviation of versus. In the United Kingdom, there is a convention that 'v' is pronounced 'and' in the name of a civil case (Smith and Jones). In a criminal case 'v' is pronounced 'against' (The Crown against Smith). In some criminal law reports and texts the 'R v' is omitted and the case may be cited merely as, for example 'Smith'

Vendor neutral citation

See *Neutral citation*

Verbatim

Latin: word for word and letter for letter

Versus

In a case name = against – see *v/vs*

Vocational training

Training towards a career. In the UK legal training this refers to training undertaken after the award of a law degree or equivalent and leading to admission into a professional body such as the Law Society or an Inn of Court or the Faculty of Advocates

Voluntary code of practice

A statement of accepted good practice designed to provide guidance drawn up by any organisation. Examples include British Standards (BS), the Accounting Standards Committee's *Statements of Standard Accounting Practice* (SSAP) and the *Association of British Travel Agents Ltd (ABTA) Tour Operators' Code of Conduct*. Voluntary codes do not have Parliamentary approval and neither are they legally enforceable in their own right. To obtain a copy of a voluntary code search the web site of the organisation responsible for drawing it up or consult a specialist looseleaf encyclopedia covering the practice/subject area. See also *statutory code of practice*

Warrant

(1) to guarantee the security of (realty or personalty or even a person)
(2) to give warranty of title
(3) to authorise
(4) a form of *Statutory Instrument*

Weekly List

Popular name for the *Weekly List of Government Publications*, a compilation of the *Daily List*. It provides publishing information for all of The Stationery Office (TSO) and some non-TSO official publications issued that week. Includes the official publications not only of *Parliament* at Westminster, but also *Parliament* in Edinburgh, and the Assemblies in Cardiff and Belfast

White Book

(1) UK: compilation published in a white hard cover of the procedural and administrative rules of the Supreme Court of England and Wales
(2) US: the National Reporter Blue and White Book series, providing parallel citations from official to unofficial case reports and vice versa
(3) US: the informal name of *A Uniform System of Citation* when the cover was white many editions ago. See *Bluebook*

White Paper
Official publication announcing a firm government policy to be implemented

Word index
See *Descriptive word index*

Words and phrases
A type of legal research task to trace the meaning of a word or phrase either used in a statute or defined by the courts. See Chapter 8

Year Book/Year-Book/year-book/yearbook
(1) UK: The Year Books are unofficial law reports dating from 1272 to 1537, compiled anonymously and probably intended for the personal use of individual members of the legal profession. The individual case reports are mainly hand written in Law French and concentrate on the pleadings rather than the *judgment*. Modern reprints with English translations have been made in the *Rolls Series* and volumes published by the Selden Society and Ames Foundation
(2) US in particular: an annual publication that reports new cases, new legislation and other legal developments that occurred during the year, usually arranged by subject. Some yearbooks report on the activities of just one organisation

APPENDIX 3

COURT DIRECTIONS RELATING TO LEGAL RESEARCH

UNITED KINGDOM: SUPREME COURT

Citation of unreported judgments

Practice Direction 6
<http://www.supremecourt.gov.uk/docs/practice-direction-06.pdf>

> 6.3.5 Transcripts of unreported judgments should only be cited when they contain an authoritative statement of a relevant principle of law not to be found in a reported case or when they are necessary for the understanding of some other authority.

Provision of authorities and hierarchy of law reports

Practice Direction 6
<http://www.supremecourt.gov.uk/docs/practice-direction-06.pdf>

> 6.5.1 **A joint set of authorities, jointly produced, should be complied for the appeal. Ten copies of the joint set of** authorities must be filed at the same time as the core volumes. The appellants have the initial responsibility for producing the authorities volumes and for filing them at the Registry but, to enable the appellants to file the volumes, the respondents must provide the appellants with 10 copies of any authorities which the respondents require but which the appellants do not, or arrange with the appellants for their photocopying. Respondents should arrange with the appellants for the delivery to them of such authorities volumes as the respondents' counsel and solicitors require.

> #### Form and content of authorities volumes
> 6.5.2 The authorities should be collected together into one or more volumes or folders. Where there are a large number of volumes, all the authorities that are likely to be referred to frequently during the oral argument should be placed together in the first volume. <u>The aim is to ensure that the materials in that volume are those that will actually be turned up and looked at most often during the hearing.</u> Each volume should have a separate index, and the authorities should appear in alphabetical order. Where there are a large number of volumes, there should be an index of indexes separate from the index contained in the first volume of the authorities.

6.5.3   Authorities should (where appropriate) be further divided into the categories: domestic, Strasbourg, foreign and academic material. Where the parties consider that a different order or arrangement would be of greater assistance to the Court, that order or arrangement should be adopted. The volumes of authorities should

    a.   be A4 size reproduced as one page per view (with any authorities smaller than A4 being enlarged);

    b.   separate each authority by numbered dividers;

    c.   contain an index to that volume; the first volume must also contain an index to all the volumes;

    d.   be numbered consecutively on the cover and spine with numerals at least point 72 in size for swift identification of different volumes during the hearing;

    e.   have printed clearly on the front cover the title of the appeal and the names of the solicitors for all parties;

    f.   have affixed to the spine a sticker indicating clearly the volume number in Arabic numerals and short title of the appeal.

Where an authority or other document extends to many pages, only those pages that are relevant to the appeal should be copied.

6.5.4   Copies of cases that have been reported should be of the case as reported in the Law Reports or Session Cases, failing which copies of the case as reported in other recognised reports should be provided. In Revenue appeals, copies of the case as reported in the Tax Cases or Simon's Tax Cases may be provided, but references to any report of the case in the Law Reports or Session Cases should be included when the case is listed in the index. Unreported copies of the judgment should only be included if the case has not been reported in any of the recognised reports.

6.5.5   The Court has on numerous occasions criticised the over-proliferation of authorities. It should be understood that not every authority that is mentioned in the parties' printed cases need be included in the volumes of authorities. They should include only those cases that are likely to be referred to during the oral argument or which are less accessible because they have not been reported in the Law Reports.

6.5.6   The volumes of authorities should be filed in the Registry, preferably in separate containers from the core volumes.

6.5.7   In order to produce the volumes of authorities, parties may download text from electronic sources; but the volumes of authorities must be filed in paper form. See Practice Direction 14 for provisions in relation to electronic volumes.

6.5.8   In certain circumstances (for example, when during the hearing it becomes apparent that a particular authority is needed but is not in the volumes of authorities), the Supreme Court Library can arrange for copies of authorities to be made available at the hearing. Parties must themselves provide ten copies of any other authority or of unreported cases. They must similarly provide copies of any authority of which notice has not been given.

6.5.9   The cost of preparing the volumes of authorities falls to the appellants, but is ultimately subject to the decision of the Court as to the costs of the appeal.

Filing documents in the Registry of the Supreme Court by electronic means

Practice Direction 14
<http://www.supremecourt.gov.uk/docs/practice-direction-14.pdf>

ENGLAND AND WALES: ALL CIVIL COURTS

Authorities which should not be cited and certification of those to be cited

Practice Direction (Citation of Authorities) [2001] 1 WLR 1001
The following authorities should not be cited unless they establish a new principle or extend the law:

- 'Applications attended by one party only

- Applications for permission to appeal

- Decisions on applications that only decide that the application is arguable

- County court cases, unless (a) cited in order to illustrate the conventional measure of damages in a personal injury case; or (b) cited in a county court in order to demonstrate current authority at that level on an issue in respect of which no decision at a higher level of authority is available.' (paragraph 6.2)

Advocates who seek to cite a judgment that contains indications given by a court delivering the judgment that it was to be seen by that court as only applying decided law to the facts of the particular case; or otherwise as not extending or adding to existing law, will be required to justify their decision to cite the case (paragraphs 7.1 and 7.2).

Cases decided in another jurisdiction 'should not be cited without proper consideration of whether it does indeed add to the existing body of law. Any advocate who seeks to cite an authority from another jurisdiction must (i) comply with rules on the certification of authorities set out in paragraph 8' (of which an extract is given below); '(ii) indicate in respect of each authority what that authority adds that is not found in authority in this jurisdiction; or, if there is said to be justification for adding to domestic authority, what that justification is; (iii) certify that there is no authority in this jurisdiction that precludes the acceptance by the court of the proposition that the foreign authority is said to establish.' (paragraphs 9.1 and 9.2).

The rules stated in paragraphs 9.1 and 9.2 do not apply to cases decided in either the Court of Justice of the European Communities or the organs of the European Convention for the Protection of Human Rights and Fundamental Freedoms. Such authorities are covered by the rules stated in paragraphs 6.2 and 6.3.

'Advocates will be required to state, in respect of each authority they wish to cite, the proposition of law that authority demonstrates, and the parts of the judgment that support that proposition. If it is sought to cite more than one authority in support of given proposition, advocates must state the reason for taking that course.' (paragraph 8.1).

The Practice Direction also states how the certification required by paragraph 8.1 is to be provided, and the detail to be included (paragraphs 8.2–8.4).

Citation of unreported judgments of the Court of Appeal (Civil Division)

Practice Note (Court of Appeal: Transcripts) [1978] 1 WLR 600
The mode of citation of unreported decisions of the Court of Appeal (Civil Division) was changed to, for example:

> *Smith v Fraser*, July 19, 1977, Court of Appeal (Civil Division) Transcript No. 178 of 1977, CA.

Note: from 1951 an official note was taken of all judgements in the Court of Appeal (Civil Division), indexed and filed in the Bar Library. From the beginning of 1978 these copies have been held in the Supreme Court Library.

Roberts Petroleum Ltd v Bernard Kenny Ltd [1983] 2 AC 192
The House of Lords decided:

> in future to decline to allow transcripts of unreported judgements of the Court of Appeal (Civil Division) to be cited on the hearing of appeals to the House unless leave is given to do so; such leave will be granted on counsel giving the assurance that the transcript contains a statement of some principle of law, relevant to an issue in the appeal to the House, that is binding on the Court of Appeal and of which the substance, as distinct from the mere choice of phraseology, is not to be found in any judgment of that court that has appeared in one of the general or special series of reports. (Headnote at pages 194 and 195)

The two weekly series of general law reports referred to in the judgment of Lord Diplock were, on the one hand, the *Weekly Law Reports*, parts 2 and 3 of which are later reproduced in the *Law Reports* and, on the other hand, the *All England Law Reports*.

Practice Statement (Court of Appeal: Authorities) [1996] 1 WLR 854
Re-iterated the principle set out in *Roberts Petroleum* (paragraph 3).

Practice Direction (Citation of Authorities) [2012] 1 WLR 780
This Practice Direction applies throughout the Senior Courts of England and Wales, including the Crown Court, in county courts and in magistrates' courts. At paragraph 10 it adds more detail and re-iterates the principles established above:

10 Where a judgment has not been reported, reference may be made to the official transcript if that is available, not the handed-down text of the judgment, as this may have been subject to late revision after the text was handed down. Official transcripts may be obtained from, for instance, BAILII (http://www.bailii.org/). An unreported case should not usually be cited unless it contains a relevant statement of legal principle not found in reported authority.

Neutral citation of judgments

Practice Direction (Judgments: Form and Citation) [2001] 1 WLR 194

To permit the unique identification on the internet of cases not or not yet published in print form a system of citation allocated to a case by the shorthand writers will come into effect from 11th January 2001 in both divisions of the Court of Appeal and the Administrative Court. The neutral citation consists of the year of the judgment, an abbreviation for the court in which the judgment was delivered and a running number from case 1 onwards. For these three courts cases will be numbered as follows:

Court of Appeal (Civil Division)	[2000] EWCA Civ 1, 2, 3, etc
Court of Appeal (Criminal Division)	[2000] EWCA Crim 1, 2, 3, etc
High Court (Administrative Court)	[2000] EWHC Admin 1, 2, 3, etc

So, a reference to paragraph 59 in *Smith v Jones*, the tenth numbered judgment of the year in the Civil Division of the Court of Appeal, would be cited: *Smith v Jones* [2001] EWCA Civ 10 at [59]:

The neutral citation will be the official number attributed to the judgment by the court and must always be used on at least one occasion when the judgment is cited in a later judgment. Once the judgment is reported, the neutral citation will appear in front of the familiar citation from the law report series. Thus *Smith v Jones* [2001] EWCA Civ 10 at [30], [2001] QB 124, [2001] 2 All ER 364 etc. The paragraph number must be the number allotted by the court in all future versions of the judgment. (paragraph 2.3)

If a judgment is cited on more than one occasion in a later judgment, it will be of the greatest assistance if only one abbreviation (if desired) is used. Thus *Smith v Jones* [2001] EWCA Civ 10 could be abbreviated on subsequent occasions to *Smith v Jones*, or *Smith's* case, but preferably not both (in the same judgement). (paragraph 2.4)

If it is desired to cite more than one paragraph of a judgment each numbered paragraph should be enclosed with a square bracket. Thus: *Smith v Jones* [2001] EWCA Civ 10 at [30]–[35], or *Smith v Jones* [2001] EWCA Civ 10 at [30], [35], and [40]–[43]. (paragraph 2.5)

Practice Direction (Judgments: Neutral Citations) [2002] 1 WLR 346

Extended the system of neutral citation initiated by Practice Direction [2001] 1 WLR 194 to the High Court in London. Neutral citations will not be automatically assigned to judgments delivered outside London, because they appear much less frequently in published reports. But, on application to the Mechanical Recording Department a citation for such a judgment will be provided to anyone wishing to include it in a published report.

The additions to the scheme are as follows:

Chancery Division	EWHC *number* (Ch)
Patents Court	EWHC *number* (Pat)
Queen's Bench Division	EWHC *number* (QB)
Administrative Court	EWHC *number* (Admin)
Commercial Court	EWHC *number* (Comm)
Admiralty Court	EWHC *number* (Admlty)
Technology and Construction Court	EWHC *number* (TCC)
Family Division	EWHC *number* (Fam)

For example, [2002] EWHC 123 (Fam); or [2002] EWHC 124 (QB); or [2002] EWHC 125 (Ch).

It is not necessary to include the descriptive word in brackets when citing the paragraph number of a judgment. Thus paragraph 59 in *Smith v Jones* [2002] EWHC 124 (QB) would be cited: *Smith v Jones* [2002] EWHC 124 at [59].

Use of a judgment in electronic form

Practice Direction (Citation of Authorities) [2012] 1 WLR 780:

13 Judgments reported in any series of reports, including those of the Incorporated Council of Law Reporting, should be provided either by way of a photocopy of the published report or by way of a copy of a reproduction of the judgment in electronic form that has been authorised by the publisher of the relevant series, but in any event (1) the report must be presented to the court in an easily legible form (a 12-point font is preferred but a 10- or 11-point font is acceptable) and (2) the advocate presenting the report is satisfied that it has not been reproduced in a garbled form from the data source. In any case of doubt the court will rely on the printed text of the report (unless the editor of the report has certified that an electronic version is more accurate because it corrects an error contained in an earlier printed text of the report).

Hierarchy of law reports

Practice Direction (Court of Appeal: Citation of Authority) [1995] 1 WLR 1096
This Direction sets down a strict hierarchy of authority. Cases must be cited from law reports in the following order:

- if a case is reported in the semi-official *Law Reports* … that report should be cited. These are the most authoritative reports;

- if a case is not (or not yet) reported in the semi-official *Law Reports*, but is reported in the *Weekly Law Reports* or the *All England Law Reports*, that report should be cited;

- if as case is not cited in any of these series of reports, a report of any of the authoritative specialist series of law reports may be cited.

If the report of a case in the specialist law reports is not readily available it is helpful if photocopies of the less frequently used series are made available to the court.

The practice outlined above need not be followed where one report is fuller than another or when there are discrepancies between reports. It is always helpful if alternative references are given.

Where a reserved judgment has not been reported, reference should be made to the official transcript (if this available) and not to the handed-down text of the judgment.

Practice Direction (Citation of Authorities) [2012] 1 WLR 780
Re-iterated the principle of 'exclusive citation' requiring that where a case is reported in the *Law Reports*, that version should be cited, and other series of reports may be used only when a case is not reported in the *Law Reports* (paragraph 5 onwards):

Preamble
1 This practice direction is issued in order to clarify the practice and procedure governing the citation of authorities and applies throughout the Senior Courts of England and Wales, including the Crown Court, in county courts and in magistrates' courts.

Repeal
2 Practice Direction (Court of Appeal: Citation of Authority) [1995] 1 WLR 1096 of 22 June 1995, Practice Statement (Court of Appeal: Authorities) [1996] 1 WLR 854 of 15 May 1996, paragraph 8 of Practice Statement (Supreme Court: Judgments) [1998] 1 WLR 825 of 22 April 1998, paragraph 3 of Practice Direction (Judgments: Form and Citation) [2001] 1 WLR 194 of 11 January 2001, and, in so far as they remain in force, paragraphs 10.1 and 10.2 of Practice Direction (Court of Appeal (Civil Division)) [1999] 1 WLR 1027 of 19 April 1999 are hereby revoked.

Variation
3 Practice Direction (Criminal Proceedings: Consolidation) [2002] 1 WLR 2870 of 8 July 2002 (as amended) is varied so that all references to paragraph 10.1 of Practice Direction (Court of Appeal (Civil Division)) [1999] 1 WLR 1027 are to read as references to paragraphs 5–13 of this practice direction.

4 Practice Direction 52 supplementing CPR Pt 52 is varied so that paragraph 15.11(2) reads as follows:

'(2)   The bundle of authorities should comply with the requirements of Practice Direction (Citation of Authorities) [2012] 1 WLR 780 and in general–

(a)   have the relevant passages of the authorities marked;
(b)   not include authorities for propositions not in dispute; and
(c)   not contain more than ten authorities unless the scale of the appeal warrants more extensive citation.'

Citation of authority
5 When authority is cited, whether in written or oral submissions, the following practice should be followed.

6 Where a judgment is reported in the official Law Reports (AC, QB, Ch, Fam) published by the Incorporated Council of Law Reporting for England and Wales, that report must be cited. These are

the most authoritative reports; they contain a summary of the argument. Other series of reports and official transcripts of judgment may only be used when a case is not reported in the official Law Reports.

7 If a judgment is not (or not yet) reported in the official Law Reports but it is reported in the Weekly Law Reports (WLR) or the All England Law Reports (All ER) that report should be cited. If the case is reported in both the WLR and the All ER either report may properly be cited.

8 If a judgment is not reported in the official Law Reports, the WLR or the All ER, but it is reported in any of the authoritative specialist series of reports which contain a headnote and are made by individuals holding a Senior Courts qualification (for the purposes of section 115 of the Courts and Legal Services Act 1990), the specialist report should be cited.

9 Where a judgment is not reported in any of the reports referred to in paragraphs 6–8 above, but is reported in other reports, they may be cited.

10 Where a judgment has not been reported, reference may be made to the official transcript if that is available, not the handed-down text of the judgment, as this may have been subject to late revision after the text was handed down. Official transcripts may be obtained from, for instance, BAILII (http://www.bailii.org/). An unreported case should not usually be cited unless it contains a relevant statement of legal principle not found in reported authority.

11 Occasions arise when one report is fuller than another, or when there are discrepancies between reports. On such occasions, the practice outlined above need not be followed, but the court should be given a brief explanation why this course is being taken, and the alternative references should be given.

12 If a judgment under appeal has been reported before the hearing but after skeleton arguments have been filed with the court, and counsel wish to argue from the published report rather than from the official transcript, the court should be provided with photocopies of the report for the use of the court.

13 Judgments reported in any series of reports, including those of the Incorporated Council of Law Reporting, should be provided either by way of a photocopy of the published report or by way of a copy of a reproduction of the judgment in electronic form that has been authorised by the publisher of the relevant series, but in any event (1) the report must be presented to the court in an easily legible form (a 12-point font is preferred but a 10- or 11-point font is acceptable) and (2) the advocate presenting the report is satisfied that it has not been reproduced in a garbled form from the data source. In any case of doubt the court will rely on the printed text of the report (unless the editor of the report has certified that an electronic version is more accurate because it corrects an error contained in an earlier printed text of the report).

14 This direction is made by Lord Judge CJ with the agreement of Lord Neuberger of Abbotsbury MR and Sir Nicholas Wall P. It is issued in accordance with the procedure laid down in Part 1 of Schedule 2 to the Constitutional Reform Act 2005.

In *Governor and Company of the Bank of Scotland v Henry Butcher & Co and others* [2003] EWCA Civ 67; [2003] 2 All ER (Comm) 557; [2003] 1 BCLC 575; (2003) 100(13) LSG 29; *The Times*, 20 February 2003, at paragraph 79 of the official transcript Mr Justice Munby criticised lawyers for using the *All England Law Reports* and the *All England Law Reports Reprint* rather than the *Appeal Cases* and the *English Reports*. These and other criticisms of the way the bundle of authorities was constituted and reports used were endorsed by the other two judges sitting, at paragraphs 95 and 97.

Provision of photocopies of authorities

Practice Direction (Citation of Authorities) [2012] 1 WLR 780:

> 12 If a judgment under appeal has been reported before the hearing but after skeleton arguments have been filed with the court, and counsel wish to argue from the published report rather than from the official transcript, the court should be provided with photocopies of the report for the use of the court.

> 13 Judgments reported in any series of reports, including those of the Incorporated Council of Law Reporting, should be provided either by way of a photocopy of the published report or by way of a copy of a reproduction of the judgment in electronic form that has been authorised by the publisher of the relevant series, but in any event (1) the report must be presented to the court in an easily legible form (a 12-point font is preferred but a 10- or 11-point font is acceptable) and (2) the advocate presenting the report is satisfied that it has not been reproduced in a garbled form from the data source. In any case of doubt the court will rely on the printed text of the report (unless the editor of the report has certified that an electronic version is more accurate because it corrects an error contained in an earlier printed text of the report).

Citation of Hansard

Practice Direction (Hansard: Citation) [1995] 1 WLR 192:

> This Practice Direction concerns both final and interlocutory hearings in which any party intends to refer to the reports of Parliamentary proceedings as reported in the Official Reports of either House of Parliament (referred to as Hansard). No other report of Parliamentary proceedings may be cited. (paragraph 2)

> Any party intending to refer to any extract from Hansard in support of an such argument as is permitted by the decisions in *Pepper v Hart* [1993] AC 593 and *Pickstone v Freemans plc* [1989] AC 66 or otherwise must, unless the judge otherwise directs, serve upon all other parties and the court copies of any such extract together with a brief summary of the argument intended to be based upon such extract. (paragraph 3)

Then follow details of the time for service, the methods of service and the result of failure to serve.

ENGLAND AND WALES: COURT OF APPEAL (CIVIL DIVISION)

Provision of photocopies of earlier judgment in a case

Practice Direction (Appeals from Reported Judgments) [1987] 1 WLR 456:

> If the judgment under appeal has been reported before the hearing and counsel wish to argue from the published report rather than from the official transcript, the court should be provided with photocopies of the report for the use of the judges in order that they may be able to annotate it as the argument proceeds.

ENGLAND AND WALES: ALL CRIMINAL COURTS

Neutral citation of judgments

The Consolidated Criminal Practice Direction 2006, unreported, Westlaw Transcript 2006 WL 1887076 Part I.12.1 incorporates material from Practice Direction (Judgments: Form and Citation) [2001] 1 WLR 194 and Practice Direction (Judgments: Neutral Citations) [2002] 1 WLR 346. See above for both Practice Directions.

Citation of Hansard

The Consolidated Criminal Practice Direction 2006, unreported, Westlaw Transcript 2006 WL 1887076 Where a party intends to refer to *Hansard* in support of argument permitted by the decisions in *Pepper v Hart* [1993] AC 593 and *Pickstone v Freeman* [1989] AC 66, he must, unless the court otherwise directs, serve upon all other parties and the court copies of any such extract together with a brief summary of the argument intended to be based upon such extract. No other report of parliamentary proceedings may be cited. (Part II.20.1)

Service of the extract and summary of argument must be effected not less that five clear working days before the first day of the hearing, whether or not it has a fixed date. Service on the court shall be effected by sending three copies to the Registrar of Criminal Appeals. (Part II.20.2)

Excessive citation of decisions in criminal appeals

R v Erskine; R v Williams [2009] EWCA Crim 1425; 2009 153 (28) SJLB 30; (2009) *The Times*, 22 July 2009:

> When the advocate is considering what authority, if any, to cite for a proposition, only an authority which establishes the principle should be cited. Reference should not be made to authorities which do no more than either (a) illustrate the principle or (b) restate it. Detailed rules are set out in paragraphs II.17 and II.19 of the Consolidated Criminal Practice Direction. (paragraph 76)

ENGLAND AND WALES: CROWN COURT

Citation of Hansard

The Consolidated Criminal Practice Direction 2006, unreported, Westlaw Transcript 2006 WL 1887076 Part IV.37.1 reiterates the text of Part II.20.1 and Part II.20.2 – see above – except that service on the court is effected by sending three copies to the chief clerk of the relevant Crown Court centre.

ENGLAND AND WALES: TRIBUNALS

Employment Appeal Tribunal

Citation of authorities

Practice Direction (Employment Appeal Procedure) [2008] ICR 889:

> It is undesirable for parties to cite the same case from different set of reports. The parties should, if practicable, agree upon which report will be used at the hearing. Where the Employment Tribunal has cited from a report it may be convenient to cite from the same report. (Citation of Authorities, 14.1)

> It is the responsibility of the party wishing to cite any authority to provide photocopies for the use of each member of the Tribunal and photocopies or at least a list for the other parties. All authorities should be indexed and incorporated in an agreed bundle. (Citation of Authorities, 14.2)

> Parties are advised not to cite an unnecessary number of authorities either in skeleton arguments or in oral argument at the hearing. It is of assistance to the EAT if parties could highlight or sideline passages relied on within the bundle of authorities. (Citation of Authorities, 14.3)

> For decision of the ECJ, the official report should be used where possible. (Citation of Authorities, 14.5)

Posting of judgments on EAT website

> All Full Hearing judgments which are transcribed or handed down will be posted on the EAT website. Any other judgment may be posted on the EAT website if so directed by the Registrar or a Judge. (EAT Website, 18.8)

First-tier Tribunal and Upper Tribunal

Neutral citation of judgments

Practice Statement – Form of Decisions and Neutral – First-tier Tribunal and Upper Tribunal on or after 3 November 2008 [2009] 1 WLR 871:

4   Decisions will be numbered in the following way:

Upper Tribunal (Administrative Appeals Chamber)	[200n] UKUT 1 (AAC)
First-tier Tribunal (Health Education and Social Care Chamber)	[200n] UKFTT 1 (HESC)
First-tier Tribunal (Special Entitlement Chamber)	[200n] UKFTT 2 (SEC)
First-tier Tribunal (War Pensions and Armed Forces Compensation Chamber)	[200n] UKFTT 3 (WPAFCC)

5   There will be consecutive numbering of decisions in each of the First-tier Tribunal and the Upper Tribunal. Thus, the first three decisions of [200n] delivered by the First-tier Tribunal would be numbered 1, 2, 3 irrespective of whether the case was allocated to HESC, SEC or WPAFCC.

6   Under these arrangements, para 77 in *Jones v Secretary of State for the Department of Work and Pensions*, the tenth numbered decision of the year in the Upper Tribunal, would be cited: *Jones v Secretary of State for the Department of Work and Pensions* [200n] UKUT 10 (AAC) at [77].

7   The paragraph number allotted by the Upper Tribunal Office should be used in all references to that decision.

8   Where anonymity was previously given to a party in a tribunal case, that practice will continue pending further review.

9   The neutral citation will be the official number attributed to the decision by the tribunal and must always be used on at least one occasion when the decision is cited in a later decision or judgment. Once the decision is reported, the neutral citation will appear in front of any citation from the law report series. Thus: *Jones v Secretary of State for the Department of Work and Pensions* [200n] UKUT 10 (AAC) at [77]; [200n] 2 All ER 364; R(AF) 3/08.

For the numbering of Social Security Commissioners and Upper Tribunal decisions see: <http://www.administrativeappeals.tribunals.gov.uk/Documents/Decisions/ GuideToNumberingDecisions2212.pdf>

Immigration Appeal Tribunal

Citation of authorities

Practice Direction (IAT: Immigration and Asylum Appeals (Procedure) Rules 2000). Also known as: Practice Direction (IAT) (2000/4) [2001] Imm AR 172:

Parties must notify the tribunal of any authorities they intend to cite and, in the case of decisions not reported in the *Immigration Appeal Reports* or the *Immigration and Nationality Reports* to provide copies of the authority. Provision of copies is particularly necessary in the case of determinations of the Tribunal. The Tribunal will not accept citations of extracts from cases without being able to see the whole decision in order to appreciate the context.

Where an authority referred to in section 2 of the Human Rights Act 1998 is to be cited at a hearing

a) the authority to be cited shall be an authoritative and complete report;
b) the tribunal must be provided with a list of the authorities it is intended to cite and copies of the reports not less than 14 days before the hearing; and
c) copies of the complete original texts issued by the European Court or the Commission, either paper based or from the Court's judgment database ('HUDOC') which is available on the internet, may be used.

Reporting of determinations

Practice Direction No 10 of 2003 (Immigration Appeal Tribunal); Practice Direction CA3 of 2003 (Chief Adjudicator) [2003] INLR 358:

From 19 May 2003 the Immigration Appeal Tribunal will cease the practice of reporting and publishing *all* its determinations. From that time, determinations will be either 'reported' or unreported. (paragraph 1)

Practice Statement of the Immigration and Asylum Chambers of the First Tier and Upper Tribunal on or after 25 September 2012
<http://www.judiciary.gov.uk/Resources/JCO/Documents/Practice%20Directions/Tribunals/iac-ut-and-f-tt-practice-statement-revised-250912.pdf>

11.1 This Practice Statement is to be read in conjunction with Practice Direction 11 (citation of unreported determinations) and Practice Statement – *Form of decisions and neutral citation First-tier Tribunal and Upper Tribunal on or after 3 November 2008* (31 October 2008).

11.2 The decision whether to report a determination is that of the Tribunal and it is not perceived to be an issue in which the parties to the appeal have an interest.

Neutral citation of judgments

Practice Direction No 10 of 2003 (Immigration Appeal Tribunal); Practice Direction CA3 of 2003 (Chief Adjudicator) [2003] INLR 358:
Reported determinations will receive a neutral citation number of the form [2003] UKIAT 00001 and will be widely available. They will be anonymous and will be cited by the neutral citation number. Determinations without a number in this form are unreported. (paragraph 2)

Unreported determinations will receive no neutral citation number. They will be sent to the parties but will not be published. Anonymous versions will be deposited in the Supreme Court Library (Negotiations for an electronic depository are in progress). (paragraph 3)

Citation of unreported decisions to the Tribunal

Practice Direction No 10 of 2003 (Immigration Appeal Tribunal); Practice Direction CA3 of 2003 (Chief Adjudicator) [2003] INLR 358:

From the date of this Practice Direction [16 May 2003] no unreported determination of the Tribunal and no determination of an adjudicator, may be cited in proceedings before any adjudicator of the tribunal unless …

then follow details on who shall give permission. (paragraph 4). Rules regarding when permission to cite an unreported decision will be given are set out in paragraph 5.

Special Commissioners for Tax

Citation of Authorities

Practice Direction (Special Commissioners: Human Rights: Citation of Authorities) [2000] STC (SCD) 465:

> If it is necessary to give evidence at a hearing of am authority referred to in section 2 of the Human Rights Act 1998 (the 1998 Act):
>
> (1)   the authority to be cited shall be an authoritative and complete report;
> (2)   the party must give to the court a list of the authorities he intends to cite and copies of the reports not less than three days before the hearing (s 2(1) of the 1998 Act requires the court to take into account the authorities listed there);
> (3)   copies of the complete original texts issued by the European Court of Human Rights and the European Commission of Human Rights either paper based or from the court's judgment database ('HUDOC'), which is available on the internet, may be used.

SCOTLAND: ALL COURTS

Citation of unreported cases

Leighton v Harland & Wolff Ltd 1953 SLT (Notes) 34
Per Lord Guthrie:

> The authority of a case depends not upon whether it is to be found in a series of reports but upon the fact that it is a judicial decision.

SCOTLAND: COURT OF SESSION

Neutral citation

Practice Note (No. 5 of 2004): Form of Opinions and Neutral Citation, 16 November 2004:
<http://www.scotcourts.gov.uk/docs/cos---practice-notes/pn05_2004.pdf?sfvrsn=2>

Neutral citation of cases
With effect form 1 January 2005 a form of neutral citation will be introduced in the Court of Session. A unique number will be given by the Deputy Principal Clerk of Session to opinions issued by the Court of session. Opinions will be numbered in the following way:

Court of Session, Outer House: [2005] CSOH 1 (2, 3 etc.)
Court of Session, Inner House: [2005] CSIH 1 (2, 3 etc.)

Under these new arrangements any particular paragraph of the case to be referred to will be cited in square brackets at the end of the neutral citation as follows:

Smith v Brown [2005] CSOH 1 [12]

The neutral citation will be the official number attributed to the opinion by the court and must always be used on at least the first occasion when the case is cited and referred to in any later opinion. Once the case is reported the neutral citation will appear in front of the citation from the law report series.

Use of opinion in electronic form

Practice Note (No. 5 of 2004): Form of Opinions and Neutral Citation, 16 November 2004: <http://www.scotcourts.gov.uk/docs/cos---practice-notes/pn05_2004.pdf?sfvrsn=2>

Citation of cases in court
It is permissible to cite a case report in a series of reports by means of a copy of a reproduction of the opinion in electronic form that has been authorised by the publisher of the relevant series, provided that the report is presented to the court in an easily legible form and the advocate presenting the report is satisfied that it has been reproduced in an accurate form from the data source. In any case of doubt the court will rely on the printed text of the report unless the editor of the report has certified that the electronic version is more accurate because it corrects an error in an earlier printed text of the report.

Hierarchy of law reports

Practice Note (No. 5 of 2004): Form of Opinions and Neutral Citation, 16 November 2004: <http://www.scotcourts.gov.uk/docs/cos---practice-notes/pn05_2004.pdf?sfvrsn=2>

Citation of cases in court
… For the avoidance of doubt, the Court of Session requires that where a case has been reported in Session Cases it must be cited from that source. Other series of reports may only be used when a case is not reported in Session Cases.

McGowan v Summit at Lloyds, 2002 S.C. 638; 2002 S.L.T. 1258 (para. 57):

In McGowan the Extra Division also stated (para 57) that where an English case has been reported in the *Law Reports* published by the Incorporated Council of Law Reporting for England and Wales it should be cited from that source. Thus, if a decision is not reported in that series, citation from the *Weekly Law Reports* is permissible as these are also published by the Council (although only cases reported in Parts 2 and 3 are intended for publication in the *Law Reports*).

From the annotation to the High Court of Justiciary Practice Note No. 2 of 2004 printed in *Renton & Brown's Criminal Procedure Legislation*.

SCOTLAND: HIGH COURT OF JUSTICIARY

Neutral citation

Practice Note (No. 2 of 2004): Form of Opinions and Neutral Citation, 16 November 2004:
<http://www.scotcourts.gov.uk/docs/cos---practice-notes/pn02_2004.pdf?sfvrsn=2>

Neutral citation of cases
With effect form 1 January 2005 a form of neutral citation will be introduced in the High Court of Justiciary and the Court of Criminal Appeal. A unique number will be given by the Deputy Principal Clerk of Justiciary to opinions issued by the High Court of Justiciary or the Court of Criminal Appeal. Opinions will be numbered in the following way:

> High Court of Justiciary: [2005] HCJT 1 (2, 3 etc.)
> Court of Criminal Appeal: [2005] HCJAC 1 (2, 3 etc.)

Under these new arrangements any particular paragraph of the case to be referred to will be cited in square brackets at the end of the neutral citation as follows:

> *Smith v Brown* [2005] HCJAC 1 [12]

The neutral citation will be the official number attributed to the opinion by the court and must always be used on at least the first occasion when the case is cited and referred to in any later opinion. Once the case is reported the neutral citation will appear in front of the citation from the law report series.

Use of opinion in electronic form

Practice Note (No. 2 of 2004): Form of Opinions and Neutral Citation, 16 November 2004:
<http://www.scotcourts.gov.uk/docs/cos---practice-notes/pn02_2004.pdf?sfvrsn=2>

Citation of cases in court
It is permissible to cite a case report in a series of reports by means of a copy of a reproduction of the opinion in electronic form that has been authorised by the publisher of the relevant series, provided that the report is presented to the court in an easily legible form and the advocate presenting the report is satisfied that it has been reproduced in an accurate form from the data source. In any case of doubt the court will rely on the printed text of the report unless the editor of the report has certified that the electronic version is more accurate because it corrects an error in an earlier printed text of the report.

Hierarchy of law reports

Practice Note (No. 2 of 2004): Form of Opinions and Neutral Citation, 16 November 2004:
<http://www.scotcourts.gov.uk/docs/cos---practice-notes/pn02_2004.pdf?sfvrsn=2>

Citation of cases in court
… For the avoidance of doubt, the High Court of Justiciary and Court of Criminal Appeal require that where a case has been reported in Justiciary Cases it must be cited from that source. Other series of reports may only be used when a case is not reported in Justiciary Cases.

SCOTLAND: TRIBUNALS

The Practice Directions listed above under England and Wales may apply in Scotland according to the jurisdiction of the individual tribunal.

NORTHERN IRELAND

The following is revealed from a search of the Practice Directions from 2001 onwards displayed on the Northern Ireland Court Service website <http://www.courtsni.gov.uk/en-GB/Judicial%20Decisions/ Practice%20Directions/Pages/default.aspx>.

Materials to accompany skeleton arguments submitted to the court

Practice Direction 6/2011 (amended with effect from 5 September 2012): Part A – Skeleton Arguments and Related Documents:

9. Each skeleton argument shall have the following schedules:

(a) A list of authorities. Full citations shall be given (including of unreported cases) in accordance with the practice set out in Annex E1. For cases, textbooks and articles, page numbers and, where available, paragraph references for the passage relied on are required. The sections of a statute or other legislative instrument relied on shall also be specified. An example is attached at Annex A.

(b) The core authorities upon which a party is relying, especially those that it is definitely intended to cite to the court, whether cases, statutes, textbooks or other material. These shall appear first in the list of authorities, and shall be differentiated from the other authorities by means of an asterisk beside the list number. The number of core authorities in a case shall only rarely exceed ten.

14. Books of Authorities shall be compiled in accordance with Annex E1. Where a party has less than fifteen authorities, they shall be submitted in hard copy. Where a party has fifteen or more authorities, they shall be submitted electronically and in hard copy, subject to any contrary direction by the Court. Skeleton arguments and schedules thereto shall, where possible, be submitted to the relevant Office in electronic format. Electronic submission shall be in accordance with Annex E and the relevant e-mail addresses are given at Annex F.

15. Electronic documents may be submitted by e-mail either as a series of Word files or as an unlocked PDF file. Electronically scanned documents should not be submitted. A read-receipt will be required as proof of lodgement. Where the skeleton argument or schedules contain sensitive information, that is information in relation to which reporting restrictions may be imposed by law or requested by a party, it should not be sent by unencrypted e-mail, but instead be lodged by submitting one CD copy or a copy on another commonly used lockable digital recording medium such as a memory-stick to the relevant Office as a PDF file. Further details are in Annex E.

16. Where it is not possible to send copies of particular authorities by e-mail, the requisite number of paper copies shall be lodged in the relevant Office no later than the date of submission of the electronic documents.

17. Any party or their solicitor, where they have one, may request that the Judges' Reference Library provide to them by e-mail a composite electronic PDF document of the skeleton arguments and authorities relied on by all parties, for their use in preparation and in court.

Annex A:

LIST OF AUTHORITIES

NAME OF PROCEEDINGS: Smith v Jones (2010 No. 200)

PARTY PROVIDING THE LIST: The Plaintiff

NAME OF COUNSEL: A N Other QC, BC Dobbs

CASES

1* *Manchester Corporation v Connolly* [1970] 1 Ch 420 at 427G to 429B

2* *Guild v IRC* [1992] 2 AC 310 at 315G to 316B

3 *Higgins v Job* [1982] EGLR 300, page 72, line 8 (copy provided)

TEXT BOOKS

1* *Chitty on Contracts* V51 (27th Edition) p.300 paragraph 3.22

2 *Cheshire, Fifoot and Furmston's Law of Contract* (13th edition) p. 217

ARTICLES

1* "Possessory title and licences" by Grabbit and Keep [1980] MLR 300, page 63, paragraph 6.36, (copy sent by hand)

STATUTES

1* The Limitation (Northern Ireland) Order 1989 Arts 100 and 89 as amended by The Limitation (NI) Order 2002 Art 3.

2* Land Registration Rules (Northern Ireland) 1994 (SRO No. 424) Rules 3 and 4

Annex E1
CITATION AND SUBMISSION OF AUTHORITIES

The following practice should be followed when an authority is cited and submitted:

1. Where a judgment is reported in the Official Law Reports (N.I.; N.I.J.B.; A.C.; Q.B.; Ch.; Fam.) on behalf of the Council of Law Reporting for Northern Ireland or the Incorporated Council of Law

Reporting for England and Wales, that report must be cited. Other series of reports and official transcripts of judgments may only be used when a case is not reported in the Official Law Reports.

2. If a judgment is not (or not yet) reported in the Official Law Reports but is reported in the Weekly Law Reports or the All England Law Reports (All ER), that report should be cited. If the case is reported in both the W.L.R and the All ER, either report may be properly cited.

3. If a judgment is not reported in the Official Law Reports, the W.L.R. or the All ER but is reported in any of the authoritative specialist series of reports which contain a headnote and are made by individuals holding a Senior Courts qualification (for the purposes of section 115 of the Courts and Legal Services Act 1990), the specialist report should be cited.

4. Where a judgment is not reported in any of the reports referred to in paragraphs 1 – 3 above but is reported in other reports, they may be cited.

5. Where a judgment has not been reported, the official transcript may be cited using the neutral citation. Official transcripts may be obtained from, for instance, www.courtsni.gov.uk and www.bailii.org. The handed down version of a judgment should not be used as it may have been subject to later revision. An unreported case should not usually be cited unless it contains a relevant statement of legal principle not found in reported authority.

6. Occasions arise where one report is fuller than another, or where there are discrepancies between reports. On such occasions, the practice outlined above need not be followed but the court should be given a brief explanation as to why this course is being taken and the alternative references should be provided.

7. Where a person is self-represented and is unable to access the Official Law reports, he/she may cite and submit the best case reports that he/she is able to access.

List of authorities and skeleton arguments

Supreme Court Practice Note No 2 of 2003: List of authorities and skeleton arguments, 27 March 2003:

2. Except where the authorities consist of standard text book in common use, or if case law, are contained in the Law Reports, the All England Law Reports, the Northern Ireland Law Reports and the Northern Ireland Judgment Bulletin, copies should be provided for the use of the Master at the hearing of the summons.

APPENDIX 4

USING DATABASES BETTER

The main search connectors and truncators for Lawtel, Lexis®Library, PLC and Westlaw UK – developed by Peter Clinch and Jon Beaumont from an original prepared by Matt Davies, Subject Librarian for Law, Cardiff University. Reproduced with permission.

Command	Function – applies to Lawtel, Lexis®Library, PLC and Westlaw UK unless otherwise stated.	Example
AND	Use when all words or phrases must appear.	EU AND budget
&	Use when all words or phrases must appear. PLC – AND is automatically inserted between words (although the connector does not appear on the screen). Westlaw UK – a space between words represents the AND connector except when using the Advanced Search screen.	EU & budget
OR	Use when at least one of the words or phrases must appear.	noise OR sound
NOT	Lawtel – use to exclude specific words. Use this connector only as the last one in a search; it has a negative influence on everything that follows it.	Barclays NOT Premier League
AND NOT	Lexis®Library – use to exclude specific words. Use this connector only as the last one in a search; it has a negative influence on everything that follows it.	Barclays AND NOT Premier League
–	PLC – use to exclude specific words. This connector does not have a negative effect on all that follows, but somewhat unhelpfully includes the function in the highlighted search terms.	Barclays – Premier League

Command	Function – applies to Lawtel, Lexis®Library, PLC and Westlaw UK unless otherwise stated.	Example
%	Westlaw UK – use to exclude specific words. Use this connector only as the last one in a search; it has a negative influence on everything that follows it.	Barclays % Premier League
"" – quotation marks	Lawtel – use quotation marks to create a phrase. Lexis®Library – no need to use quotation marks unless a connector appears in a phrase. PLC – use quotation marks to create a phrase. Westlaw UK – use quotation marks to create a phrase.	"unfair dismissal" "landlord and tenant"
/N W/N	Lawtel and Westlaw UK – use to specify the proximity between words. Lexis®Library – use to specify the proximity between words. PLC – proximity search not available.	Microsoft /15 internet Microsoft W/15 internet
/s W/S	Lawtel and Westlaw UK – use to find specified words within the same sentence – only effective if lower case /s used. Lexis®Library – use to find specified words within the same sentence. PLC – proximity search not available.	Microsoft /s internet Microsoft /s internet
/p W/P	Lawtel and Westlaw UK – use to find specified words within the same paragraph – only effective if lower case /p used. Lexis®Library – use to find specified words within the same paragraph. PLC – proximity search not available.	Microsoft /p internet Microsoft W/P internet

Command	Function – applies to Lawtel, Lexis®Library, PLC and Westlaw UK unless otherwise stated.	Example
*	Lawtel – place the asterisk at the start or end of a word to search for a common centre with different beginnings and endings.	*legal – retrieves *illegal, legality* acqui* – *acquires, acquired, acquiring,* and *acquisition*
	Lexis®Library and Westlaw UK – use the asterisk to replace one or more letters in a word. You can use more than one asterisk and you can use it anywhere in a word, except as the first letter.	object*** – retrieves *object, objects, objected, objective, objection* and *objecting* but not *objectionable*
	PLC – insert an asterisk in place of a missing word or words, which is most useful with an exact phrase search.	wom*n – *woman, women* Share * agreement – retrieves both *share sale agreement* and *share purchase agreement*
!	Lawtel – use * for the same purpose – see above.	
	Lexis®Library and Westlaw UK – use to replace any number of letters at the end of a word. You may use only one exclamation mark in a word.	acqui! – *acquires, acquired, acquiring,* and *acquisition*
	PLC – automatically applies truncation. The user has no choice.	Contract – *contracts, contracted, contracting,* and *contraction*
?	Lawtel – use as a wildcard character, to replace a letter within a word.	Licen?e – retrieves licence and license

Some additional advice

Singular or plural?

Lexis®Library and *Westlaw UK* – always use the singular. The database will look automatically for the plural. But if you type in the plural, it will search only for the plural. Remember that some plurals which are irregular will need to be spelled out using an appropriate connector or truncator, for example: mouse OR mice; wife OR wives; m*n [for man or men]; child! [for child or children]

Lawtel – will search only for the exact words typed in. It does not assume the plural. So, singular and plural must be specifically typed in.

PLC – automatically searches for synonyms and alternative forms of common words, although using a specific phrase will override this function.

APPENDIX 5

POPULAR NAMES INDEX TO UK CASES AND EU LEGISLATION AND CASES

It should be noted that this list:

- excludes UK legislation – there is a list of the popular names of legislation passed up to the late 19th century published in an appendix to *Craies on Statute Law*, up to the 7th edition, 1971;

- excludes the popular titles of most treaties and conventions (usually the place where the document was concluded, eg the Geneva Convention), since this type of search may be carried out successfully on the free FLARE Index to Treaties:
  <http://193.62.18.232/dbtw-wpd/textbase/treatysearch.htm>

- excludes references to ship's names since *Current Law Case Citator* (Sweet & Maxwell) carries a Ship's Names Index in Part III, with law report citations;

- files titles and abbreviations in letter-by-letter order;

- is arranged so that the nth Company Law Directive, for example, is filed under Company Law, in Directive number order;

- refers to the Official Journal (OJ) in the order: year, series letter, issue number/page number.

The following book was consulted during preparation of the list:

- Fong, C and Rodwell, J, *Popular Australian and English Case Names* (Australian Law Librarians' Group, New South Wales Branch, 1994).

For help in compiling the list special thanks are due to Masoud Gerami, Managing Director of Justis, who placed the Justis popular EU names index at our disposal. Other contributions, gratefully received, were made by (in alphabetical order) Viv Burfitt, Philip Duffy, Sue Fuller, Vivian Grange, Natasha Hammond-Browning, Dean Mason, Professor David Miers, Patrick Overy, Patricia Pritchard, Diane Warren.

1990 World Cup Clips Case
British Broadcasting Corporation v British Satellite Broadcasting Ltd [1991] 2 All ER 833

Aarhus Convention
Convention on access to information, public participation and access to justice in environmental matters adopted 25 June 1998 at the UN/ECE Fourth Ministerial Conference held in Aarhus Denmark <http://www.unece.org/env/pp>

Abba Case
Lynstad v Anabas Products Ltd [1975] FSR 488

Access Directive
Directive 2002/19/EC of the European Parliament and of the Council of 7 March 2002 on access to, and interconnection of, electronic communications networks and associated facilities (OJ 2002 L108/7)

Access to Environmental Information Directive
Council Directive 90/313/EEC of 7 June 1990 on the freedom of access to information on the environment (OJ 1990 L158/56)

Accounting Directives
Collective term for the Fourth Company Law Directive and the Seventh Company Law Directive – see Company Law Directives

Acquired Rights Directives
See Transfer of Undertakings Directives

Active Implantable Medical Device Directive
Council Directive 90/385/EEC of 20 June 1990 on the approximation of the laws of the Member States relating to active implantable medical devices (OJ 1990 L189/17)

Addinell's Case
Re Leeds Banking Co (1865) LR 1 Eq 225

Additives Framework Directive
See Food Additives Framework Directive

ADR Framework Directive
Council Directive 94/55/EC of 21 November 1994 on the approximation of the laws of the Member States with regard to the transport of dangerous goods by road (OJ 1994 L319/7)

Advocaat Case
Erven Warnink BV v John Townend & Sons (Hull) Ltd [1979] AC 731

Air Quality Framework Directive
Council Directive 96/62/EC of 27 September 1996 on ambient air quality assessment and management (OJ 1996 L296/55)

Airspace Regulation
Regulation (EC) No 551/2004 of the European Parliament and of the Council of 10 March 2004 on the organisation and use of the airspace in the single European sky (the airspace Regulation) (Text with EEA relevance) – Commission statement (OJ 2004 L96/20)

Alconbury Case
R (on the application of Holding & Barnes Plc) v Sec. of State for the Environment, Transport and the Regions and related applications [2001] UKHL 23; [2003] 2 AC 295

Amsterdam Treaty
Treaty establishing the European Community (Amsterdam consolidated version) (OJ 1997 C340/173)

Amstrad Case
CBS Songs Ltd v Amstrad Consumer Electronic plc [1988] AC 1013

Anderson's Case
Re Wedgwood Coal and Iron Co (1887) 7 Ch D 75

Angostura Bitters Case
Siegert v Findlater (1878) 7 Ch D 801

Animal Experiments Directive
Council Directive 86/609/EEC of 24 November 1986 on the approximation of laws, regulations and administrative provisions of Member States regarding the protection of animals used for experimental and other scientific purposes (OJ 1986 L358/1)

Annual Accounts Directive
See Company Law Directives, Fourth Directive

Anti-Discrimination Directives
See Equal Treatment Directives

Anti-Dumping Regulation
Council Regulation (EC) No 384/96 of 22 December 1995 on protection against dumped imports from countries not members of the European Community (OJ 1996 L56/1)

Anti-Raider Directive
Council Directive 88/627/EEC of 12 December 1988 on the information to be published when a major holding in a listed company is acquired or disposed of (OJ 1988 L348/62)

Anti-Spam Directive
See Privacy and Electronic Communications Directive

Anti-Subsidy Regulation
Council Regulation (EC) No 2026/97 of 6 October 1997 on protection against subsidized imports from countries not members of the European Community (OJ 1997 L288/1)

Anti-Trust Regulation
Council Regulation (EC) No 1/2003 of 16 December 2002 on the implementation of the rules on competition laid down in Articles 81 and 82 of the Treaty (Text with EEA relevance) (OJ 2003 L1/1)

Appliances Burning Gaseous Fuels Directive
Council Directive 90/396/EEC of 29 June 1990 on the approximation of the laws of the Member States relating to appliances burning gaseous fuels (OJ 1990 L196/15)

Architects' Directive
Council Directive 85/384/EEC of 10 June 1985 on the mutual recognition of diplomas, certificates and other evidence of formal qualifications in architecture (OJ 1985 L223/15)

Asbestos Case
Asbestos Insurance Coverage Cases, In re [1985] 1 WLR 331

Asbestos Directive
Council Directive 83/477/EEC of 19 September 1983 on the protection of workers from the risks related to exposure to asbestos at work (second individual Directive within the meaning of Article 8 of Directive 80/1107/EEC) (OJ 1983 L263/25)

Ashford Case
R v Ashford Borough Council ex parte Shepway District Council [1999] PCLR 12; [1998] JPL 1073

Asylum Procedures Directive
Council Directive 2005/85/EC of 1 December 2005 on minimum standards on procedures in Member States for granting and withdrawing refugee status (OJ 2005 L326/13)

Asylum Seekers Directive
Council Directive 2003/9/EC of 27 January 2003 laying down minimum standards for the reception of asylum seekers (OJ 2003 L31/18)

ATEX Directives
From the French title for Directive 94/9/EC: 'Atmosphere explosible'
Directive 94/9/EC of the European Parliament and the Council of 23 March 1994 on the approximation of laws of Member States concerning equipment and protective systems intended for use in potentially explosive atmospheres (OJ 1994 L100/1)
Directive 1999/92/EC of the European Parliament and of the Council of 16 December 1999 on minimum requirements for improving the safety and health protection of workers potentially at risk from explosive atmospheres (15th individual Directive within the meaning of Article 16(1) of Directive 89/391/EEC) (OJ 2000 L23/57)

Austin Rover Case
HM Inspector of Factories v Austin Rover Group Ltd [1989] IRLR 404

Authorisation Directive
Directive 2002/20/EC of the European Parliament and of the Council of 7 March 2002 on the authorisation of electronic communications networks and services (Authorisation Directive) (OJ 2002 L108/21)

Avonridge Case
Avonridge Property Co Ltd v Mashru
Also known as:
Mashru v Avonridge Property Co Ltd; Avonridge Property Co Ltd v London Diocesan Fund; London Diocesan Fund v Avonridge Property Co Ltd; London Diocesan Fund v Phithwa, [2005] UKHL 70; [2005] 1 WLR 3956

BALAI Directive
Council Directive 92/118/EEC of 17 December 1992 laying down animal health and public health requirements governing trade in and imports into the Community etc (OJ 1993 L62/43)

Bank Accounts Directive
Council Directive 86/635/EEC of 8 December 1986 on the annual accounts and consolidated accounts of banks and other financial institutions (OJ 1986 L372/1)

Bank Branches Directive
Council Directive 89/117/EEC of 13 February 1989 on the obligations of branches established in a Member State of credit institutions and financial institutions having their head offices outside that Member State regarding the publication of annual accounting documents (OJ 1989 L44/40)

Banking Directives
First Council Directive 77/780/EEC of 12 December 1977 on the coordination of the laws, regulations and administrative provisions relating to the taking up and pursuit of the business of credit institutions (OJ 1977 L322/30)
Second Council Directive 89/646/EEC of 15 December 1989 on the coordination of laws, regulations and administrative provisions relating to the taking up and pursuit of the business of credit institutions and amending Directive 77/780/EEC (OJ 1989 L386/1)

Barcelona Convention
Convention on the protection of the Mediterranean Sea against pollution (OJ 1977 L240/3)

Barings Liquidation Cases

Barings plc (in liquidation) v Coopers & Lybrand (No 1), Court of Appeal (Civil Division), 5 May 2000 [2000] 1 WLR 2353

Barings plc (in liquidation) v Coopers & Lybrand (No 2), Chancery Division, 9 February 2001, [2001] Lloyd's Rep Bank 85

Re Barings plc (in liquidation) (No 1), Chancery Division, 18 June 2001, [2001] 2 BCLC 159

Barings plc (in liquidation) v Coopers & Lybrand (No 3), Court of Appeal (Civil Division), 20 July 2001 [2001] EWCA Civ 1163; [2001 CPLR 451

Barings plc No 006303 of 1996, Chancery Division (Companies Court), 20 September 2001, unreported

Barings plc (in liquidation) v Coopers & Lybrand (No 4), Chancery Division), 23 November 2001, [2002] 2 BCLC 364

Re Barings plc (in liquidation) (No 2), Chancery Division (Companies Court), 13 December 2001 [2002] 1 BCLC 401

Barings plc (in liquidation) v Coopers & Lybrand (No 5), Chancery Division, 20 March 2002, [2002] EWHC 461 (Ch); [2002] BCLC 410

Basic Safety Directive

Council Directive 80/836/Euratom of 15 July 1980 amending the Directives laying down the basic safety standards for the health protection of the general public and workers against the dangers of ionizing radiation (OJ 1980 L246/1)

Bathing Water Directive

Directive 2006/7/EC of the European Parliament and of the Council of 15 February 2006 concerning the management of bathing water quality and repealing Directive 76/160/EEC (OJ 2006 L64/37)

Batteries Directives

Council Directive 91/157/EEC 18 March 1991 on batteries and accumulators containing certain dangerous substances (OJ 1991 L78/38)

Directive 2006/66/EC of the European Parliament and of the Council of 6 September 2006 on batteries and accumulators and waste batteries and accumulators and repealing Directive 91/157/EEC (OJ 2006 L266/1)

Directive 2006/66/EC of the European Parliament and of the Council of 6 September 2006 on batteries and accumulators and waste batteries and accumulators and repealing Directive 91/157/EEC (Text with EEA relevance) (OJ 2006 L266/1)

BCCI Cases

Of the numerous cases here is a selection:

Cloverbay Ltd v Bank of Credit and Commerce International SA [1991] Ch 90

Bank of Credit and Commerce International SA, re (No 2) [1992] BCC 715

Bank of Credit and Commerce International SA, re (No 3) [1993] BCLC 1490

Bank of Credit and Commerce International SA, re (No 9) [1994] 3 All ER 764

Three Rivers District Council and Others v Bank of England [2006] EWHC 816 (Comm)

Biotechnology Directive

Directive 98/44/EC of the European Parliament and of the Council of 6 July 1998 on the legal protection of biotechnological inventions (OJ 1998 L213/13)

Birds Directive

See Wild Birds Directive

Birmingham Six Case

Hunter v Chief Constable of the West Midlands [1982] AC 529

R v McIlkenny (1991) 93 Cr App Rep 287

Biocidal Products Directive

Directive 98/8/EC of the European Parliament and of the Council of 16 February 1998 concerning the placing of biocidal products on the market (OJ 1998 L123/1)

Biocides Directive

See Biocidal Products Directive

Biofuels Directives
Directive 2003/30/EC of the European Parliament and of the Council of 8 May 2003 on the promotion of the use of biofuels or other renewable fuels for transport (OJ 2003 L123/42)
Directive 2009/28/EC of the European Parliament and of the Council of 23 April 2009 on the promotion of the use of energy from renewable sources and amending and subsequently repealing Directives 2001/77/EC and 2003/30/EC (OJ 2009 L140/16)

Biological Agents Directive
Directive 2000/54/EC of the European Parliament and of the Council of 18 September 2000 on the protection of workers from risks related to exposure to biological agents at work (seventh individual directive within the meaning of Article 16(1) of Directive 89/391/EEC) (OJ 2000 L262/21)

Biotechnology Directive
Directive 98/44/EC of the European Parliament and of the Council of 6 July 1998 on the legal protection of biotechnological inventions (OJ 1998 L213/13)

Black List
Council Directive 76/464/EEC of 4 May 1976 on pollution caused by certain dangerous substances discharged into the aquatic environment of the Community (OJ 1976 L129/23)

Bland Case
Airedale NHS Trust v Bolland [1993] AC 789

Blood Directive
Directive 2002/98/EC of the European Parliament and of the Council of 27 January 2003 setting standards of quality and safety for the collection, testing, processing, storage and distribution of human blood and blood components and amending Directive 2001/83/EC (OJ 2003 L33/30)

Blue Arrow Case
R v Cohen (1992) 142 NLJ 1267

Boilers Directive
Council Directive 92/42/EEC of 21 May 1992 on the efficiency requirements for new hot-water boilers fired with liquid or gaseous fuels (OJ 1992 L167/17)

Bolland Case
Airedale NHS Trust v Bolland [1993] AC 789

Bosman Case
Union royale belge des sociétés de football association ASBL v Jean-Marc Bosman, Royal club liégeois SA v Jean-Marc Bosman and others and Union des associations européennes de football (UEFA) v Jean-Marc Bosman. Case C-415/93 in the European Court of Justice on the freedom of movement for footballers [1995] ECR I-4921

BPI/MCPS Case
British Phonographic Industry Ltd v Mechanical Copyright Protection Society Ltd (No 2) [1993] EMLR 86

Braking Directive
Council Directive 71/320/EEC of 26 July 1971 on the approximation of the laws of the Member States relating to the braking devices of certain categories of motor vehicles and of their trailers, English special edition: Series I Chapter 1971(III) P. 0746–0783

British Sherry Case
Vine Products Ltd v Mackenzie & Co Ltd [1969] RPC 1

Broadwater Farm Murder Case
R v Silcott; R v Braithwaite [1987] Crim LR 765; *The Times*, 6 December 1991

Brussels I Regulation
Council Regulation (EC) No 44/2001 of 22 December 2000 on jurisdiction and the recognition and enforcement of judgments in civil and commercial matters (OJ 2001 L12/1)

Brussels II Regulation
Council Regulation (EC) No 2201/2003 of 27 November 2003 concerning jurisdiction and the recognition and enforcement of judgments in matrimonial matters and the matters of parental responsibility, repealing Regulation (EC) No 1347/2000 (OJ 2003 L338/1)

Budweiser Case
Anheuser-Busch Inc v Budejovicky Budvar Narodni Podnik (1984) 4 IPR 260; [1984] FSR 413

Bulger Case
See James Bulger Case

Bullock Order Case
Bullock v London General Omnibus Co [1907] 1 KB 264

Burden of Proof Directive
Council Directive 97/80/EC of 15 December 1997 on the burden of proof in Cases of discrimination based on sex (OJ 1998 L14/6)

Camel-Hair Belting Case
Reddaway v Banham [1896] AC 199

Cann Case
Abbey National Building Society v Cann [1991] 1 AC 56

Cannibalism Case
R v Dudley and Stephens (1884) 14 QBD 273

Capital Adequacy Directive
Council Directive 93/6/EEC of 15 March 1993 on the capital adequacy of investments firms and credit institutions (OJ 1993 L141/1)

Capital Transfer Directive
Council Directive 88/361/EEC of 24 June 1988 for the implementation of Article 67 of the Treaty (OJ 1988 L178/5)

Car Recycling Directive
Directive 2000/53/EC of the European Parliament and of the Council of 18 September 2000 on end-of life vehicles – Commission Statements (OJ 2000 L269/34)

Carnot Decision
Council Decision 1999/24/EC of 14 December 1998 adopting a multiannual programme of technological actions promoting the clean and efficient use of solid fuels (OJ 1999 L7/28)

Cartel Regulation
See Anti-Trust Regulation

Carcinogens Directive
Council Directive 90/394/EEC of 28 June 1990 on the protection of workers from the risks related to exposure to carcinogens at work (Sixth individual Directive within the meaning of Article 16 (1) of Directive 89/391/EEC) (OJ 1990 L196/1)

Cassis de Dijon Case
Case 120/78 in the European Court of Justice which established that any product lawfully produced and marketed in one member state must (in principle) be admitted to the market of any other member state (ECR 1979/1)

CCC
Community Customs Code: Council Regulation (EEC) No 2913/92 of 12 October 1992 establishing the Community Customs Code (OJ 1992 L302/1)

CCSU Case
Council of Civil Service Unions v Minister for the Civil Service [1985] 1 AC 374

CE Marking
Council Directive 93/68/EEC of 22 July 1993 amending Directives 87/404/EEC (simple pressure vessels), 88/378/EEC (safety of toys), 89/106/EEC (construction products), 89/336/EEC (electromagnetic compatibility), 89/392/EEC (machinery), 89/686/EEC (personal protective equipment), 90/384/EEC (non-automatic weighing instruments), 90/385/EEC (active implantable medicinal devices), 90/396/EEC (appliances burning gaseous fuels), 91/263/EEC (telecommunications terminal equipment), 92/42/EEC (new hot-water boilers fired with liquid or gaseous fuels) and 73/23/EEC (electrical equipment designed for use within certain voltage limits) (OJ 1993 L220/1)
Council Decision 93/465/EEC of 22 July 1993 concerning the modules for the various phases of the conformity assessment procedures and the rules for the affixing and use of the CE (Conformité Européenne) marking, which are intended to be used in the technical harmonization directives (OJ 1993 L220/23)

Cereals Directive
Council Directive 86/362/EEC of 24 July 1986 on the fixing of maximum levels for pesticide residues in and on cereals (OJ 1986 L221/37)

Champagne Cases
Champagne Heidsieck et Cie Monopole Society Anonyme v Buton [1030] 1 Ch 330
J Bollinger Ltd v Costa Brava Wine Co Ltd (No 1) [1960] Ch 262
J Bollinger Ltd v Costa Brava Wine Co Ltd (No 2) [1961] 1 WLR 277

Channel Tunnel Case
Channel Tunnel Group Ltd v Balfour Beatty Construction Ltd [1993] AC 334

Chapman's Case
Re General Rolling Stock Co (1886) LR1 Eq 346

Character Reference Case
Spring v Guardian Assurance plc [1994] 3 WLR 354

Chariots of Fire Case
EMI Music Publishing Ltd v Papathanasiou [1993] EMLR 306

Charter of Fundamental Rights
Codification of rights deriving mainly from the European Convention on Human Rights, the European Social Charter and general principles on Community law, Nice 2000 <http://ec.europa.eu/justice_home/unit/charte/index_en.html>

Chemical Agents Directive
Council Directive 98/24/EC of 7 April 1998 on the protection of the health and safety of workers from the risks related to chemical agents at work (fourteenth individual Directive within the meaning of Article 16(1) of Directive 89/391/EEC) (OJ 1998 L131/11)

Chicago Pizza Case
My Kinda Town Ltd v Soll [1983] RPC 15

CHIP
Chemicals (Hazard Information and Packaging) Regulations 1993, SI 1993/1746, as amended

Chocolate Directive
Directive 2000/36/EC of the European Parliament and of the Council of 23 June 2000 relating to cocoa and chocolate products intended for human consumption (OJ 2000 L197/19)

CHP Directive
Directive 2004/8/EC of the European Parliament and of the Council of 11 February 2004 on the promotion of cogeneration based on a useful heat demand in the internal energy market and amending Directive 92/42/EEC (OJ 2004 L52/50)

CITES
Convention on International Trade in Endangered Species of Wild Fauna and Flora:
Council Regulation (EC) No 338/97 of 9 December 1996 on the protection of species of wild fauna and flora by regulating trade therein (OJ 1997 L61/1)

Clayton's Case
Devaynes v Noble (1816) 1 Mer 572

Clinical Trials Directive
Directive 2001/20/EC of the European Parliament and of the Council of 4 April 2001 on the approximation of the laws, regulations and administrative provisions of the Member States relating to the implementation of good clinical practice in the conduct of clinical trials on medicinal products for human use (OJ 2001 L121/34)

Clinical Trials Regulations
Medicines for Human Use (Clinical Trials) Regulations 2004, SI 2004/1031

Clinical Practice Directive
Directive 2001/20/EC of the European Parliament and the Council of 4 April 2001 on the approximation of the laws, regulations and administrative provisions of the Member States relating to the implementation of good clinical practice on the conduct of clinical trials on medicinal products for human use (OJ 2001 L121/34)

Clockwork Orange Case
Time Warner Entertainments LP v Channel Four Television Corporation plc [1994] EMLR 1; (1994) 28 IPR 459

Cogeneration Directive
Directive 2004/8/EC of the European Parliament and of the Council of 11 February 2004 on the promotion of cogeneration based on a useful heat demand in the internal energy market and amending Directive 92/42/EEC (OJ 2004 L52/50)

Collective Redundancies Directive
Council Directive 98/59/EC of 20 July 1998 on the approximation of the laws of the Member States relating to collective redundancies (OJ 1998 L225/16)

Coloroll Case
Coloroll Pension Trustees v James Richard Russell and others, European Court of Justice, 28 September 1994, [1994] ECR I-4389

Columbia Trademark Case
EMI Records v CBS UK [1976] ECR 811; 1976] 2 CMLR 235

COMAH Directive
See Seveso Directives – Second Directive

Commercial Agents Directive
Council Directive 86/653/EEC of 18 December 1986 on the coordination of the laws of the Member States relating to self-employed commercial agents (OJ 1986 L382/17)

Community Customs Code Regulation
Council Regulation (EEC) No 2913/92 of 12 October 1992 establishing the Community Customs Code (OJ 1992 L302/1)

Community Patent Convention
76/76/EEC: Convention for the European patent for the common market (Community Patent Convention) (OJ 1976 L17/1)
89/695/EEC: Agreement relating to Community patents – Done at Luxembourg on 15 December 1989 (OJ 1989 L401/1)

Community Trade Mark Regulation
Council Regulation (EC) No 40/94 of 20 December 1993 on the Community trade mark (OJ 1994 L11/1)

Company Law Directives
First Council Directive 68/151/EEC of 9 March 1968 on co-ordination of safeguards which, for the protection of the interests of members and others, are required by Member States of companies within the meaning of the second paragraph of Article 58 of the Treaty, with a view to making such safeguards equivalent throughout the Community (OJ 1968 L65/8)
Second Council Directive 77/91/EEC of 13 December 1976 on coordination of safeguards which, for the protection of the interests of members and others, are required by Member States of companies within the meaning of the second paragraph of Article 58 of the Treaty, in respect of the formation of public limited liability companies and the maintenance and alteration of their capital, with a view to making such safeguards equivalent (OJ 1977 L26/1)
Third Council Directive 78/855/EEC of 9 October 1978 based on Article 54 (3) (g) of the Treaty concerning mergers of public limited liability companies (OJ 1978 L295/36)
Fourth Council Directive 78/660/EEC of 25 July 1978 based on Article 54 (3) (g) of the Treaty on the annual accounts of certain types of companies (OJ 1978 L222/11)
Fifth Company Law Directive
Proposal for a fifth Directive on the coordination of safeguards which for the protection of the interests of members and outsiders are required by Member States of companies within the meaning of Article 59, second paragraph, with respect to company structure and to the power and responsibilities of company boards (OJ 1972 C131/49) – never enacted
Sixth Council Directive 82/891/EEC of 17 December 1982 based on Article 54 (3) (g) of the Treaty, concerning the division of public limited liability companies (OJ 1982 L378/47)
Seventh Council Directive 83/349/EEC of 13 June 1983 based on the Article 54 (3) (g) of the Treaty on consolidated accounts (OJ 1983 L193/1)
Eighth Council Directive 84/253/EEC of 10 April 1984 based on Article 54 (3) (g) of the Treaty on the approval of persons responsible for carrying out the statutory audits of accounting documents (OJ 1984 L126/20)
Eleventh Council Directive 89/666/EEC of 21 December 1989 concerning disclosure requirements in respect of branches opened in a Member State by certain types of company governed by the law of another State (OJ 1989 L395/36)
Twelfth Council Company Law Directive 89/667/EEC of 21 December 1989 on single-member private limited-liability companies (OJ 1989 L395/40)
[Thirteenth Company Law Directive] Directive 2004/25/EC of the European Parliament and of the Council of 21 April 2004 on takeover bids (Text with EEA relevance) (OJ 2004 L142/12)

Company Statute
See European Company Statute

Comparative Advertising Directive
Directive 97/55/EC of European Parliament and of the Council of 6 October 1997 amending Directive 84/450/EEC concerning misleading advertising so as to include comparative advertising (OJ 1997 L290/18)

Compliance Directive
Council Directive 89/665/EEC of 21 December 1989 on the coordination of the laws, regulations and administrative provisions relating to the application of review procedures to the award of public supply and public works contracts (OJ 1989 L395/33)

Computer Programs Directive
Council Directive 91/250/EEC of 14 May 1991 on the legal protection of computer programs (OJ 1991 L122/42)

Conditional Access Directive
Directive 98/84/EC of the European Parliament and of the Council of 20 November 1998 on the legal protection of services based on, or consisting of, conditional access (OJ 1998 L320/54)

Conformity Assessment Procedures and CE Marking Rules Decision
Council Decision 93/465/EEC of 22 July 1993 concerning the modules for the various phases of the conformity assessment procedures and the rules for the affixing and use of the CE conformity marking, which are intended to be used in the technical harmonization directives (OJ 1993 L220/23)

Conglomerates Directive
Directive 2002/87/EC of the European Parliament and of the Council of 16 December 2002 on the supplementary supervision of credit institutions, insurance undertakings and investment firms in a financial conglomerate and amending Council Directives 73/239/EEC, 79/267/EEC, 92/49/EEC, 92/96/EEC, 93/6/EEC and 93/22/EEC, and Directives 98/78/EC and 2000/12/EC of the European Parliament and of the Council (OJ 2003 L35/1)

Consolidated Accounts Directive
See Company Law Directives – Seventh Directive

Consolidated Supplies Directive
See Public Sector Supply Directive

Contractual Obligations Convention
80/934/EEC: Convention on the law applicable to contractual obligations opened for signature in Rome on 19 June 1980 (OJ 1980 L266/1)

Construction Products Directive
Council Directive 89/106/EEC of 21 December 1988 on the approximation of laws, regulations and administrative provisions of Member States relating to construction products (OJ 1989 L40/12)

Consumer Credit Directive
Council Directive 87/102/EEC of 22 December 1986 for the approximation of the laws, regulations and administrative provisions of member states concerning consumer credit (OJ 1987 L42/48)

Consumer Guarantees Directive
Directive 1999/44/EC of the European Parliament and of the Council of 25 May 1999 on certain aspects of the sale of consumer goods and associated guarantees (OJ 1999 L171/12)

Consumer Protection Cooperation Regulation
Regulation (EC) No 2006/2004 of the European Parliament and of the Council of 27 October 2004 on cooperation between national authorities responsible for the enforcement of consumer protection laws (the Regulation on consumer protection cooperation)Text with EEA relevance (OJ 2004 L364/1)

Contractual Netting Directive
Directive 96/10/EC of the European Parliament and of the Council of 21 March 1996 amending Directive 89/647/EEC as regards recognition of contractual netting by the competent authorities (OJ 1996 L85/17)

Copyright Directives
Council Directive 93/98/EEC of 29 October 1993 harmonizing the term of protection of copyright and certain related rights (OJ 1993 L290/9)
Directive 2001/29/EC of the European Parliament and of the Council of 22 May 2001 on the harmonisation of certain aspects of copyright and related rights in the information society (OJ 2001 L167/10)

Copyright Term Directive
See Copyright Directives

Cosmetics Directive
Council Directive 76/768/EEC of 27 July 1976 on the approximation of the laws of Member States relating to cosmetic products (OJ 1976 L262/169)

Costa Case
Flaminio Costa v E.N.E.L. European Court of Justice Case 6/64 [1964] ECR 1141

Council Swaps Case
Hazell v Hammersmith and Fulham London Borough Council [1991] 2 AC 1

CPC
See Community Patent Convention

CPD
See Construction Products Directive

Crazy Horse Case
Alain Bernardin v Pavillion Properties Ltd [1967] RPC 581

Credit Institutions Reorganisation and Winding Up Directive
Directive 2001/24/EC of the European Parliament and of the Council of 4 April 2001 on the reorganisation and winding up of credit institutions (OJ 2001 L125/15)

Crossman Diaries Case
Attorney-General v Jonathan Cape Ltd [1976] QB 752

Cuban Sugar Case
Empressa Exportardora de Azucar v Industria Azucarera Nacional SA [1983] 2 Lloyd's Rep 171

Dalmia Industries Case
Dalmia Dairy Industries Ltd v National Bank of Pakistan [1978] 2 Lloyd's Rep 223

Dangerous Goods Training Directive
See ADR Framework Directive

Dangerous Preparations Directive
Council Directive 67/379/EEC of 7th June 1988 on the approximation of the laws, regulations and administrative provisions of the Member States relating to the classification, packaging and labelling of dangerous preparations (OJ 1988 L187/14)

Dangerous Substances Directives
Council Directive 67/548/EEC of 27 June 1967 on the approximation of laws, regulations and administrative provisions relating to the classification, packaging and labelling of dangerous substances (OJ 1967 L196/1)
Directive 2006/121/EC of the European Parliament and of the Council of 18 December 2006 amending Council Directive 67/548/EEC on the approximation of laws, regulations and administrative provisions relating to the classification, packaging and labelling of dangerous substances in order to adapt it to Regulation (EC) No 1907/2006 concerning the Registration, Evaluation, Authorisation and Restriction of Chemicals (REACH) and establishing a European Chemicals Agency (OJ 2006 L396/850)
Regulation (EC) No 1907/2006 of the European Parliament and of the Council of 18 December 2006 concerning the Registration, Evaluation, Authorisation and Restriction of Chemicals (REACH), establishing a European Chemicals Agency, amending Directive 1999/45/EC and repealing Council Regulation (EEC) No 793/93 and Commission Regulation (EC) No 1488/94 as well as Council Directive 76/769/EEC and Commission Directives 91/155/EEC, 93/67/EEC, 93/105/EC and 2000/21/EC (OJ 2006 L396/1)

Dangerous Substances and Preparations Directive
Council Directive 76/769/EEC of 27 July 1976 on the approximation of the laws, regulations and administrative provisions of the Member States relating to restrictions on the marketing and use of certain dangerous substances and preparations (OJ 1976 L262/201)

Dangerous Substances in Water Directive
Council Directive 76/464/EEC of 4 May 1976 on pollution caused by certain dangerous substances discharged into the aquatic environment of the Community (OJ 1976 L129/23)

Dassonville
Procureur du Roi v Benoît and Gustave Dassonville. European Court of Justice, Case 8/74 [1974] ECR 837

Data Protection Directive
Directive 96/9/EC of the European Parliament and of the Council of 11 March 1996 on the legal protection of databases (OJ 1996 L77/20)

Database Directive
See Data Protection Directive

Design Directive
See Design Protection Directive

Design Protection Directive
Directive 98/71/EC of the European Parliament and of the Council of 13 October 1998 on the legal protection of designs (OJ 1998 L289/28)

Diane Pretty Case
R (on the application of Pretty) v DPP [2001] UKHL 61; [2002] 1 AC 800

Diplock's Case
Re Diplock [1948] Ch 468
Ministry of Health v Simpson [1951] AC 251

Diplomas Directives
Council Directive 89/48/EEC of 21st December 1988 on a general system for the recognition of higher education diplomas awarded on completion of professional education and training of at least three years' duration (OJ 1989 L19/16)
Council Directive 92/51/EEC of 18 June 1992 on a second general system for the recognition of professional education and training to supplement Directive 89/48/EEC (OJ 1992 L209/25)

Distance Marketing Directive
Directive 2002/65/EC of the European Parliament and of the Council of 23 September 2002 concerning the distance marketing of consumer financial services and amending Council Directive 90/619/EEC and Directives 97/7/EC and 98/27/EC (OJ 2002 L271/16)

Disclosure Requirements Directive
See Company Directives – Eleventh Directive

Discrete Selling Case
Greenwich (London Borough) v Discrete Selling Estates Ltd [1990] EG 113

Discharge of Dangerous Substances Directive
See Dangerous Substances in Water Directive

Dispatches Case
Terrence Higgins Trust v Channel 4. Broadcasting Complaints Commission, Finding of 23 May 1991

Display Screen Equipment Directive
Council Directive 90/270/EEC of 29 May 1990 on the minimum safety and health requirements for work with display screen equipment (fifth individual Directive within the meaning of Article 16 (1) of Directive 89/391/EEC) (OJ 1990 L156/14)

Distance Selling Directive
Directive 97/7/EC of the European Parliament and of the Council of 20 May 1997 on the protection of consumers in respect of distance contracts – Statement by the Council and the Parliament re Article 6 (1) – Statement by the Commission re Article 3 (1), first indent, (OJ 1997 L144/19)

Dolly Blue Case
Edge & Sons Ltd v Gallon & Son [1990] 17 RPC 557

Doorstep Selling Directive
Council Directive 85/577/EEC of 20 December 1985 to protect the consumer in respect of contracts negotiated away from business premises (OJ 1985 L37/31)

Downing Street Years Case
Times Newspapers Ltd v MGN Ltd [1993] EMLR 443

Drinking Water Directive
Council Directive 80/778/EEC of 15 July 1980 relating to the quality of water intended for human consumption (OJ 1980 L229/11)

Drinks Cases
J Bollinger Ltd v Costa Brava Wine Co Ltd (No 1) [1960] Ch 262
J Bollinger Ltd v Costa Brava Wine Co Ltd (No 2) [1961] 1 WLR 277
John Walker & Sons Ltd v Henry Ost & Co Ltd [1970] 1 WLR 917
Vine Products Ltd v Mackenzie & Co Ltd [1969] RPC 1

Dual Pricing Directive
Directive 98/6/EC of the European Parliament and the Council of 16 February 1998 on consumer protection in the indication of the prices of products offered to consumers (OJ 1998 L80/27)

Dublin II Regulation
Council Regulation (EC) No 343/2003 of 18 February 2003 establishing the criteria and mechanisms for determining the Member State responsible for examining an asylum application lodged in one of the Member States by a third-country national (OJ 2003 L50/1)

Dublin Convention
Convention determining the State responsible for examining applications for asylum lodged in one of the Member States of the European Communities – Dublin Convention (OJ 1997 C 254/1)

Duke of Westminster Case
Inland Revenue Commissioners v The Duke of Westminster [1936] AC 1

Dundalk Case
Commission of the European Communities v Ireland. European Court of Justice, Case 45/87 [1988] ECR 4929

Duration Directive
Council Directive 93/98/EEC of 29 October 1993 harmonising the term of protection of copyright and certain related rights (OJ 1993 L290/9)

E-Commerce Directive
See Electronic Commerce Directive

E-Money Directive
See Electronic Money Directive

E-Privacy Directive
See Privacy and Electronic Communications Directive

E-Signatures Directive
See Electronic Signatures Directive

Eastenders Case
BBC v Celebrity Centre Productions Ltd (1990) 15 IPR 333

EAEC Treaty
See EURATOM Treaty

EC Treaty
Name for the EEC treaty following the entry into force of the Treaty on European Union on 1 November 1993

ECI
See European Chemicals Inventory

ECS
See European Company Statute

ECSC Treaty
European Coal and Steel Community Treaty. Signed in Paris on 18 April 1951, entered into force 23 July 1952, expired 23 July 2002

Eco-Labelling Regulation
Regulation (EC) No 1980/2000 of the European Parliament and of the Council of 17 July 2000 on a revised Community eco-label award scheme (OJ 2000 L237/1)

EEA Agreement
Agreement on the European Economic Area (OJ 1994 L1/3)

EEC Treaty
Treaty establishing the European Economic Community. Signed in Rome on 25 March 1957, entered into force 1 January 1958. Later renamed the EC treaty

EIA Directive
See Environmental Impact Assessment Directives

Elderflower Champagne Case
Tattinger SA v Allber Ltd [1992] FSR 641; [1993] 2 CMLR 741; [1994] 4 All ER 75

Electric Velveteen Case
In re Van Duzer's Trade-Mark; In re Leaf, Sons, & Co's Trade-Mark (1887) 34 Ch D 623

Electricity Market Access Directive
Directive 96/92/EC of the European Parliament and of the Council of 19 December 1996 concerning common rules for the internal market in electricity (OJ 1997 L27/20)

Electricity Regulation
Regulation (EC) No 1228/2003 of the European Parliament and of the Council of 26 June 2003 on conditions for access to the network for cross-border exchanges in electricity (Text with EEA relevance) (OJ 2003 L176/1)

Electromagnetic Compatibility Directive
Directive 2004/108/EC of the European Parliament and of the Council of 15 December 2004 on the approximation of the laws of the Member States relating to electromagnetic compatibility and repealing Directive 89/336/EEC Text with EEA relevance (OJ 2004 L390/24)

Electronic Commerce Directive
Directive 2000/31/EC of the European Parliament and of the Council of 8 June 2000 on certain legal aspects of information society services, in particular electronic commerce, in the Internal Market ('Directive on electronic commerce') (OJ 2000 L178/1)

Electronic Communications Directive
See Privacy and Electronic Communications Directive

Electronic Money Directive
Directive 2000/46/EC of the European Parliament and of the Council of 18 September 2000 on the taking up, pursuit of and prudential supervision of the business of electronic money institutions (OJ 2000 L275/39)

Electronic Signatures Directive
Directive 1999/93/EC of the European Parliament and of the Council of 13 December 1999 on a Community framework for electronic signatures (OJ 2000 L3/12)

Elton John Case
Elton John v James [1991] FSR 397

ELV Directive
See Car Recycling Directive

EMC Directive
See Electromagnetic Compatibility Directive

Emissions Trading Directive
Directive 2003/87/EC of the European Parliament and of the Council of 13 October 2003 establishing a scheme for greenhouse gas emission allowance trading within the Community and amending Council Directive 96/61/EC (Text with EEA relevance) (OJ 2003 L275/32)

Encrypted Services Directive
See Conditional Access Directive

Energy Performance of Buildings Directive
Directive 2002/91/EC of the European Parliament and of the Council of 16 December 2002 on the energy performance of buildings (OJ 2003 L1/65)

Energy Tax Directive
Council Directive 2003/96/EC of 27 October 2003 restructuring the Community framework for the taxation of energy products and electricity (Text with EEA relevance) (OJ 2003 L283/51)

Enforcement of Judgments Convention
See Brussels Convention

Environmental Impact Assessment Directives
Council Directive 85/337/EEC of 27 June 1985 on the assessment of the effects of certain public and private projects on the environment (OJ 1985 L175/40)
Directive 2002/49/EC of the European Parliament and of the Council of 25 June 2002 relating to the assessment and management of environmental noise – Declaration by the Commission in the Conciliation Committee on the Directive relating to the assessment and management of environmental noise (OJ 2002 L189/2)

Environmental Liability Directive
Directive 2004/35/CE of the European Parliament and of the Council of 21 April 2004 on environmental liability with regard to the prevention and remedying of environmental damage (OJ 2004 L143/56)

Equal Pay Directive
Council Directive 75/117/EEC of 10 February 1975 on the approximation of the laws of the Member States relating to the application of the principle of equal pay from men and women (OJ 1975 L45/19)

Equal Treatment Directives
Council Directive 76/207/EEC of 9 February 1976 on the implementation of the principle of equal treatment for men and women as regards access to employment, vocational training and promotion, and working conditions (OJ 1976 L39/40)
Council Directive 2000/43/EC of 29 June 2000 implementing the principle of equal treatment between persons irrespective of racial or ethnic origin (OJ 2000 L180/22)
Council Directive 2000/78/EC of 27 November 2000 establishing a general framework for equal treatment in employment and occupation (OJ 2000 L303/16)
Directive 2006/54/EC of the European Parliament and of the Council of 5 July 2006 on the implementation of the principle of equal opportunities and equal treatment of men and women in matters of employment and occupation (recast) (OJ 2006 L204/23)

Establishment Directive
Directive 98/5/EC of the European Parliament and of the Council of 16 February 1998 to facilitate practice of the profession of lawyer on a permanent basis in a Member State other than that in which the qualification was obtained (OJ 1998 L77/36)

EUCD
See Copyright Directives

Euratom Treaty
Treaty establishing the European Atomic Energy Community (EAEC – EURATOM) 25 March 1957

Eurodac Regulation
Council Regulation (EC) No 2725/2000 of 11 December 2000 concerning the establishment of 'Eurodac' for the comparison of fingerprints for the effective application of the Dublin Convention (OJ 2000 L316/1)

Eurodisc Directive
See Eurovignette Directive

Eurolist Directive
Council Directive 80/390/EEC of 17 March 1980 coordinating the requirements for the drawing up, scrutiny and distribution of the listing particulars to be published for the admission of securities to official stock exchange listing (OJ 1980 L100/1)

European Chemicals Inventory
96/335/EC: Commission Decision of 8 May 1996 establishing an inventory and a common nomenclature of ingredients employed in cosmetic products (Text with EEA relevance) (OJ 1996 L132/1)

European Company Statute (Societas Europea)
Council Regulation (EC) No 2157/2001 of 8 October 2001 on the Statute for a European company (SE) (OJ 2001 L294/1)
Council Directive 2001/86/EC of 8 October 2001 supplementing the Statute for a European company with regard to the involvement of employees (OJ 2001 L294/22)

European Works Council Directive
Council Directive 94/45/EC of 22 September 1994 on the establishment of a European Works Council or a procedure in Community-scale undertakings and Community-scale groups of undertakings for the purposes of informing and consulting employees (OJ 1994 L254/64)

Eurovignette Directive
Directive 1999/62/EC of the European Parliament and of the Council of 17 June 1999 on the charging of heavy goods vehicles for the use of certain infrastructure (OJ 1000 L187/42)

EWC Directive
See European Works Council Directive

Excise Duty Directive
Council Directive 92/12/EEC of 25 February 1992 on the general arrangements for products subject to excise duty and on the holding, movement and monitoring of such products (OJ 1992 L76/1)

Excise Duty Regulation
Council Regulation (EC) No 2073/2004 of 16 November 2004 on administrative cooperation in the field of excise duties (OJ 2004 L359/1)

Explosive Atmospheres Directives
Dir 76/117/EEC and 79/196/EEC on electrical equipment for use in potentially explosive atmospheres (OJ L24/76 and OJ L43/79)

Fair Value Directive
Directive 2001/65/EC of the European Parliament and of the Council of 27 September 2001 amending Directives 78/660/EEC, 83/349/EEC and 86/635/EEC as regards the valuation rules for the annual and consolidated accounts of certain types of companies as well as of banks and other financial institutions (OJ 2001 L283/28)

Fares Fair Case
Bromley London Borough Council v Greater London Council [1983] 1 AC 768

Fish Water Directive
Council Directive 78/659/EEC of 18 July 1978 on the quality of fresh waters needing protection or improvement in order to support fish life (OJ 1978 L222/1)

Fixed-Term Work Directive
Council Directive 1999/70/EC of 28 June 1999 concerning the framework agreement on fixed-term work concluded by ETUC, UNICE and CEEP (OJ 1999 L175/43)

Fleetwood Mac Case
Clifford Davis Management Ltd v WEA Records Ltd [1975] 1 WLR 61

Flegg Case
City of London Building Society v Flegg [1988] AC 54

Food Additives Framework Directive
Council Directive 89/107/EEC of 21 December 1988 on the approximation of the laws of the Member States concerning food additives authorized for use in foodstuffs intended for human consumption (OJ 1989 L40/27)

Food Hygiene Regulation
Regulation (EC) No 852/2004 of the European Parliament and of the Cou_cil of 29 April 2004 on the hyg_ene of foodstuffs (OJ 2004 L139/1)

Food Labelling Directive
Directive 2000/13/EC of the European Parliament and of the Council of 20 March 2000 on the approximation of the laws of the Member States relating to the labelling, presentation and advertising of foodstuffs (OJ 2000 L109/29)

Food Supplements Directive
Directive 2002/46/EC of the European Parliament and of the Council of 10 June 2002 on the approximation of the laws of the Member States relating to food supplements (OJ 2002 183/51)

Foot and Mouth Disease Directive
Council Directive 2003/85/EC of 29 September 2003 on Community measures for the control of foot-and-mouth disease repealing Directive 85/511/EEC and Decisions 89/531/EEC and 91/665/EEC and amending Directive 92/46/EEC (Text with EEA relevance.) (OJ 2003 L306/1)

Forty Eight Hour Directive
See Working Time Directive

Framework Directive
Directive 2002/21/EC of the European Parliament and of the Council of 7 March 2002 on a common regulatory framework for electronic communications networks and services (Framework Directive) (OJ 2002 L108/33)

Francovich Case
Francovich v Italy [1991] ECR I-5357

Francs Case
Ironmonger & Co v Dyne (1928) 44 TLR 497

Free Markets Directive
Directive 2004/38/EC of the European Parliament and of the Council of 29 April 2004 on the right of citizens of the Union and their family members to move and reside freely within the territory of the Member States amending Regulation (EEC) No 1612/68 and repealing Directives 64/221/EEC, 68/360/EEC, 72/194/EEC, 73/148/EEC, 75/34/EEC, 75/35/EEC, 90/364/EEC, 90/365/EEC and 93/96/EEC (Text with EEA relevance) (OJ 2004 L158/77)

Freedom of Movement for Workers Directive
Directive 2004/38/EC of the European Parliament and of the Council of 29 April 2004 on the right of citizens of the Union and their family members to move and reside freely within the territory of the Member States amending Regulation (EEC) No 1612/68 and repealing Directives 64/221/EEC, 68/360/EEC, 72/194/EEC, 73/148/EEC, 75/34/EEC, 75/35/EEC, 90/364/EEC, 90/365/EEC and 93/96/EEC (OJ 2004 L158/77)

Fresh Meat Directive
Council Directive 91/497/EEC of 29 July 1991 amending and consolidating Directive 64/433/EEC on health problems affecting intra-Community trade in fresh meat to extend it to the production and marketing of fresh meat (OJ 1991 L268/69)

Fruit and Vegetables Directive
Council Directive 76/895/EEC of 23 November 1976 relating to the fixing of maximum levels for pesticide residues in and on fruit and vegetables (OJ 1976 L340/26)

Fuel Quality Directive
Directive 98/70/EC of the European Parliament and of the Council of 13 October 1998 relating to the quality of petrol and diesel fuels and amending Council Directive 93/12/EEC (OJ 1998 L350/58)

Fusion Treaty
See Merger Treaty

Gas and Electricity Price Transparency Directive
Council Directive 90/377/EEC of 29 June 1990 concerning a Community procedure to improve the transparency of gas and electricity prices charged to industrial end-users (OJ 1990 L185/16)

Gay News Case
R v Lemon [1979] 1 QB 10
Whitehouse v Lemon [1979] AC 617

GCHQ Case or Government Communications Headquarters Case
Council of Civil Service Unions v Minister for the Civil Service [1985] 1AC 374

General Framework Equal Treatment Directive
See Equal Treatment Directives

Gender Directive
Council Directive 2004/113/EC of 13 December 2004 implementing the principle of equal treatment between men and women in the access to and supply of goods and services (OJ 2004 L373/37)

General Electromagnetic Compatibility Directive
See Electromagnetic Compatibility Directive

General Product Safety Directive
Directive 2001/95/EC of the European Parliament and of the Council of 3 December 2001 on general product safety (Text with EEA relevance) (OJ 2002 L11/4)

General Tractor Directive
Council Directive 74/150/EEC of 4 March 1974 on the approximation of the laws of the Member States relating to the type-approval of wheeled agricultural or forestry tractors (OJ 1974 L84/10)

Genetically Modified Food and Feed Regulation
Regulation (EC) No 1829/2003 of the European Parliament and of the Council of 22 September 2003 on genetically modified food and feed (Text with EEA relevance) (OJ 2003 L268/1)

Genetically Modified Organisms Directive
Directive 2001/18/EC of the European Parliament and of the Council of 12 March 2001 on the deliberate release into the environment of genetically modified organisms and repealing Council Directive 90/220/EEC - Commission Declaration (OJ 2001 L106/1)

George Michael Cases
Morrison Leahy Music Ltd v Lightbond Ltd, 21 March 1991 [1993] EMLR 144 (Ch)
Panayiotou v Sony Music Entertainment (UK) Ltd, 21 June 1994 [1994] EMLR 229 (Ch)
Panayiotou v Sony Music Entertainment (UK) Ltd, 15 July 1993 [1994] Ch 142 (Ch)

Ginger Beer Bottle Case
Donoghue v Stevenson [1932] A.C. 562

GLC Fares Fair Case
Bromley London Borough Council v Greater London Council [1983] AC 768

GM Food and Feed Regulation
See Genetically Modified Food and Feed Regulation

GMO
See Genetically Modified Organisms Directive

GPSD
See General Product Safety Directive

Gramophone Cases
Gramophone Co Ltd's Application (1910) 27 RPC 689
Portagram Radio Electrical Co Ltd's Application (1952) 69 RPC 241

Grey List
Council Directive 76/464/EEC of 4 May 1976 on pollution caused by certain dangerous substances discharged into the aquatic environment of the Community (OJ 1976 L129/23)

Grissell's Case
Re Overend, Gurney & Co (1886) 1 Ch App 528

Groundwater Directive
Council Directive 80/68/EEC of 17 December 1979 on the protection of groundwater against pollution caused by certain dangerous substances (OJ 1980 L20/43)

Guildford Four Case
R v Bow Street Stipendary Magistrate, ex parte Director of Public Prosecutions (UK CA Crim, 19 October 1989) and (1992) 95 Cr App R 9 (QBD)

Guinness Case
R v Panel on Takeovers and Mergers, ex parte Guinness plc [1989] BCLC 255

Habitats Directive
Council Directive 92/43/EEC of 21 May 1992 on the conservation of natural habitats and of wild fauna and flora (OJ 1992 L206/7)

Hag Trademark Case
Van Zuylen frères v Hag AG [1974] ECR 731; [1974] 2 CMLR 127

Hague Rules
The International Convention for the Unification of Certain Rules of Law Relating to Bills of Lading, 1924

Hague-Visby Rules
International Convention (1968 & 1979) governing the carriage of cargo by sea under a bill of lading – amends the Hague Rules

Hamburg Rules
United Nations Convention on the Carriage of Goods by Sea, 1978

Hansard Case
Pepper v Hart [1993] AC 593 (HL)

Hazardous Waste Directive
Council Directive 91/689/EEC of 12 December 1991 on hazardous waste (OJ 1991 L377/20)

Health and Safety Framework Directive
Council Directive 89/391/EEC of 12 June 1989 on the introduction of measures to encourage improvements in the safety and health of workers at work (OJ 1989 L183/1)

Herald of Free Enterprise Ferry Disaster Case
R v HM Coroner for East Kent, ex parte Spooner (1987) 88 Cr App Rep 10

Heyday Case
Incorporated Trustees of the National Council on Ageing (Age Concern England) v Secretary of State for Business, Enterprise and Regulatory Reform (C-388/07) ECR 2009 as yet unpublished

Hickling Broad Case
Micklethwait v Vincent (1982) 67 LT 225

High Trees Case
Central London Property Trust Ltd v High Trees House Ltd [1947] KB 130

Hillsborough Stadium Disaster Cases
Alcock v Chief Constable of South Yorkshire Police [1992] 1 AC 310
Frost v Chief Constable of South Yorkshire; White v Chief Constable of South Yorkshire [1999] 2 AC 455

Himalaya Clause Case
Adler v Dickson [1955] 1 QB 158

'The Hit Factory' Case
Pete Waterman Ltd v CBS United Kingdom Ltd [1993] EMLR 45

Holly Hobbie Case
In re American Greetings Corporation's Application [1984] 1 WLR 189; [1984] RPC 329

Holly Johnson Case
Zang Tumb Tuum Records Ltd and another v Johnson [1993] EMLR 61

Hull Prison Visitors Case
R v Board of Visitors of Hull Prison, ex parte St Germain [1979] QB 425

Hyde Park Bomber Case
R v McNamee (Gilbert Thomas Patrick) Court of Appeal (Crim) 17 December 1989, unreported

IAS Regulation
See International Accounting Standards Regulation

IMO Carwash Case
In the matter of Bluebrook Ltd and others [2009] EWHC 2114 (Ch)

Impact Directive
See Environmental Impact Directive

In Vitro Diagnostic Directive
Directive 98/79/EC of the European Parliament and of the Council of 27 October 1998 on in vitro diagnostic medical devices (OJ 1998 L331/1)

Incinerator Case
Gateshead MBC v Secretary of State for the Environment and Northumbrian Water plc Court of Appeal (Civil Division) [1995] Env LR 37; (1996) 71 P&CR 350; [1994] 1 PLR 85; [1995] JPL 432

Indoor Management Rule Case
Royal British Bank v Turquand (1856) 6 El & Bl 327; 119 ER 886

Information and Consultation Directive
Directive 2002/14/EC of the European Parliament and of the Council of 11 March 2002 establishing a general framework for informing and consulting employees in the European Community – Joint declaration of the European Parliament, the Council and the Commission on employee representation (OJ 2002 L80/29)

Information Society Directive
Directive 2001/29/EC of the European Parliament and of the Council of 22 May 2001 on the harmonisation of certain aspects of copyright and related rights in the information society (OJ 2001 L167/10)

Injunctions Directive
Directive 98/27/EC of the European Parliament and of the Council of 19 May 1998 on injunctions for the protection of consumers' interests (OJ 1998 L166/51)

Insider Dealing Case
In re An Inquiry under the Company Securities (Insider Dealing) Act 1985 [1988] AC 660

Insider Dealing Directive
Council Directive 89/592/EEC of 13 November 1989 coordinating regulations on insider dealing (OJ 1989 L334/30)

Insurance Block Exemption Regulation
Commission Regulation (EC) No 358/2003 of 27 February 2003 on the application of Article 81(3) of the Treaty to certain categories of agreements, decisions and concerted practices in the insurance sector (Text with EEA relevance) (OJ 2003 L53/8)

Insurance Mediation Directive
Directive 2002/92/EC of the European Parliament and of the Council of 9 December 2002 on insurance mediation (OJ 2003 L9/3)

Integrated Pollution Prevention and Control Directive
Council Directive 96/61/EC of 24 September 1996 concerning integrated pollution prevention and control (OJ 1996 L257/26)

Intellectual Property Rights Enforcement Directive
Directive 2004/48/EC of the European Parliament and of the Council of 29 April 2004 on the enforcement of intellectual property rights (Text with EEA relevance) (OJ 2004 L157/45)

Interconnections Directive
See Open Network Provision Interconnections Directive

Interest and Royalties Directive
Council Directive 2003/49/EC of 3 June 2003 on a common system of taxation applicable to interest and royalty payments made between associated companies of different Member States (OJ 2003 L157/49)

International Accounting Standards Regulation
Regulation (EC) No 1606/2002 of the European Parliament and of the Council of 19 July 2002 on the application of international accounting standards (OJ 2002 L243/1)

Interoperability Regulation
Regulation (EC) No 552/2004 of the European Parliament and of the Council of 10 March 2004 on the interoperability of the European Air Traffic Management network (the interoperability Regulation) (Text with EEA relevance) (OJ 2004 L96/26)

Investment Services Directive
Council Directive 93/22/EEC of 10 May 1993 on investment services in the securities field (OJ 1993 L141/27)

Investor Compensation Directive
Directive 97/9/EC of the European Parliament and of the Council of 3 March 1997 on investor-compensation schemes (OJ 1997 L84/22)

IPC Directive
See Integrated Pollution Prevention and Control Directive

IPPC Directive
See Integrated Pollution Prevention and Control Directive

IPR Enforcement Directive
See Intellectual Property Rights Enforcement Directive

Isoglucose Case
SA Roquette Frères v Council of the European Communities, Case 138/79 of the European Court of Justice [1980] ECR 333

IVD Directive
See In Vitro Diagnostic Directive

James Bulger Case
R v Venables; R v Thomson (Preston Crown Court 1993, unreported)
Subsequent appeals against sentence culminating in:
R v Secretary of State for the Home Department Ex p Venables; R v Secretary of State for the Home Department Ex p Thompson, House of Lords [1998] AC 407; [1997] 3 WLR 23

Jaws Case
Universal City Studios Inc v Mukhtar Ltd [1976] FSR 252

Jeanette Sterilisation Case
In re B (a minor) (Wardship: Sterilisation) [1988] 1 AC 199

Jif Lemon Case
Reckitt and Colman (Products) Ltd v Borden Inc [1990] 1 WLR 491

John Berry Case
R v Berry [1991] 1 WLR 125

Kenyan Sugar Case
Astia SA v Aztec AG [1983] 2 Lloyds Rep 579

Know-How Licensing
See Technology Transfer Regulations

Kodak Case
Eastman Kodak Co v Kodak Cycle Co (1898) 15 RPC 105

Kojakpops Case
Tavener Rutledge Ltd v Trexapalm Ltd [1975] FSR 479

Labelling Directive
Usually refers to Directive 2000/13/EC on the approximation of the laws of member states relating to the labelling, presentation and advertising of foodstuffs (OJ 2000 L109/29). But there are several other Directives relating to particular industries: Directive 98/6/EC: prices to consumers (OJ 1998 L80/70); Directive 1999/45/EC: dangerous preparations (OJ 1999 L200/1); Directive 1999/94/EC: fuel economy and CO_2 emissions of new cars (OJ 2000 L2/16); Directive 2001/37/EC tobacco products (OJ 2001 L194/26)

Laeken Declaration
European Council declaration on the future of the European Union, 2001

Landfill Directive
Council Directive 1999/31/EC of 26 April 1999 on the landfill of waste (OJ 1999 L182/1)

Large Combustion Plant Directive
Council Directive 94/66/EC of 15 December 1994 amending Directive 88/609/EEC on the limitation of emissions of certain pollutants into the air from large combustion plants (OJ 1994 L337/83)

Late Payment Directive
Directive 2000/35/EC of the European Parliament and of the Council of 29 June 2000 on combating late payment in commercial transactions (OJ 2000 L200/35)

Lawyers' Services Directive
Council Directive 77/249/EEC of 22 March 1977 to facilitate the effective exercise by lawyers of freedom to provide services (OJ 1977 L78/17)

LCP Directive
See Large Combustion Plant Directive

Lead-Free Directive
Directive 2002/95/EC of the European Parliament and of the Council of 27 January 2003 on the restriction of the use of certain hazardous substances in electrical and electronic equipment (OJ 2003 L37/19)

Leased Lines Directive
Council Directive 92/44/EEC of 5 June 1992 on the application of open network provision to leased lines (OJ 1992 L165/27)

Lego Cases
Lego Systems Atkieselskab v Lego M Lemelstricht [1983] FSR 155
Interlego AG v Tyco Industries Inc [1989] AC 217

Life Assurance Directives
First Council Directive 79/267/EEC of 5 March 1979 on the coordination of laws, regulations and administrative provisions relating to the taking up and pursuit of the business of direct life assurance (OJ 1979 L63/1)
Council Directive 90/619/EEC of 8 November 1990 on the coordination of laws, regulations and administrative provisions relating to direct life assurance, laying down provisions to facilitate the effective exercise of freedom to provide services and amending Directive 79/267/EEC (OJ 1990 L330/50)

LIFE Regulation
Regulation (EC) No 1682/2004 of the European Parliament and of the Council of 15 September 2004 amending Regulation (EC) No 1655/2000 concerning the Financial Instrument for the Environment (LIFE) (OJ 2004 L308/1)

Lifts Directive
European Parliament and Council Directive 95/16/EC of 29 June 1995 on the approximation of the laws of the Member States relating to lifts (OJ 1995 L213/1)

Lisbon Treaty
See Treaty of Lisbon

Loads Directive
See Manual Handling Directive

Lomé Convention
Agreement between ACP countries and the EU on trade and cooperation ACP-EEC Convention of Lomé (OJ 1976 L25/2)
First Lomé Convention
Second ACP-EEC Convention signed at Lomé on 31 October 1979 (OJ 1980 L347/1)
Third ACP-EEC Convention signed at Lomé on 8 December 1984 (OJ 1986 L86/3)
Fourth ACP-EEC Convention signed at Lomé on 15 December 1989 (OJ 1991 L229/3)
Replaced by the Cotonou Agreement

Low Voltage Directive
Council Directive 73/23/EEC of 19 February 1973 on the harmonization of the laws of Member States relating to electrical equipment designed for use within certain voltage limits (OJ 1973 L77/29)

Lord Lonsdale's Case
Earl of Lonsdale v Curwen (1799) 3 Bli (OS) 168

Lugano Convention
Convention of 16 September 1988 on jurisdiction and the enforcement of judgments in civil and commercial matters (88/592/EEC) (OJ 1988 L319/9)

Luxembourg Convention
89/695/EEC: Agreement relating to Community patents, done at Luxembourg on 15 December 1989 (OJ 1989 L401/1)

Luxembourg Protocol
Protocol concerning the interpretation by the Court of Justice of the Convention of 27 September 1968 on jurisdiction and the enforcement of judgments in civil and commercial matters, signed in Luxembourg on 3 June 1971 (OJ 1975 L204/28)

Maastricht Treaty
Treaty on European Union (OJ 1992 C191/1/)

MAC Directive
See Multiplex Analogue Components Directive

Machinery Directive
Directive 2006/42/EC of the European Parliament and of the Council of 17 May 2006 on machinery, and amending Directive 95/16/EC (recast) (Text with EEA relevance) (OJ 2006 L157/24)

MAD
See Market Abuse Directive

Maguire Seven Case
R v Maguire [1972] QB 936

Manual Handling Directive
Council Directive 90/269/EEC of 29 May 1990 on the minimum health and safety requirements for the manual handling of loads where there is a risk particularly of back injury to workers (fourth individual Directive within the meaning of Article 16 (1) of Directive 89/391/EEC) (OJ 1990 L156/9)

Market Abuse Directive
Directive 2003/6/EC of the European Parliament and of the Council of 28 January 2003 on insider dealing and market manipulation (market abuse) (OJ 2003 L96/16)

Markets in Financial Instruments Directive
Directive 2004/39/EC of the European Parliament and of the Council of 21 April 2004 on markets in financial instruments amending Council Directives 85/611/EEC and 93/6/EEC and Directive 2000/12/EC of the European Parliament and of the Council and repealing Council Directive 93/22/EEC (OJ 2004 L145/1)

Marmite Case
Beecham Group plc v J Sainsbury plc High Court, 6 April 1987, unreported

Maxwell Cases
Bishopsgate Investment Management Ltd v Maxwell [1993] Ch 1; (No 2) [1994] 1 All ER 261

McKenzie Friend Case
McKenzie v McKenzie [1971] P 33

Measuring Instruments Directive
Directive 2004/22/EC of the European Parliament and of the Council of 31 March 2004 on measuring instruments (Text with EEA relevance) (OJ 2004 L135/1)

Meat Labelling Directive
Dir 2000/13/EC of the European Parliament and of the Council of 20 March 2000 on the approximation of the laws of the Member States relating to labelling, presentation and advertising of foodstuffs (OJ 2000 L109/29)

Mechanical Copyright/Royalty Case
British Phonograph Industry Ltd v Mechanical Copyright Protection Society Ltd (No 2) [1993] EMLR 86

Medical Devices Directive
Council Directive 93/42/EEC of 14 June 1993 concerning medical devices (OJ 1993 L169/1)

Melrose Hair Restorer Case
In re Van Duzer's Trademark; In re Leaf, Sons & Co's Trade-Mark (1887) 34 ChD 623

Merger Control Regulations
Council Regulation 4064/89 of 21 December 1989 on the control of concentrations between undertakings (consolidated text including corrigenda: OJ 1990 L257/90; original text: OJ 1989 L395/1)
Council Regulation (EC) No 139/2004 of 20 January 2004 on the control of concentrations between undertakings (the EC Merger Regulation) (Text with EEA relevance) (OJ 2004 L24/1)

Merger Directive
Council Directive 90/434/EEC of 23 July 1990 on the common system of taxation applicable to mergers, divisions, transfers of assets and exchanges of shares concerning companies of different Member States (OJ 1990 L225/1)

Merger Treaty
Establishing a single European Community Council and a single Commission, signed on 8th April 1965

Metric Directive
Council Directive 80/181/EEC of 20 December 1979 on the approximation of the laws of the Member States relating to units of measurement and on the repeal of Directive 71/354/EEC (OJ 1980 L39/40)

MFK Case
R v Inland Revenue Commissioners, ex parte MFK Underwriting Agents Ltd [1990] 1 WLR 1545

MiFID
See Markets in Financial Instruments Directive

Mignonette Case
R v Dudley and Stephens (1884) 14 QBD 273

Milk Hygiene Directive
Directive 2004/41/EC of the European Parliament and of the Council of 21 April 2004 repealing certain Directives concerning food hygiene and health conditions for the production and placing in the market of certain products of animal origin intended for human consumption and amending Council Directives 89/662/EEC and 92/118/EEC and Council Decision 95/408/EC (OJ 2004 L157/33)

Mineral Oils Rates Directive
Council Directive 92/82/EEC of 19 October 1992 on the approximation of the rates of excise duties on mineral oils (OJ 1992 L316/19)

Mineral Transporter Case
Candlewood Navigation Corp Ltd v Mitsui OSK Ltd [1986] AC 1

Mini Schengen
Refers to the Nordic Passport Union: Denmark, Finland, Iceland, Norway and Sweden

Misleading Advertising Directive
Council Directive 84/450/EEC of 10 September 1984 relating to the approximation of the laws, regulations and administrative provisions of the Member States concerning misleading advertising (OJ 1984 L250/17)

Mocambique Rule Case
British South Africa Co v Companhia de Mocambique [1893] AC 602

Modernisation of Accounts Directive
Directive 2003/51/EC of the European Parliament and of the Council of 18 June 2003 amending Directives 78/660/EEC, 83/349/EEC, 86/635/EEC and 91/674/EEC on the annual and consolidated accounts of certain types of companies, banks and other financial institutions and insurance undertakings (Text with EEA relevance) (OJ 2003 L178/16)

Modernisation Regulation
See Anti-Trust Regulation

Money Laundering Directives
Council Directive 91/308/EC of 10 June 1991 on prevention of the use of the financial system for the purpose of money laundering (OJ 1991 L166/77)
[Third Money Laundering Directive] Directive 2005/60/EC of the European Parliament and of the Council of 26 October 2005 on the prevention of the use of the financial system for the purpose of money laundering and terrorist financing (Text with EEA relevance) (OJ 2005 L309/15)

Moneylender Case
Harrods Ltd v R Harrod Ltd (1923) 41 RPC 74

Motor Insurance Directives
Council Directive 72/166/EEC of 24 April 1972 on the approximation of the laws of Member States relating to insurance against civil liability in respect of the use of motor vehicles, and to the enforcement of the obligation to insure against such liability (OJ English special edition: Series I Chapter 1972(II) P. 0360)
Second Council Directive 84/5/EEC of 30 December 1983 on the approximation of the laws of the Member States relating to insurance against civil liability in respect of the use of motor vehicles (OJ 1984 L8/17)
[Fourth Motor Insurance Directive] Directive 2000/26/EC of the European Parliament and of the Council of 16 May 2000 on the approximation of the laws of the Member States relating to insurance against civil liability in respect of the use of motor vehicles and amending Council Directives 73/239/EEC and 88/357/EEC (OJ 2000 L181/65)
[Fifth Motor Insurance Directive] Directive 2005/14/EC of the European Parliament and of the Council of 11 May 2005 amending Council Directives 72/166/EEC, 84/5/EEC, 88/357/EEC and 90/232/EEC and Directive 2000/26/EC of the European Parliament and of the Council relating to insurance against civil liability in respect of the use of motor vehicles (Text with EEA relevance) (OJ 2005 L149/14)

Motor Vehicle Framework Directive
Council Directive 70/156/EEC of 6 February 1970 on the approximation of the laws of the Member States relating to the type-approval of motor vehicles and their trailers (OJ English special edition: Series I Chapter 1970(I) P. 0096)

Multiplex Analogue Components Directive
Council Directive 92/38/EEC of 11 May 1992 on the adoption of standards for satellite broadcasting of television signals (OJ 1992 L137/17)

Mutual Recognition of Qualifications Directives
See Diplomas Directives

Natural Habitats Directive
See Habitats Directive

'Neighbours' Defamation Case
Charleston v News Group Newspapers Ltd [1995] 2 AC 65

'Neighbours' Television Series Case
Grundy Television Pty Ltd v Startrain Ltd (1988) 13 IPR 585

Nicol's Case
Re Florence Land & Public Works Co (1885) 29 Ch D 421

Nice Treaty
Treaty of Nice amending the Treaty on European Union, the Treaties establishing the European Communities and certain related acts, signed at Nice, 26 February 2001 (OJ 2001 C80/1)

Nickel Directive
European Parliament and Council Directive 94/27/EC of 30 June 1994 amending for the 12th time Directive 76/769/EEC on the approximation of the laws, regulations and administrative provisions of the Member States relating to restrictions on the marketing and use of certain dangerous substances and preparations (OJ 1994 L188/1)

Ninja Turtles Case
Mirage Studios v Counter-Feat Clothing Ltd [1991] FSR 145

Nitrates Directive
Council Directive 91/676/EEC of 12 December 1991 concerning the protection of waters against pollution caused by nitrates from agricultural sources (OJ 1991 L375/1)

Noise Directive
Directive 2000/14/EC of the European Parliament and of the Council of 8 May 2000 on the approximation of the laws of the Member States relating to the noise emission in the environment by equipment for use outdoors (OJ 2000 L162/1)

Non-Life Insurance Directives
First Council Directive 73/239/EEC of 24 July 1973 on the coordination of laws, regulations and administrative provisions relating to the taking-up and pursuit of the business of direct insurance other than life assurance (OJ 1973 L228/3)
Second Council Directive 88/357/EEC of 22 June 1988 on the coordination of laws, regulations and administrative provisions relating to direct insurance other than life assurance and laying down provisions to facilitate the effective exercise of freedom to provide services and amending Directive 73/239/EEC (OJ 1988 L172/1)
Third Council Directive 92/49/EEC of 18 June 1992 on the coordination of laws, regulations and administrative provisions relating to direct insurance other than life assurance and amending Directives 73/239/EEC and 88/357/EEC (OJ 1992 L228/1)

Non-Road Mobile Machinery Directive
Directive 97/68/EC of the European Parliament and of the Council of 16 December 1997 on the approximation of the laws of the Member States relating to measures against the emission of gaseous and particulate pollutants from internal combustion engines to be installed in non-road mobile machinery (OJ 1998 L59/1)

Nottinghamshire Case
R v Secretary of State for the Environment ex parte Nottinghamshire County Council [1986] AC 240

Novel Food Regulation
Regulation (EC) No 258/97 of the European Parliament and of the Council of 27 January 1997 concerning novel foods and novel food ingredients (OJ 1997 L43/1)

Office Cleaning Case
Office Cleaning Services Ltd v Westminster Window and General Cleaners Ltd [1946] RPC 39

ONP Framework Directive
See Open Network Provision Framework Directive

ONP Interconnections Directive
See Open Network Provision Interconnections Directive

ONP Leased Lines Directive
See Leased Lines Directive

Open Network Provision Framework Directive
Council Directive 90/387/EEC of 28 June 1990 on the establishment of the internal market for telecommunications services through the implementation of open network provision (OJ 1990 L192/1)

Open Network Provision Interconnections Directive

Directive 97/33/EC of the European Parliament and of the Council of 30 June 1997 on interconnection in Telecommunications with regard to ensuring universal service and interoperability through application of the principles of Open Network Provision (ONP) (OJ 1997 L99/32)

Open Networks Directive

See Open Network Provision Framework Directive

Overseas Association Decision

2001/822/EC: Council Decision of 27 November 2001 on the association of the overseas countries and territories with the European Community ('Overseas Association Decision') (OJ 2001 L314/1)

Own Funds Directive

Directive 2000/12/EC of the European Parliament and of the Council of 20 March 2000 relating to the taking up and pursuit of the business of credit institutions (OJ 2000 L126/1)

Package Travel Directive

Council Directive 90/314/EEC of 13 June 1990 on package travel, package holidays and package tours (OJ 1990 L158/59)

Packaging Waste Directive

European Parliament and Council Directive 94/62/EC of 20 December 1994 on packaging and packaging waste (OJ 1994 L365/10)

Paints Directives

Council Directive 1999/13/EC of 11 March 1999 on the limitation of emissions of volatile organic compounds due to the use of organic solvents in certain activities and installations (OJ 1999 L85/1)

Directive 2004/42/CE of the European Parliament and of the Council of 21 April 2004 on the limitation of emissions of volatile organic compounds due to the use of organic solvents in certain paints and varnishes and vehicle refinishing products and amending Directive 1999/13/EC (OJ 2004 L143/87)

Parallel Convention

See Lugano Convention

Paramount Airways Cases

Bristol Airport plc v Powdrill [1990] Ch 744
Powdrill v Watson [1994] 2 All ER 513

Parent and Subsidiary Directive

Council Directive 90/435/EEC of 23 July 1990 on the common system of taxation applicable in the Case of parent companies and subsidiaries of different Member States (OJ 1990 L225/6)

Parental Leave Directive

Council Directive 96/34/EC of 3 June 1996 on the framework agreement on parental leave concluded by UNICE, CEEP and the ETUC (OJ 1996 L145/4)

Paris Treaty

See ECSC Treaty

Parma Ham Case

Consorzio del Proscuitto di Parma v Marks & Spencer plc [1991] RPC 351

PARNUTS

Council Directive 89/398/EEC of 3 May 1989 on the approximation of the laws of the Member States relating to foodstuffs intended for particular nutritional uses (OJ 1989 L186/27)

Part-Time Work Directive
Council Directive 97/81/EC of 15 December 1997 concerning the Framework Agreement on part-time work concluded by UNICE, CEEP and the ETUC – Annex: Framework agreement on part-time work (OJ 1998 L14/9)

Patent Convention
See Community Patent Convention

PCB Directive
Council Directive 96/59/EC of 16 September 1996 on the disposal of polychlorinated biphenyls and polychlorinated terphenyls (PCB/PCT) (OJ 1996 L243/31)

PED
See Pressure Equipment Directive

Pensions Fund Directive
Directive 2003/41/EC of the European Parliament and of the Council of 3 June 2003 on the activities and supervision of institutions for occupational retirement provision (OJ 2003 L235/10)

Personal Protective Equipment Directives
Council Directive 89/656/EEC of 30 November 1989 on the minimum health and safety requirements for the use by workers of personal protective equipment at the workplace (third individual directive within the meaning of Article 16 (1) of Directive 89/391/EEC) (OJ 1989 L393/18)
Council Directive 89/686/EEC of 21 December 1989 on the approximation of the laws of the member states relating to personal protective equipment (OJ 1989 L 399/18)

Pesticides Directive
Council Directive 90/642/EEC of 27 November 1990 on the fixing of maximum levels for pesticide residues in and on certain products of plant origin, including fruit and vegetables (OJ 1990 L350/71)

Pesticide Residues Directive (1976)
See Fruit and Vegetables Directive

Pet Passport Regulation
Regulation (EC) No 998/2003 of the European Parliament and of the Council of 26 May 2003 on the animal health requirements applicable to the non-commercial movement of pet animals and amending Council Directive 92/65/EEC (OJ 2003 L146/1)

Peter Pan Cases
Hospital for Sick Children (Board of Governors) v Walt Disney Productions [1968] Ch 52
Peter Pan Manufacturing Corporation v Corsets Silhouette Ltd [1963] RPC 45

Peter Sellers Case
Rickless v United Artists Corporation [1988] QB 40

Petrol Storage Directive
European Parliament and Council Directive 94/63/EC of 20 December 1994 on the control of volatile organic compound (VOC) emissions resulting from the storage of petrol and its distribution from terminals to service stations (OJ 1994 L365/24)

PGI
See Protected Geographical Indication Directive

Phyto Directive
Council Directive 77/93/EEC of 21 December 1976 on protective measures against the introduction into the Member States of harmful organisms of plants or plant products (OJ 1977 L26/20)

Pillars
Metaphor describing the European Union structure as resting on a number of supporting policies, concepts or pillars. The first is the European Community, the second the Common Foreign and Security Policy and the third deals with Justice and Home Affairs. The second and third pillars are based on inter-governmental co-operation.

Pink Panther Case
Rickless v United Artists Corporation [1988] QB 40

Plain Language Directive
See Unfair Contract Terms Directive

Plant Health Directive
See Phyto Directive

Plant Protection Products Directive
Council Directive 91/414/EEC of 15 July 1991 concerning the placing of plant protection products on the market (OJ 1991 L230/1)

Plant Variety Rights Regulation
Council Regulation (EC) No 2100/94 of 27 July 1994 on Community plant variety rights (OJ 1994 L227/1)

Plastics Directive
Commission Directive 90/128/EEC of 23 February 1990 relating to plastic materials and articles intended to come into contact with foodstuffs (OJ 1990 L75/19)

Plating Directive
Council Directive 76/114/EEC of 18 December 1975 on the approximation of the laws of Member States relating to statutory plates and inscriptions for motor vehicles and their trailers, and their location and method of attachment (OJ 1976 L24/1)

Plumber Regulations
Council Regulation (EEC) No 3/84 of 19 December 1983 introducing arrangements for movement within the Community of goods sent from one Member State for temporary use in one or more other Member States (OJ 1984 L2/1)
Council Regulation (EEC) No 1292/89 of 3 May 1989 amending Regulation (EEC) No 3/84 introducing arrangements for movement within the Community of goods sent from one Member State for temporary use in one or more other Member States, (OJ 1989 L130/1)
Council Regulation (EEC) No 718/91 of 21 March 1991 amending Regulation (EEC) No 3/84 introducing arrangements for movement within the Community of goods sent from one Member State for temporary use in one or more other Member States (OJ 1991 L78/4)

Polish Sugar Case
C Czarnikow Ltd v Centrala Handlu Zagranicznego Rolimpex (CHZ) [1979] AC 351

Popeye Case
King Features Syndicate Inc v Kleeman [1941] AC 417

Port State Control Directive
Council Directive 95/21/EC of 19 June 1995 concerning the enforcement, in respect of shipping using Community ports and sailing in the waters under the jurisdiction of the Member States, of international standards for ship safety, pollution prevention and shipboard living and working conditions (port State control) (OJ 1995 L157/1)

Portuguese Bank Note Case
Banco de Portugal v Waterlow and Sons Ltd [1932] AC 452

Post-BCCI Directive
European Parliament and Council Directive 95/26/EC of 29 June 1995 amending Directives 77/780/EEC and 89/646/EEC in the field of credit institutions, Directives 73/239/EEC and 92/49/EEC in the field of non-life insurance, Directives 79/267/EEC and 92/96/EEC in the field of life assurance, Directive 93/22/EEC in the field of investment firms and Directive 85/611/EEC in the field of undertakings for collective investment in transferable securities (Ucits), with a view to reinforcing prudential supervision (OJ 1995 L168/7)

Postal Directive
Directive 97/67/EC of the European Parliament and of the Council of 15 December 1997 on common rules for the development of the internal market of Community postal services and the improvement of quality of service (OJ 1998 L15/14)

Posted Workers Directive
Council Directive 96/71/EC of the European Parliament and of the Council of 16 December 1996 concerning the posting of workers in the framework of the provision of services (OJ 1997 L18/1)

PPE Directive
See Personal Protection Equipment Directive

Pregnant Edinburgh Fish Wife's Case
Bourhill (Hay) v Young [1943] AC 92

Pregnant Workers Directive
Council Directive 92/85/EEC of 19 October 1992 on the introduction of measures to encourage improvements in the safety and health at work of pregnant workers and workers who have recently given birth or are breastfeeding (tenth individual Directive within the meaning of Article 16 (1) of Directive 89/391/EEC) (OJ 1992 L348/1)

Pressure Equipment Directive
Directive 97/23/EC of the European Parliament and of the Council of 29 May 1997 on the approximation of the laws of the member states concerning pressure equipment (OJ 1997 L181/1)

Price Labelling Directive
See Unit Prices Directive

Prison Visitors Case
R v Board of Visitors of Hull Prison ex parte St Germain [1979] QB 425

Privacy and Electronic Communications Directive
Directive 2002/58/EC of the European Parliament and of the Council of 12 July 2002 concerning the processing of personal data and the protection of privacy in the electronic communications sector (Directive on privacy and electronic communications) (OJ 2002 L201/37)

Private Eye Cases
Beloff v Pressdram [1973] 1 All ER 47
Sutcliffe v Pressdram Ltd [1991] 1 QB 153

Procurement Directive
Council Directive 92/13/EEC of 25 February 1992 coordinating the laws, regulations and administrative provisions relating to the application of Community rules on the procurement procedures of entities operating in the water, energy, transport and telecommunications sectors (OJ 1992 L76/14)

Product Liability Directive
Council Directive 85/374/EEC of 25 July 1985 on the approximation of the laws, regulations and administrative provisions of the member states concerning liability for defective products (OJ 1985 L210/29)

Product Safety Directive
See General Product Safety Directive

Prohibition Directive
Council Directive 79/117/EEC of 21 December 1978 prohibiting the placing on the market and use of plant protection products containing certain active substances (OJ 1979 L33/36)

Prospectuses Directive
Directive 2003/71/EC of the European Parliament and of the Council of 4 November 2003 on the prospectus to be published when securities are offered to the public or admitted to trading and amending Directive 2001/34/EC (Text with EEA relevance) (OJ 2003 L345/64)

Protected Geographical Indication Directive
Council Regulation (EEC) No 2081/92 of 14 July 1992 on the protection of geographical indications and designations of origin for agricultural products and foodstuffs (OJ 1992 L208/1)

Protection of Workers Directive
Council Directive 90/679/EEC of 26 November 1990 on the protection of workers from risks related to exposure to biological agents at work (seventh individual Directive within the meaning of Article 16 (1) of Directive 89/391/EEC) (OJ 1990 L374/1)

PSI Directive
See Public Sector Information Directive

Public Sector Information Directive
Directive 2003/98/EC of the European Parliament and of the Council of 17 November 2003 on the re-use of public sector information (OJ 2003 L345/90)

Public Sector Services Directive
Council Directive 92/50/EEC of 18 June 1992 relating to the coordination of procedures for the award of public service contracts (OJ1992 L209/1)

Public Sector Supply Directive
Council Directive 93/36/EEC of 14 June 1993 coordinating procedures for the award of public supply contracts (OJ 1993 L199/1)

Public Works Directive
Council Directive 93/37/EEC of 14 June 1993 concerning the coordination of procedures for the award of public works contracts (OJ 1993 L199/54)

Pye Cases
J A Pye (Oxford) Ltd v Graham [2003] 1 AC 419
J A Pye (Oxford) Ltd v United Kingdom [2005] 3 EGLR 1; [2007] ECHR 700

Queen's (The) Case
(1820) 2 Brod & Bing 286; 129 ER 976 (Court of Common Pleas)

R&TTE Directive
See RTTE Directive

Race Directive
Council Directive 2000/43/EC of 29 June 2000 implementing the principle of equal treatment between persons irrespective of racial or ethnic origin (OJ 2000 L180/22)

Railway Safety Directive
Directive 2004/49/EC of the European Parliament and of the Council of 29 April 2004 on safety on the Community's railways and amending Council Directive 95/18/EC on the licensing of railway undertakings and Directive 2001/14/EC on the allocation of railway infrastructure capacity and the levying of charges for the use of railway infrastructure and safety certification (Railway Safety Directive) (OJ 2004 L164/44)

Raise the Red Lantern Case
Century Communications Ltd v Mayfair Entertainment UK Ltd [1993] EMLR 335

REACH Directive
See Dangerous Substances Directives

Reception Directive
See Asylum Seekers Directive

Red Hot Dutch Case
R v Secretary of State for the National Heritage ex parte Continental Television BVI [1993] EMLR 389

Red Label Cigarette Case
John Walker & Sons Ltd v Rothmans International Ltd and John Sinclair Ltd [1978] FSR 357

Refrigerator Directive
Directive 96/57/EC of the European Parliament and of the Council of 3 September 1996 on energy efficiency requirements for household electric refrigerators, freezers and combinations thereof (OJ 1996 L236/36)

Regent Oil Case
Strick v Regent Oil Co Ltd [1966] AC 295

Remedies Directives
Council Directive 89/665/EEC of 21 December 1989 on the coordination of the laws, regulations and administrative provisions relating to the application of review procedures to the award of public supply and public works contracts (OJ 1989 L395/33)
European Parliament and Council Directive 97/52/EC of 13 October 1997 amending Directives 92/50/EEC, 93/36/EEC and 93/37/EEC concerning the coordination of procedures for the award of public service contracts, public supply contracts and public works contracts respectively (OJ 1997 L328/1)

Renewables Directive
Directive 2009/28/EC of the European Parliament and of the Council of 23 April 2009 on the promotion of the use of energy from renewable sources and amending and subsequently repealing Directives 2001/77/EC and 2003/30/EC (OJ 2009 L140/16)

Rental Right Directive
Council Directive 92/100/EEC of 19 November 1992 on rental right and lending right and on certain rights related to copyright in the field of intellectual property (OJ 1992 L346/61)

Residues Directive
Council Directive 86/469/EEC of 16 September 1986 concerning the examination of animals and fresh meat for the presence of residues (OJ 1986 L275/36)

Restriction of Hazardous Substances Directive
Directive 2002/95/EC of the European Parliament and of the Council of 27 January 2003 on the restriction of the use of certain hazardous substances in electrical and electronic equipment (OJ 2003 L37/19)

Risk Assessment Regulation
Commission Regulation (EC) No 1488/94 of 28 June 1994 laying down the principles for the assessment of risks to man and the environment of existing substances in accordance with Council Regulation 793/93 (OJ 1994 L161/3)

Road Transport Directive
Directive 2002/15/EC of the European Parliament and of the Council of 11 March 2002 on the organisation of the working time of persons performing mobile road transport activities (OJ 2002 L80/35)

Robin Hood Case
Standard Camera Company Ltd's Application for a Trade Mark (1952) 69 RPC 125

ROHO Case
Hodgkinson & Corby Ltd v Wards Mobility Services Ltd [1995] FSR 169

RoHS Directive
See Lead-Free Directive

Romalpa Case
Aluminium Industrie Vaasen BV v Romalpa Aluminium Ltd [1976] 1 WLR 676

Rome II Regulation
Regulation (EC) No 864/2007 of the European Parliament and of the Council of 11 July 2007 on the law applicable to non-contractual obligations (Rome II) (OJ 2007 L199/40)

Rome Convention
See Contractual Obligations Convention

Rome Statute
The Rome Statute of the International Criminal Court, 1998

Rome Treaty
Establishing the International Criminal Court
Or
See EEC Treaty

RTTE Directive
Directive 1999/5/EC of the European Parliament and of the Council of 9 March 1999 on radio equipment and telecommunications terminal equipment and the mutual recognition of their conformity (OJ 1999 L91/10)

(The) Satanic Verses Case
R v Chief Metropolitan Stipendiary Magistrate ex parte Choudhury [1991] 1 QB 429

S, re
St George's Healthcare NHS Trust v S; R v Collins and Others, ex parte S, Court of Appeal (Civil Division) [1999] Fam 26

Sampling Drinking Water Directive
Council Directive 79/869/EEC of 9 October 1979 concerning the methods of measurement and frequencies of sampling and analysis of surface water intended for the abstraction of drinking water in the Member States (OJ 1979 L271/44)

Satellite and Cable Directive
Council Directive 93/83/EEC of 27 September 1993 on the coordination of certain rules concerning copyright and rights related to copyright applicable to satellite broadcasting and cable retransmission (OJ 1993 L248/15)

Savings Tax Directive
Council Directive 2003/48/EC of 3 June 2003 on taxation of savings income in the form of interest payments (OJ 2003 L157/38)

Scaffolding Directive
Directive 2001/45/EC of the European Parliament and of the Council of 27 June 2001 amending Council Directive 89/655/EEC concerning the minimum safety and health requirements for the use of work equipment by workers at work (second individual Directive within the meaning of Article 16(1) of Directive 89/391/EEC) (Text with EEA relevance) (OJ 2001 L195/46)

Schengen Acquis
See Schengen Agreement

Schengen Agreement
The Schengen acquis – Agreement between the Governments of the States of the Benelux Economic Union, the Federal Republic of Germany and the French Republic on the gradual abolition of checks at their common borders (OJ 2000 L239/13)

Schengen Convention
See Schengen Agreement

Schengen Treaty
See Schengen Agreement

Scotch Whisky Case
John Walker & Sons Ltd v Henry Ost & Co Ltd [1970] 1 WLR 917

SEA Directive
See Strategic Environmental Assessment Directive

Sellafield Cancer Case
Reay v British Nuclear Fuels Ltd; Hope v British Nuclear Fuels Ltd [1994] Env LR 320; [1994] PIQR P171

Semi-Conductor Topographies Directive
Council Directive 87/54/EEC of 16 December 1986 on the legal protection of topographies of semiconductor products (OJ 1987 L24/36)

Service Provision Regulation
Regulation (EC) No 550/2004 of the European Parliament and of the Council of 10 March 2004 on the provision of air navigation services in the single European sky (the service provision Regulation) (Text with EEA relevance) (OJ 2004 L96/10)

Seveso Directives
Council Directive 82/501/EEC of 24 June 1982 on the major accident-hazards of certain industrial activities (OJ 1982 L230/1)
Council Directive 96/82/EC of 9 December 1996 on the control of major-accident hazards involving dangerous substances (OJ 1997 L10/13)

Shadow Directive
An unofficial text produced to serve as a model for an officially- produced Directive.

Sharp's Case
Ministry of Housing and Local Government v Sharp [1970] 2 QB 223

Shelley's Case
(1581) Moore KB 136; 72 ER 490

Shellfish Water Directive
Council Directive 79/923/EEC of 30 October 1979 on the quality required of shellfish waters (OJ 1979 L281/47)

Sherry Case
Vine Products Ltd v Mackenzie & Co Ltd [1969] RPC 1

Shirley Bassey Case
Millar v Bassey [1994] EMLR 44

Simplification Directives
See VAT Simplification Directives

Single European Act
OJ 1987 L169/1

Single-Member Company Directive
See Company Directives – Twelfth Directive

Shipbuilding Directive
Council Directive 87/167/EEC of 26 January 1987 on aid to shipbuilding (OJ 1987 L69/55)
[Seventh] Council Directive 90/684/EEC of 21 December 1990 on aid to shipbuilding (OJ 1990 L380/27)

Sir Henry Constable's Case
Constable's Case (1601) 5 Co Rep 106a; 77 ER 218

Six Carpenters' Case
(1610) 8 Co Rep 146A; 77 ER 695

Sky Framework Regulation
Regulation (EC) No 549/2004 of the European Parliament and of the Council of 10 March 2004 laying down the framework for the creation of the single European sky (the framework Regulation) (Text with EEA relevance) – Statement by the Member States on military issues related to the single European sky (OJ 2004 L96/1)

'Slip-on' Case
Burberry's v JC Cording & Co Ltd (1909) 26 RPC 693

Snail in the Ginger Beer Bottle Case
Donoghue v Stevenson [1932] AC 562

Social Charter
See European Social Charter

Software Directive
See Computer Programs Directive

Solio Case
Eastman Photographic Material Co Ltd v Comptroller General of Patents, Designs and Trade Marks [1898] AC 571

Solo Case
Cadbury Schweppes Pty Ltd v The Pub Squash Co Ltd [1981] RPC 429

Solvency Ratio Directive
Council Directive 89/647/EEC of 18 December 1989 on a solvency ratio for credit institutions (OJ 1989 L386/14)

Solvent Emissions Directive
Council Directive 1999/13/EC of 11 March 1999 on the limitation of emissions of volatile organic compounds due to the use of organic solvents in certain activities and installations (OJ 1989 L85/1)

Spalding's Case
A G Spalding & Bros v A W Gamage (1915) 84 LJ Ch 449

Spanish Champagne Case
J Bollinger Ltd v Costa Brava Wine Co Ltd [1960] Ch 262

Spanish Fishing Fleet Case
R v Secretary of State for Transport ex parte Factortame (No 2) [1991] 1 AC 603

Spargo's Case
Re Harmony and Montague Tin and Copper Mining Co (1873) 8 Ch App 407

Spycatcher Cases
Attorney-General v Guardian Newspapers Ltd [1987] 1 WLR 1248
Attorney-General v Observer Ltd [1988] 1 All ER 385

St Martin's Corporation Case
Linden Gardens Trust Ltd v Lenesta Sludge Disposals Ltd; St Martins Corporation Ltd v Sir Robert McAlpine Ltd [1994] 1 AC 85

Stack Case
Stack v Dowden [2007] AC 432

Stage 1 Directive
See Petrol Storage Directive

Stage 2 Directive
See Paints Directives

Stone Roses Case
Silvertone Records Ltd and Zomba Music Publishers Ltd v Mountfield [1993] EMLR 152

Strasbourg Court
European Court of Human Rights

State Aid Regulation
Council Regulation (EC) No 659/1999 of 22 March 1999 laying down detailed rules for the application of Article 93 of the EC Treaty (OJ 1999 L83/1)

Strawberry Regulation
Council Regulation (EC) No 2679/98 of 7 December 1998 on the functioning of the internal market in relation to the free movement of goods among the Member States (OJ 1998 L337/8)

Strategic Environmental Assessment Directive
Directive 2001/42/EC of the European Parliament and of the Council of 27 June 2001 on the assessment of the effects of certain plans and programmes on the environment (OJ 2001 L197/30)

Stringfellows Nightclub Case
Stringfellow v McCain Foods (GB) Ltd [1984] RPC 501; (1984) 128 SJ 701 (CA), reversing Chancery Division decision [1984] FSR 175

Striped Toothpaste Cases
Unilever Ltd's (Striped Toothpaste) Trade Mark [1980] FSR 280 (Ch)
Unilever Ltd's (Striped Toothpaste No 2) Trade Marks [1987] RPC 13 (Ch)

Subcontractors Directive
See Posted Workers Directive

The Suez Cases
Carapanayoti & Co v ET Green Ltd [1959] 1 QB 131
Albert D Gason & Co v Soc Interprofessionalle des Oleagineaux Fluides Alimentaires [1960] 2 QB 348
Tsakiroglous & Co Ltd v Noblee Thorl Gmbh [1962] AC 93; [1962] QB 348

Summer Time Directives
Eighth Directive 97/44/EC of the European Parliament and of the Council of 22 July 1997 on summer-time arrangements (OJ 19967 L206/62)
[Ninth] Directive 2000/84/EC of the European Parliament and of the Council of 19 January 2001 on summer-time arrangements (OJ 2001 L31/21)

Sunday Times Thalidomide Cases
Attorney-General v Times Newspapers Ltd [1974] AC 273 (HL)
Case of the Sunday Times v United Kingdom, ECHR judgment: 26 April 1979, Series A No 30

Sunday Trading Cases
WH Smith Do it All Ltd v Peterborough City Council (No 3); Payless DIY Ltd v Peterborough City Council [1991] 1 QB 304 (DC)
Kirklees Metropolitan Borough Council v Wickes Building Supplies Ltd; Mendip DC v B&Q plc [1993] AC 227 (HL)

Superstores Cases
Gateshead Metropolitan Borough Council v Secretary of State for the Environment [1995] Env LR 37; (1996) 71 P&CR 350 (CA Civil); [1994] Env LR 11; (1994) 67 P&CR 179 (QBD)

Surface Water Abstraction Directive
See Sampling Drinking Water Directive

Surface Water Quality Directive
See Sampling Drinking Water Directive

Swaps Cases
Hazell v Hammersmith and Fulham London Borough Council [1991] 2 AC 1
Westdeutsche Landesbank Girozentrale v Islington London Borough Council [1994] 1 WLR 938

Sweeteners Directive
European Parliament and Council Directive 94/35/EC of 30 June 1994 on sweeteners for use in foodstuffs (OJ 1994 L237/3)

Table A
Also Tables B to G, SI 1985/805 Regulations relating to the setting up and formation of a company in the United Kingdom

Takeover Bids Directive
See Company Law Directives [Thirteenth Company Law Directive]

Taxation of Mergers Directive
See Merger Directive

Taxation of Savings Directive
See Savings Tax Directive

Taylforth Cases
Attorney General v MGN Ltd [1997] 1 All ER 456; [1997] EMLR 284 (Divisional Court)
Attorney General v MGN [2002] EWHC 907 (QB)

Technology Transfer Regulations
Commission Regulation (EC) No 240/96 of 31 January 1996 on the application of Article 85 (3) of the Treaty to certain categories of technology transfer agreements (Text with EEA relevance) (OJ 1996 L31/2)
Commission Regulation (EC) No 772/2004 of 27 April 2004 on the application of Article 81(3) of the Treaty to categories of technology transfer agreements (Text with EEA relevance) (OJ 2004 L123/11)

Teenage Mutant Ninja Turtles Case
Mirage Studios v Counter-Feat Clothing Company Ltd [1991] FSR 145

Telecom Terminal Equipment Directive
Council Directive 91/263/EEC of 29 April 1991 on the approximation of the laws of the Member States concerning telecommunications terminal equipment, including the mutual recognition of their conformity (OJ 1991 L128/1)

Telecoms and Data Protection Directive
Directive 97/66/EC of the European Parliament and of the Council of 15 December 1997 concerning the processing of personal data and the protection of privacy in the telecommunications sector (OJ 1998 L24/1)

Telecommunications Licensing Directive
Directive 97/13/EC of the European Parliament and of the Council of 10 April 1997 on a common framework for general authorizations and individual licences in the field of telecommunications services (OJ 1997 L117/15)

Telecommunications Terminal Equipment Directive
See RTTE Directive

Telesales Directive
Directive 97/7/EC of the European Parliament and of the Council of 20 May 1997 on the protection of consumers in respect of distance contracts – Statement by the Council and the Parliament re Article 6 (1) – Statement by the Commission re Article 3 (1), first indent (OJ 1997 L144/19)

Teletubbies Case
BBC Worldwide v Pally Screen Printing [1998] FSR 665

Television Without Frontiers Directives
Council Directive 89/552/EEC of 3 October 1989 on the coordination of certain provisions laid down by Law, Regulation or Administrative Action in Member States concerning the pursuit of television broadcasting activities (OJ 1989 L298/23)
Directive 97/36/EC of the European Parliament and of the Council of 30 June 1997 amending Council Directive 89/552/EEC on the coordination of certain provisions laid down by law, regulation or administrative action in member states concerning the pursuit of television broadcasting activities (OJ 1997 202/60)

Temporary Work at Height Directive
Directive 2001/45/EC of the European Parliament and of the Council of 27 June 2001 amending Council Directive 89/655/EEC concerning the minimum safety and health requirements for the use of work equipment by workers at work (second individual Directive within the meaning of Article 16(1) of Directive 89/391/EEC) (Text with EEA relevance) (OJ 2001 L195/46)

Terminals Directive
Directive 98/13/EC of the European Parliament and of the Council of 12 February 1998 relating to telecommunications terminal equipment and satellite earth station equipment, including the mutual recognition of their conformity (OJ 1998 L74/1)

Thalidomide Cases
Satherley v Distillers Co (Biochemicals) Ltd, 7 November 1962 unreported
Distillers Co (Biochemicals) v Times Newspapers Ltd [1975] QB 613 (QBD)
Attorney-General v Times Newspapers Ltd [1974] AC 273 (HL)
Case of the Sunday Times v United Kingdom, ECHR judgment: 26 April 1979, Series A No 30

Thatcher Memoirs Case
Times Newspapers Ltd v MGN Ltd [1993] EMLR 443

Thunderball Case
Baron O'Neill and United Artists Corp v Paramount Pictures Corp, High Court, 2 December 1982, unreported

Tichbourne Case
Castro v The Queen (1880–81) L.R. 6 App. Cas. 229

Timeshare Directive
Directive 94/47/EC of the European Parliament and the Council of 26 October 1994 on the protection of purchasers in respect of certain aspects of contracts relating to the purchase of the right to use immovable properties on a timeshare basis (OJ 1994 L280/83)

Tissue and Cells Directive
Directive 2004/23/EC of the European Parliament and of the Council of 31 March 2004 on setting standards of quality and safety for the donation, procurement, testing, processing, preservation, storage and distribution of human tissue and cells (OJ 2004 L102/48)

Titanium Dioxide Directive
Council Directive 92/112/EEC of 15 December 1992 on procedures for harmonizing the programmes for the reduction and eventual elimination of pollution caused by waste from the titanium dioxide industry (OJ 1992 L409/11)

Tobacco Advertising Directive
Directive 2003/33/EC of the European Parliament and of the Council of 26 May 2003 on the approximation of the laws, regulations and administrative provisions of the member states relating to the advertising and sponsorship of tobacco products (OJ 2003 L152/16)

Tony Bland's Case
Airedale NHS Trust v Bolland [1993] AC 789

Toy Safety Directive
Council Directive 88/378/EEC of 3 May 1988 on the approximation of laws of member states concerning the safety of toys (OJ 1988 L187/1)

Trade Barriers Regulation
Council Regulation (EC) No 3286/94 of 22 December 1994 laying down Community procedures in the field of the common commercial policy in order to ensure the exercise of the Community's rights under international trade rules, in particular those established under the auspices of the World Trade Organization (OJ 1994 L349/71)

Trade Mark Directive
First Council Directive 89/104/EEC of 21 December 1988 to approximate the laws of the member states relating to trade marks (OJ 1989 L40/1)

Transfer of Undertakings Directives
Council Directive 77/187/EEC of 14 February 1977 on the approximation of the laws of the Member States relating to the safeguarding of employees' rights in the event of transfers of undertakings, businesses or parts of businesses (OJ 1977 L61/26)
Council Directive 2001/23/EC of 12 March 2001 on the approximation of the laws of the Member States relating to the safeguarding of employees' rights in the event of transfers of undertakings, businesses or parts of undertakings or businesses (OJ 2001 L82/16)

Transfers Directive
See Acquired Rights Directive

Transit of Electricity Directive
Council Directive 90/547/EEC of 29 October 1990 on the transit of electricity through transmission grids (OJ 1990 L313/30)

Transit of Natural Gas Directive
Directive 2003/55/EC of the European Parliament and of the Council of 26 June 2003 concerning common rules for the internal market in natural gas and repealing Directive 98/30/EC (OJ 2003 L176/57)

Transparency Directive
Commission Directive 80/723/EEC of 25 June 1980 on the transparency of financial relations between Member States and public undertakings (OJ 1980 L195/35)

Treaty of Amsterdam
Signed in Amsterdam on 2 October 1997 and entered into force on 1 May 1999 making significant changes to the Treaty on European Union

Treaty of Lisbon
Signed in Lisbon on 13 December 2007 (text at OJ 2007 C306/1)

Treaty of Maastricht
See Treaty on European Union

Treaty of Nice
Signed in Nice on 26 February 2001 (text in OJ 2001 C80/1)

Treaty of Paris
See ECSC Treaty

Treaty of Rome
See EEC treaty and EURATOM treaty

Treaty on European Union
Signed at Maastricht on 7 February 1992, entered into force 1 November 1993. Often referred to as the Maastricht Treaty. Amended the text of the ECSC and EEC treaties and set a date for European and Monetary Union and established other new structures and procedures (consolidated version: OJ 2002 C325/145)

Turquand's Case
Royal British Bank v Turquand (1856) 6 El & Bl 327; 199 ER 886

Turtles Case
See Teenage Mutant Ninja Turtles Case

TV Listings Cases
News Group Newspapers Ltd v Independent Television Publications Ltd [1993] EMLR 1; [1993] RPC 173 (Copyright Tribunal)
News Group Newspapers Ltd v Independent Television Publications Ltd (No 2) [1993] EMLR 133 (Copyright Tribunal)

TWAHD
See Temporary Work at Height Directive

UDITS Directive
Council Directive 85/611/EEC of 20 December 1985 on the coordination of laws, regulations and administrative provisions relating to undertakings for collective investment in transferable securities (UCITS) (OJ 1985 L375/3)

Under Milk Wood Case
Ex parte Sianel Pedwar Cymru [1993] EMLR 251

Unfair Contract Terms Directive
Council Directive 93/13/EEC of 5 April 1993 on unfair terms in consumer contracts (OJ 1993 L95/29)

Unit Prices Directive
See Dual Pricing Directive

Universal Service Directive
Directive 2002/22/EC of the European Parliament and of the Council of 7 March 2002 on universal service and users' rights relating to electronic communications networks and services (Universal Service Directive) (OJ 2002 L108/51)

Urban Waste-Water Directive
See Urban Waste-Water Treatment Directive

Urban Waste-Water Treatment Directive
Council Directive 91/271/EEC of 21 May 1991 concerning urban waste-water treatment (OJ 1991 L135/40)

Utilities Remedies Directives
Council Directive 90/531/EEC of 17 September 1990 on the procurement procedures of entities operating in the water, energy, transport and telecommunications sectors (OJ 1990 L297/1)
Council Directive 92/13/EEC of 25 February 1992 coordinating the laws, regulations and administrative provisions relating to the application of Community rules on the procurement procedures of entities operating in the water, energy, transport and telecommunications sectors (OJ 1992 L76/14)
Council Directive 93/38/EEC of 14 June 1993 coordinating the procurement procedures of entities operating in the water, energy, transport and telecommunications sectors (OJ 1993 L199/84)
Directive 98/4/EC of the European Parliament and of the Council of 16 February 1998 amending Directive 93/38/EEC coordinating the procurement procedures of entities operating in the water, energy, transport and telecommunications sectors (OJ 1998 L101/1)

VAT Directives
First Council Directive 67/227/EEC of 11 April 1967 on the harmonisation of legislation of Member States concerning turnover taxes (OJ 1967 L71/301)
Second Council Directive 67/228/EEC of 11 April 1967 on the harmonisation of legislation of Member States concerning turnover taxes – Structure and procedures for application of the common system of value added tax (OJ 1967 L71/1303)
Third Council Directive 69/463/EEC of 9 December 1969 on the harmonisation of legislation of Member States concerning turnover taxes – introduction of value added tax in Member States (OJ English special edition: Series I Chapter 1969(II) P. 0551)
Fourth Council Directive 71/401/EEC of 20 December 1971 on the harmonization of the laws of the Member States relating to turnover taxes – Introduction of value added tax in Italy (OJ 1971 L 283/41)
Cinquième directive 72/250/CEE du Conseil, du 4 juillet 1972, en matière d'harmonisation des législations des États membres relatives aux taxes sur le chiffre d'affaires. Introduction de la taxe à la valeur ajoutée en Italie (OJ 1972 L162/18)
Sixth Council Directive 77/388/EEC of 17 May 1977 on the harmonization of the laws of the Member States relating to turnover taxes – Common system of value added tax: uniform basis of assessment (OJ 1977 L145/1)
Eighth Council Directive 79/1072/EEC of 6 December 1979 on the harmonization of the laws of the Member States relating to turnover taxes – Arrangements for the refund of value added tax to taxable persons not established in the territory of the country (OJ 1979 L331/11)
Ninth Council Directive 78/583/EEC of 26 June 1978 on the harmonization of the laws of the Member States relating to turnover taxes (OJ 1978 L194/16)
Tenth Council Directive 84/386/EEC of 31 July 1984 on the harmonization of the laws of the Member States relating to turnover taxes, amending Directive 77/388/EEC – Application of value added tax to the hiring out of movable tangible property (OJ 1984 L208/58)
Eleventh Council Directive 80/368/EEC of 26 March 1980 on the harmonization of the laws of the Member States relating to turnover taxes – exclusion of the French overseas departments from the scope of Directive 77/388/EEC (OJ 1980 L90/41)

VAT Rates Directive
Council Directive 92/77/EEC of 19 October 1992 supplementing the common system of value added tax and amending Directive 77/388/EEC (approximation of VAT rates) (OJ 1992 L316/1)

VAT Simplification Directives
Council Directive 92/111/EEC of 14 December 1992 amending Directive 77/388/EEC and introducing simplification measures with regard to value added tax (OJ 1992 L384/47)
Council Directive 95/7/EC of 10 April 1995 amending Directive 77/388/EEC and introducing new simplification measures with regard to value added tax – scope of certain exemptions and practical arrangements for implementing them (OJ 1995 L102/18)

VCM Directive
See Vinyl Chlorid_ Monomer Directive

VDU Directi_e
See Display Screen Equipment Directive

Veterinary Checks Directive
Council Directive 91/496/EEC of 15 July 1991 laying down the principles governing the organization of veterinary checks on animals entering the Community from third countries and amending Directives 89/662/EEC, 90/425/EEC and 90/675/EEC (OJ 1991 L268/56)

Vibrations Directive
Directive 2002/44/EC of the European Parliament and of the Council of 25 June 2002 on the minimum health and safety requirements regarding the exposure of workers to the risks arising from physical agents (vibration) (sixteenth individual Directive within the meaning of Article 16(1) of Directive 89/391/EEC) – Joint Statement by the European Parliament and the Council (OJ 2002 L177/13)

Vinyl Chloride Monomer Directive
Council Directive 78/610/EEC of 29 June 1978 on the approximation of the laws, regulations and administrative provisions of the Member States on the protection of the health of workers exposed to vinyl chloride monomer (OJ 1978 L197/12)

Visegrad Agreements
Poland (OJ 1993 L348); Hungary (OJ 1993 L347); Czech Republic (OJ 1994 L360); Slovak Republic (OJ 1994 L359)

VOC Paints Directive
See Paints Directive

Voice Telephony Directive
Directive 98/10/EC of the European Parliament and of the Council of 26 February 1998 on the application of open network provision (ONP) to voice telephony and on universal service for telecommunications in a competitive environment (OJ 1998 L101/24)

Vredeling Initiative
Proposal for a Directive on procedures informing and consulting the employees of undertakings with complex structures (Bulletin EC Supplement 3/180, with revision in Supplement 2/1983 and a Council Conclusion in OJ 1986 C203)

Wagon Mound Case (No 1)
Overseas Tankship (UK) Ltd v Morts Dock and Engineering Co Ltd [1961] AC 388

Wagon Mound Case (No 2)
Overseas Tankship (UK) Ltd v Miller Steamship Co Pty Ltd [1967] 1 AC 617

Waste Directive
Council Directive 75/442/EEC of 15 July 1975 on waste (OJ 1975 L194/39)

Waste Electrical and Electronic Equipment Directive
Directive 2002/96/EC of the European Parliament and of the Council of 27 January 2003 on waste electrical and electronic equipment (WEEE) – Joint declaration of the European Parliament, the Council and the Commission relating to Article 9 (OJ 2002 L37/24)

Waste Electronic and Electrical Equipment Regulations

Waste Electronic and Electrical Equipment Regulations 2006, SI 2006/3315 (England & Wales); SI 2006/3289; SI 2007/172 (Scotland).

Implementing European Parliament and Council Directive 2002/96/EC on waste electrical and electronic equipment (OJ 2002 L37/03) and Dir 2002/95/EC on the restriction of the use of certain hazardous substances in electrical and electronic equipment (OJ 2002 L37/03)

Waste Incineration Directive

Directive 2000/76/EC of the European Parliament and of the Council of 4 December 2000 on the incineration of waste (OJ 2000 L332/91)

Waste Oils Directive

Council Directive 75/439/EEC of 16 June 1975 on the disposal of waste oils (OJ 1975 L194/23)

Water Framework Directive

Directive 2000/60/EC of the European Parliament and of the Council of 23 October 2000 establishing a framework for Community action in the field of water policy (OJ 2000 L327/1)

Water Quality Directive

Council Directive 80/778/EEC of 15 July 1980 relating to the quality of water intended for human consumption (OJ 1980 L229/11)

Wednesbury Case

Associated Provincial Picture Houses Ltd v Wednesbury Corporation [1948] 1 KB 223

WEEE Directive

See Waste Electrical and Electronic Equipment Directive

WEEE Regulations

See Waste Electronic and Electrical Equipment Regulations

West Tankers Case

West Tankers Inc v RAS Riunione Adriatica di Sicurta SpA [2007] UKHL 4; [2007] 1 All ER (Comm) 794 (HL)
Allianz SpA (formerly Riunione Adriatica di Sicurta SpA) v West Tankers Inc (C-185/07) [2009] All ER (EC) 491; [2009] 1 All ER (Comm) 435 (ECJ)

White's Case

In re Government Security Fire Insurance Co (1879) 12 Ch D 511

Wild Birds Directive

Council Directive 79/409/EEC of 2 April 1979 on the conservation of wild birds (OJ 1979 L103/1)

Winding-Up Directive

Directive 2001/17/EC of the European Parliament and of the Council of 19 March 2001 on the reorganisation and winding-up of insurance undertakings (OJ 2001 L110/28)

Women's Ordination Case

Ex parte Williamson, The Times, 9 March 1994 (CA Civ), transcript on Westlaw UK

Work Equipment Directive

Council Directive 89/655/EEC of 30 November 1989 concerning the minimum safety and health requirements for the use of work equipment by workers at work (OJ 1989 L393/13)

Workers' Charter

See European Social Charter

Working Hours Directive
See Working Time Directive

Working Time Directives
Council Directive 93/104/EC of 23 November 1993 on certain aspects of the organisation of working time (OJ 1993 L30718)
Directive 2003/88/EC of the European Parliament and of the Council of 4 November 2003 concerning certain aspects of the organisation of working time (OJ 2003 L299/9)

Workplace Directive
Council Directive 89/654/EEC of 30 November 1989 concerning the minimum safety and health requirements for the workplace (first individual directive within the meaning of Article 16 (1) of Directive 89/391/EEC) (OJ 1989 L393/1)

Works Council Directive
See European Works Council Directive

World Cup Case
British Broadcasting Corporation v British Satellite Broadcasting Ltd [1992] 2 Ch 141

Yeast-Vite Case
Irving Yeats-Vite v Horsenail (1934) 51 RPC 110

Yorkshire Relish Case
Birmingham Vinegar Brewery Co Ltd v Powell [1897] AC 710

Yorkshire Ripper Case
Sutcliffe v Pressdram Ltd [1991] 1 QB 153

Young Workers Directive
Council Directive 94/33/EC of 22 June 1994 on the protection of young people at work (OJ 1994 L216/12)

Zeebrugge Ferry Disaster Case
R v HM Coroner for East Kent ex parte Spooner (1987) 88 Cr App R 10

Zoonoses Directive
Council Directive 92/117/EEC of 17 December 1992 concerning measures for protection against specified zoonoses and specified zoonotic agents in animals and products of animal origin in order to prevent outbreaks of food-borne infections and intoxications (OJ 1993 L62/38)

ZTT Records Case
Zang Tumb Tuum Records Ltd and another v Johnson [1993] EMLR 61 (CA (Civ))

Subject Index

Index of Published Materials

Index to Databases and Organisations

References are to page numbers